Administering SAP™ R/3: The FI-Financial Accounting and CO-Controlling Modules

Administering SAP™ R/3: The FI-Financial Accounting and CO-Controlling Modules

ASAP World Consultancy

Jonathan Blain
and Bernard Dodd
with David Sandison

Contributions by
Anthony Kudzin
Ian Henderson

que®

Administering SAP R/3: The FI-Financial Accounting and CO-Controlling Modules

Library of Congress Catalog Number: 97-80938
ISBN: 1-7897-1548-1

Printed in the United States of America 1 2 3 4 5 6 7 8 9 0

00 99 98   6 5 4 3 2 1

Interpretation of the printing code: the rightmost double-digit number is the year of the book's printing; the rightmost single-digit number, the number of the book's printing. For example, a printing code of 98-1 shows that the first printing of the book occurred in 1998.

"SAP" is a trademark of SAP Aktiengesellschaft, Systems, Applications and Products in Data Processing, Neurottstrasse 16, 69190 Walldorf, Germany. The publisher gratefully acknowledges SAP's kind permission to use its trademark in this publication. SAP AG is not the publisher of this book and is not responsible for it under any aspect of press law.

Warning and Disclaimer

Trademark Acknowledgments

Contents at a Glance

Contents

I Preparing the Public Accounts

II Planning and Controlling

6 Controlling by Cost Management   187

7 Costing on the Basis of Activities   223

Credits

PUBLISHER
Joseph B. Wikert

EXECUTIVE EDITOR
Bryan Gambrel

MANAGING EDITOR
Patrick Kanouse

ACQUISITIONS EDITOR
Tracy Dunkelberger

DEVELOPMENT EDITOR
Scott Warner

TECH EDITORS
Gurpreet Bhui
David Sandison

PROJECT EDITOR
Dayna Isley

COPY EDITOR
Krista Hansing

TEAM COORDINATOR
Michelle Newcomb

COVER DESIGNER
Dan Armstrong

BOOK DESIGNER
Ruth Harvey

PRODUCTION TEAM
Carol Bowers
Mona Brown
Julie Geeting
Ayanna Lacey
Gene Redding
Elizabeth San Miguel

INDEXER
Bront Davis

Visit Macmillan Computer Publishing's Web site at **http://www.mcp.com**

I dedicate this book to my dear wife, Jennifer, and our beautiful daughter, Kezia.
—Jonathan Blain

About the Authors

ASAP World Consultancy is an international SAP consulting company and is part of the ASAP International Group. The ASAP International Group comprises of the following:

ASAP World Consultancy—SAP/Enterprise Transformation Consultancy

ASAP Worldwide—Recruitment and Resourcing

ASAP Institute—Education, Training, and Research

ASAP Standards and Assessment Board—Quality Standards and Assessment Services

ASAP World Consultancy is in the business of selling high-quality products and services relating to SAP and other enterprise applications, computing systems, and implementations. The company specializes in "Enterprise Transformation Management," delivering integrated business solutions.

ASAP International Group operates globally and its activities include the following:

- Introductory SAP Courses for Corporate Clients Globally
- SAP Implementation Consultancy
- SAP Permanent, Temporary, and Contract Recruitment
- Business Process Re-engineering, Renewal, Change Management, and Transformation Consultancy
- SAP Human Issues Consultancy
- SAP Internal and External Communications Consultancy
- SAP Project and Resource Planning Consultancy
- SAP Skills Transfer to Your Employees
- SAP Education and Training
- SAP System Testing Consultancy and Resourcing
- SAP Documentation Consultancy
- SAP Procurement Consultancy
- SAP Access and Security Consultancy
- Hardware and Installation Consultancy
- Development of SAP Complementary Solutions
- SAP Market Research
- SAP Product and Services Acquisitions, Mergers, and Joint Ventures

The company is known for:

- Accelerated Skills Transfer

- Maximizing Retained Value

- Transformation Management

- ASAP World Consultancy Implementation Methodology

- ASAP Institute—Comprehensive Education and Training

The company prides itself on the quality of its people. It uses a combination of its own employees, International Sovereigns, and associates, who bring a wealth of experience and skills to meet the needs of its customers.

ASAP has a commitment to quality and is focused on meeting the business objectives of its clients through a number of highly specialized divisions and companies.

ASAP International Group can be contacted at the following address:

ASAP House
P.O. Box 4463
Henley on Thames
Oxfordshire
RG9 1YW
UK

Tel: +44 (0)1491 414411
Fax: +44 (0)1491 414412
email: **enquiry@asap-consultancy.co.uk**
Author comments: **info@asap-consultancy.co.uk**
Web site: **http://www.asap-consultancy.co.uk/**

ASAP 24-Hour Virtual Office, New York, USA
Voice mail: 212-253-4180; Fax: 212-253-4180

See the advertisements at the back of this book for more details.

Jonathan Blain is the founder of the ASAP group of companies. He has been working with SAP products since 1991. He has a strong business background, having spent 10 years in the oil industry working in a variety of different roles in the downstream sector for the Mobil Corporation. He has specialist knowledge of large-scale SAP implementations, project management, human issues, planning, communications, security, training, documentation, and SAP recruitment. He has benefited from professional business training with the Henley Management College and other institutions.

As a management consultant, he has specialized in matching corporate business strategies to IT strategies. He has a special interest in business engineering and the effective management of change when implementing large-scale IT systems.

Coming from a business rather than systems background, he is focused on providing business solutions. He believes that the implementation of SAP can improve the way that companies do business and that, provided common sense and logical thinking are applied, SAP implementations need not be daunting.

Jonathan is a keen yachtsman and is the vice-chairman of the Yacht Owners Association in the UK. He has been instrumental in the development of the *Hy-Tech Sprint* yacht, a revolutionary 43-foot light displacement, water-ballasted ocean cruiser.

Bernard Dodd, after graduating in psychology at Aberdeen University, built and directed an industrial training research unit over a period of nine years at the Department of Psychology, University of Sheffield. Two years with an international business consultancy led to an open competition direct entry to the specialist Civil Service, where he served the Royal Navy for 17 years to become the senior psychological advisor to the Second Sea Lord.

Since 1990, he has specialized in technical interviewing of experts and the writing of system documentation and user handbooks for the computer-intensive industries.

David Sandison M.A., C.A., gained accountancy degree at University of Aberdeen in 1985 and was trained as a Chartered Accountant with Deloitte, Haskins & Sells, Aberdeen. He also worked on engineering, travel, media, university, and public sector audits. He was admitted to the Scottish CA Institute in November 1988 and then worked in the upstream oil industry for over five years between audit, contracts, finance, and technical support for SAP R/2. He consulted for 2 years in FI and CO in SAP R/3 while working with 121 Consulting. In his 2-year career with SAP UK Ltd., he has worked in the training department as an FI and CO instructor, instructor manager, and, currently, as relationship manager.

Contributions by:

Ian Henderson trained as a production engineer with Rolls Royce Aeroengines and has had over 25 years experience working with enterprise application systems around the world. During the last three years, he helped establish a successful consultancy business in the SAP market. He is a founder of the ASAP International Group.

Anthony Kudzin is a certified accountant and an experienced FICO consultant.

Acknowledgments

In writing this book, we have benefited from the help and support of many people. There would not be space here to acknowledge everyone. They have each given their time and effort freely to make this book thorough, accurate, and useful to readers. Equally, there are many companies who have given us much of their valuable time and shared their thoughts and opinions.

Our heartfelt thanks go to everyone who has helped. The writing of this book has been a team effort, and just praise should go to each and every team member.

CHAPTER 1

Reviewing the Processes of Accounting in SAP R/3

In this chapter

Outlining This Book

Traditional accounting methods have evolved into sophisticated means of keeping track of the ways in which value is altered by the processes of work and commerce. These methods not only have been built into the finance and control modules of the SAP R/3, but they also have been integrated so as to yield a global enterprise-management system capable of both discerning important events and trends and taking timely action to deal with problems and reap the rewards of opportunities. This volume demonstrates that the process of installing a sophisticated enterprise-control system need not fall beyond the reach of medium-sized companies if the constituents are drawn from the SAP R/3 business object repository that holds only items that can be seamlessly integrated into a total enterprise-management support system.

In this book you will learn how to use the SAP R/3 FI-Financial Accounting and the Co-Controlling applications, which are integrated with the SAP R/3 Basis system at the code level. These applications can be configured according to the requirements of your company.

This introduction reviews the processes of accounting so as to clarify the way in which the SAP R/3 system uses the concepts and terminology of accounting and financial controlling. Some differences exist in naming processes, and sometimes variations arise in how responsibility is assigned to specific departments.

Part I, "Preparing the Public Accounts," focuses on the balance sheet and the profit and loss statement. These financial documents are legal requirements for companies that might incur tax liabilities when using borrowed money. The financial documents also provide a window on the recent performance and financial viability of a company so that shareholders and potential investors can assess the potential profitability of the enterprise.

Part II, "Planning and Controlling," looks forward from the public accounts to the processes of planning for a company's future by studying the data collected in the past and applying it, where appropriate, to a model of the enterprise's future physical and financial activities. The purpose of this modeling exercise is to prepare for the next set of financial documents by making sure that the planned activities are profitable.

Part III, "Funding, Investment, and Development," recognizes the importance of having funds available for planned activities and also maintaining contingency resources, which can be applied to anticipated developments in market opportunities based on trends already discernible.

Appreciating Developments in Financial Accounting

Accounting offers a source of support for working people. At its best, accounting sheds light on the value of what people do and uncovers the value of the materials and other resources that are used and thrown away. Accounting should help people waste less and add more value by using information and skill. Those who have invested in the company also want to see how things are going and will look at the annual accounts for a start. At its worst, accounting is the painful process of collecting a confusing blanket of numbers to throw over an enterprise that could be a waste of time and resources. The law requires the publication of financial documents, but it may take an expert to discern just which elements of the business contribute to the value of the material and information passing through the company.

The possibility of managing the accounts on a computer opens an opportunity to make one of two mistakes at the software design and implementation stage.

The first mistake involves overlooking the many ways in which the computer can add value to the information and material work items passing through the company. For example, the computer can make sure that the customer is provided with exactly what he needs and is properly billed so that he pays for it. Manual systems can be used to serve this purpose if the person in charge of them is diligent and energetic. In contrast, the computer can be diligent and energetic in a business in which everything is going according to plan, or the computer can detect slow responses in billing and customer service. Then the computer can call attention to this imperfection, not simply by ringing an alarm bell but by gathering together the pertinent information and presenting it to a human decision-maker.

The second mistake in conceiving a computer-assisted accounting system is to assume that such a system is simply a matter of mechanized books.

The computer can be made to work well at what it does only if it is endowed with impeccable behavior. As much as possible, the computer must be incorruptible. Of course, entry errors may occur that are not detected at the time. When the problem is uncovered, it must be possible to trace the origin of the error, make corrections to the accounting, and perhaps take steps to make this type of error less likely in the future—or at least detectable at the time it occurs. The SAP system takes this moral stand very seriously. Each time a transaction takes place between SAP and the outside world, an SAP document is created and stamped with the date and time. The terminal device signs the document, and the user also is obliged to record his or her identification. From this moment of formal entry launching the transaction, no further opportunity exists to annotate or adjust anything illegally. The time-stamped SAP document recording the entry event remains locked. Therefore, it is best if the document is checked before it is launched. The user also should append any annotations or explanatory remarks at this stage.

N O T E   When dealing with an SAP document, you usually will have a choice of standard annotations to cope with most eventualities. You also might be able to enter a free-text explanation.

If the transaction is legal but in error, a correcting transaction must be enacted. This, too, leaves its mark on the audit trail by generating an SAP document.

Accruals are an essential part of modern online accounting. Costs and charges (and possibly profits as well) are linked to the time period and the cost or profit center to which they belong, rather than to any general fund. The aim is to reveal the true value to the company of whatever activity uses its resources.

There is no doubt that the cycle time of the financial management process is decreasing. (A financial year may take too long!) If your company manufactures only to a specific customer order, you necessarily work within a different time frame than if you manufacture identical items in bulk and sell them by shipping mass quantities. However, given the immediacy of electronic communication (of product information and orders, for instance), you may find that customers increasingly drive your production. If your assembly or manufacturing teams are quick and responsive, you might be able to persuade the customer to wait for delivery if he or she will obtain the exact configuration or product variant desired. In another potential situation, your product mix may be transformed because of customer demand before you have time to compile the annual accounts. You might have to keep running cost accounts and rolling plans developed on the basis of current information. You need a financial system designed for this change of pace, and even a small enterprise needs a proper financial system. The future directions for accounting are touched on in Chapter 12, "Developments in Financial Management."

Rendering the External Accounts

A company is accountable to its owners, investors, host country, host taxation authority, and employees. Groups of companies can combine to form a group enterprise. Most legal systems insist on being able to scrutinize a set of financial documents for the group as a whole and for each of the constituent companies. When the accounts have been certified, they must be made public so that anyone may read the balance sheet and the profit and loss statement for each corporate entity.

Under the discipline of an SAP R/3 financial system, every financial transaction is recorded as an electronic document that identifies the following information:

- Date and time of the transaction
- Commercial content
- Company code of the corporate entity that will account for this transaction in its balance sheet and profit and loss statement

Using Subsidiary Accounts

The General Ledger stores the values needed to compile the balance sheet and the profit and loss statement for one company code.

A subsidiary ledger, or a subledger, is a company code ledger designated for storing values of accounting transactions of a particular category. The Debtors and Creditors categories are two such subledgers. Both are sometimes referred to as the personal ledgers or the Accounts Receivable and Accounts Payable ledgers. Another subledger account is often named "Assets" because it is used to compile the entries of this category in the company code balance sheet.

Using Client*

Client (or Client*) is a data object in the SAP Enterprise Data Model that generally encompasses all other data objects in the system. This Client* entity can be specialized based on whether it is used for a single enterprise or to summarize accounts across several Client*s. For example, the Client* could span several corporate groups.

The Client* entity represents a self-contained business system that has the purpose of acquiring, producing, arranging, or distributing goods or services.

The data fields in the client records can be differentiated according to legal or administrative viewpoints, and they usually map readily to business concepts. For example, the Plant field is used to record details of physical assets holding materials such as manufacturing plants and warehouses.

N O T E   Each item of Plant must belong to just one client because the public accounts do not allow the value of this plant to be assigned to more than one owner. ▨

Using Company Codes

A client can be used to consolidate the accounts of several associated companies in a group. Each of these companies is legally allowed to publish its own set of financial documents. If some of these member companies operate in overseas taxation regimes or in other countries from the Client*, then these separate sets of accounts are obligatory. However, the enterprise corporate headquarters will want to publish a set of financial documents that represents the group as a whole. In SAP terminology, the Client* comprises one or more company codes.

A company code is a data object that appears on every transaction document to signal how that transaction is to be used in the preparation of the public accounts. The term "company code" is used to denote a self-contained unit, such as an autonomous division or a decentralized business department that can differentiate its own account transactions.

N O T E   Company codes usually represent separate legal companies. ▨

Using Business Areas

Some enterprises span many types of businesses and are composed of many constituent companies. The Client* has many company codes because each constituent company needs to keep its accounts separate. The company codes also can be classified as operating in a specific business area. There is no legal obligation to use business areas as part of your system of labeling transaction documents. However, you may find it useful to assign some of your customers, for example, to the business area Retail and others to the business area Wholesale. If your business is differentiated by geographical region or by type of product or by type of final user, you can set up business areas that make sense in your particular circumstances by using any combination of such factors.

If you want to use a particular set of business areas in your financial accounting, the SAP R/3 system can maintain a separate set of accounts for each business area and can automatically print individual documents for each division if a transaction involves more than one. The result is the final breakdown of a company's balance sheet and profit and loss statement into a statement for each business area, to be used for internal information purposes.

Using Profit Centers

A profit center is a real or conceptual structure, internal to your company, that you designate to bear the responsibility for financial accounting, insofar as it concerns specific operating capabilities of part of your company. You need not nominate any profit centers—in such a case, the company code is treated as the natural focus for profitability computations and acts as a profit center.

You may nominate any cost objects to be the responsibility of a particular profit center. However, each cost object may be assigned to only one profit center.

Using Cost Accounting Areas

If you need collate transaction data across profit centers or across company codes, you can declare one or more cost accounting areas within a Client*. This enables you to inspect the flows of values and services within each area of cost accounting responsibility, to and from the cost objects contained within the cost accounting area.

N O T E   If your enterprise is multinational, you may have to apply different accounting conventions to some cost accounting areas.

Using Distributed Accounting Systems

A business scenario can be distributed in the sense that the separate accounting mechanisms can reside in different locations and hardware complexes. For example, one or more integrated logistics systems could be partnered with a centralized financial accounting system. The ALE (Application Link Enabling) technology allows any of the partnered systems to make controlled linked calls to any other partner. These links are used to initiate business transaction elements that must be executed by one partner to complete the transaction begun by the other. The ALE links can be processed in batch mode and supported by intelligent reconciliation of aggregated data to initiate "ledger rollup." This process minimizes wasted data storage by holding the same data in more than one location.

Often the distributed system is composed of several company codes, not all of which may be using SAP systems. The ALE protocols accommodate the aggregation of data from many different types of accounting systems and the consolidation modules. These protocols then are used to present the data in the most useful form for corporate group ledger reporting, as well as for national or regional analysis and summary.

Using Costing and Revenue Element Accounting

One method of costing involves adding all the payments and dividing by the number of items to arrive at the average cost of an item. The cost element in this method is the item. This information is not very meaningful, however, if you have purchased several different kinds of items, such as raw materials and services. How can you average across unlike entities?

If you have truly been able to record all your costs over a settlement period, then you are well on the way toward setting up a database from which you can build cost elements.

Recording costs is not a problem if you run an SAP R/3 system because every transaction (including purchasing goods and services) leaves a time and dated document that can be accessed to compile costs as necessary. This same document notes the account assignment object used for the transaction (for example, a cost center). Therefore, consumption of a quantity of a certain material for production or sales leaves a record in the General Ledger profit and loss account cost element. The system also records a corresponding entry on the account assignment object in the controlling application. This system ensures that updating an account in the General Ledger also causes a corresponding update in the controlling application records.

A cost element is an item in the chart of accounts that is used to accumulate value changes arising as primary costs or sales revenue. These chart of accounts items classify a cost according to a scheme that can include categories such as the following:

- Consumption of bought-out raw materials, or raw material costs
- Basic personnel costs in fixed wages or salary in production
- Basic variable personnel costs in production
- Personnel costs for administration
- Commissions to employees
- Cost of sales
- Imputed rent
- Settled job order costs
- Christmas bonuses

 N O T E The chart of accounts item for cost and revenues records sales revenue as the main category of revenue.

A chart of accounts item can be a profit/loss value category in Financial Accounting and, at the same time, a primary cost type in Cost Accounting. The Cost Accounting module provides a wide range of standard cost objects to which you may add your own category if none of the standard objects is suitable. The purpose is to enable you to see how costs flowed through your organization. Where did the costs arise? How were they passed on along the value-added chain? These issues are discussed in Chapter 6, "Controlling by Cost Management."

Using Cost Centers

The place in which costs are incurred, however you define it, is represented by a data object of the type Cost Center. This is a unit within your company distinguished in some way by area of responsibility, location, or accounting method, and perhaps all three.

You might find it useful to assign certain types of cost objects to a cost center. A cost center is an extension of the system of dividing costs into, say, raw materials, labor, and overheads. No limit exists as to the number of cost centers or the way in which they are construed and defined.

Using Orders

An order is an instrument for monitoring the costs of an internal job. An order describes the job and accepts transactions that are concerned with planning the job and monitoring its progress. The order also accepts transactions that specify how the costs of this job are to be allocated to cost elements in the chart of accounts. Therefore, an order is also a cost object.

Orders can be assigned an internal order type, of which the following are examples:

- Repair orders
- Investment orders
- Public relations and trade fair orders

See Chapter 7, "Costing on the Basis of Activities," for additional information on this topic.

Using Projects

A project is a series of jobs that are directed to the achievement of a set of objectives according to a detailed plan. The type of objectives amenable to project management include the following:

- Engineer-to-order manufacturing
- Plant maintenance
- Installation of the plant
- Installation of information technology systems and hardware with associated training
- Research and development
- General investment programs

Usually, a time constraint and some form of constraint on the use of resources affect project management. The SAP R/3 PS-Project System is a fully integrated part of the R/3 system that supports efficient project management in every type of industry. The work to be done is specified as a WBS (work breakdown structure) and the dependencies between WBS elements can be portrayed as a network of activities. Either a WBS or a network can be used independently of the other.

The WBS can be used on its own to track the costs of a project that is treated as a cost object. This use is discussed in Chapter 8, "Controlling by the PS-Project System."

Using the Reconciliation Ledger

When an actual posting occurs for a controlling object such as a cost object, a reconciliation ledger is updated at the same time. The reconciliation ledger holds summary information about all transactions in the cost accounting system, which then can be used in reporting functions. This ledger also is used to identify cost accounting allocations that must be shown in the General Ledger, and it automatically generates these entries for financial reporting.

In distributed systems, a reconciliation ledger is maintained locally. From time to time, the data in each of these reconciliation ledgers is transmitted to the central company code system, or to the controlling area system if this is not the company code. The central system then can aggregate the distributed system data and can perform a complete analysis of all controlling objects of a company code or controlling area.

Using Special Purpose Ledger Accounting

If the analysis you require cannot be conducted using the General Ledger accounts of debit and credit transactions for each month, you may be able to find what you want in the CO-Controlling system database. For example, the CO system could keep accounts that reflect value flows between internal responsibility centers. If you cannot get the analytical result you require using the General Ledger or the CO systems, you can set up special purpose ledgers to be maintained in addition to the standard traditional accounts based on the general ledger.

You can define the data for a special purpose ledger on the basis of any combination of the data elements held in the SAP R/3 system or its applications. In addition, your implementation can be configured to receive data from non-SAP third-party systems.

The special purpose ledger facility is supported by a very flexible reporting system that is built specifically to report on the changes of these values. For example, you may want to have extra reporting on the quantity and value of certain materials, together with an analysis of which customers contribute the most business involving these materials.

User-defined special purpose ledgers can be specified so as to selectively record transaction data from a set of nominated accounts or by filtering on the basis of account groups. Individual cost elements or cost element groups can be targeted. Similarly, revenue elements or revenue element groups can contribute to a special purpose ledger.

Value components could be the focus of a special purpose ledger system. Your company could set up a specific ledger in which you perform planning, allocation, and currency conversions. Any business transaction relevant to the value components in this ledger would update it so that you would always be able to scrutinize those aspects of your business that you had assigned to the special ledger.

N O T E Although the company code is the usual unit for profit center accounting, the SAP R/3 system accepts profit centers defined in any way that suits the reporting needs of your company.

You can, of course, compute the profitability of your activities as a whole using the accounts already compiled for the general ledger. The concept of statistical profitability analysis is used to draw attention to the fact that the computations generally are based on aggregated data from many transactions. The result should be interpreted as an average or an estimate of profitability across this sample of transactions rather than a definite calculation of the profitability of any one instance.

Using Parallel Costing Systems

The SAP R/3 arrangement has a Financial Accounting system supported by a CO system that maintains a separate database. One of the benefits of this arrangement is the availability of planning data and actual data at all times. The planning data, for instance, can include historical information from which estimates of future values can be developed. As a result, it is possible to run a suite of parallel costing systems and draw reports from them to inform management decisions.

Comparing Cost Accounting Methods

Parallel costing systems may or may not use the same method to assign costs. More than likely however, the different systems will use different methods. Table 1.1 describes the cost accounting methods.

Table 1.1   Cost Accounting Methods

Method	Description
Actual Cost Accounting	The costs posted to the General Ledger can be assigned to a cost component without modification. You then know what you have paid for this component in this accounting period.
Standard Cost Accounting	If your costs are variable, you can decide to allocate to your cost component only the standard costs that you have established on the basis of historical data and a trend factor. The difference between the actual costs for this component and the standard costs that have been assigned to it can be assigned to period profitability analysis.
Absorption Costing	By arranging for the system to roll over the actual costs (from whatever cause) to the cost object, you can set up absorption costing. You can attribute some or all of the overhead costs to some or all of the cost objects, for example.
Marginal Costing	If your main costs have been calculated, you can elect to separate the variable costs that arise from differences in particular items or from differences in the quantities. These variable costs can be assigned to the cost object as marginal costs. For example, you could ask how much one extra production quantity would cost, given that you had already accounted for the costs of the current run.
Direct Cost Accounting and Contribution Margin Accounting	If you have planned for a particular set of cost objects, you can decide to assign all the indirect costs entirely to these planned cost objects. If you then consume or produce a greater quantity than planned, you can determine the direct costs without factoring in the indirect cost. The same type of calculation can be used to determine the revenue contribution of the marginal quantities.

Method	Description
Cost-of-Sales Accounting	The accounting definition of "sales" is the total value of all the goods and services sold in the accounting period. The valuation takes place at the respective applicable selling price of each item sold. The cost-of-sales accounting technique assigns costs only to the goods and services sold in the period.
Period Accounting	Period accounting assigns the costs to the accounting period, regardless of the sales, if any, in that period.

Accounting for Forward Commitments and Prospects of Revenue

In parallel with the cost accounting methods using the financial and controlling databases, the planning function and the computation of profitability must take note of the various transactions that have committed funds without yet leading to any costs. For example, your purchasing department might have placed an order for stock from a vendor. The associated costs generally do not enter the system until the invoice is presented.

N O T E Commitments also arise from internal orders and projects. ⬚

On the revenue side, your sales department might have information about incoming orders that should be brought into the picture if you are using the integrated Financial Accounting and Controlling system to assess the medium-term prospects for your business.

Understanding Treasury and Financing

The treasury is recognized in English-speaking countries as the function that ensures that an enterprise has funds for its activities and commitments. The treasury department also makes sure that surplus funds are invested wisely. In European businesses, these functions are carried on as part of financial accounting.

In the English-speaking structure, the following statements are true:

- "Finance" manages controlling and public accounts.
- "Treasury" manages financing.

The European structure uses different terms for these functions:

- "Controlling" manages controlling.
- "Financial Accounting" manages financing.

The SAP R/3 system comprises a software system, integrated at the code level, that can be configured to carry out financial, controlling, and treasury functions according to the requirements of the client user. The various functions are grouped as application modules for ease of use. The treasury application therefore can be configured to support either the English-speaking or the European structure.

Using Cash Management

The needs of your company for efficient check entry and clearing and for cash forecasting are met by the TR-CM Treasury-Cash Management component. Short-term cash management is improved by automatic or manually created memos to supplement the planning data regarding anticipated payments.

The following functions are covered by the TR-CM component:

- Electronic banking
- Check deposit and clearing
- Short-term cash management
- Cash concentration
- Cash budget management
- Long-term financial budgeting

Using Treasury Planning and Active Treasury Management

The TR-TM Treasury-Treasury Management component is the planning module for the treasury functions. This module supports the following activities:

- Liquidity management
- Currency position management
- Market risk management
- Financial planning and portfolio management

See Chapter 10, "Managing the Treasury," for details of this module.

Using Funds Management

Budgeting on a local basis for all company codes is supported by the TR-FM Treasury-Funds Management component. A separate fund can be set up for each specific purpose, with budgets distributed over fiscal years. This component enables you to see how the funds are being utilized.

The IS-PS is an Industry Solution developed from TR-FM, with the intended users working in the public sector, essentially on budgets.

Using Investment Management

The domain of the IM Investment Management-application is the enterprise with capital-intensive investment programs. This application provides support from initial planning to settlement. A depreciation forecast is realized by internal orders and projects that control activities during the construction phase. Capitalization values can be accrued automatically to fixed assets. Chapter 11, "Managing Investments," discusses this module.

Understanding Controlling

In the context of business data processing and business management, controlling is the process of planning the value flows in an organization and then recording the actual values for comparison with the plan. The controlling tasks are essentially planning, monitoring, reporting, advising, and informing. These tasks address any activities that affect or could affect the profitability of the enterprise. Therefore, the controlling functionality must include such duties as the following:

- Cost control
- Profitability analysis
- Financial control
- Investment control

The basic controlling tasks depend on thorough and complete documentation of the consumption of materials and other resources in terms of the quantities used and their value. Equally thorough must be the documentation of the quantity and market value of all the goods produced and the services generated.

To assist in maximizing the profitability of the enterprise, the control function must monitor the efficiency of all operations and make sure that they are contributing the maximum to the value added chain. For the same reason, the controlling department will want to provide good support for decision-making of all kinds.

The SAP R/3 controlling functions are explained in the following chapters:

- Chapter 6, "Controlling by Cost Management"
- Chapter 7, "Costing on the Basis of Activities"
- Chapter 8, "Controlling by the PS-Project System"
- Chapter 9, "Analyzing Profitability"

Planning and Controlling the Enterprise Business

The basic profit center is the company code, and an enterprise can comprise one or more such component business units. For the enterprise as a whole to remain viable, it must consider the viability of all the constituent parts. The financial documents of the company codes must be consolidated. Chapter 5, "Consolidating Company Accounts," discusses this topic in more detail.

Management consolidation is the process of aggregating accounts to form a legal consolidation that represents the financial position of the group as a whole. The phrase also denotes the process of making sure that the management decisions of the enterprise controllers are faithfully transmitted to the company code managements. An integrated enterprise-wide business data processing system can be a powerful vehicle for this communication.

The EIS (Executive Information System) is a comprehensive reporting and analysis module that can draw data from any component of SAP R/3 and its applications. With appropriate links, the EIS can also utilize data from associated third-party systems. ◉

I

Preparing the Public Accounts

Understanding the General Ledger

In this chapter

Understanding SAP Accounting

The SAP R/3 system is an integrated financial and controlling software complex in which the components comprise standard business processes programmed to accept the details of a specific client company. The components cannot be altered by the user in their essential integrated functions. The specific components or modules configured in your particular implementation can be determined by your business requirements and by the pricing agreement you have with the supplier.

This chapter focuses on the essential of any accounting system: a book of accounts known as the General Ledger.

The SAP R/3 accounting functionality can support the following three essential component systems:

- Accounting (FI)
- Controlling (CO)
- Treasury (TR)

The following supplementary accounting applications are also configurable:

- Investment Management (IM)
- Business Planning and Control (EC), formerly named Enterprise Controlling
- Executive Information System (EIS)

Understanding the Principles of SAP R/3 General Ledger Accounting

The General Ledger is a series of account balances. Modern online accounting maintains the General Ledger balances continuously. Data that has been entered is posted immediately to the General Ledger (and also to the CO-Controlling system if it has been installed and configured). The balance sheet and the profit and loss account are based on the General Ledger.

> **CAUTION**
> If your system handles very large volumes of small-value transactions with many corrections and adjustments, you might have to weigh the value of remaining up-to-date against the costs of processing and data storage. On the other hand, processing and data storage costs likely will continue to fall, whereas the penalties of outdated accounting will not lessen.

Each business transaction creates a record in the format of an SAP document. The transaction may be part of a batch input, or it may be the result of a dialogue transaction at a terminal. The transaction is checked and validated as far as possible and then returned for corrections, if necessary.

When the transaction is acceptable, it is posted and stored on the record log as an SAP document. The system updates the daily journal file and posts the transaction to the appropriate reconciliation account of the General Ledger. From that moment, up-to-date account balances, trial balances, the balance sheet, and the profit and loss statement reports are accessible on the screen.

Special document types and posting keys provide access to compilations of particular types of transactions, such as the following:

- Customer or vendor invoices
- Cash receipts and disbursements
- Inventory transactions
- Allocations or distributions for cost accounting
- Transactions involving two or more profit centers
- Transactions involving two or more company codes
- Statistical postings (noted items, guarantees, and so on)
- Special business transactions (down payments, bills of exchange, and so on)

Entering and posting a transaction document immediately updates both financial accounting and cost accounting. The General Ledger and its subledgers use the information, as do the cost analyses elaborated from the data.

The transaction log is available to feed the General Ledger and the subsystems managing asset accounting, inventory accounting, cost accounting, order and project accounting, product costing, profitability analysis, and the subledgers of Accounts Receivable and Payable. The same transaction log can be available for updating any special ledger accounts that you decide to maintain. From any or all of this, the finance and controlling information system can extract and present whatever primary or derived information is required.

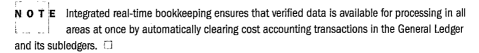

N O T E   Integrated real-time bookkeeping ensures that verified data is available for processing in all areas at once by automatically clearing cost accounting transactions in the General Ledger and its subledgers. ☐

In keeping with the principle that any number that appears on the public external accounting documents should be amenable to analysis into its constituents, the cost accounting system must be supplied with all the expense and revenue entries. Costing data allocated to period or product line is also posted to the General Ledger via a common chart of accounts shared by both the financial (external) accounting system and the cost control (internal) accounting system.

The accounts named in the General Ledger are called General Ledger accounts. One or more General Ledger account balances can be derived from a corresponding subledger specified in the chart of accounts.

Using the Extended General Ledger Concept

An extended General Ledger uses accounts based on a range of subledgers that enable analyses from different points of view. For example, accounts can focus on cost centers, product costs, or activities. These options are provided by using the CO-Controlling system as an internal accounting system. Entered data posted to the General Ledger is posted to the CO system and its components as part of the extended General Ledger.

The financial and cost accounting systems are constantly reconciled at the level of the individual General Ledger accounts. These accounts are named in the common chart of accounts.

Using the Chart of Accounts

The chart of accounts is a legal requirement that is enacted in the SAP R/3 environment as a master data record according to the specification of entity type 2001. This specification declares a valid chart of accounts to be a detailed and ordered list of value categories in which the economic situation of your company can be recorded. The chart of accounts is used to configure any account in the General Ledger so that it serves two purposes:

- To permit entry of transaction details required by the business
- To provide for any balance sheet or profit and loss statement required by law

Generally, the business wants to plan and operate some logistical processes and exercise internal financial control. In addition, the law demands proper external accounting practice so that shareholders can value their holdings and see that taxes are paid.

The processes of a business often can be classified broadly according to the focus of the activities of the various departments and their managers. The chart of accounts master record in the SAP R/3 system can differentiate many chart of accounts items, including the following:

- Undeveloped real estate
- Long-term portfolio investments
- Equity capital for each shareholder
- Receivables from sales and services, domestic debtors
- Receivables from sales and services, receipt uncertain
- Payables for goods and services, domestic creditors
- Interest revenues from loans to business partners
- Semifinished products
- Raw materials, group 1
- Auxiliary materials
- Consumption of bought-out raw materials (raw materials costs)
- Basic personnel costs (wage and salary) in production, fixed
- Basic personnel costs (wage and salary) in production, variable
- Personnel costs, administration

- Commissions to employees
- Sales costs
- Imputed rent
- Settled job order costs
- Christmas bonus
- Cafeteria generation
- Sales revenue for company-produced products and services

The significance of having a large number of chart of accounts items is that any transaction is identified with a chart item and, therefore, with a specific purpose and accounting procedure. The system can deal with any sequence of transactions because each transaction addresses specific chart of accounts items. It is not necessary to additionally classify transactions according to their accounting function.

N O T E The chart of accounts items are maintained in only one language. This language may be used for some or all charts of accounts in an enterprise. However, any user may read the item descriptions in any of the languages supported in the particular implementation.

The first group of General Ledger accounts monitors the following activities, which are concerned with building the productive resources of the company:

- Procurement of investment items, such as fixed assets, current assets, and financial assets
- Extraordinary expense or revenue

The next group of accounts deals with how the day-to-day production and processing activities affect the value of the company:

- Procurement of materials
- Consumption of company resources
- Valuation of finished or semifinished products

The third group is made up of activities with their own accounts in the General Ledger to show how sales of products are set against costs to yield the financial statements:

- Sales revenue or sales deductions
- Closing to the balance sheet and profit and loss statement

The sales and revenue items represent the value flows in the company, as do the cost items.

Using Account Classes

External accounting balances are classified into account classes using the chart of accounts. The following are examples:

- Fixed assets and long-term capital
- Finances, current assets, and short-term capital
- Non-operating expense and revenue
- Materials or stock
- Primary cost elements
- Secondary cost elements
- Job order cost elements
- Stock of finished and semifinished products
- Yield or changes to stock or capitalized internal activity
- Closing balances

The accounts needed to satisfy the GAAP principles (the Generally Accepted Accounting Principles that set the standard for a reliable accounting system) may be arranged and supplemented to suit the management requirements of your company. You may want to have reports generated to select data for a business area defined in terms of geographical operating regions, according to product grouping, or as product groups per region. You could also define profit centers to report separate financial data as a second accounting process supplementary to that required by law to render the external accounts.

Using Internal Controlling Account Classes

Controlling balances achieved by internal accounting fall into one of the following four categories:

- Project cost settlement
- Job order costing
- Cost center accounting
- Profitability analysis

Project cost settlement and job order costing recognize that purchases and allocations of resources may be needed to carry out projects and complete specific job orders that may not yield any financial return during the current accounting period. These costs are therefore treated as investment.

Cost center accounting is used to gather specified types of cost under the heading most useful for business purposes. These cost centers may correspond to departments, or they may be used to associate costs with, for example, a specific plant or item of equipment considered crucial for understanding and managing the enterprise.

Job order and product costing are the traditional techniques of associating costs with specific orders from customers or for internal production work. The manufacture of goods for inventory provides a common example of this type of costing.

Profitability analysis is the process of relating the financial yield of part of the enterprise to the costs of owning and running it. No restrictions on how the parts to be analyzed are defined.

The profitability of a work unit may be of interest, or the value of carrying out procedure change may be the target. The wisdom of all business decisions may have to be assessed in relation to the short- and long-term profitability of the consequences.

N O T E To illustrate integration of accounting, consider the fact that the common chart of accounts can record all the costs and revenues and can also provide all the factors needed for financial control via internal accounting.

The chart of accounts installed in a specific implementation must comply with statutory requirements under company law, as it is practiced in the host country. The chart must also embody the essential GAAP elements.

Understanding General Ledger Account Master Data Areas

The master data held for General Ledger purposes is arranged in two areas, which are both accessed as needed in any transaction. The chart of accounts area contains the master formats needed by all companies in the group. The company code area contains the masters that are not necessarily common to all the affiliated companies.

Using the Chart of Accounts Area

General data, such as the following, is maintained for each account in this master area:

- Account number
- Account name
- Type of General Ledger account, as determined by the chart of accounts item specified for it (such as income statement account or balance sheet account)
- Control information to specify how master records are created in the corresponding company code area
- Account group assignment
- Screen layout for master record creation

Using Company Code Area

The General Ledger masters hold separate data for each company code that defines the standard accounting environment. These include the following:

- Currency in which values are recorded
- Whether managed on an open item basis or not
- Sort basis, when line items are displayed

▨ Tax category

▨ Reconciliation account

▨ Screen layout for data entry DS

By arranging the General Ledger account master records in these two areas, you can control the use of the chart of accounts. For instance, you could specify how new accounts are to be assigned to the chart of accounts system and then open this policy to modification by only a small number of authorized users. Different sets of users can access the areas of the master data that deal with specific company codes without interfering with the main chart of accounts policy.

N O T E   If several accounts groups share attributes such as bank accounts or reconciliation accounts, you can specify a numerical range within which new accounts must be assigned. ▨

The user screen, which appears when you open a new account, can be controlled by the General Ledger master record by specifying mandatory and optional attributes for display. By this means, the user does not have to view unnecessary entry fields.

Creating Charts of Accounts

You can copy and edit any charts of accounts in your system to create one that suits the way your company prefers to set out its accounts. Additionally, you can prepare the names of the accounts that you want to use and then assign them to the accounts provided in the master reference system. The accounts you need are created automatically with new account numbers and the names you assign.

If you have an existing General Ledger chart of accounts, you can transfer all the account master data to your R/3 system by means of a standard SAP interface that invites you to confirm that the intended transfer will correctly interpret the data in your existing system.

If you have several company codes in your enterprise, you may find it convenient to define the values for the attributes of your General Ledger accounts and then instruct the system to use sample accounts to generate appropriate new accounts for each company code.

Maintaining General Ledger Master Data

You can enter General Ledger master data through the FI system for each account, either separately or by groups of accounts. Your installation may have a configured SAP data interface to enable direct input of master data under controlled conditions.

Accounts can be added to the General Ledger, and certain parameters can be modified. You can block and delete accounts during the fiscal year. As in all SAP R/3 directories, match codes set up by the individual user can be used to find specific accounts by entering an easily remembered name or title.

N O T E As with all transactions, your activities with General Ledger accounts are logged so that all modifications can be traced. ▨

Checking the Data

Checks at every stage automatically assess whether the incoming information is reasonable. The following types of questions are asked:

▨ Do the figures balance?

▨ Is this transaction legal?

▨ Has this decision-maker been authorized to deal with value changes this large?

SAP standard business software is built to provide continuous measurement of the profitability of all actions. Each business function records how often it is used and how long it takes to do its work. This kind of performance information is available to illuminate resource use.

This sophistication in accounting performance measurement, provided as standard in the SAP systems, is additional to GAAP elements.

The ideal accounting system can recreate an unbroken audit trail from each and every transaction that involves the company's balance sheet and profit and loss account. The auditor should be able to point to any number on the financial documents of the company and ask to see how it was computed, right back to the original paper documents.

N O T E SAP FI-Financial Accounting can always deliver an unbroken audit trail because every external and internal transaction creates a record in the form of an SAP document. This document can be called to substantiate the audit and prove the credentials of the company's accounts. ▨

Upon this foundation, it is possible to demonstrate just how the system complies with the GAAP tenets applied to computerized accounting systems. The GAAP requirements arise from a set of statutory regulations, decrees, and ordinances that embody the experience of accounting professionals and serve as the basis upon which each nation may develop additional accounting traditions and requirements.

Implementing GL Financial Accounting

The SAP R/3 system with the FI-Financial Accounting application installed is configured for particular countries, with the features specific to the accounting laws and customs configured to operate correctly. The system also is configured to comply with GAAP tenets, modified, if necessary, for region-specific regulations.

A national chart of accounts usually exists. If you have a multinational installation, you can install the necessary additional charts of accounts. If you install another SAP application, the system generates the additional FI-General Ledger accounts required automatically.

Part I Ch 2

Using the FI-GL General Ledger Module

The internal accounting system of a company is designed to control costs. Investors want to know how the capital of the company is assigned in the external accounting system that comprises the General Ledger.

For convenience, the General Ledger is supported by a set of subledgers, including Accounts Receivable, Accounts Payable, Fixed Assets, Human Resources, and Materials.

N O T E   An external accounting system should show what a company is worth. ▨

Integrating Accounting Through the General Ledger

The General Ledger is the source of the data used to build the external accounting documents, the balance sheet, and the profit and loss statement. Because this information is audited, it must be supported by audit trails that show how each summary total has been computed.

Anticipating the Year-End Results   If a complete audit trail exists, the possibility also exists of using the information therein to make some decisions before the end-of-year results are derived. Making interim decisions on the basis of accounting information is the province of business controlling, for which the SAP CO-Controlling module was developed.

Controlling depends on detailed record-keeping, in which the individual transactions retain their identity, their date, their sources, and the identification of the users who worked on them. Only if the accounting information is retained in this fine detail can the controlling functions assemble it and then use it to discern what is happening in the business. If the decision-makers cannot establish what is happening, they will be prone to take no action when they should, to take action when they should not, or to take the wrong action.

The work units of a business controller probably are the line items of the business transactions, as well as the journal statements, the accounts, the trial balance, and the final statements. These provide fundamental monitoring of business direction in terms of movement and progress, strategic goals, and operating tactics. These are the primary results achieved as a result of investing human and financial capital in the company.

Calling Up the Standard Transaction Data   The copious and comprehensive data gathered from the SAP standard procedure of capturing all transaction information in the form of SAP documents can subsequently be analyzed. For example, there can be valuable additions to primary results in the form of data interpretations that examine the company from various points of view. For example, you might consider taking a look at profit and loss for each activity over each operating period.

These additional analyses of the accounting data can serve to prompt and direct an interim change of direction or emphasis. However, they may also form the essential inputs to business planning. Profit centers may focus the analysis; geographical business areas may be of interest; and product groups may be worth assessing in terms of profit contributions.

Viewing Profitability from the Center   Clearly, data should be held centrally if you seek widespread analyses. Furthermore, if you want up-to-date information, records of every transaction must be available to contribute to the analysis if required. The General Ledger and its subledgers in the SAP online accounting system provide this central source. From this source in the General Ledger, you can extract comprehensive analyses of important ratios such as cash flow proportions and workload per person.

Be sure to watch liquidity. With General Ledger accounting, you can forecast liquidity by examining projected short- and medium-term cash disbursements and receipts. If you have created a business plan in the SAP system and have efficient tools available to assist, then you can compare the actual results to planned ones in whatever dimensions and ratios are of interest. Planning that is integrated across an entire company must include plans for the balance sheet and for the profit and loss statements. Cash plans that include project receipts and payments are also required.

Controlling from the Accounts   Controls over the ongoing activities of the company begin by comparing the balance sheet and the profit and loss statements, year on year. Short-term cash management using projected cash payments, receipts, and a daily financial statement may well be essential. Control of ongoing business can also make good use of financial analyses, comparisons, and ratios based on the organization's structure of business areas or units.

Subledgers can be the means of exercising control over the entities they represent. Receivables and Payables can be managed by inspecting analyses of due dates, amounts, selected customers, regions, and so on. Assets may attract the attention of controllers because of automatic reports of their ratios, depreciation, capitalized cost, and net book value. Inventory transactions, invoices, and personnel expenses are other examples of business aspects that can be made available to controllers—the SAP system captures all transactions from all system components in the form of SAP documents that can be collated and analyzed into whatever informative structure is feasible.

Of course, data not entered into the SAP system at some stage cannot take part in subsequent analysis. You may have interfaces installed to link with third-party systems that hold important business information, but it will not affect your reporting system unless these links successfully transmit the accurate and timely information you require.

However, if the necessary primary data is in the system, then automatic profit and loss information can be computed. Overheads can be monitored and attributed to such headings as Cost Center and Order Settlement. Product cost accounting can shed light on the costs of ongoing jobs. Technical and commercial projects can be monitored, controlled, and brought into the plans. Profitability analysis can be conducted on the basis of cost of sales and period accounting.

TIP At any time, it is possible to clear individual line items in business transactions to reconcile separate controlling units with the General Ledger.

Part
I

Ch
2

Identifying the Two Primary Functions of the General Ledger

The FI-GL General Ledger component recognizes two main reasons for asking for reports from a General Ledger:

- To discern the financial viability of the company
- To seek opportunities to improve profitability by controlling some or all activities of the company

Shareholders may be very interested in the financial statements required by law—the balance sheet and the profit and loss statement. These two financial documents serve as the basis of external accounting because they reveal a company's financial health.

The profit and loss computations depend on closing the accounts in the General Ledger at the end of the financial year. One of the primary functions of the General Ledger is to accommodate this year-end closing in an orderly manner.

The other primary function of the General Ledger is financial accounting for the current fiscal year. The function of collecting and recording data from transactions is one part of financial accounting. Posting data and effecting reconciliation on a continuous basis make up the other part. Reconciliation takes place at the transaction level before an entry is posted, but a closing of the reconciliation accounts at the end of the month and then at the end of the year also must occur. A facility exists in R/3 to call up daily or monthly reports at any time.

Using Special General Ledger Transactions

The accounts in the special General Ledger are reconciliation accounts for special subledger transactions that do not directly involve sales or purchases and that may not be balanced with the Receivables and Payables. The special General Ledger indicator is a single character code to distinguish these transactions from sales to customers or purchases from vendors. The following transaction types are examples of special General Ledger transactions:

- Acquisitions
- Dispositions
- Depreciation
- Transfers
- Down payments
- Bills of exchange
- Period closing entries

Performing Year-End Closing

The law for closing a fiscal year requires entries to closing accounts for the balance sheet and profit and loss statement. The SAP FI System ensures that year-end closing entries are transferred from subledgers such as the following:

- Accounts Receivable
- Accounts Payable
- Fixed assets

Provision is also made for closing entries manually and individually. You can close a fiscal year at any time. The flexible online reporting system offers separate formats of the financial documents for tax authorities, stockholders, legal consolidation of associated companies, and so on.

Understanding Complex Organizations and the Chart of Accounts

The chart of accounts must include all General Ledger accounts in an accounting system. You can specify what transaction data goes where so that each account contains all the required details for closing. Internal accounting usually requires that certain types of data be sent to each of the accounts used in the controlling functions.

Two possibilities exist for using a common chart of accounts in a complex organization:

- You may have a centralized organization in which the maximum number of accounts at group level is displayed in a uniform chart of accounts that applies to all company codes in the group.
- You may have a decentralized organization in which each company code has its own chart of accounts.

In either case, it is possible to use sample accounts taken from the reference system paired with transfer rules for individual company codes. This grants each company some flexibility while operating on a common chart of accounts.

Understanding International Taxation

The SAP system is international. Common taxation functions have been programmed as standard business functions, with tables of parameters available for customization of specific operational features.

When you use the SAP system, you signify both the country in which your company is located and the country in which your vendor or customer is located. The system adopts the taxation regimes appropriate to each of these countries.

The system calculates tax or adjusts it automatically. When you enter the transaction, the system creates the SAP document that contains all the details and then immediately posts the taxes as it updates the accounts. The required tax reports are generated automatically.

Using Standard Taxation Functions

The FI-Financial Accounting module includes the following standard international taxation functions:

- Taxes on sales and purchases
- Bills of exchange tax
- Tax base for tax calculation
- Definitions of all required tax rates
- Methods for the determination of due dates for tax payment
- Tax calculation procedures
- Tax base for cash discount
- Dependent taxes as surcharges or deductions
- European Community acquisition tax
- Division into deductible and nondeductible taxes

Withholding tax can be programmed to suit your requirements. The process makes use of the following functions:

- Tax base
- Definition of all required tax rates
- Flagging of all vendors affected
- Determination of due dates for tax payments

The system verifies withholding tax when you enter a vendor invoice and payment. You do not have to check the tax entries later. The necessary reports are prepared automatically.

Although the system adopts the appropriate standard tax regime as soon as you indicate the country, you can adjust parameters to meet your specific tax requirements. For instance, you may have to make adjustments to the standard procedure because of a change in the national taxation regulations, or because you are working in a country that does not exactly follow any of the standard tax regimes programmed into the system.

 N O T E   Country-specific tax requirements are notified in the SAP INT International component and can be used to customize your particular implementation.

Using Country-Specific Taxation Requirements

Specific taxation rules for charging, disclosing, and paying tax are accommodated by customizing each company code operating in that country. Specific forms of payment and common payment media are prepared for each country.

The following examples illustrate the range of differences that can be handled by the system:

- German-speaking countries in Europe require a tax adjustment if the payment for an invoice is net of cash discount. Other countries calculate tax liability on the invoiced amount.
- Different countries have their own arrangements for tax exemptions and delay of liability.
- Withholding tax is subject to wide differences in scope and method.

Using Intercompany Accounting

A group of two or more individual companies has an organizational structure designed to facilitate day-to-day operations. For example, each company may buy material and manage a warehouse. Each may run a Sales and Distribution division. To increase the complexity of the organization somewhat, suppose there is also a head office that functions as a separate company.

As a company, the head office may oversee the two other companies. Each of these business units incurs expenses and probably enjoys revenue. For the sake of business convenience, two or even three of these units might combine to make a purchase, perhaps at a discount because of the size of the order. In this case, one payment to the vendor is made against one invoice.

Again for good business reasons, the units may join forces to provide a service to a customer. For example, Purchasing may provide the material goods, and Distribution may look after their delivery. Again, one payment from the customer is made against one invoice.

If each of these business units is managed as an individual company, all intercompany transactions within the group and with customers and vendors must obey the rules of intercompany accounting. In particular, transactions must leave records that enable intercompany business to be legally audited to give a true picture of the group as a whole, as well as of the individual companies, when it comes to drawing up the financial documents.

The principles of intercompany accounting are applied when your company is part of a group; they also apply when your customer or your vendor is part of another group. The SAP accounting system uses methods that support intercompany transactions and comply with GAAP codes.

N O T E With modern online computerized accounting systems, the balance sheets and the profit and loss statements of the group and each individual company are readily available at any time.

Using Intercompany Expense and Revenue Postings

Two divisions of a group, each with a separate company code, may jointly make a purchase or issue goods. The same principles apply if more than two company codes are involved. You must enter and post the expense item in both company codes, but you post only one vendor account in one of the company codes (it does not matter which one).

The system automatically calculates and posts the Receivables and Payables between company codes, just as if you entered a regular transaction in one company code. The system creates line items for Receivables and Payables between company codes. It also generates an SAP document in each company code. As it does so, the system assigns a unique intercompany transaction number, which appears on all documents and vouchers.

N O T E The debits do not have to equal the credits in each company code; they must balance only within the entire intercompany transaction. Transaction documents in each company are balanced by the automatic entries made by SAP R/3.

Paying for Intercompany Purchases

Several companies in a group may purchase from the same vendor. You can pay for the purchase by making a single payment, with the vendor account number being the same in the vendor master record in each company in the group. One company must keep a central bank account to be used to pay on behalf of the other companies.

Using Cash Receipt for Two or More Company Codes

Some companies in a group may have customers in common. If one of these customers offers payment for two or more company codes in the group, you can use this procedure:

1. Match open items to the amount of the payment.
2. Process the selected items, sharing the payments flexibly if necessary.
3. Apply cash discount calculations in each company.
4. Clear documents for each of the companies.

The system automatically posts the required clearing account in each company.

Using Head Office and Branch Accounts

Your supplier may be a branch with its own account, but its head office may want to receive your payment. In this case, you can enter its head office account number in the master record for the branch vendor. When you enter a transaction to the branch account, the system posts the transaction to the head office account, leaving a cleared entry on the branch account to show who supplied the goods or service.

The master includes data about the branch and a reference to another master to give details to the head office. By this means, dunning letters can be sent to the head office, the branch, or both for overdue refunds.

Making Vendor Payments to an Alternative Recipient

Your supplier may not have to deal with its payments due. For example, it may have a head office that receives payment. You can record in its master data the account number of this alternative recipient. The system then processes return transfers and other vendor payment business through the banks to the alternative recipient.

If you do post vendor invoices to an affiliate, you must record in the master data of the branch vendor a group-wide company account number to be used during consolidation to eliminate the invoices that would otherwise appear twice in the company accounts. The system can look at the transaction documents bearing this group-wide company account number and identify any entries that are replicated because the payment was made to an affiliate that was not the original vendor.

Making Intercompany Payments

One vendor may have supplied several company codes in the same group. The payment system can make one payment and then settle the intercompany accounts by calculating and posting Receivables and Payables between company codes.

You must define one of the company codes and enter it as a normal paying company. The system assigns the document a unique intercompany identification number, used to ensure that the other members of the company code group pay their shares.

Eliminating Intercompany Payables and Receivables

FI-Financial Accounting eliminates intercompany balances by open item only if each trading partner has been marked in the vendor master record. You must also ensure that the reporting procedures inform the consolidating department of the numbers of these trading partners, at least on the items relating to intercompany Payables and Receivables, revenues and expenses.

The law requires that all intercompany balances be eliminated before presenting the balance sheet and the profit and loss statement. All possible pairs of individual companies must be investigated to prove that they have been trading with each other.

In practice, significant differences in the way individual companies keep their records may make complete elimination impractical. The most frequent causes of discrepancies in elimination are as follows:

- Currency translation differences
- Differences in the timing of entries for goods in transit between individual companies
- Specific reserves set aside for doubtful accounts
- Liabilities that are not acknowledged in the records

The cause that is most difficult to handle is currency translation; the others can usually be resolved by applying corporate policies in a thorough manner.

If the individual companies have installed and configured SAP accounting applications, automatic dual currency accounting occurs. In this type of accounting, every transaction is documented at the time it occurs, in both the local currency and the currency designated for all transactions in the group.

If the FI-LC Consolidation component is installed and configured in your company, you can trace any currency translation differences between the local currency, at the prevailing rate of exchange, and the transaction currency. An exchange rate difference correction then is posted automatically in the balance sheet account designated for this purpose, therefore updating the consolidated financial statement.

Dealing with Language Differences

R/3 is an international system. The names of all General Ledger accounts can be translated if the language key is entered together with the name of the account in the target language. This process can be repeated for all languages in the group. By this means you might add or modify General Ledger account names in the language of the holding company and later log in and call for the account balances in the language of your login profile.

N O T E In a listing of the charts of accounts, each chart is annotated to show the main language and all the alternatives available. ☐

Defining Currency

The following operational currencies have been defined, and their codes are assigned to each function by default (you can alter the default settings):

- Local currency is also the reporting currency for the company code.
- Document currency is the currency specified for entry on SAP documents.
- Group currency is an alternative to document currency for group reporting.
- Updating currency is defined for posting debits and credits to the General Ledger in parallel with the local currency.
- Credit limit currency is the currency chosen to maintain the credit limit.
- Ledger currency is an alternative to the updating currency for that ledger.

Additional currency assignments are available in the SAP Foreign Exchange Management component. R/3 also offers the possibility of recording hard currency, index currency, and global currency in the standard FI-GL General Ledger.

Using Currencies in Transactions

Each company code has a local currency for reporting. The system records amounts in this local currency, as well as in the document currency, which will be used on all documents in addition to the local currency.

N O T E You can enter documents in any currency. ☒

You have two options for converting currencies:

- You can enter an exchange rate when you enter the transaction document.
- The system can translate between document and local currencies by referring to a table of daily exchange rates, which is either updated manually or maintained automatically by a link to a separate database.

The system can be customized in various ways, including the following:

- A specific user must enter amounts in a particular currency, which can be the local currency or the document currency.
- A specific user can be permitted to enter amounts in either local or document currency.

Regardless of the customizing arrangements, the system displays amounts in both local and document currencies. Minor differences are rounded, using rules established for this purpose. These differences can occur when several line items are converted and then added in both currencies.

Customer monthly debits and credits are kept by the system only in local currency. The reconciliation account for the Accounts Receivable subledger is kept in local currency and in all the other currencies posted.

Dealing with Currency Exchange Differences

A line item can be expressed in a currency other than the local or document currency. You can enter payments to clear such foreign currency line items using either local or document currency.

The payment expressed in the document currency is converted from the local currency at an exchange rate adopted by the system (according to rules for assigning the daily exchange rate). If this rate has changed from the rate prevailing when the invoice was written, the payment amount may not match the open item amount. In such cases, the system automatically calculates and posts an exchange difference entry to a separate account established for this purpose.

Specifying Rules for Administering General Ledger Accounts

An open item is one that can be partially settled; it remains open until the item has been fully cleared. If an item is not to be managed on an open item basis, the settlement has to be in full or not at all. Rules can be established, for example, in the partial payment of accounts outstanding, to determine that the largest items should be settled first, or perhaps those that have been open longest.

Such manipulations may not be permitted in some General Ledger accounts because that would destroy their informative nature. By and large, if you have authority to manipulate the General Ledger accounts, you will not have any restrictions-only obligations.

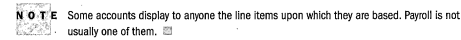 N O T E   Some accounts display to anyone the line items upon which they are based. Payroll is not usually one of them.

Another example of attaching instructions to a data object representing a General Ledger account involves how the line items are to be displayed. This includes their sort order and any masks applied to conceal certain values.

Using Daily Journals and Interim Statements

Certain SAP programs can help you prepare your system for year-end closing. For daily and monthly closings, however, you face no special requirements and no extra entries because the account balances are maintained all the time.

At the end of each day, you can review a report of the exact closing balances for the day, based on the line items and the total debits and credits entered. For periods of a day or more, you can ask for data reports posted over the period, sorted by date or by any of the fields that appear in the relevant SAP documents created for the transactions.

These journals can help you decide how to close posting periods and account for accruals. You may wish to define two accounting periods open for this purpose.

 T I P The practice of calling daily or short-period journals can be helpful. You can validate data entry soon after it occurs, so you can control it.

Performing Year-End Closing Tasks

Monthly and interim closing entails no technical requirements. Year-end closing, however, must be anticipated by running a series of SAP programs that include the foreign currency conversions. These year-end programs serve two main purposes:

- They reorganize SAP documents into more convenient groupings.
- They reconcile summary records with the individual documents upon which they are based.

The year-end closing sequence must include the following tasks, which do not necessarily have to be completed in this order:

1. Close posting periods.
2. Re-value all line items and General Ledger account balances to adjust for foreign currencies.
3. Sort open and closed Receivables by their due dates.
4. Sort open and closed Payables by their due dates.
5. Identify and adjust vendor accounts with debit.
6. Identify and adjust customer accounts with credit balances.
7. Post re-evaluations.
8. Post adjustments.
9. Post accruals.
10. Print the balance sheet with the profit and loss statement.

Automatic closing programs compile a series of reports that support you by preparing what you need to close the year. These supporting reports include the following:

- Reconciliation of documents with monthly debits and credits
- Posting totals
- Accumulated balance trail
- Balances carried forward from the balance sheet of the previous year

Planning in the General Ledger

Throughout the SAP R/3 system, a distinction is maintained between two values: numerical and monetary values that are the result of operational transactions, and values that have been generated for planning purposes. As far as the user is concerned, the planning entries are maintained in a database separate from the operational data of the live production system. These two types of value are brought together in the comparison of planned and actual values. This can take place at any time for the purpose of exercising closer control over business processes. It is also customary to amplify the presentation of the balance sheet and the profit and loss statement by showing how well the company performed in relation to the target planning values.

The natural structure for building a plan of anticipated or targeted business activity is the one used for the profit and loss statement. The R/3 system includes examples that you may copy and edit to formulate a first draft plan. These profit and loss statement examples can be displayed as a tree structure that you can modify to suit your company's requirements.

You can establish planned values for the whole profit and loss structure, or you can decide to enter planned values for only part of the structure. Any value is open to copying, overwriting, editing, and selecting as a member of a group of values subjected to a logical or arithmetical operation, such as an increase of 5% for next year's target.

If you enter a planned value, you may subject it to any of the following operations:

- Copy the planned value to other locations
- Append a reference text to a particular value or group of values
- Carry forward a value to successive time periods of the plan
- Assign a value to certain time periods of the plan
- Have the system distribute the entered value across a group of selected periods according to a particular distribution scheme, such as "evenly to all periods" or "linear increase from zero to the value entered"

Each plan you make is identified by the date and time you post it and by any other text that you use to title it. In particular, the document management system ensures that if you change a plan in any way, the new version is identified as such and is kept separate from the previous version. By this means, you can formulate several plans and see how the values change if you switch from one to another on your display.

Using the FI-SL Special Purpose Ledger

From SAP R/3 Release 3.0, the FI-SL module has been assigned the functions previously identified as the FI-GLX Extended General Ledger. The FI-GL General Ledger module includes access to the full reporting facilities of the SAP R/3 Basis system with which it is fully integrated at the code level. However, you can elect to exclude some of the components of R/3 from your implementation by specifying this at configuration. For example, if you do not require the full CO-Controlling application to be installed and configured, you may nevertheless opt to have some planning functionality available with your General Ledger. This option may be presented as the FI-SL Special Purpose Ledger module. An implementation that opts for the full CO-Controlling application does not need the FI-SL component because all these functions are provided by CO-Controlling.

For historical and legal reasons, the General Ledger has been the primary means by which an auditor or an investor might see how well or badly a company has been managed. The results of this management are extracted to form the balance sheet, showing the end-of-year value of the company's assets, and the trading report or profit and loss statement, revealing how the assets either have generated profit or have diminished through losses. The General Ledger is therefore the basis for external accounting, but it does not show all the useful information that has been collected in the course of the trading year, such as who bought what.

The manager must submit to the procedures of internal accounting to see more closely how resources might be used for a better outcome. Perhaps it would be informative if the financial summaries contained breakdowns of activities by geographical business areas, by type of business, by product, and so on. These other ways of collating business information for the benefit of exercising better control of a company have been provided with standard business functions in the CO-Controlling module.

The FI-Financial Accounting module primarily serves the requirements of external accounting. The CO-Controlling module accommodates internal accounting. Both serve the same company by sharing a common chart of accounts that includes accounts that are not necessary to meet the legal requirements of the financial statement—those requirements that are met by the General Ledger, from which the balance sheet and the profit and loss statement are derived.

These extra accounts are there to improve the usefulness of the financial system in controlling the company. The FI-GL General Ledger accounts and these extra accounts and account subtotals comprise the FI-SL Special Purpose Ledger. The General Ledger is extended through integration with the common chart of accounts to take advantage of the facilities offered by the CO-Controlling module.

Although the Controlling System is specialized for internal accounting procedures, it maximizes the favorable values and minimizes the unfavorable values summarized in the formal legal documents of external accounting (namely, the balance sheet and the profit and loss statement). After all, the purpose of the company is to realize profit from its activities and its use of invested capital invested. The CO-Controlling module represents a comprehensive application of the SAP system to all the elements of a company's business.

Using the FI-GLX Standalone Special Purpose Ledger

The Special Purpose Ledger is an SAP product that can stand alone and accept data from external systems using software from other suppliers. This product can also be installed to integrate with the SAP R/3 system and interact with components of the FI-Financial Accounting module and the CO-Controlling module. Either directly or via the CO-Controlling module, the Special Purpose Ledger module can link up with any of the SAP R/3 components.

The bridge between other applications and the Special Purpose Ledger comprises one or more ledgers. Not all transaction data from other applications can find a corresponding account in the Special Purpose Ledger. The system ensures that updates from another application correspond with at least one ledger, however. A standard program is supplied with the Special Purpose Ledger to check that this reconciliation does in fact take place.

N O T E   You can reconcile the Special Purpose Ledger with the transaction data at any time.

Planning in the FI-SL Special Purpose Ledger

A plan comprises three operations and a reporting stage, which can occur at any time and be repeated as often as required. The following sections explain these processes.

Specifying Planning Objects   Controlling in business usually means that the controlling person has a plan or objective that is used to influence decisions in situations where common sense is not sufficient. A production target is an example. You could set up a plan to produce as much as possible, or an amount for which you had positive orders. You could set a sales target in units or total value. But if your resources are not unlimited, or if your markets are restricted, then you may be advised to choose and plan for a target that takes these factors into consideration.

The first step is to set out the planning cost objects or the levels at which planning is to take place. These could include the following:

- Business area
- Cost centers
- General Ledger accounts
- Months or other posting periods

Many businesses can predict season variations by choosing posting periods to which target values can be assigned to match the expected variations.

Assigning Values   Entering target values and budgets to be assigned to the planning cost objects can be done manually or with assistance from automatic distribution functions. For example, you could divide your annual planned sales evenly across the months, or you could use a standard function to distribute your target according to a predefined set of parameters in proportion to your expected variations. You might use last year's monthly figures plus 5% for these parameters. The more market intelligence you can apply, the better your plan.

Collating Data   SAP R/3 automatically saves transaction data. But collecting this transaction data and collating the individual items to match planning levels and objects is the most intensive operation in terms of information flow. This function can be assigned to batch processing and off-peak scheduling.

Reporting   The standard SAP R/3 flexible reporting functions can show you, for any combinations of planning cost objects that you require, how actual values stack up against plans and targets. Any or all of these procedures can be automated by setting parameters under the control of the Special Purpose Ledger component.

Enabling Functionalities with the Special Purpose Ledger

The following actions can be carried out through the Special Purpose Ledger program:

- Specifying General Ledger account subtotals to collect data on chosen periods or another focus of interest
- Naming the account subtotals
- Specifying the criteria for posting entries to each subtotal
- Recording and updating account subtotals from the transaction information entered in SAP documents
- Accepting data from other SAP applications
- Accepting data from systems that do not use SAP software
- Entering financial plans in the form of planned values for each relevant account and account subtotal of the Extended General Ledger
- Reporting on the planned and actual account totals and subtotals for the period or other focus of interest
- Designing reports based on flexible fiscal years
- Providing parallel reports in up to three currencies

You could regard these extra reporting functions as a waste of time and resources because they are concerned with events that have already happened. However, the more carefully you plan your business year, the more accurately the automatic SAP R/3 functions can report on how the performance of your company corresponds to your anticipation.

Specifying Inflow of Data to the Special Purpose Ledger

Data reaching the Special Purpose Ledger system arises mainly from transactions in other systems, other SAP applications, or systems provided by other suppliers. SAP provides a comprehensive suite of standard interfaces.

The flow can take place immediately after a transaction is posted, at regular intervals, or via batch transfers. Validation can take place to ensure that the incoming data complies with the conditions imposed by the Special Purpose Ledger. Substitution of transaction data can take place so that what is retained is amenable to further processing by the client systems using the facilities provided by the Special Purpose Ledger module.

Checking for consistency also must occur. For example, master data in the Special Purpose Ledger must have elements to name and specify all the necessary data objects used to store data generated by the associated applications. Account identification, cost center, product identification, and any other attribute of interest must find a place in the Special Purpose Ledger. Of course, such information can be retrieved and identified even though, in the case of non-SAP systems, it may no longer be easily traced in the system that first created it.

One solution is to have the Special Purpose Ledger acquire master data from the transferring system. This imposes the requirement that transactions in the transferring system include all the information of interest as either optional or required entries. Obviously, information that has not been collected by the transferring system cannot subsequently be accessed from the Special Purpose Ledger.

A set of master data shared by all applications ensures consistency of data across all systems using the Special Purpose Ledger.

From other SAP R/3 applications, the preliminaries of data transfer include establishing the following specifications:

- Determining which transactions update the Special Purpose Ledger. Sources might include Financial Accounting, Material Management, or Job Order Accounting.
- Determining which particular ledger is to be updated and how.
- Determining whether each ledger is to be updated immediately or at regular intervals.

SAP R/3 guides and prompts you to set up the validation rules in each case, based on rules and combinations of fields that you can define. The system then validates transaction data, subtotals, or totals in the ledgers specified.

It is customary to have other SAP applications automatically transfer the data for the Special Purpose Ledger. A direct data entry function is also provided to enable the entry of notes or consolidation entries, for instance. As is normal practice, these entries create SAP documents. These SAP documents can be flagged to show that they are records of direct entries to the Special Purpose Ledger. If necessary, these documents can be displayed separately.

Making an Assessment in the Special Purpose Ledger

In this context, assessment refers to the process of gathering cost information from a number of sources. Consider freight charges across all warehouses for all products in a particular group or on a particular list of products. Assessment is the process of seeking out the details and calculating the total of these charges.

This task lies in the province of the Special Purpose Ledger. Needless to say, you cannot complete such a task successfully if the master data of the Extended General Ledger makes no mention of freight charges or any data field that could be used to make a proper substitution (such as delivery charges.)

Using Distribution in the Special Purpose Ledger

Distribution is sharing. For example, the total of freight charges across the group can be distributed by sharing it as some kind of overhead charge imposed by the accounting system. Who should share this burden may be hotly debated, but in the end the Special Purpose Ledger must be told to divide this cost between various accounts.

Part II
Ch 2

Two types of distribution exist:

- Single-dimension
- More than one dimension or level of detail

Single-dimension distribution takes place when a value is credited to the sender and debited to a single receiving account. For example, a cost center can be created so that certain costs can be reported under the name of that center. Administration Costs might be the name of such a cost center.

Distribution can also be directed at more than one receiving entity. The set of recipients might include all production departments. The costs can be distributed across specific products in a product group, for example.

Whether the distribution involves a single receiver (such as a cost center) or a set of receivers, three methods exist for computing how much is attributed to each:

- *Fixed amount method.* You decide how much to charge each individual recipient. A fixed amount is debited to each, and the sender is credited with the total.
- *Fixed share method.* You decide what percentage share of the amount to be distributed shall be charged to each recipient. Each recipient is debited with the fixed share, and the sender is credited with the total of these shares, which need not equal 100% of the assessed charge. The sender may retain a share.
- *Dynamic method.* The amount to be distributed is automatically calculated by the system on the basis of the subtotals already recorded in the Special Purpose Ledger.

Using the Set Concept

The logical concept of a set is used in the Special Purpose Ledger for reporting, planning, and ledger processing. A set refers to a data structure and its relationships with other data structures. A set of numbers may be defined, where the numbers are the identification codes of bank accounts, for example. A list of cost centers also can constitute a set.

The actual members of a set may not be known until the set definition is called into use. A set definition of this kind is, "The top three operating divisions for gaining new customers in the current month." The definition of a set may include relationships between specific firms or companies in a group, not necessarily at the same level. A set may comprise any collection of data objects that meet the logical criteria forming the definition for membership of that set.

Specific business functions can call on a set definition that has been stored for later use. Assessment and distribution often take place under the control of sets.

Using Planned Amounts in the Special Purpose Ledger

The basic concept is to set target values for account totals or subtotals for one or more periods. Actual values totaled from the transaction data are then compared with these planned targets. The method is to enter a planned total and then have it allocated to periods by various standard functions. Special functions and tools in the Special Purpose Ledger provide flexible planning and controlling facilities.

In practice, planning usually requires several iterations in which suggested budgets and target values are distributed in various ways until an agreed distribution is effected. The starting point for a plan is a set of plan parameters, such as the following:

- Basic data and targets to be entered
- Planned currency for transactions, and the local and group currencies
- Planned types of main and additional quantities
- Standard period allocation keys
- Input units (hundreds, thousands, millions)
- Planned number of decimal places
- Plan version identification
- Data objects to be used

The plan parameters are dependent on the authorization profiles of the users. Not all users are allowed to alter certain parameters.

N-O-T-E   You can specify for display at any time sets of plan parameters to be used as the basis for planning and for suggesting more appropriate amounts to be set as targets. ▢

Planning Perspectives

Centralized planning entails planning cost elements, such as for all cost centers. Decentralized planning plans for each cost center individually. The Special Purpose Ledger accommodates both perspectives, and you can switch between perspectives online.

The technique of setting up plan parameters enables you to begin the planning process with a complete plan that can be used without altering anything. On the other hand, any of the parameter values can be changed if the user is so authorized.

The distribution functions can be changed, as can the sets of account totals and subtotals upon which they act. Individual amounts can be overwritten.

N O T E   Each version of a plan can be stored for later comparison. ▢

Many standard ways exist for distributing planned amounts. Annual or quarterly input values are usually distributed to planning periods by using one or more distribution keys.

A distribution key is a tag or code that can be used simply as a label, or it may refer to a complex data object that serves as a distribution formula. A standard distribution key distributes an amount equally to every working day in the current month, for example. SAP R/3 offers a wide variety of standard distribution keys, and the user can define unique keys available for use with other planning periods or other versions of the plan.

Other distribution keys can be used with various planning objects, such as sales, personnel expenses, and so on. There are standard keys for product groups and for product types such as semifinished products. Such keys can be used to plan for production cost centers so that, in this example, the value of semifinished products appears in the Special Purpose Ledger reports under that heading. In this case, such a value also attracts a designated share of the cost of warehousing or other assessments.

This system of distribution keys can be used with the suite of distribution functions and the logical concept of sets to arrange for a flexible and focused planning system that can be adjusted to suit changing business conditions.

Posting Technique in the General Ledger

The General Ledger is a primary recording mechanism that must be maintained at the highest standards of propriety. The SAP R/3 system complies with the U.S. GAAP principles and with the legal requirements of more than 40 industrialized nations. This standard can be reached only if there is complete recording of all the necessary data at the point of origin. It will not suffice to assign posting data to origins and accounts at some later time.

To be reliable, precise, and comprehensive, every element of data must be associated and recorded together at the time the transaction is posted. This record, an SAP transaction document, is then locked against further editing to that it can be recalled in an audit trail with the assurance that the information it contains is truly the original data.

The posting data must include sufficient information to achieve the following standards:

- ☐ The organization and person who originated the transaction must be identifiable
- ☐ The date and time of the transaction must be recorded
- ☐ The organizational unit or department responsible for the accounting aspects must be designated
- ☐ The details of the transaction items must be unequivocally specified

Understanding Origins of General Ledger Postings

A posting to a General Ledger account can occur as a result of any of several types of events, such as the following:

- ☐ An operational transaction occurring in an active and integrated application module
- ☐ A posting transaction in a subsidiary ledger
- ☐ A transaction assigned to a General Ledger account

For example, if the MM-Materials Management system is active and integrated with the General Ledger, an issue of goods automatically posts a transaction that prompts an inventory reduction posting to document the corresponding reduction in value.

If you install and configure the FI-AA Asset Accounting module, when you acquire a new asset (such as a plant item or a warehouse), automatic posting of the change of value can be arranged in the Asset Acquisition account of the fixed assets subledger. If you have the authorization and the FI-GL General Ledger module is active, you might be able to post directly to a General Ledger account.

Understanding the Relationship of Subledgers to the General Ledger

The existence of subsidiary ledgers is a matter of convenience for the users rather than a legal requirement. Subledgers are completely and comprehensively integrated as part of the General Ledger. This means that there are several ways in which the subsidiary and General Ledger can be treated as a single system:

- Master data is common to general and subsidiary ledgers.
- Master data parameters can be shared across general and subsidiary ledgers.
- Transaction data is shared.
- Data can be mutually verified for correctness and validity.
- Reporting automatically uses both general and subsidiary ledgers, as necessary.
- The chart of accounts is shared.
- All the account assignment elements of the subsidiary ledgers are integrated with the General Ledger, including cost accounting elements.

Transaction data is held in a database that makes no distinction between general and subsidiary ledgers. A line item of subledger accounting is in complete correspondence with the original data and the account assignment, as recorded in any central document.

The effect of using a shared uniform database for all ledger data is to provide the following advantages:

- Data is created and maintained without redundancy.
- The database is accessible in the same way by all the installed and configured applications.
- All transaction documentation can be verified and reviewed.
- Any customized reporting and information systems can access all the data.

The integration of data is facilitated by the SAP system of standard account assignment terms. These are provided by the system and can be edited during customization. Thereafter, however, the terms are used as fixed codes that are assigned to all transaction documents. If a document flows through a business transaction sequence, it is processed with the standard assignment code.

One of the advantages of this mechanism is that each posting is identified by its assignment code when records are selected for any evaluation or reporting purpose. By this means, all the relevant data sources are collated when the uniform database is accessed.

Part
II

Ch
2

To the user, the common integrated database is apparent only by implication, so it appears that data is reliably communicated to all the necessary places. From the accounting point of view, the shared database ensures that the General Ledger and the subsidiary ledgers are always reconciled.

Financial information compiled from the shared database automatically includes the very latest postings to assets and profit and loss accounts. Conversely, you can see immediately how any particular transaction posting affects the assets or profit and loss positions.

N O T E   For the compilation of reports, the possibility always exists of using the balance sheet and
profit and loss statement data from the subsidiary ledgers. You also have the option of
allowing the user to drill down the data to the single document level, if necessary.

Understanding Data Entry Techniques

The entry of data is subject to authorization. As an added benefit, a user can set up posting facilities that will be reconstructed every time the user profile is evoked. Each user and each piece of information can be scrutinized so that data entry is permitted or blocked according to a wide variety of filtering principles, such as the following:

- Users can be confined to or restricted from a particular account.
- A user can be allowed to post only to accounts belonging to a specific company code.
- A user can be confined to a business area but not to specific company codes.
- A user can be confined to a cost center or a cost object.

N O T E   Before a document posting is accepted, data is checked for validity against related data in
the document.

Closing the General Ledger During the Fiscal Year

The SAP R/3 system includes programs to automate year-end closing so that it can be generated quickly and reliably. The following tasks must be performed to close the General Ledger and the subsidiary ledgers:

- Close the posting period to prevent further postings to the accounts.
- Evaluate open items.
- Evaluate balances in foreign currencies.
- List by due dates all incoming payments, including open items.
- List by due dates all outgoing payments, including open items.
- Determine vendors with a debit balance.
- Determine customers with a credit balance.
- Post re-valuations.

☐ Post adjustments.

☐ Post accruals and deferrals.

☐ Print the balance sheet and the profit and loss statement.

Reporting at Closing

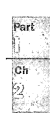

The reporting system of the General Ledger is particularly flexible. You can use it to report by any field that is already defined for accumulating subtotals.

Installations of SAP R/3 differ according to the needs of the customer, but there may be account subtotals for planned data and actual data, for product groups and business areas, and for individual products and cost centers. Many permutations could make business sense for a particular user. Even the choice of time period may be an important matter for individual purposes. SAP R/3 can work with up to 365 time periods a year.

Using Standard Reports Available at Closing

Standard reports are available for the main tasks:

☐ Reconciling and controlling account subtotals

☐ Providing an audit trail for internal and external auditors

Many reports are available to be compiled in real time to provide information on the elements of the closing process. These elements include the following:

☐ Posting totals reports

☐ Open item account balance audit trails

☐ Transfer balance sheet account balances with multiple carry-forwards

 T I P When posting to the previous year, it is useful to call for a report on the permanent standardizing of balance carry-forwards.

All the closing reports can be executed at any time for monitoring and analysis. They may be examined interactively to provide a current business accounting service. The main reports in the General Ledger are available online, with a range of sorting and presentation options to help in year-end closing and final reporting:

☐ Chart of accounts

☐ Account statements

☐ Balance sheet with profit and loss statement

☐ General Ledger

☐ Advance return for tax on sales and purchases

☐ Document journal

☐ Posting totals

- Balance sheet adjustments
- Reconciliation of documents with monthly debits and credits
- Customer open items
- Customer open items by General Ledger indicator code
- Overdue Receivables
- Open checks
- Open item account balance audit trails
- Line item journal
- Accumulated balance audit trial
- Vendor open items
- Accounts Payable in local currency
- Bill of Exchange Register

Using Report Writer and Report Painter for Custom Reporting

Many of the standard reports are available to call without additional parameter entries. However, if you require reporting from user-defined ledgers, or if your presentation needs are not best served by a standard report, then you have available a flexible system of designing custom reports.

Short reports can be generated interactively. Large volume reports are scheduled for offline output. The normal output media are screen, printer, sequential file, PC file, and the SAP Business Graphics component.

The advantage of interactive reporting is that you can change the report structure and explore the data immediately. The SAP system of using a table of parameters to specify report design enables you to make the following revisions online:

- Change the level of detailing
- Change the subtotaling
- Change the content of the columns
- Output all or parts of the report to file or to a printer

Display controls enable you to change what you see, such as with these functions:

- Switch to another report with another perspective
- Select a row in the report and see the whole of the SAP document upon which it is based

The Report Writer is a component that enables you to select from a menu any reported total and evaluate it along any of the dimensions that were used to compile it. To exercise the full functionality of this tool, it is best to use the extensive and powerful control elements called by keyboard entries and special function keys.

The Report Painter provides a graphical interface to most of the functions of Report Writer. Both systems require you to select or enter the parameters for the report you are designing.

The column and line layout of a report are designed independently of the individual report and can be maintained separately even though they are shared by several reports.

In designing a custom report, you must make decisions on the following options:

- Which standard or user text elements should appear in the report
- Which column width layout to adopt from a set of predefined system standards
- Which dimensions appear in the lines
- Which summation levels to include
- Which values should appear in the columns (such as actual, planned, monthly, quarterly, or total year values)
- Which data to use
- How the key figures should be derived, and what formulas to use

The reporting system of the General Ledger gives you the ability to extract pertinent data and process that data so you can present it in the ways that best serve effective decision making.

The following possibilities illustrate the range of functions:

- Print part of the onscreen report
- Generate graphics from part of the onscreen report
- Select an area of the report (a group of row items and some of the columns) and call on SAP Business Graphics to present the data in one of a range of graphical styles that you can subsequently adjust and annotate before storing or consigning them to one or more of the output routes
- Drill down on report lines to inspect the individual documents
- Change the parameters to alter the content of the columns
- Change the level of detail and the summation levels
- Evaluate the same data using another report structure and take a different point of view

N O T E Any onscreen report can be saved to a file for inspection by other users.

Understanding Report Output Media

Reports can be produced online or in batches. They can be stored for later analysis or printing, possibly by other users or through specialized output devices. The range of output routes available for reporting includes the following:

- Online screen listing with user control of format and content
- Printing in accord with ad hoc designs to replicate screen reports
- Printing to standard report formats
- Printing to customized report formats and selected destination printers

- Printing to sequential files in the system for subsequent processing or printing
- Printing to local PC files available to selected network users
- Sending graphic reports to screen or printers with SAP Business Graphics

Understanding Financial Statement Report Formats

Taken together, the main reports in the General Ledger satisfy the legal requirement that a company publish an annual financial statement. The essential components of the company financial statement are as follows:

- Fixed assets
- Current assets
- Equity
- Debt
- Profit and loss statement

These essential requirements relate to the basic elements of the chart of accounts, from which the financial statement is constructed. A complex company is required by law to present a financial statement for each of its components separately and a consolidated statement for the group or company as a whole.

There may be a different chart of accounts for each company in a group. SAP FI-GL General Ledger accommodates all these variations of organizational structures when preparing the financial statement.

The process of designing or customizing the format of the balance sheet and the profit and loss statement entails specifying the following details for each account:

- Levels of account detail
- Headings and subheadings
- Text
- Subtotaling and totaling

Separate formats can be designed according to the target readership of the financial documents, such as the following:

- Stockholders and tax authorities
- Group requirements
- Profit centers

Facilities have been provided as extensions to the balance sheet functions. They enable you to draft financial statements in a wide range of formats to suit all types of company organization. These facilities have been integrated and placed under the control of a sophisticated user interface.

N O T E Balances on all accounts are always current. Therefore, a profit and loss statement or a balance sheet can be prepared at any time. ▫

Reporting Operational Control Data at Closing

In some companies, the reporting structure used for the legal financial documents, the balance sheet, and the profit and loss statement is the same as the structure through which the company is organized and managed. However, mergers and restructuring may cause the operational structure of the enterprise to differ from the legal reporting hierarchy. In other words, the balance sheet elements may not correspond to the controlling elements.

For example, there may be separate groups of investors in the corporate enterprise as a whole and in some of the constituent companies. For balance sheet purposes, each of these investor groups requires a separate set of financial documents. However, efficient management of the enterprise on a day-to-day basis may be better served by a structure of formally defined business areas, profit centers, and cost centers. This operational structure is the one used for transaction accounting and controlling. The various accounts are then reconciled and consolidated to provide the balance sheet and profit and loss statements directed at the company structure and its investor groups.

In the SAP R/3 system, both types of structures can be supported at all times. You can nominate a business area and call for reports to show the cash flows across all company codes. You can nominate a company code and see how it has operated across all business areas.

Any of these reports can be predefined or copied from sample master designs for the standard reports, and the periods can be defined to suit your requirements. All the reports can be generated offline or online because they evaluate and analyze the posted account data directly.

Understanding Balance Sheet Reporting Principles

The main elements of the General Ledger are the balance sheet and the profit and loss statement. These elements must be defined specifically for each of the company's operations so that they correctly portray in the closing report the assets, liabilities, expenses, and revenues of the company over the reporting period.

The SAP R/3 General Ledger facilities enable you to specify the following parameters:

- Level of detail to be reported
- Account classification structure
- How the items and subitems are to be assigned to each of the accounts
- What standard text elements are to be printed, and how they are to be arranged and formatted
- Which totals and subtotals are to be computed, and how they are to be captioned

A complex multinational enterprise must be able to generate financial documents in several versions to suit the target readership and the legal requirements of the nation that is host to the company code being reported. The following versions of the balance sheet and the profit and loss statement can be generated in parallel:

☐ Commercial law edition

☐ Tax law edition

☐ Corporate group financial document set

☐ Operational group balance sheet and profit and loss statement

N O T E   If your corporate enterprise operates with more than one chart of accounts, you can instruct the financial system to generate reports that select accounts from any of the charts.

Using the Financial Document Interface

The balance sheet and the profit and loss statement are generated from the posting data. Therefore, you can call for them at any time. You can also recall data from previous periods so that your display shows the differences. If you call for planned data for any past or future period, you can again view the comparison and have the display reformatted to highlight the significant aspects.

You always have a choice between tabular and graphic representation of any data assembled for a report. You can also send this data to a specialized evaluation and analysis system, for instance, to apply statistical techniques to it.

If you become interested in the movements of values through time or through the accumulation of transactions, you can command the system to step through the data using increments of your choice. What's more, you could also display the movements of value in graphical form. Your viewing focus can be the accounts themselves or the stream of transaction documents that have contributed to them.

If a subledger is of interest, you can inspect summaries of the data across periods or product divisions, or across profit centers or cost elements. You can drill down through the data until you reach the line items themselves.

An existing item may include text. A summary may have had text added by a previous user. You may wish to append text to comment on or explain some aspect of the data that you think important. You can use standard texts for the common business names and phrases to conserve data storage and processing resource. You may also generate and append free text.

The financial documents can be generated in different versions that can use up to 10 hierarchy levels to differentiate the details of any particular account. By this means, you can accommodate the readers who need detail as well as those who are content to see only summary values at one or more of the hierarchy levels.

The period results of accounting calculations can be drafted according to different conventions, such as the following:

- Alternative versions for different currencies
- Comparisons of actual and planned values
- Comparisons of current and previous reporting period
- Comparisons shown as absolute differences, percentages, or index figures
- Transaction accounting using a flexible start and finish date to define the reporting period
- Opening balance sheet with progress shown as a balance carried forward
- Cumulative balance carry-forward to the reporting period

Any of these accounting conventions can be combined, and the design can be saved as a report specification version.

Using the Financial Information System

The Financial Information System (FIS) is a subset of the functions available in the Enterprise Information System (EIS) developed to integrate all the reporting functions of the SAP R/3 applications. The FIS creates separate reporting databases, which summarize the main FI-GL, FI-AP, and FI-AR databases.

Analyzing a Balance Sheet

The profit and loss system of Financial Accounting can be seen as a hierarchy in which the summaries of profit or loss are based on many layers of subsidiary data sources, down to the level of the individual transaction document. It is a legal requirement that these pathways back to the sources be traceable, if necessary, using audit trail methods. The SAP R/3 system is prepared for this because the component data elements of any balance sheet total can be identified by selecting from the database all transaction documents bearing the code of the chart of accounts item on which that balance sheet total is accumulated.

A parallel set of data is maintained for planning purposes in the General Ledger application, and this set is also used by the CO-Controlling application. From the EIS or the General Ledger application, you can call for multiple variance analyses to compare actual and planned values on the following bases:

- Annual planned versus actual
- Semi-annual planned versus actual
- Quarterly planned versus actual
- Monthly planned versus actual

Using Balance Sheet Key Figure Reports

If you are accustomed to reading balance sheet reports that include presentations of key figures computed in a manner particular to your company, you can set up such reports in the General Ledger system. You may find it convenient to use as your starting point one or more of the many standard balance sheet key figure reports that are available as models you can copy and edit.

Part

II

Ch

2

Understanding Reporting Options

Evaluations of key figures, subtotals, ratios, and similar arithmetical formulas can be performed on demand or to schedule for all organizational units, such as Client*, company code, and business area. The period of these reports can be based on a fiscal year, a settlement period, or any time period you have established as significant for your enterprise. The currency of a report is under your control. You can generate reports with currencies in parallel from the following list of currency types:

- Group or Client* reporting currency
- Hard currency on a specific currency market
- Indexed currency
- Company currency for each company code
- Global currency for cross-system reporting and interface

Any SAP R/3 report can be generated anew from the most recent postings relevant to it. You may also have a database system installed to collate the necessary documents in preparation for reporting. This arrangement enables you to conserve the system resources in favor of more urgent processing that cannot be delayed.

Although the data for reports can be collated from the original document sources, two techniques are popular because they save work and minimize errors. The first is to define reports as standard entities that effectively specify the data storage pathways that must be traversed to find the sources of information needed. The second technique is to have the database system locate only those records that have changed since their previous use in a report. This technique is sometimes referred to as Delta database management because the Greek symbol is often used to represent a very small change in a quantity.

All the functions described in connection with the FI-SL Special Purpose Ledger component are available from the FIS. The information systems provide additional control over the reporting procedures of the extended General Ledger.

In summary, the FIS enables you to operate flexibly on any subcomponent of the constituent reporting functions. You can therefore access any data element in your system, assuming you have the authorization to do so. If you have a distributed database system that includes third-party systems, there may be some restrictions concerning the level of detail to which you can return in the event of an auditing query on the original transaction documentation.

The FIS offers the following manipulative options on financial report objects:

- All standard reporting functions can be deployed.
- Customized procedures can be called upon to define, select, evaluate, and analyze financial and planning data.
- Data on the screen can be highlighted by the user and is subject to drill-down, which is a sequence of recursively more detailed reporting of the data set identified by the cursor.

- Any defined data set can be integrated with evaluations that have been set up for specific company operations and that take part in customized analysis and reporting. This may entail using particular reporting interfaces to associated systems.
- Any reporting procedure can be integrated with operational processes by using text, code, and standard messages to and from the operational facilities.

Taking Advantage of the FI-SL Functions

The facilities of the Special Purpose Ledger enable you to simultaneously run ledgers that can instantly portray the business situation from any or all of the following points of view:

- Profit and loss
- Effective drivers of the balance sheet movements
- Departments responsible for the best and worst profitability evaluations
- Comparative performance of the company codes
- How individual business areas are being served by different company codes
- Locations of the units that add the most value and consume the most resources
- How costs are incurred by the products and services provided
- How costs are incurred by particular projects

The currency of a Special Purpose Ledger is that used for the original entry of the business transactions. Two additional currencies can be designated by the user to be maintained in parallel. You can choose from company code, index, group, global, and ledger currencies.

Conversion between currencies always uses the exchange rate prevailing when the transaction document was first entered. You can also arrange for other conversions to be applied to the data.

The quantity units of SAP R/3 can be supplemented by units you have specified for your own purposes. Any of these units can be designated for use in a Special Purpose Ledger. For example, you could generate totals of some materials expressed in the units used when purchasing. You may also require totals to be drafted in terms of the delivery units.

The posting period of a Special Purpose Ledger can be any length. The General Ledger maintains weekly and daily sales analyses. But you can set up a Special Purpose Ledger to have the same transaction data assigned to monthly periods, and another that separates the data according to time periods you have defined. A Special Purpose Ledger can use more than 365 posting periods per fiscal year if this suits your reporting requirements.

Your financial control and reporting arrangements probably include the following services:

- Management reporting
- Individual account closing
- Consolidated financial statements
- Statistical reporting

For these services, your General Ledger and your Special Purpose Ledger store the information that can be identified and reported to illuminate the following aspects of your business:

- Expenditures
- Commitments
- Statistical summaries of relationships that represent value flows of importance to your particular situation
- Salaries
- Depreciation
- Interest
- Vendor invoices
- Sales invoices
- Closing data on particular accounts
- Orders
- Cash receipts
- Disbursements
- Receivables
- Asset acquisitions
- Asset transfers

A standard program is available for comparing and reconciling General Ledger accounts and the accounts in user-defined ledgers. This function can be called at any time. If some of the data required by your Special Purpose Ledger is entered in an external third-party system, it can be transferred through a standard interface. You can apply validation and authorization checks to data flows for the Special Purpose Ledger. For example, you could restrict posting to a cost center so that only a certain group of users could update that particular ledger.

When data is transferred, the Special Purpose Ledger function expands the account assignment allocation key so that all necessary postings can be affected. The function accesses the master data of the transferring system so that all the fields available can be copied.

Additional controls over the updating and reconciliation of Special Purpose Ledgers include the following options:

- Update at each posting from financial accounting
- Update at every transaction in MM-Materials Management
- Update at every order settlement
- Update according to specified logical conditions

A logical condition is stored as a master record and can be applied for many purposes. For the control of Special Purpose Ledgers, you can define logical conditions that are automatically consulted so that transactions of particular types are assigned to update specific ledgers. The parameters of the logical condition can be data from any available data field in the system, and no restrictions exist for the complexity of the numerical or logical operations to be applied. As a result, the Special Purpose Ledgers are updated according to the rules you define.

Using Direct Data Entry to Special Purpose Ledgers

Although updating Special Purpose Ledgers is largely automatic in an integrated system of R/3 and its applications, you can enter data directly in the form of a special document recognized as a record of direct data entry. You may want to use this facility if you are inputting statistical data, perhaps in connection with planning or when simulating a what-if situation. You may also need to input data directly to one or more Special Purpose Ledgers when consolidating company code accounts. Two other common examples of direct update include planning and currency translation posted directly to the ledger.

Using Standalone Special Purpose Ledger Systems

The FI-SL Special Purpose Ledger system includes a standard interface for processing external data transferred from non-SAP systems. This means that the module can be used independently of any SAP R/3 implementation. This configuration can be seen in the banking and insurance industries.

Using Allocation in Special Purpose Ledgers

FI-SL includes an allocation function that can automatically allocate or distribute currency amounts and quantity values from sender objects to receiver objects. Two types of allocation and distribution are supported:

☐ Allocation by distribution within a dimension or level of detail

☐ Allocation by assessment

For example, one cost center could be credited and the amount distributed to other cost centers, which would be debited on perhaps an equal-share basis. The administration cost center may have paid for customer hospitality, and this cost could be shared across other departments by the Special Purpose Ledger module.

Distributing Costs

Three main methods of distribution exist:

☐ Fixed amount distribution

☐ Fixed percentage distribution

☐ Dynamic distribution

In fixed amount distribution, you define the amount to be debited to each receiver object. The total of these values is credited to the sender object.

In fixed percentage distribution, each receiver is debited with a percentage of the total that you specify. It is not necessary to distribute the entire amount.

When using dynamic distribution, you specify certain values that have been totaled in the database of the FI-SL system. These values are then used automatically to determine how much to allocate to the receivers. For instance, you may distribute certain overhead costs in proportion to the sales revenues of designated cost centers.

Using the Set Concept in Ledger Processing

Many of the ledger processing functions accept as valid attributes any combination of single values, intervals, and sets.

In logical terms, a single value is a set with only one member. An interval is a set of values taken from an ordered sequence by specifying the lowest and highest values.

Another way of specifying a set is to name or nominate the members individually.

SAP R/3 stores many set definitions as master records so that they can be referred to by any of the integrated functions. The FI-SL module accepts set definitions as a way of identifying senders and receivers.

Special Purpose Ledger processing takes advantage of the set concept to allocate and distribute among the following types of data structure:

- ☐ Single accounting objects, such as individual bank accounts
- ☐ Hierarchies of cost centers
- ☐ Multilevel relations between individual business entities

By using the set concept, it is possible to echo in the Financial Accounting system any configuration of companies and business partners so that planning and reporting can be carried out precisely over the same structure. If the elements of this structure do not correspond exactly with the accounts of the General Ledger, the Special Purpose Ledger functionality can be installed and configured to build a faithful accounting model for your enterprise.

Planning in the Special Purpose Ledgers

The essentials of a business planning system are the accumulated actual values and a method of setting planned or target values that map to the categories used to accumulate the actual values. For example, you can take your most recent sales total and declare a planned sales total that equals the actual total.

The FI-Financial Accounting system is based on transaction data. Every precaution is taken to ensure that no user can enter values that could be mistaken for actual transaction data, unless they do indeed result from a valid business transaction—such data will be present in the chart of accounts and therefore in the company balance sheet and the profit and loss statement.

Planning data is always identified as such. It is entered as a total value for one or several accounting periods, among which it can be distributed by a variety of standard functions. These distribution functions are the same as those used by the Special Purpose Ledger module, which is capable of serving as an extensive planning tool.

Using General Planning Parameters in FI-SL

A master record is established for each version of a plan so that it can store general data and requirements for the planning process. These values, referred to as the planning parameters, both describe how your plan is to be constructed and suggest values to be used in it. The planning parameters cannot be altered by a user who lacks the requisite authorization profile. Each user can have access to only a limited set of planning parameters.

A planning parameter is a data object that stores the following types of information:

- How the planning total is to be entered or derived by calculation, perhaps using cost center areas that do not correspond exactly to the accounts to which the actual data is assigned
- The transaction currency, as well as the second and third currencies
- Primary and additional quantities suggested for this plan
- Standard or user-defined distribution keys used to specify the method of allocating the total across the receiver objects
- The units assumed for the total when it is entered, such as hundreds, thousands, or millions
- The number of decimal digits in the planned values
- The plan version number to which this parameter belongs
- The receiver objects to which this parameter applies, such as work days per month

You can change any of these parameter values temporarily during a planning session if you want to conduct a flexible what-if experiment. You can save your experimental plan, but it will not recognize a new or revised parameter unless you have an authorization profile that enables you to release planning parameters for use by others.

Using Distribution Keys

A distribution key is a record of a defined procedure used to allocate values from a sender to one or more receivers. Each key can have a name that suggests where it is used, although you can use any distribution key in any planning activity. You can take a standard distribution procedure, or one you elaborated earlier, and assign a name to it that then appears in any planning parameter you design.

If an appropriate distribution key is not available, you can enter the individual planning values directly for each period.

Understanding the Scope of Special Purpose Ledger Planning

The planning perspective is defined as the combination of the planning periods and the method of selecting or nominating planning objects. The FI-SL module is completely flexible in this respect.

For example, you can set up central planning in which you establish a set of planning cost types that apply to all cost centers in your corporate enterprise. You can also use the same FI-SL module to conduct decentralized planning, in which you designate a set of planning cost types separately for each cost center.

Reporting from the Special Purpose Ledgers

You can regard the Special Purpose Ledger system as a dedicated support facility for management reporting. Suppose you settle on the following set of reporting requirements:

- Product results for each product
- Weekly and daily reports on demand
- Monthly, quarterly, and annual reports
- Comparisons of monthly, quarterly, and annual totals
- Key figures and ratios
- Short- and long-term projections
- Elimination of intercompany sales on selected reports

If such a list corresponds, even approximately, to your reporting diet, the Special Purpose Ledger module would seem to be an essential element of your business data processing arrangements.

Two data structures must be collated to feed such an extensive reporting requirement:

- Each cost center must identify the transaction data by account assignment, by accounting period, and by product for all the business within its responsibility.
- The data in all the cost centers must be consolidated and arranged by product group and business area.

Each entry of actual values in such a system of data structures must be matched with a planned value.

Using Workflow with the Financial Calendar

The Financial Calendar is a planning and monitoring tool specialized for the preparation of closings and the efficient conduct of the recurring tasks associated with financial management. The Financial Calendar can be used in conjunction with SAP Workflow to plan the following kinds of accounting tasks:

- Periodic dunning runs
- Periodic payment runs
- Periodic evaluations of specific accounts or groups of accounts
- Automatic messages and instructions for key period closing functions.

If you install and configure the Human Resources module and note in it the skills and capabilities of your employees, the workflow can be arranged to assign a suitable and available person to each task as it becomes due. The workflow schedule is available at all times to authorized users so that the workloads and task assignments are apparent beforehand.

The Financial Calendar component is responsible for the following functions associated with future tasks:

- Displaying all planned tasks in preview format
- Displaying all planned tasks in overview format

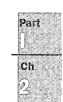

The Financial Calendar component is responsible for the following functions associated with previous tasks:

- Displaying all planned tasks to determine how and by whom they have been accomplished
- Reviewing all planned tasks that have been executed automatically
- Tracking specific sequences of completed tasks

If you plan tasks to be carried out as manual activities, the Financial Calendar can provide the following support facilities:

- Displaying the status of any task
- Assigning tasks to a specific user
- Assigning tasks to a group of users defined by their authorization and experience or qualification
- Defining recurring standard tasks
- Distributing assigned tasks among available users

The Financial Calendar can operate in either of two modes:

- Given a date or period, the Financial Calendar can list the scheduled activities.
- Given a preconfigured activity or set of activities, the Financial Calendar can report the time of the scheduled tasks and the name or the qualifying attributes of the person assigned to each.

The Financial Calendar component can be installed and configured to integrate with the Financial Accounting system, with or without the Human Resources link. The SAP Workflow module is a standard application that can be used with the financial activities alone, or as a cross-application scheduling tool that can be controlled over an intranet or through the Internet. These configuration possibilities provide a flexible means of adjusting your company's activities to the nature of the work and the workloads in relation to your available resources. ◉

CHAPTER 3

Using Subledger Accounts

In this chapter

Understanding Ledgers and Accounting

Various traditions of accounting have developed concepts and assigned titles to the departments responsible for carrying out the work activities. Thus Accounts Receivable or Receivables are recognized as departments that keep track of value owed to your company. These may also be the titles of ledger accounts in your Financial Accounting system.

This chapter sets out the pivotal functions of the FI-AR Accounts Receivable and FI-AP Accounts Payable modules of SAP R/3 that manage these subledgers of the General Ledger. These functions address the following questions:

- How does money come?
- How does money go?
- How can my company organize these processes?

You will find that most accounting activities can be automated without losing control because the FI-AR and FI-AP modules reliably report any difficulties and suggest how you can remove them.

The SAP R/3 system uses the following structure of accounting function entities.

- General Ledger is the master record maintained using the defined entity type 2107 in the enterprise data model, upon which the R/3 operates.
- Each account in the General Ledger is recorded in a record of the type General Ledger Account–Transaction Figure.
- If there are many creditors, a Subsidiary Ledger–Creditor is defined as an entity of type 2108, which is reserved for the company code credits account records.
- A subsidiary ledger, or subledger, is an integral part of the General Ledger and is regarded as a legal extension of it for balance sheet purposes.
- A special ledger or special purpose ledger is a grouping of accounts that are held separately from the General Ledger and are used for alternative reporting purposes specified according to the requirements of your company. This type of ledger is not subject to legal restrictions.

Understanding Accounts Receivable

FI-AR Accounts Receivable is a module of the SAP R/3 Basis system. It is specialized to maintain the Accounts Receivable subledger of the FI-GL General Ledger and completely integrated with it at the following levels:

- Master Data
- Transaction Data
- Reporting System

The General Ledger and its subledgers share the common chart of accounts with all applications and also share all the details of master records. Reporting can draw from the General Ledger and the Accounts Receivable subledger.

The purpose of the Accounts Receivable subledger is to keep track of customers and the transactions that involve them. Its job is to collect money, to process cash receipts, and to dun customers who are late in paying. This subledger shares the same accounting needs as the SD-Sales and Distribution module, which is also a core module of the SAP R/3 Basis, and IT is fully integrated with it at the software code level.

Transaction data is stored centrally in the document database, and the corresponding line items and details are stored in the appropriate subledgers. The system automatically updates a subtotal of a balance sheet account for every business transaction and reconciles the account subtotals and the line items to ensure that the financial information is always correct and current.

Every transaction creates an SAP document, and the data is immediately posted to the General Ledger. Every business transaction recorded in this way automatically updates the balance sheet or the profit and loss statement. This is the defining characteristic of an up-to-date accounting and controlling system.

 N O T E The SAP system maintains account balances by debits and credits for up to 16
periods.

Using the Customer Master Record

The Accounts Receivable functions are shared with the SD-Sales and Distribution application. The customer master record is maintained as a common reference for all the information about a customer that could be of use within the company. Access to this data can be controlled through the Authorization Profile System, which can also regulate the updating of customer information.

N O T E The central database of customer information is the source for decisions on automatic
dunning and automatic payment.

The sales organization need not have the same organizational structure as the legal structure of the company. One sales department can handle products from two or more associated companies. The system of customer master records makes provision for this.

Master data is organized into the following three parts:

- General data
- Data applicable only for specific company codes
- Sales data

General data about each customer is available to every company code and every sales department. It includes such items as the following:

- Name, address, telephone, fax, and modem number
- Customer registration number
- Line of business and business group
- Bank account data

For each individual company using a shared sales organization, there may be different entries for each company code to reflect their different business methods and any existing agreements. These can include the following:

- Standard payment terms
- Data for dunning overdue accounts
- Data for direct debit or automatic payment
- Data for correspondence, such as the account number and name

If more than one sales department in your group sells to the same customer, you must specify a General Ledger reconciliation account for that customer. This is identified in the customer master record.

Sales data in the customer master records may be helpful in initiating a relationship between a sales representative and a customer. For example, a sales representative may want to retrieve from the database the name and title of the customer company buyer responsible for purchasing a specific range of products or services. This kind of information can also be held as part of a sales support function.

The sales information section of a customer master record also includes the order processing, shipping, and invoicing data required by the SD-Sales and Distribution application.

Strategic sales data can be held in the customer master record. For instance, you can specify whether a new customer master is to be made available to all your departments or only within specific areas. One alternative is to make the general customer data central and maintain individual database records for the departments, such as accounting and sales.

Making Sales to an Affiliated Company

Among your customers you may have one or more affiliated company code departments of your own corporate group. If you wish to use the SAP Consolidation module in reporting, any intercompany sales achieved through business transactions with such customers must be eliminated from the company accounts before closing. Therefore, the ID code of other members of your group must be entered on the customer master record so that it is automatically transferred to the document when posting.

Processing Master Data Records

Access to customer master data records must be controlled by limiting the staff authorized to modify certain data fields. This method involves using the system of authorizations to restrict certain functions that can affect the critical fields of the customer master records.

 T I P   Separate functions can be authorized individually to create, change, or simply display customer master records. These restrictions can then be applied to general data, accounting data, and sales data.

When a new or prospective customer is identified, a new master record is created and assigned to an account group. The account group determines whether you may assign account numbers within specified ranges or whether the system does this automatically. Your implementation can include a supporting system that generates account numbers that are then adopted by your SAP R/3 accounting application. Your system is not allowed to assign the same account number more than once, but both customers and vendors can exist within the same range of numbers. The numbers can also be assigned on the basis of a hierarchy or classification of customer accounts.

The account group also controls the fields that are active in this master record. You can pick the fields offered by the account group and assign them to one of three categories:

- Fields into which the user must make a valid entry
- Fields the user can either leave blank or make an entry into (optional fields)
- Suppressed fields that do not appear on the screen

N O T E   A whole screen of fields can be suppressed if it is not needed for a particular transaction. You can use field groups to control certain fields of sensitive information within a customer master record to specify authorized users. □

The FI-AR Accounts Receivable system makes it easy to create master records by offering various options.

- By using a search function, you can inspect the master records of customers similar to the one you are entering.
- You can copy the master record of an existing customer and edit the unwanted details to make it into a new master record.
- You can copy a master record from a reference record that has been established for the purpose. You must make at least one alteration to it before you post it as a new master record.
- You can create the new customer master record by entering all the necessary details.

After you enter and store a customer master record, you can call it back again and change almost any of the fields. You have a choice of whether to go through all the fields or work on a single subset of fields, such as the payment details. Master records can be selectively displayed so that you see only those fields of interest to you.

Part
I

Ch
3

N O T E Any changes you make to any record in the customer master database automatically leaves
a change record that can be accessed to form an updated history. ⌐⌐

Using One-Time Accounts

If you think a customer probably will not become a regular purchaser, you can set up a one-time account by selecting a special function. This creates a master record that contains only the essential control data, such as the number of the reconciliation account to which this sale will be posted. The system can provide the customer name, address, telephone number, and bank account data when an invoice is entered. This information then arrives in the one-time account master record, where the dunning and payment programs can find it.

Using Customer Head Office and Branch Accounts

Your customer contact may be a branch with its own account, but the head office may foot the bill. In this case, you can enter the head office account number in the master record for the branch customer. When you enter a transaction to the branch account, the system posts the transaction to the head office account, leaving a cleared entry on the branch account to show who received the goods or services.

The master record includes data about the branch and a reference to another record to give details of the head office. By this means, dunning letters can be sent to the head office, the branch, or both.

Receiving Payments from an Alternate Payer

Your customer may not have to deal with his own payments. You can record in his master data the account number of the alternate payer, and the system then processes direct debits, return transfers, and other customer payment business through the banks of the other payer.

If you post customer invoices to an affiliate, you must record in the master data of the branch customer a group-wide company account number to be used during consolidation to eliminate the invoices that would otherwise appear twice in the company accounts. The system is capable of looking at the transaction documents bearing this group-wide company account number and then identifying any entries that are replicated because the payment was made by an affiliate that was not the original customer.

N O T E A customer may have an arrangement whereby any overdue payments must be dunned to
an alternative address. This is recorded in the customer master record and is used if
dunning is necessary. ⌐⌐

Understanding Customer Transactions in Accounts Receivable

As soon as the master data is stored for a customer, a customer transaction can occur. If the master record is for a one-time account, the data will be sparse.

If you installed and configured SAP SD-Sales and Distribution with the SAP FI-Financial Accounting system, invoices entered in the SD system are automatically posted to General Ledger accounts in FI. Otherwise, the route to the FI-GL General Ledger accounts runs through an SAP open interface, which transfers and posts invoice data to General Ledger accounts automatically. If you must manually enter an invoice that has not been posted automatically, SAP R/3 provides all possible help. You can enter and post a check received and match the payment to specific open items in the customer account, all in one operation.

The successful posting of a transaction does not occur until the necessary data is recorded as an SAP document and is complete and error-free. You can set aside a transaction document before it is ready for posting, in which case the system validates any information you have already entered and reports to you any discrepancies.

The SAP document must end up with a document header showing posting date, document date, document reference number, and currency key. The body of the document contains one or more line items that show the amount and identify the product and terms of payment. The system generates certain line items, such as tax entries, cash discounts, and exchange rate differences, as applicable.

You can set up helping routines and use standard data entry functions such as the following:

- Offering default values that you can edit at the time of entry
- Recalling for copying and editing a previous screen
- Retaining data for individual users for several transactions
- Adapting a copy of a data entry screen so that it is better suited to a set of expected transactions
- Searching for an account number by using matchcodes to narrow the search

An SAP document that records a previous transaction can be copied to act as a sample or a model to be edited. This sample can be a regular document that has been set aside, perhaps as an incomplete transaction document. The posting date and new values may have to be changed before posting.

Handling Recurring Entries

If you expect to make a series of entries in which the amounts are always the same, you can set up a recurring entry. For example, one of your customers may be paying in monthly installments. The entries will be posted to accounts only when they occur, not when the recurring entry original document was first created.

A recurring entry is a set of data that will not be used until the due dates. Until then, the entries will not update account balances. You must specify the first and last dates and the frequency or time interval, and you must supply a deadline date. The system automatically posts the required transaction on each of the due dates.

Using Invoice and Credit Memo Entry Tools

An invoice, a credit memo, or a transfer cannot be successfully posted unless it is complete and free of errors. However, an incomplete Receivables document can be saved, and you can resume work on it when the required information becomes available. If the document is then posted, it is checked immediately, and adjustments are suggested for your rejection or confirmation. The criteria for accepting a transaction include the following:

- The debit and credit balance is zero.
- The assignment account data is complete.
- The mandatory entry fields are complete.

The assignment account data includes at least the following entries:

- Document date
- Posting date
- Document type
- Posting key
- Account number
- Amounts to be posted

Using Entry Currencies

Any currency can be used for document entry to Accounts Receivable. A local currency will have been assigned to each company code, which is automatically computed. Two other currencies can be indicated, if required, and are handled in parallel. The records store the entered amounts in both local and document currencies. An exchange rate table is consulted to convert between them.

You can also indicate a specific exchange rate when posting. The entry document master will have been coded to control whether the local currency is open to posting in addition to the document currency, which is always open for input during document entry.

A document must have a zero balance in both the local and the document currency before it can be successfully posted. Small rounding differences are automatically taken into account. Transaction amounts are kept only in the local currency of the customer area. The reconciliation account for Receivables From Goods and Services is kept in local currency and in all the foreign currencies used in posting.

The system can be customized in various ways, which include the following:

- A specific user is obliged to enter amounts in a particular currency, which can be the local currency or the system document currency.
- A specific user can be permitted to enter amounts in either the local or the document currency.

Whatever the customizing arrangements, the system displays amounts in both local and document currencies. It rounds off minor differences, using rules established for this purpose. These differences can occur when several line items are converted and then added in both currencies.

The system keeps customer monthly debits and credits only in local currency. The reconciliation account for the Accounts Receivable subledger is kept in local currency and in all the other currencies that have been posted.

Dealing with Currency Exchange Differences

A line item can be expressed in a currency other than the local or document currency. You can enter payments to clear such foreign currency line items using either the local or the document currency.

The payment expressed in the document currency will have been converted from the local currency at an exchange rate adopted by the system according to the approved rules for assigning the daily exchange rate. If this rate has changed from the rate prevailing when the invoice was written, the payment amount may not match the open item amount. In such cases, the system automatically calculates and posts an exchange difference entry to a separate account established for this purpose.

Processing Incoming Payments

The usual paper form of a payment is a check, a transfer, or a bill of exchange. Regardless of the form, the processing of an incoming payment must include two processes.

- Posting the payment to the assigned account
- Matching open invoice lines for this customer with payment line items and then clearing them if they correspond

Understanding the Basic Procedure for Receiving Payments

A payment for clearing is indicated as a transfer slip or a payment advice note. Credit memos are indicated in a similar fashion.

Your payment receipt actions are best carried out in a logical order. You must perform the following steps:

1. Enter the bank general ledger account number.
2. Enter the amount of the payment.
3. Enter any bank charges.

4. Enter the document numbers of the unpaid items to be cleared by this payment.

5. Apply the rules for cash discount, and deduct it from the total of the indicated invoices.

6. Confirm that the total of the indicated invoice, minus cash discount if appropriate, agrees with the input payment amount.

If the totals agree, the payment receipt is then posted. The cleared items should be annotated to show the clearing date and which incoming payment was responsible.

Searching for Invoices to Be Cleared

If necessary, you can search for all the outstanding unpaid invoices for the customer using any document-specific search term, such as the following:

▢ Amount of the invoice

▢ Reference number of the invoice

▢ Posting date

You can assemble a list of open items by specifying single values or intervals for your search criteria. You can combine the results of several searches, and you can remove items from the list if you do not want to consider them for clearing against the incoming payment.

 TIP It may be helpful to have the list sorted, in either direction, on any of the values that appear in the listing.

NOTE If you are focusing on a single line item, you can call for all the data in summary form, or you can retrieve the entire document. ▢

Minor differences might exist between the payments and the invoices to be cleared against them. In such instances, you can arrange to adjust values less than a certain amount through the cash discount, or you can post them to a separate differences account. You may wish to grant some users permission to exercise more discretion in this respect than others. You can control this through their authorization profiles.

Searching for Open Items

If the customer has not told you which invoices are being paid (by writing their numbers on the check or by including an advice note or an allocation notice), you must use the system to determine this information.

For example, you can call for a search for open items for this customer, but there may be too many to decide which are being settled by this payment. In such a case, you can narrow the search by giving exact values or ranges of values for almost any of the header fields and line item fields that appear on a transaction document.

It is recommended that you use no more than a handful of search fields. The most useful fields for narrowing a search for open items for a customer include the following:

- Document Reference Number
- Posting Date
- Invoice Amount
- Posting Key

For any of your searching criteria, you can accept a range of values, such as the following:

- Any document number between two given numbers
- Any posting date over a specified interval
- Any invoice amount greater than or less than a given amount
- Any posting key out of a short list that you specify

The system's first response to a search command is to display a summary screen showing the items found. The summary totals the amounts. If this equals your customer's payment, your search is over. If not, you must refine the search.

You might select a few items from the summary screen and examine their details to find some better entries for a more focused search. The summary screen layout may be more useful to you if you change its display format by moving or replacing some of the columns until you are looking at only the details that interest you.

 T I P At any time, you can switch the display between showing the details of a line item and showing the entire document. This includes the entry offsetting this customer line item, if there is one.

If your search for open items is successful, you arrive at a list of invoices that add up to the same amount offered as payment by the customer. The system calculates allowances for cash discounts, and you can check this from the display. Differences also might arise because of the conversions between currencies.

When your system is being customized, you can specify the limits within which the system posts minor payment differences automatically. You can also establish special rules for each user so that any differences larger than a certain amount must be referred to a user with authorization to deal with them.

N O T E When the selected open items balance the payment, you can post the document. ▨

Dealing with Open Items

The following are several different types of open items:

- Vendor open items
- Open items for different customers
- Open items with different company codes

Because the FI-GL General Ledger accounts are fully integrated, vendor open items can be cleared at the same time as customer payments.

The integrated FI-AR Accounts Receivable component accepts each item as an independent task because each item has access to the complete set of data objects needed to process it. Therefore, open items can be found for several customers and cleared by the appropriate payments in the same session.

Open items bearing different company codes can be cleared at the same time. The system records a clearing document in each company code.

Using Automatic Clearing in Accounts Receivable

If your customer allows you to collect by direct debit, you can use the FI-AR payment program component, which collects all invoices when due. Reimbursing customers with checks or by bank transfers follows the FI-AP Accounts Payable procedures for automatic payment.

If you installed and configured the FI-CM Cash Management component, you can clear payments automatically. A file transfer can provide your bank statement, and the system automatically posts the entries to the FI-GL General Ledger as it clears the matching open items in the customer accounts. Only if the data from the transfer is incomplete must you intervene.

Automatic incoming payment processing can be supported by the following specific techniques:

- Electronic account statement
- Lockbox (in the United States)
- POR procedures (in Switzerland)
- Check scans and deposit transactions initiated automatically if the checks are valid

The requirements for an acceptable electronic business transaction system are defined in part by the national standards that depend on the legal monetary instruments in that region. The payer must assign value to a check or other instrument that can be taken as a contract. The validation of this assignment must be conducted at the same time as the receiver is notified of the transaction details. The loop is completed when the receiver acknowledges a valid transfer of value.

The SAP organization is developing improved methods of electronic banking to further develop this aspect of business data processing.

Using Payment Procedures for Particular Countries

Variations in the legal payment procedures exist for different countries. These have been encapsulated in the standard business procedures of the FI-AR Accounts Receivable component. For example, there are differences between national accounting conventions concerning whether a transaction should be dated for tax and accounting purposes according to the invoice or to correspond to the confirmation of payment received.

NOTE   National payment procedures can be specified for your implementation during the
        customizing process.

Receiving Partial Payments

If the open items do not balance the payment after cash discounts, you have three options.

- You can post a payment on account.
- You can clear an open item and post a residual item.
- You can enter a partial payment with a reference to the open item that remains open.

If you cannot find any amounts to match with the payment, your only option is to post the payment on account. If you cannot closely match the payment to the open items, the best option remains posting the payment on account.

If you know the open item concerned and the payment is only partial, you can clear the full amount of the open item but open a residual item to cover the difference still unpaid. Alternatively, you can enter the payment with a note that marks the open item as only partially settled.

If many possible open items exist, you can direct the system to pick open items without defining any search criteria. The system will try various combinations of open items to try to match the amount paid. It will suggest a set of items that together add up to an amount as close as possible to the amount paid.

NOTE   If a bank charge is associated with a cash receipt, you can enter it at the same time. The
        system automatically generates and displays a line item for the bank fee.

Understanding the Payment Advice Note Procedure

If the system finds a relevant payment advice note during clearing, it uses that to settle the incoming payments on the appropriate accounts. A payment advice note can be entered manually by copying the details from an existing advice note. EDI (electronic data interchange) can also submit payment advice notes.

If you carry out the manual procedure for receiving payments, you can create a payment advice note to record the current processing status of any items that are exceptions, such as those that cannot be cleared directly. You can configure automatic generation of payment advice notes to take place during the processing of account statements, check deposit transactions, or Lockbox data, if any of the items cannot be directly cleared.

The system requires only the payment advice note number to begin to use it for clearing. If differences exist between the payment advice note and the open items, the system automatically creates residual items and payments on account. You can subsequently cancel these if you assign the differences manually or post them as a total.

Understanding the Debit Memo Procedure

If a customer agrees to operate the debit memo procedure, your system can automatically collect all invoices according to their due date. The payment program generates debit memos in accordance with the agreement. Refunds to customers can similarly be made by automatically generated checks or transfers initiated by the same program. These functions are described in the section on Accounts Payable.

Using Fast Incoming Payment Entry Techniques

Two features are designed to accelerate the processing of incoming payments.

 ▧ Manual check deposit
 ▧ Manual account statement

Neither feature requires user intervention, but the automatic procedure replicates the manual clerical activities used in the absence of computer processing.

The incoming payment is registered as a check identification code, a check number, and a payment amount. The payment is automatically posted to the bank and to the customer account. The payment is settled automatically.

Using Automatic Electronic Banking

The fast entry methods that seek open items in a customer's account and clear them against incoming payments can work automatically until the system detects a difference that exceeds the acceptable limits. At this point, a review by an authorized user is necessary.

Data can be provided by a bank or the post office in any agreed on format. For example, the Swiss POR procedure uses a protocol that can be accepted by the SAP R/3 financial system and posted directly. The United States operates on a Lockbox system from which SAP R/3 can receive payments and post directly to clear open items.

A check scanner can be used to acquire payment data for direct and automatic posting to clear open items.

Using Electronic Account Statements

The purpose of the electronic account statement is to obtain information for clearing from a Note to Payee field. This indicates the document number so that the incoming payment associated with an open item for that customer can be cleared if it balances and is correct in other respects. For example, you can set up a validation procedure that uses a code particular to your industry. This method is used in the insurance industry, where the policy identification code is the key reference.

No limit exists as to the complexity of the security measures in your system. For example, if you have a particular device or software system that carries out your identification and security validation, you can arrange to use an SAP User Exit. This is a software gateway to an external system that can be used as a step in a workflow sequence without disturbing any of the SAP R/3 system's standard business software.

The account statement facility enables you to post payment transaction information in any of the supported languages and to transmit this information to any country for clearing against the appropriate items. Transaction information can be transmitted and received in any of the following international formats:

- BACS (Great Britain)
- ETEBAC (France)
- SWIFT MT 940 (United States)
- MultiCash (United States)
- CODA (Belgium)
- CSB43 (Spain)
- FIDES (Switzerland)
- ZENGINKYO (Japan)
- Various formats (Czech Republic)
- Various formats (Sweden)

N O T E The SAP R/3 architecture allows additional transaction information formats to be defined and used in an integrated manner without difficulty.

Using Special Transactions in Accounts Receivable

Transactions that are posted to a customer's account automatically update the FI-AR General Ledger Accounts Receivable (a reconciliation account) if they are invoices, credit memos, or payments. Some transactions posted to the customer account can update FI-GL General Ledger accounts other than FI-AR Accounts Receivable.

A special operation or special transaction is so named because the item is posted to the customer but does not cause an update in the General Ledger's Receivables From Goods and Services line-item account. The value is not actualized in the reconciliation account from the customer master record but in a general ledger account set up specifically for this purpose.

These accounts are a type of Special General Ledger Account. They are reconciliation accounts recording business that is neither a sale to a customer nor a purchase from a vendor. Special General Ledger Transactions include the following:

- Down payments
- Bills of exchange
- Security deposits
- Guarantees

Using Down Payments

A down payment is a payment for a product or service not yet supplied or performed. Down payments must be reported in the balance sheet separately from other Receivables or

Payables. Down payments made are reported as assets; down payments received are reported as liabilities.

A request for a payment that is the first of a series of partial payments can be identified as a down payment and is recorded as such. The item remains open, and the amount is posted to an account established for the purpose of accumulating such payments until full payment is received. Only then is the item cleared and the holding account cleared by the same amount.

The receipt of a down payment from a customer is entered into the system as a down payment request, which is a statistical posting. A down payment request is recorded as a note that is displayed with other open items for each customer. As a note, this request does not update account balances. However, as with any other open item, you can dun the request for a down payment with the dunning program and collect the down payment by direct debit.

The payment program automatically generates a down payment posting for each bank collection. When a down payment request is posted, the system assigns the line items to a special General Ledger account. You can call for a list of all expected down payments.

A customer down payment account can display net of tax or gross:

- Net display shows the down payment minus the tax.
- Gross display shows the tax included in the line item, but an additional line item is generated in the tax clearing account as a clearing entry.

When a final payment is posted, an automatic note appears detailing the existing down payments. The down payment total can be transferred in full or in part, but the invoice is not cleared unless the full payment is received.

N O T E The down payment facility can also be used to assign values to accounts set up for internal orders, cost centers, and projects.

Using Bills of Exchange Receivables

A bill of exchange is a document with a written promise to pay a certain amount on a certain date in exchange for a specific business transaction that has taken place. A Bill of Exchange Receivable is a promise that payment can be collected from a customer on the expiration date record on the bill. This is a form of IOU ("I owe you") with a date set for payment. When a customer submits a bill of exchange, you can use the search facilities to find open items to match it if you have any doubt regarding the invoice to which it belongs.

A Bill of Exchange Receivable is an open item until the bill itself is deposited at the bank and discounted there against your account. Alternatively, your customer could pay cash to the amount of a bill of exchange. Either method of concluding the payment permits you to close the open invoice item.

Because the Bill of Exchange Receivable is a promise and not a payment, it is posted to a special General Ledger account set up for this purpose, the Bills of Exchange Receivables account. If the customer offers you a cash or check payment before the Bill of Exchange Receivable has expired, you can reverse the deposit in the Bills of Exchange Receivable account and post the cash against the open item in the normal way.

Using the Bills of Exchange Discount Ledger

Discounting is the process of depositing bills of exchange that are not yet due. The system can prepare a deposit slip for bills of exchange. Discounting also refers to the process of depositing a post-dated check and deducting interest on the amount (the discount) until the due date.

N O T E Commission or collection fees can be charged on both bills of exchange and checks. ⬚

The system can prepare the discount ledger, a journal in which all bills of exchange are entered. The following data fields are mandatory:

- Due date
- Amount
- Name and address of the drawer
- Name and address of the previous holder
- Place of payment
- Name and address of the drawee
- Discount

You can specify default values for each company code for the following:

- Discount percentage
- Collection fees or charges
- Bill of exchange tax indicator

The charges must be posted to separate accounts in the General Ledger. The system can prepare a bill for the customer that details these charges.

Bills of exchange deposits can be recorded and annotated as follows:

- Discounted before the due date
- Collected on the due date
- Factored—an exporter gets cash immediately from a bank or other financial institution that takes responsibility for collecting the receivable amounts or the amounts due on the bills of exchange

Using Security Deposits and Guarantees

A security deposit is a payment made in advance against the possibility of poor performance by one of the parties to a transaction. Some examples are the payment by the buyer or the performance of the seller.

Security deposits are reported as noted items in the financial statements.

A guarantee is a contract entered into by a third party to pay up to a specified limit if one of the parties to a transaction either fails to deliver the contracted materials or service or fails to pay the amount due.

Guarantees are reported as noted items in the financial statements.

Understanding Document and Account Processing

An SAP R/3 business transaction is posted to an assigned account in which the account balance is immediately updated. At the same time, the system records the items on the transaction document that contributed to the update. If you later query the balance of this account, you can inspect the document items that formed it, right back to the beginning of the accounting period. Furthermore, you can display an overview of the transaction figures, separated into debits and credits, for each period.

You can also inspect sales totals per period, as well as the General Ledger accounts for special transactions such as down payments and bills of exchange. In each case, you can drill down to see the individual line items.

A line item display provides a summary of open and cleared items. The format of the summary display of line items can be customized by the user at the time.

Understanding Item Display in Accounts Receivable

Within each line item, it is possible to select the constituent document items and display a variety of totals, such as separate summations for each type of document. Documents can be selected according to their account in a company code, or as related to a group of accounts in a group of company codes. Totals can be displayed to this structure.

You can switch between a display of all line items and a view of the constituent documents of any chosen item. If necessary, you can search for a specific document according to posting date or document type.

If you want to view transactions that cross company codes, the system offers you a list of relevant documents. You can alternate between displaying all line items belonging to a particular transaction and all line items on individual documents.

Standard summary displays are available for the most frequently used analyses and reviewing tasks. These include the following:

- Displaying the credit limit for one account or a group of accounts
- Tabulating a set of items by the number of days in arrears
- Displaying an overview of the net and cash discount situation
- Displaying a customer's payment history to assess liquidity
- Simulating a payment history by entering trial values and assessing the consequences

The most helpful screen display can be saved so that you can use it again. You can save the exact display with the data, or you can save the pathway or analytical route used to arrive at it. If you save the pathway as a report design, you can use the same analysis on other data next time because the totals will be generated from the data you specify.

 TIP The quickest way to access account documents is to begin at the individual account display and then drill down in whatever direction is most fruitful.

Changing Documents Already Posted

The procedures for controlling the display on your screen can also be used in preparation for changing a document. There are four main methods of accessing documents for the purpose of making changes.

- Display an individual document by selecting it according to one or more data fields in it.
- Display a document that involves more than one company code by choosing from the list offered by the system when you identify a cross-company code transaction.
- Select a document from a list of all the documents for a specific vendor.
- Select all the documents for a specific vendor and perform a mass change for certain fields, such as a release of payment.

You cannot make any changes to a data field on a document if that field has already been used to update the transaction database. For example, the following fields are not open to alteration after the document in which they appear has been posted.

- Account number
- Posting key
- Amount
- Tax information

Some fields in a document are locked against updating only if your system has installed and configured a certain SAP R/3 component. For instance, a cost center field cannot be changed if your system has already used it to update a cost center account in the cost accounting component.

The status of a document can also affect the fields that are amenable to alteration after posting. For example, you cannot alter the terms of payment after an item has been cleared.

In addition to the logical rules that prevent you from changing a document to invalidate SAP R/3 compliance with the Generally Accepted Accounting Principles (GAAP) standards, you can institute other rules that make sense for your particular business.

If you have set up additional account assignments for a special purpose ledger or for a particular controlling reason that requires an accumulation of values, you can declare a rule that prevents anyone from changing an additional account assignment unless the document is still open for posting. After the month or other accounting period is closed for accounting purposes,

Part
1

Ch
3

the posting data may be relayed to other systems for evaluation. In these circumstances, you probably won't want anyone to alter the originals and destroy the validity of the audit trail or any other operation that referenced the posting documents. Such rules that should be obeyed across your system can be established through adjustments of the system settings, which are permitted only to suitably qualified users.

Dunning Accounts Receivable

Each customer's master data includes a field to indicate what is to be done about overdue invoices. This dunning code identifies an established dunning procedure. This procedure has the task of preparing a dunning proposal, which it does in the following related stages, not necessarily in this order:

- Identifies the accounts and the items to be dunned
- Establishes the dunning level of the account
- Selects the text of the dunning letter or dunning notice according to the dunning level of the account
- Computes the interest on arrears and any charges due
- Edits the text to include interest and charges
- Adds the details of the items overdue
- Adds the totals in the document currency and the local currency, as required
- Addresses the dunning proposal to the customer's head office or to another addressee the customer approves
- Submits the dunning proposal for approval
- Prints or otherwise dispatches the dunning notice
- Stores the dunning particulars in the records of the items and the dunned accounts
- Compiles lists and reports of the dunning activities

A standard dunning procedure can be independent of company codes. This procedure records the grace period, the dunning level principle, and the number of dunning levels.

Understanding Dunning Levels   The dunning level principle is the formula or logical conditions used to determine a set of dunning levels. A debt is allowed a number of days of grace before it is dunned. If the debt is not cleared after the grace period, the dunning begins at the first level. Subsequent levels of dunning are assigned to the debt according to the dunning level principle so that the text of the dunning notice reflects the seriousness of the overdue payment. You can establish the dunning levels on the basis of number of days in arrears, and you can add other conditions based on such factors as the following:

- The absolute amount of the overdue item
- The percentage of overall sales to this customer represented by the open item overdue
- The absolute amount of the total of all overdue items on this account
- The total of all overdue items on this account as a percentage of the sales on this account

Each item in arrears on a particular account can be assigned to a separate dunning area and, for this reason, can be subject to the dunning notice and procedure for that area. A dunning area is confined to a single company code. Several dunning areas in a company code can correspond to the profit centers or sales organization of that company.

Preparing and Using Dunning Letters   The SAPscript word processing program is available to design and change the format of dunning letters. During customization, the system provides you with some model letters at each dunning level. You can change and edit the text of the letter and also the company logo, position of the address window, and footers. You can give open items referred to in the letter a special format and content for this purpose.

A dunning proposal is a set of suggestions assembled by the system, which you can accept as is or alter in various ways. The system initially creates a dunning proposal by using due dates and some method of selecting the accounts to be dunned. You may have defined these methods previously and specified dunning levels and dunning areas.

You can then edit the dunning proposal list online. You can target the dunning letters at particular individuals in your customer's organization. You may decide to change the dunning level of an item. The dunning level of the whole account is changed automatically to the highest dunning level of any open item. You can release specific open items and accounts to be referenced in the dunning letters. The system records all changes to open items to be dunned.

The dunning data in an individual item is not changed, nor is the customer account updated when you generate a dunning proposal. You can generate a proposal several times and reject it without affecting the accounts. However, if you accept a proposal, the dunning data is updated in the item and in the account as soon as you release the printing proposal and therefore dispatch the letter to the customer.

You can use the same letter forms throughout the group, or you can customize different forms for each company code. If your customer is recorded as a business partner, you can instruct the system to automatically consult a master to determine details of the dunning procedure. In particular, your system can be configured to issue dunning notices in the language specified in the business partner master.

Certain text may appear only for particular company codes. You can decide for each company code whether an individual dunning letter is to be prepared for each dunning level. If this is to be the case, only the items with that dunning level appear on the dunning letter.

Individual accounts can have their own dunning letters. Customer items can be assigned to different dunning areas, each of which receives a separate dunning letter.

N O T E   If the SD-Sales and Distribution System has been installed and configured, the dunning areas can be made to correspond to the areas of the sales organization, the distribution channel, or the division.

Refunds overdue from a vendor can be dunned, and you can instruct the dunning program to subtract vendor items from customer items when they concern the same company, if the master records specify that this is permitted.

Part
II

Ch
3

The dunning program can direct dunning letters to the EDI system on the basis of individual customer or vendor accounts, or in accordance with a group or dunning area policy. You can also use the office system to send the letters by telex, messenger, or postal delivery.

The system always prepares a standard processing log. It can also offer the following reports pertaining to dunning:

- ☐ Lists of blocked items
- ☐ Lists of blocked accounts
- ☐ Lists of items with special dunning keys
- ☐ Dunning statistics
- ☐ Reports of dunning runs

Using Automatic Dunning   Automatic dunning can be initiated if you have determined the key date for a maturity check and identified the accounts to be scrutinized. The automatic dunning program checks the due dates of open items in these accounts.

If you have installed and configured the Financial Calendar, you can schedule dunning runs and assign the proposal lists they generate to the appropriate person for editing and release. This person is notified automatically when a dunning proposal list is about to be generated.

Using Automatic Correspondence from Accounts Receivable

Dunning notices are a type of automatic correspondence that must be first submitted as a dunning proposal to a person authorized to edit and release the dunning notices. This causes the dunning data to be updated in the records of the dunned items and accounts.

You can call for a proposal for automatic correspondence at virtually any time while you are processing accounts and documents. You can set up a cycle of automatic correspondence, and you can initiate individual items manually.

N O T E   Any type of correspondence can be generated in the language of the business partner. ☐

Sending Automatic Payment Notices to Business Partners

The business partner who has submitted a payment is automatically notified by a notice that details the items cleared by this payment. If the system detects a discrepancy, the business partner can be automatically asked to clarify the discrepancy or pay the differences. Should it prove impossible to identify an item that could be cleared by the payment received, the customer again can be automatically asked to clarify.

You can use an automatic reply slip to permit payments on account to be assigned to specific open items. This procedure can also be used to deal with any credit memos that cannot be automatically assigned to items and posted in the clearing procedure.

The automatic payment notice also lists any customer items still open after the payment has been assigned. The payment program can be used to identify the open items to be paid and can append additional remarks that are standard phrases or text entered by the supervisor.

Using Account Statements and Open Item Lists

The customer account statement is a standard report generated by the system and addressed to a business partner. The account statement shows the following entities:

- ☐ The balance carried forward
- ☐ All items, both open and cleared, for the selected time period
- ☐ The account closing balance

An open item list is a form of account statement that includes only the open items up to the specified date. This can be sent as a reminder, for reconciliation, or simply for information.

Both account statements and open item lists specify the following information:

- ☐ Document number
- ☐ Document date
- ☐ Document type
- ☐ Currency
- ☐ Amount for each item
- ☐ Balance of open items on the key date
- ☐ Clearing document number, if applicable
- ☐ Addresses of the customer's head office and branch offices, as appropriate

N O T E The number of days in arrears per item can be included in the account statement or the open item list. ☐

Using Standard and Individual Letters

A standard letter can be added to an account statement or open item list automatically. You may wish to notify customers of a relevant change in your organization that could affect their payment and reconciliation activities. This could be the occasion to use a standard letter.

You can use the accounting events of the SAP R/3 system to trigger the insertion of standard texts in a standard letter. You can also assign specific texts to particular segments of your business; some of your customers could be sent particular forms of your standard letters. Furthermore, an individual letter can be added and edited to suit each customer.

Part
II
Ch
3

Using Other Types of Automatic Correspondence

A balance confirmation is a standard report mailed to a customer. You can operate conditions that automatically arrange for the customers with the highest balances to be notified first. In addition, you can arrange for a random selection of the remaining customers to be notified of their balances.

A document extract is a standard report in which you inform customers of specific line items that you have extracted from a transaction document. For example, you might inform a customer of a credit memo and append a listing of the line items involved.

A customer can clear invoices by submitting a bill of exchange. This incurs charges that you can notify and explain in the form of an automatic letter. This is generated from a master form in the language of the business partner.

Interest can be charged on items that have not been paid and are overdue, or on items that were not paid before the due date for net payment. Interest also can be charged on the account balance and notified by an automatic letter. This could arise, for example, in cases when employees have loan accounts on which interest is charged.

 TIP The SAP R/3 system contains a form letter for interest notification. You can modify this letter and store it as the standard.

With appropriate authorization, an in-house or internal document that contains any data fields in your system can be generated. You might want to create an internal document using customer or product data, for example, because no suitable original document was entered. All the standard text phrases and word-processed free text stand at your disposal. An internal document can be saved and used as a standard.

Reporting Customer Accounts

SAP R/3 reporting is executed by identifying the source records and subsequently processing them. This two-stage process means that any standard reports can be run virtually in parallel to a file that identifies the set of sources. Memory considerations do not usually allow online storage of all information, so a separate file is assembled containing only information from customer line items.

This line-item file is typically sorted so that all the cleared items appear at the beginning of each account. Clearing transactions are sorted by clearing date and clearing document number so that the context can be ascertained. Items still open on the key date appear at the end of each account. Reconciliation totals are output for each customer account and for each reconciliation account. This means that the Accounts Receivable position can be integrated with other R/3 modules.

The online reporting facilities of the Accounts Receivable module can be supplemented by printed outputs in single or batch modes. These reports can be sent to file or to a printer. Three main classes of reports exist.

- Standard master record lists
- Customer account statements and open item lists
- Audit trails of individual accounts

Customers can be selected by various criteria, singly or in the form of logical expressions that isolate customers on the basis of one or more attributes of their master records, combined with attributes computed from their accounts up to a key date.

The content of a report falls under your control. You can mix master data and account data, subject to authorization. If the items remain in the system, you can call for reports of customer open items that sort the items by ranges of due dates or by values according to the report specification that you build or copy from a previous design.

A legally valid financial accounting system must have a method of demonstrating all the transactions that contributed to each of the balances on the balance sheet. The system must show the balance at the beginning of the accounting period and all the debits and credits applied to the account to reach the balance at the close of the period.

Every computer system has limits to the amount of storage space that it can make available for any particular purpose. The SAP approach to the management of storage space is to archive all the line items needed for a balance audit trail separately from the document data that recorded the transactions. When a balance audit trail is required, usually at the end of the accounting period, the line-item archive can be scanned without also having to read all the document data.

The balance audit trail report contains a list of customer line items and a control total for each customer account. Reconciliation account totals are also shown so that the accounts can be matched with accounts in other parts of your accounting system.

TIP The customer line items for accounts that are not managed on an open-item basis can be sorted in chronological order to assist in tracking.

When open-item accounting is in practice, the balance audit trail procedure sorts the cleared line items to the beginning of each account, arranged in clearing date order and then by clearing document number. This helps the auditor trace how and when an item was cleared. The uncleared open items fall at the end of each account listing.

Managing Customer Credit

A credit limit is assigned to a customer based on an assessment of his or her creditworthiness. If an order leaves the customer balance within the credit limit, the order is accepted.

N O T E Customers can have a credit limit of zero.

The Sales module checks the credit limit when the order is posted, as does the Financial Accounting module. If the limit is exceeded, the system either issues a warning or an error message, depending on the key held in the customer master. The document can still be posted, but precautionary measures must be taken by examining the customer position, and possibly by blocking the account at the master record.

You can set up a credit control area that covers one or more company codes, and you can specify a standard credit limit for each credit control area. Under these circumstances, a new customer master record is assigned the credit limit according to the credit control area of the company code in which the account is opened.

You can assign a credit limit to a single customer or to several customers according to specific criteria. For example, you can assess customers and potential customers according to your estimate of the business risk of associating with them. You can assign your business partners to risk classes and check their position in a certain way before accepting an order.

A customer can also be assigned to a group of companies that define an industry or industrial sector. A customer can also be classified according to the country in which it operates or according to the area of the world that shares its business conventions.

The procedure for monitoring customer credit limits in a credit control area automatically assembles and summarizes the following information for each customer account:

- The Receivables from sales not in dispute
- The Receivables from special General Ledger transactions that affect the credit limit calculation, such as down payments
- The total order value comprising open orders, open deliveries, and open invoices

These totals are added to yield the total liabilities for each customer. When a customer invoice is posted, the total liabilities display increases automatically by the amount of the invoice. When a payment is received, the total liabilities display decreases. If the posting of a customer invoice will cause an increase that exceeds the credit limit, a warning is issued and the system records the date on which the credit limit was exceeded.

Each credit control area has a credit limit currency in which all credit calculations are conducted. This currency is independent of the local currency of the company code. The system updates the credit limit data using an amount calculated by converting the invoice amount to the credit limit currency. This control currency update does not affect the transaction figures or the posting to the General Ledger.

Using Credit Limit Displays

The detailed monitoring of credit generally is focused on one customer account at a time. For example, you might find it helpful at times to use one or more of the following standard reports:

- Changes in the master record reflecting some aspects of the customer account history
- Oldest due items to see whether there is a reasonable explanation or a pattern to the items still owed

- Customer order value distributed among open orders, open deliveries, and open invoices
- The date and details of the most recent payment
- The line items of some or all unpaid orders
- The dunning history and the payments in response to dunning

One of the best ways to discover unusual patterns in your customers' payment behavior is to have alert people use the display facilities and think about possible interpretations of what they see. You can use an internal memo that references a stored display or a display specification, along with a more detailed examination of customer data. This could come from other sources, such as sales support, perhaps with a block imposed on further orders from this customer until the payment situation is resolved.

One of the benefits of an integrated accounting system is that you can move effortlessly from credit control to financial information. You can display the sales and payment histories. You can perform due date analysis and ask for a calculation of day sales outstanding (DSO), a figure that combines the time overdue with the magnitude of the amount outstanding. DSO represents the seriousness of the debt from the cash flow perspective of your company.

Any combination of variables and display features can be deployed to help you facilitate business intelligence. Business intelligence is defined as the capability of discerning relationships in the data and the capability of working out what they mean and what should be done. If you find a particular display or computation useful, you can identify it and save it for future use.

Creating a Credit Master Sheet

As you move through the process of interpreting a customer credit situation, you can build a credit master sheet to inform others or to document your decision processes. The system enables you to assemble the line-item display, the account analysis, and the credit management data on a document that also is automatically annotated with the following information:

- The address and data for communication with the customer
- The credit limit and the date when the customer was last notified
- Selected fields from the credit management master record
- The totals of open deliveries, invoices, and orders
- The balance, the days in arrears of each item, and the texts sent to the customer for each item
- The customer's payment history

Your credit management module generally is integrated with the SD-Sales and Distribution module, so it is possible to access any sales information and use it to amplify the credit master sheet. The integration with SD enables you to perform what may be complex credit checks in at least the two most critical moments:

- Before an order is accepted
- Just before the goods are delivered

Part II

Ch 3

If the customer has been assigned to a risk class or a credit control area, the following checks can be mandated:

- A statistical check on the credit limit
- A dynamic check on the credit limit that takes into account the delivery deadlines and the due date for all open items on the customer account
- The absolute value of the order
- Changes in critical fields, such as terms of payment during the customer's payment history
- The structure of overdue items in terms of amounts and time patterns

The credit limit management functions of FI-AR Accounts Receivable require a policy to be elaborated and recorded as a set of master records for one or more credit limit control areas. Standard dunning notices and credit limit documents are available for editing. In total, a comprehensive and flexible system ensures that no customers can deplete the value flows in your company by failing to settle.

Using the Accounts Payable Module

The role of the SAP R/3 FI-AP Accounts Payable module is to maintain and manage accounting data for all vendors of goods, materials, and services and to pay for them in support of an integrated purchasing system. Information about orders, deliveries, and invoices is stored according to vendor.

Accounts Payable is a subledger of the General Ledger and is completely integrated with it at the following levels:

- Master data
- Transaction data
- Reporting system

Master data entered or modified in one application is available to all the others. Transaction data is accessible to all. Reporting can draw from the General Ledger and the Accounts Payable subledger.

Transaction data is stored centrally in the document database, and the corresponding line items and details are stored in the subledgers, as appropriate. The system automatically updates a subtotal of a balance sheet account for every business transaction and reconciles the account subtotals and the line items to ensure that the financial information is always correct and current.

Every transaction creates an SAP document, and the data is immediately posted to the General Ledger. As such, every business transaction recorded in this way automatically updates the balance sheet or the profit and loss statement. This is the defining characteristic of an up-to-date networked accounting and controlling system.

Understanding the Business Functions of Accounts Payable

Accounts Payable includes a program that records orders, deliveries, and invoices for each vendor. Operating transactions automatically update accounts in the FI-GL General Ledger system. When you post a vendor transaction, the system immediately updates the Accounts Payable account.

Accounts Payable is directly integrated with Cash Management, which supports cash planning and dunning. An automatic payment program can be called from Accounts Payable. SAP Purchasing is a group of components used by the MM-Materials Management module that can be installed and configured to integrate with Accounts Payable.

Reporting on matters concerned with FI-AP Accounts Payable follows the SAP standard business functions to yield the following reports, for example:

- List of due dates for Accounts Payable
- Currency lists
- Hit list

Correspondence concerning Accounts Payable can be set to provide automatic letters and messages for the following purposes:

- Balance confirmation
- Information
- Interest calculation

You can also customize correspondence to suit individual vendors.

The Accounts Payable module is designed to maximize available cash discounts. You can set up an invoice receipt with information that is incomplete or that has not been assigned to an account. The necessary details can then be added when they become available.

FI-AP is also integrated with the business workflow functions so that invoices can be routed automatically to those who are authorized and qualified to complete or release them. The payment process sequence can be partly or completely computerized. The module supports all customary payment modes for the countries for which your implementation is configured.

Complying with GAAP

The methods used by SAP FI-AP Accounts Payable to adhere to GAAP standards are the methods used throughout the SAP system. These methods also comply with the account conventions of most industrial nations.

Vendor information is stored in vendor master data records, which are the only source of this information and which are kept up-to-date by all users and applications with reason to interact with them. The master data is entered once and stays in only one place. Everyone knows where to find the data and can discover when it was last updated.

Transactions concerning vendors automatically create SAP documents that can be used to keep track of the transactions and any resulting actions. These SAP documents can be used to compile a legal audit trail for each balance amount in the balance sheet. The documents can also be used to record other information used by controlling systems with interests in vendor transactions.

SAP documents must comply with GAAP in the matter of capturing information essential to the proper and legal analysis and control of business. These documents, which are automatically created during vendor transactions under the Accounts Payable system, can be displayed and altered in a controlled manner using the SAP standard business functions for manipulating SAP documents.

The vendor accounts and other accounts such as Payables and down payments integrated with the Accounts Payable system are updated in accordance with GAAP recommendations, and the proper record must be created whenever any changes are made to the account balances by the SAP documents that record such activities. In particular, a company must be capable of disclosing its debts when closing an accounting period.

The R/3 Accounts Payable accounting system uses balance confirmations, journals, balance audit trails, and custom valuation reports to document and manage transactions with vendors. The main activities of deadline analysis are as follows:

- Revaluation of foreign currency items
- Identification of vendors with debit balances
- Lists of the calculated balance amounts on the vendor accounts, sorted according to the terms of payment still obtainable

A thorough Accounts Payable accounting system not only meets legal obligations, but it can also serve as a database for optimizing purchases. If they are directly linked to Cash Management and Cash Forecasting, the Accounts Payable functions can provide valuable support for efficient liquidity planning.

Working with Vendor Master Records

In accordance with the SAP principle of redundancy-free data storage, standard practice involves using master records for the control of basic data that seldom changes. The system designers have ensured that a vendor master data object has a data field for every item of information needed to record and post business transactions with vendors.

N O T E   If the information you require for any business process can be supplied by the system, you should not have to enter it by hand every time you attempt to carry out a transaction. SAP should obtain it from the master data object and supply it for you to confirm or edit.

Information in a master record is not necessarily available to anyone interested in it. Certain data objects can be closed to a user who does not have access authorization. The vendor's bank balance is an example of data that is not available for scrutiny by just anyone.

The Purchasing components of MM-Materials Management must be installed and configured to make use of information directed at a Purchasing department. In these circumstances, both the Purchasing department and the Accounting department use the vendor master record at times. Data fields must be present to suit them both, including the following data.

- General vendor data that any company code in your enterprise might need, such as vendor address, telephone number, and telex and network addresses
- Company code data about the vendor, such as terms of payment and other arrangements that have been agreed upon only between that company code and the vendor
- Purchasing organization data about the vendor that might vary from one purchasing department of your company to another, such as the products of interest and the relevant section of the vendor accounting structure

The vendor master record stores the data needed to control payment transactions, and this record can provide the basic information needed to generate a preliminary invoice posting without waiting for final details. Vendor master data for each of your company codes includes the following:

- Payment terms agreed upon with the vendor
- The vendor account number under that company code
- The reconciliation account number in Payables
- The payment methods agreed upon
- The dunning procedure
- Correspondence information and prepared texts
- How the vendor line items are to be sorted on displays under that company code

Creating and Maintaining Vendor Master Records

If your enterprise has more than one purchasing organization, each one could maintain information that is of no particular interest to the other. For example, both organizations could be responsible for the purchasing of different types of materials and services. They might have a different set of purchasing contacts and might operate through different sales departments of the vendor organization. Each purchasing organization may need to maintain separately such items as inquiry information, order information, and data required to verify invoices.

If your Financial Accounting and Materials Management applications are integrated, the following possibilities are available for maintaining vendor master records:

- Maintaining company code data on vendor masters separately at each company code
- Maintaining purchasing organization data on vendor masters separately in each purchasing area
- Maintaining all data on vendor masters from a central location

When a new or prospective vendor is identified, a new master record is created. This record must be assigned to an account group.

The account group determines whether you can assign account numbers within specified ranges or whether this is done automatically by the system. You cannot assign the same account number more than once, but you can have both customers and vendors within the same range of numbers.

The account group also controls which fields are active in this master record. You can pick the fields offered by the account group and assign them to one of three categories:

- Fields into which the user must make a valid entry.
- Fields the user can either leave blank or make an entry into (optional fields).
- Fields suppressed so they do not appear on the screen. An entire screen of fields can be suppressed if they are not needed for a particular master record.

Field groups enable you to subdivide the control over groups of fields such as address and bank information. Accounts Payable also can add fields that contain specific information about the supplier.

The FI-AP Accounts Payable system makes it easy to create vendor master records by offering various options.

- You can copy and edit a master record from a reference record established for the purpose.
- You can copy the master record of an existing vendor and edit the unwanted details to make it into a new master record.
- You can create the new vendor master record by entering all the necessary details.

After you have entered and stored a vendor master record, you can recall it and change almost any field. Master vendor records can be selectively displayed so that you can see only those fields of interest. You have the choice of whether to go through all the fields or to work on only one set of fields, such as the product or service details.

N O T E The system automatically maintains a log of all changes made to vendor master records.

Using One-Time Transaction Accounts

If you think a vendor probably will not become a regular supplier, you can set up a one-time account by selecting a special function. This creates a master record that contains only the essential control data, such as the number of the reconciliation account to which this purchase is posted.

You can supply the address and the bank account data when you enter an invoice received. This information then arrives in the one-time account master record, where the dunning and payment programs can find it.

Using Vendor Head Office and Branch Accounts

Your supplier could be a branch with its own account, but the head office may want to receive your payment. In this case, you can enter the head office account number in the master record for the branch vendor. When you enter a transaction to the branch account, the system posts the transaction to the head office account, leaving a cleared entry on the branch account to show who supplied the goods or service.

The master record includes data about the branch and a reference to another master record to give details of the head office. By this means, dunning letters can be sent to the head office, the branch, or both for overdue refunds, for example.

Sending Vendor Payments to an Affiliate

Your supplier may not have to deal with his payments due. You can record in his master data the account number of the alternative recipient. The system then processes return transfers and other vendor payment business through the banks to the alternate recipient.

If you have a credit balance in one or more affiliates of a vendor and you post vendor invoices to an affiliate account, your accounting system also must record the single head office vendor company account number to be used during consolidation to eliminate the invoices that would otherwise appear twice in the accounts. The system can look at the transaction documents bearing this group-wide company account number and identify any entries that are replicated because the payment was made to an affiliate that was not the original vendor.

Part

Ch

Understanding Transactions in Accounts Payable

When you post a transaction to a vendor account, the reconciliation account for Accounts Payable is updated immediately in the General Ledger. The system updates a separate account for each type of vendor transaction, such as the following:

- [ ] Purchases
- [ ] Down payments
- [ ] Bills of exchange payable
- [ ] Guarantees

Orders to and invoices from vendors also update financial planning and cash management data.

Using Vendor Invoices

The SAP FI-Financial Accounting system can be integrated with the MM-Materials Management system. An invoice with an order and delivery data can be entered and validated in Materials Management. Validated invoices are posted automatically to the General Ledger accounts in the FI-Financial Accounting system, if the two systems are suitably configured.

If your financial system is not integrated with a Materials Management system, you can carry out the invoice receipt function in the Financial Accounting module using the following steps:

1. Enter the invoice document header.
2. Enter one or more line items.
3. Verify the line items entered automatically by the system, such as input tax postings.
4. Correct any details on the invoice receipt document.
5. Post the invoice receipt.

Using Electronic Data Interchange

Vendor invoices can be received by EDI. Data entry starts automatically, and the system creates an SAP document that receives the incoming data and is posted when complete. If any errors are detected, the invoice receipt document is forwarded to a suitable person for verification.

One of the advantages of this kind of system is that the invoices can be processed at off-peak times, and the problem items can be presented in batches when a suitable person is available.

Scanning Invoices

The ArchiveLink standard interface can be used to scan incoming invoices. The interface will have been customized to recognize the type of document and the vendor company. The scanning will also be primed to identify standard materials and services, with the corresponding quantities. If the recognition cannot be completed automatically, the system forwards each image to an appropriate person for verification.

Supporting Manual Invoice Entry

If you must manually enter or edit an invoice that has not been posted automatically, SAP R/3 provides all possible help. The successful posting of a transaction does not occur until the necessary data is recorded as an SAP document and is complete and error-free. You can set aside a transaction document before it is ready for posting, in which case the system validates any information you have already entered and reports any discrepancies in the form of a detailed list of the error sources. If you have the authority, you can access the source document to seek clarification.

The SAP document must end up with a document header showing posting date, document date, document reference number, and currency key. The body of the document contains one or more line items showing the amount and identifying the product and terms of payment. The system generates certain line items such as tax entries, cash discounts, and exchange rate differences, as applicable.

You can set up helping routines and use standard data entry functions such as the following:

- Setting default values that you can edit at the time of entry
- Recalling for copying and editing a previous screen

- Retaining data for individual users for several transactions
- Adapting a copy of a data-entry screen so that it is better suited to a set of expected transactions
- Searching for an account number by using matchcodes to narrow the search

An SAP document that records a previous transaction can be copied to act as a sample or model to be edited. This sample can be a regular document that has been set aside, perhaps as an incomplete transaction document. The posting date and new values may have to be changed before posting.

Handling Recurring Entries

If you expect to make a series of entries in which the amounts are always the same, you can set up a recurring entry. Monthly service charges under contract would be one example.

A recurring entry is a set of data that is not used until the due dates. Until then, the entries do not update account balances. You must specify the first and last dates and the frequency or time interval. The system automatically posts the required transaction on each of the due dates.

Using Account Assignment Models

An account assignment model is a document entry template that can take a variety of forms. Unlike a sample document, a document entry template need not be a complete and valid document. You may have to add or edit details before posting it.

The advantage of using an account assignment model is that you can enter invoices and credit memos quickly and safely. For example, you may have to repeatedly divide amounts between several company codes, between accounts, or between cost centers. If you have a suitable document entry template, you can arrange for the General Ledger account items to be in place so that when you enter the total amount, the system can apportion it automatically between the various receiver accounts. Your account assignment models can include fixed distribution ratios to control the assignments between General Ledger items.

You do not have to accept the suggestions of an account assignment model. You can amend any details before you release it by entering the total and posting the template as a complete document.

Using Control Totals and Checks for Duplication

If you post any document that is in error, the system immediately reports it and suggests a correction. Control totals are maintained at suitable levels that are entered, automatically where possible, on the basis of the expected values. A built-in function ensures that you do not generate duplicate invoices. Should you mistakenly post a transaction to the wrong vendor, you can reverse this transaction and the associated SAP document. The system automatically generates a reversing entry for each item wrongly posted.

Working with Incomplete and Preliminary Documents

If you are interrupted before completing a transaction document, or if you want to set the document aside for the moment, you can save it as an incomplete document and recall it when you are ready to resume work on it. If you have an invoice that needs to be reviewed or assigned to an account, you can enter it as a preliminary document. Creating a preliminary document does not update transaction figures, even if the document is complete. However, the posting of a preliminary document is treated as a statistical transaction and is displayed along with other accounts.

The data in a preliminary document, or in a set of preliminary documents, can be analyzed and used in various ways, as long as you do not try to update the transaction database with them. For example, you could create a preliminary invoice to calculate and print an advance sales tax return, perhaps in response to a question from a business partner. Another use of preliminary invoices might involve payment requests to assure that your customer or your accounting department pays on time and qualifies for a cash discount.

A preliminary or incomplete invoice receipt document can be generated by one person and then forwarded to a cost center for payment release by someone with the required authorization. The document could then be returned to the originating person for completion and posting.

Another main use for a preliminary document is to register an invoice when there is insufficient information to have the amount correctly assigned in cost accounting, for example. The invoice can still be recorded and reported for tax purposes, ensuring there is no loss in cash flow resulting from taxes levied on supplier invoices.

The task of processing incoming invoices can be summarized in the language of the SAP workflow system, as follows:

1. A trigger event arises on receipt of an EDI invoice, a scanned invoice, or a manual invoice entry.
2. Accounting entry is affected by posting a preliminary document with the payment-blocking indicator set.
3. The responsible organizational unit releases the preliminary document for payment.
4. The responsible employee workplace processes the document through to completion.

The authority for actions at each stage of the workflow is defined in terms of authorization paths that represent the stages of approval for payments of different kinds and amounts.

The flexibility of the workflow concept, as it is elaborated in the SAP R/3 system, is demonstrated by the infinite variety of workflow paths that can be established to ensure that your work activities are performed in the correct order and with the utmost dispatch.

Using Centralized Open Items

You can support centralized open items by allowing more than one company code to post to them. For example, you might wish to hold a central stock of a material and permit each company code to draw on it as planned or as required. Under these circumstances, an invoice can refer to goods and services destined for different company codes. The invoice must be entered in the Accounts Payable of only one company code. The General Ledger account items must therefore be distributed among the various company codes that make withdrawals of the central item.

When a multicompany open item of this kind is posted, the system automatically creates line items for Payables and Receivables arising between the individual company codes. The system also generates a separate document for each so that their individual accounts can be correctly updated to record their particular withdrawal from the central open item. Each document carries its unique document number, but they all refer to a joint transaction number that links them. This joint transaction number can be used to acquire a summary of the joint transaction data.

Understanding the Net Posting Procedure

A net vendor invoice records the liability to the vendor after the cash discount. When you process a net vendor invoice, you must enter the gross amount. The system calculates the net amount on a line-by-line basis.

When this type of invoice is posted, the General Ledger entries in the Accounts Payable subledger include the offsetting amounts net of the cash discount. The amount of the cash discount is automatically posted to a discount clearing account. This figure remains there until you pay the invoice, at which time it is released.

When a vendor invoice is entered using net posting, the cash discount is taken into account at the time the vendor invoice is entered. A net posting anticipates that the payment will be made before the due date and will attract the cash discount. The cost of the goods or services bought on a net posting transaction is recorded in the materials or expense account, with an additional line item to allow for the discount.

If you use the payment program to pay invoices, the system applies the cash discount rate when the payment is made and posts the net amount. This discount therefore might differ from the discount anticipated and posted when the invoice was received. If this difference arises, it is posted to a separate expense account.

The gross posting procedure and the net posting procedure are used side by side in the SAP R/3 system. In both cases, even after posting, you can make changes to the cash discount terms in the invoice document or in the payment proposal. In both types of posting, you enter gross values and the system automatically corrects the line items and posts any differences to the clearing account.

The purchase of a fixed asset can be recorded as a net vendor invoice. By this means, the amount representing the value of the fixed asset is net of the cash discount and can be depreciated in the normal way. The discount clearing account carries the amount of the cash discount, but it does not have to be cleared later because it was released when payment was made for the fixed asset.

Using Credit and Debit Memos

A transaction that reduces Amounts Receivable from a customer is a credit memo. For example, the customer could return damaged goods. A debit memo is a transaction that reduces Amounts Payable to a vendor because, for example, you send damaged goods back to your vendor.

When you post credit memos, the payment program processes them automatically. If the credit memo is specifically related to a particular open invoice item, the payment program automatically attempts to offset the credit memo against the open item. If it is not possible to completely offset the credit memo against an invoice, you can post a debit memo to the vendor, who is to reimburse the amount. Then you can apply a multilevel dunning program.

Dealing with Down Payment Requests

The standard general-purpose data-entry function can be called from the Accounts Payable module to General Ledger entries such as credit memos and adjustments. However, down payments, bills of exchange, and security deposits are examples of special General Ledger transactions. Separate account balances are maintained for them.

A down payment to a vendor can be made by the payment program if you have entered to the system a down payment request document that includes all the necessary payment data and the due date before which the down payment must be made. The system stores the request without updating any account balances. At any time, you can call for a report to display an individual request, all requests for a given vendor, or all requests for down payment entered.

You have the option to display down payments in the vendor or General Ledger as either gross (including sales tax) or net (excluding sales tax). The net amount is reported in the balance sheet, and the tax appears in the tax account.

When the payment program carries out all the down payments requested and you receive the final invoice from the vendor, you can enter it. The system displays all the down payments made on this invoice, and you can apply them to offset the invoice in whole or in part. The payment program then pays any amount outstanding to the vendor.

Using Automatic Payment Functions

Manual entering of payments is necessary, for example, if a vendor is to collect from you by direct debits. The most effective time-saver in Accounts Payable, however, is the automatic payment program. The payment program proceeds in three stages:

1. Generating a payment proposal list
2. Presenting a payment proposal for editing
3. Executing the approved payment proposal by posting payment documents to clear the Payables and link them to the payment, creating payment forms and other payment media as required

You can also have a payment triggered automatically without considering a payment proposal.

Editing a Payment Proposal

The purpose of a payment proposal is to maximize cash discounts within the constraints set by the control strategy specified in the vendor master records and also by the way the payment program has been set up. The following options are available for editing a payment proposal:

- Replace the proposed payment procedure with another
- Substitute a different bank to receive the payment
- Change the cash discount terms for the items to be paid
- Block certain payment items
- Add open items to the payment proposal

Displaying vendor open items shows you who is yet unpaid; you must decide who to choose for payment. You can choose who to pay on the basis of due dates, according to the outstanding amounts of magnitude, according to your preferred vendor policy, and so on.

The system checks the due dates of vendor open items and proposes a method of payment for each, depending on the vendor master data and the requirement to maximize cash discount. The system also chooses one of your banks to provide the funds for each payment, as well as a bank to receive it on behalf of the vendor.

The system can generate a form for a check or automatic payment medium, such as disk or an online electronic transfer. You must assign a medium of this kind for each payment, either individually, based on the default values suggested by the system, or based on the data in the vendor master records. You can directly specify the choice of medium prior to a batch of payment proposals.

Execution of a valid payment proposal is largely automatic. The payment program generates SAP payment documents and posts payments to the appropriate General Ledger accounts. The vendor items in the payment proposal are marked as cleared and are given a reference number that links them to the SAP payment document.

For each country and payment method combination, a specific program prints the checks or payment forms in the language and accounting style for that country and, if a disk or other electronic payment notification channel is used, in the format for that medium. The system compiles a log of each payment run and all payment methods applied so that you can see the effects and exercise control.

Maximizing Cash Discounts

The default payment principle operated by the system is to pay open items as late as possible without losing any available cash discounts. Each vendor open item carries a base amount, which is the payment due before applying cash discounts. Each vendor master record contains information about the payment terms that that vendor has agreed upon with the purchasing company. Under the control of the purchasing group, different payment terms can be negotiated between a vendor and each business entity defined by the company codes.

Part I Ch

The payment terms for each company code purchasing from a vendor each include at least one cash discount term, expressed as a percentage discount, and a cash discount date related to the date of the invoice. For example, the following are cash discount payment terms:

- 3% if paid within 14 days of the date of the invoice
- 2.5% if paid on or before the 15th of the month following the date of the invoice

For each open item, you can enter one or two payment terms and a date for net payment. The system can calculate the due discount date by referring to the payment terms and the invoice date. You might wish to enter a date for net payment within a discount period on a date that suits your requirements.

You may find national differences in the practice of settling accounts. In France, for instance, it is customary to pay an invoice with a bill of exchange immediately so that the due dates of the bill of exchange and the invoice are the same.

Controlling the Payment Program

The SAP payment program can be set to pay, by bill of exchange, all invoices due within a specific time period. Many other different payment methods could be available in the system. The payment program can also be used to make payments by check, by bank transfer, by postal check, and by other methods such as notes payable that are specific to particular countries or trading areas.

Multinational accounting is supported by the SAP INT-International Development module that manages accounting according to the areas of legal force listed in Table 3.1.

Table 3.1 SAP Accounting Areas of Legal Force

Abbreviation	Area
IN-APA	Asian and Pacific Area
IN-EUR	Europe
IN-NAM	North America
IN-AFM	Africa and the Middle East
IN-SAM	South America

No limits exist as to the number of different payment methods you can use for each country. Many of the forms are supplied via an SAP script, which is then used to control the printing in the language of the destination country.

N O T E You can edit the forms that are supplied so that they precisely suit your payment
format.

You can ask the system to select the payment method from a list of up to 10 methods that have been nominated in the vendor master record. The automatic selection of payment method can be governed by such factors as the following:

- Amount to be paid
- Number of open items paid
- Currency of the receiver
- Location of the vendor
- Amount available in the bank account

Open items can be grouped for payment, and individual items can be marked to be paid separately. You can nominate a specific open item to be paid in a particular way.

Your system may be set up to choose one of the vendor's banks on the basis of the bank's capability of paying, for example, by bills of exchange. The choice could rest on your bank's capability of making a direct transfer to the vendor's bank. Banks are given group codes to indicate who can transfer to whom.

Part

II

Ch

3

The payment system can be asked to choose one of your banks from which to make a payment. You can rank-order your banks and have the system work down the list to look for sufficient cash and the appropriate means of paying. You can instruct the system to choose one of your banks because it has a branch near the vendor. You can also override the automatic selection by commanding it through an entry in the open line item or by changing the vendor master data.

If payment must go to a recipient other than the vendor, you can arrange it in various ways:

- All payments in all company codes can be redirected by entering the new account number in the general data of the vendor master record.
- All payments in a specific company code can be redirected by entering the new account number in the company code section of the vendor master record.
- Payments for specific open items can be redirected by marking each open item by a code, but only if this is expressly permitted by an entry in the vendor master record that specifies the alternate account number.

Receiving Intercompany Payments

One vendor might supply several company codes in the same group. The payment system can make one payment and then settle the intercompany accounts by calculating and posting Receivables and Payables between company codes.

The transaction requires you to define one of the company codes and enter it as a normal paying company. The system assigns the document a unique intercompany identification number used to ensure that the other members of the company code group pay their shares.

Clearing Sales Contra Purchases by Offsets

If a vendor is also a customer, you can offset vendor and customer open items against each other via a Contra account. The vendor and customer master records must be capable of identifying each other by holding the respective account numbers in the company code areas. This sort of dealing must be explicitly permitted by the appropriate master data items, which enable you to control which of your company codes is permitted to operate offsets between sales and purchases. This practice is forbidden in certain countries by their insolvency (bankruptcy) laws.

Using Reverse Documents

Should you mistakenly post a transaction to the wrong vendor, you can reverse this transaction and the associated SAP document. The system automatically generates a reversing entry for each item wrongly posted.

Managing Data Media

Standard forms printed for particular banks or countries can be supplemented by custom forms created by word processing through SAPscript. A disk for data medium exchange is made from a file that contains all payment information the destination country requires. The system includes a data medium management function to support the data media created during payment transaction runs. You can ask for an overview of each data medium object that includes the following elements:

- ☐ Payment run identification
- ☐ The house bank
- ☐ The clearing center
- ☐ The calculated amount

A data medium comprises a collection of stored documents that can be individually inspected or selectively output to screen or printer.

Managing Checks

The significance of the check management function is that it can issue checks without using the payment document number. There are two situations of relevance:

- ☐ Where banks supply checks that are uniquely prenumbered, such as in Australia, Canada, France, Great Britain, and the United States
- ☐ Where the banks or the company require checks to be numbered in a particular way, such as when the payment document number is too long or where there is a possibility of check numbers recurring over the years

Checks or payment document forms from a printer are divided into stacks, which are assigned number ranges. The check print program chooses the next available check number or payment document number and stores the details of the payment assigned to this number.

Posting from the outgoing checks account to the bank account is an automatic process. The check register file stores the date on which each check was cashed. Checks that have been cashed or voided can be archived and recalled for subsequent scrutiny through the check or payment document number, or by a search for other attributes such as payee or date of issue.

If the bank supplies electronic information about the checks that have been presented and canceled, the system updates automatically. If the bank returns a hard copy of canceled checks, you must use the Manually Cashed Checks input function.

N O T E The system can be set up to generate a list of all incoming checks for each house bank and a register of all check information stored in the database. ☐

4

Accounting for Assets

In this chapter

Defining Assets

Assets are legally defined as an organization's property plus its accrued income. Assets are shown on the left side of the balance sheet. A balance sheet account is used to record acquisitions and retirements of assets through the fiscal year. The balance is carried forward to the same account for the following year.

Assets are identified as a separate accounting area and are assigned an account type in a scheme that usually includes such account types as the following:

- General Ledger accounts
- Fixed assets
- Customer accounts
- Vendor accounts

Accounts assigned to different accounting types can have the same account numbers because they are differentiated by their type code.

N O T E   In practice, it is sometimes useful to discriminate between fixed assets and financial assets.

This chapter concentrates on the processes of balance sheet accounting for all types of assets, although the main concepts were developed in connection with fixed asset accounting. Chapter 11, "Managing Investments," develops the ideas of investing in financial assets and details the strategies for managing their acquisition and disposal.

Structuring Asset Records in Financial Accounting

The R/3 system is designed to support any legal accounting convention and to comply with the Generally Agreed Accounting Practice (GAAP) and similar national standards. Among their many functions, asset records support the compilation of balance sheets for specific closing dates and for inclusion in the annual financial documents. Different balance sheets can be drafted to display lists of balances and to report funds flow analysis.

Asset transactions are subject to the receipt principle, in which the system notices and remembers all business events because they generate SAP documents that record the time, date, and all relevant aspects of the event. The structure of the asset records is flexible within a formal scheme that ensures that all system modules are compatible and fully integrated.

Like all SAP R/3 data processing, asset accounting is based on data elements that are defined in master records. If you engage in manual entry, for example, you can proceed almost entirely by a sequence of multiple selections presented by a list of options. Even if you enter the required field as a key sequence, the system probably validates your entry by referring to a set of masters that define acceptable entries for this field. For complex entities, you need complex master records. For businesses that change over time, you need the ability to recombine your established master entities to represent the concepts that make business sense.

The defining reference source for SAP R/3 data elements is the enterprise data model. In this model, entity types are specified as patterns to which all instances must conform if they are to be successfully processed by the system. This effectively imposes an immutable logical structure on data and ensures the integrity of data processing.

Understanding the Hierarchical Classification of Assets

A tree structure, or better, the structure of the roots of a tree, can be interpreted as a hierarchy. At each level, every item is connected to one of the items in the level above, although it may not be connected to any item in the level below. The balance sheet items in SAP R/3 are classified in a hierarchical fashion, starting at the items that typically appear in a balance sheet:

- Intangible assets
- Fixed assets
- Financial assets

Of these three elements of a balance sheet, the fixed asset category is assigned the most complex record structure. Fixed assets are classified, depending on the requirements of your company, into such categories as the following:

- Real estate
- Machinery
- Fixtures and fittings
- Assets under construction

To ensure that these categories of fixed assets are served with the appropriate transaction data, a system of General Ledger accounts is established with such headings as the following:

- Land
- Commercial buildings
- Residential buildings
- Production machinery
- Packing and packaging machinery
- Transportation machinery
- Vehicles
- Data processing equipment
- Office fittings
- Buildings under construction
- Production facilities under construction
- Miscellaneous assets under construction

Assigning these categories to fixed asset classes at the level above may be different for your company. For instance, do you regard data processing equipment as fixtures and fittings, machinery, or even as assets under construction?

Identifying Assets

The word "asset" is used in two senses:

- "Assets" is a legally defined heading in the balance sheet that records an organization's property plus its accrued income.
- Assets are the individual economic units that a company uses in permanent business operations that can be identified on the closing key date for accounting purposes.

The concept of a fixed asset is useful in manufacturing industries to differentiate these individual economic units from assets such as currency holdings. The distinction is not so clear, however, if the business of your company is largely concerned with holding currencies.

Developing Asset Classes

An asset class is defined by entity type 3008, which specifies that an asset class is a grouping or classification of complex fixed assets, according to statutory or enterprise-specific requirements.

Although the asset class structure is designed to support balance sheet accounting, it can also include categories established purely for the convenience of the enterprise or one of its company codes. Control parameters and default values for calculating depreciation must be defined for each asset individually within an asset class. An asset master record is assigned to only one asset class.

N O T E Each asset class can be assigned a different set of custom or standard reporting formats.

Using Asset Classes to Manage Different Types of Assets

The reason for having a complex classification of assets is to facilitate their subtle and simple management. You can account for your assets in legal procedures that also suit your company.

The main idea is to manage different types of assets by using the characteristics of the asset classes to which they have been assigned. You are free to design asset classes on any basis, provided that every asset class can be related to one of the main types of assets as defined on your balance sheet (such as intangible, tangible, and financial).

The asset class is the main classification criterion for dividing the fixed assets. This class also uses its relationship to the fixed assets balance sheet account to serve as a bridge between the reconciliation accounts of financial accounting and the records of the fixed assets. No restrictions exist as to the number of reconciliation accounts you set up to receive account allocations that arise as the result of purchasing and other transactions in the system. However, if you arrange these allocations based on account class membership, you ensure that the allocations remain the same throughout the class.

Several asset classes can use the same account allocation so that you can classify a fixed asset by the asset classes that contribute to it. This enables you to select fixed assets for special reports and evaluations to suit your company's requirements. Furthermore, you can use the account class relationship as a control factor that determines how master records screens and field displays are formatted. New asset master records can be created by assigning as defaults the values held in the asset class master. Assigning main asset numbers can be controlled at the asset class level, either automatically or as proposals that await confirmation from an authorized user.

Individual tangible assets can have different uses. For this reason, you might prefer to allocate them to different balance sheet items. It may be sensible to apply different depreciation procedures to them, and these can be designated by their asset class.

If you have an asset under construction, you can arrange that no further acquisitions be assigned to it after it has been completed and settled on another asset. The IM-Investment Management module is specialized in the control and management of large asset investments.

You can lease one or more of your assets. The capital lease method can be applied to determine and capitalize future payment debits for the leased assets. The lessor's Accounts Payable account is posted with leasing liabilities with the correct due dates.

Many of your assets may have low value. You can manage them individually or collectively, and you can set a limit to the check amount. By assigning a special depreciation key, either individually or as part of the asset class definition, you can write off the acquisition value as soon as the item is acquired.

If you install and configure the PM-Plant Maintenance application, you can closely couple the asset accounting to manage the necessary technical asset maintenance for the assets and asset classes that need it. Financial asset management and real estate management can be arranged by functions from the TR-Treasury application, which is discussed in Chapter 10, "Managing the Treasury."

Understanding Asset Class Master Records and the Asset Class Catalog

A catalog of defined asset classes is created and maintained at the client level and is available to all associated company codes. An asset class master can store primary valuation parameters and default values that can be used to create master records for assets in that class. More than one set of valuation parameters can be specified for each asset class. This enables you to define country-specific valuation parameters in the asset class master.

If you need to classify asset class masters that are specific to particular organizations, you can use multipurpose fields in the master record that are available for customizing as any of the following key types:

- Evaluation groups for reporting purposes
- Access criteria for match codes
- Validation criteria for master record maintenance

Using Asset Master Records

You can create a fixed asset master record by entering selected information that is specific to the asset. One asset could be represented in the system by several asset master records that refer to parts of the assets and are assigned asset subnumbers. In such circumstances, the asset is referred to as a complex fixed asset and is recorded as an entity of type 3002. You can specify during customizing whether you permit values to be changed individually for asset subnumbers or whether you prefer to change the values uniformly throughout a complex fixed asset. The following examples of complex fixed assets illustrate the possibilities for exercising this option:

- All low-value fixed assets in the company could be treated as a single complex fixed asset and depreciated uniformly.
- All company vehicles could be classified as subnumbers of a complex fixed asset, but individual vehicles could be assigned specific depreciation rates.

A complex fixed asset can contain only a single fixed asset. However, the subnumber system is useful for a variety of purposes, as demonstrated by the following examples:

- Subsequent acquisitions to a complex fixed asset can be tracked separately or in groups for changes in value.
- Individual fixed assets that are constituents of a complex fixed asset can be allocated to different cost centers.
- The components of a complex fixed asset can change their relative values in ways that are not reflected by applying a uniform depreciation formula.
- Constituent individual or groups of fixed assets can be differentiated for technical reasons, such as the qualifications of a person able to diagnose malfunctions.

CAUTION

A fixed asset cannot be considered a constituent of more than one complex fixed asset.

Using Group Assets and Super-numbers

A complex fixed asset is assigned a main number and is stored as an entity of type 3002. This asset type can be used to represent one or more fixed assets, each stored in entity type 3001 format. These have asset subnumbers as the asset components of the complex asset, which has the main number.

If you need to represent the fixed assets of an economic unit or group that does not coincide with the scope of an account already established in the General Ledger or any supporting ledgers, you can assign asset super-numbers to any asset master records to form a representation of the desired economic unit or group. A group asset, defined by assigning assets an asset super-number, is used in reporting to add up any desired number of asset master records.

For most controlling and planning purposes, depreciation calculated and posted at the level of asset components is sufficiently precise. The FI-AA Asset Accounting module therefore calculates depreciation by main asset number or by asset subnumber. To perform such calculations at a higher group level, you must assign super-numbers and create a virtual asset super-class. This may be necessary if legal requirements mandate summaries at a level higher than the economic unit represented by the main asset number.

Using Asset Line Items

Each transaction concerning an asset creates a line item for every depreciation area to be posted. The following data elements can be included in an asset line item:

- Transaction type, such as acquisition or retirement
- Asset value date
- Posted amount
- Depreciation and interest pertaining to the transaction for each relevant depreciation area
- Proportionate value adjustments, if appropriate

No limits are imposed on the number of transaction line items posted to an asset master record, so you can continue to use the same record throughout the lifecycle of an asset. By selecting line items for particular depreciation areas, such as book valuation or tax valuation, you can report on the transaction history of an asset from different points of view.

Using Asset History Reporting

An asset history sheet is a standard report delivered at year-end closing. This sheet must be included in the Notes to the Balance Sheet in the financial documents. The asset history sheet gives an overview of expansion costs and points out the changes in value of the individual balance sheet items comprising the fixed assets.

An asset history report or asset chart is a special customized report that collates master data and changes in value of particularly important assets. Each asset class can be assigned SAPscript forms that can be adjusted by word processing to give the list layout and associated information required by the target readership.

Maintaining Asset Master Data

An economic unit is represented as a complex fixed asset made up of one or more subassets. The master record system must store the following types of information:

- The fundamentals of memory-based orderly accounting, as needed for the legal financial documents
- Long-term documentation of the fixed assets of your company

Part
I

Ch
4

- Information needed for internal decision making, such as the legal acquisition costs and depreciation, together with information used in controlling and profitability assessment
- Information needed to process transactions relevant to the life cycle of each asset

Using Asset Master Record Elements

Each asset master can be viewed as a series of screens that you can reformat according to asset class and the data to be displayed. One screen contains information that is likely to change frequently during the lifecycle of an asset, such as information relevant to cost accounting that can be maintained as a function of time. Other screens show information that is relevant to particular management functions. The selection of this information can be controlled by the asset class of the asset master displayed.

The following types of master record displays are standard screens or screen components:

- Time-dependent data
- Real estate data
- Leased asset data
- Origin or supplier of the asset
- Insurance data
- Inventory and warehouse management data
- Customized organization-specific asset sorting criteria

The requirements of an asset master data system include the following:

- Detailed and comprehensive information must be available on each asset.
- Data can be changed only under strict authorization code and is subject to document change management procedures that can trace all changes and recover them if necessary.
- Different asset types should be accessible without displaying irrelevant fields.
- Users should be able to view only the screens that are needed for their task and are compatible with their authorization profiles.

Controlling Asset Class Screens

The screens available and their structure are determined by the asset class to which the asset belongs. Under this regime, the following classification of master data elements can be affected:

- Data fields that do not appear on the screen
- Data fields that are mandatory
- Data fields that are optional

This scheme enables you to specify some fields to be optional in the master and optional in the screen as displayed. An asset class master that includes mandatory fields ensures that these fields appear in any copy of this master.

Understanding Asset Master Maintenance Levels

An economic unit always belongs to an asset class and therefore does not need a separate maintenance level. Instead, an economic unit can be maintained by updating the main and subnumber assets that comprise it.

The function of a maintenance level is to control how each data field in an asset master can be altered. Some can be changed at the asset class level, some at the main asset number level, some at the asset subnumber level. Within an economic unit, data can be changed uniformly across asset components at the subnumber level.

Using Validation Conditions and Substitution Conditions

A validation condition is a rule (additional to the standard checks) that governs how an asset master can be created. For example, you could specify that masters for certain asset classes are to be limited in the permissible depreciation keys.

A substitution condition is an if-then rule that automatically inserts particular default values if certain fields contain specified entries. For example, you could set up a condition that automatically enters the correct business area according to the content of the Plant field by referring to a table of correspondences.

Creating and Viewing Asset Master Records

In the absence of any other command, a new asset master inherits the default values of the principal control parameters of the asset class to which you assign it. If you reference an existing asset master record, whatever its asset class, the parameters are copied to your new master.

You have two choices in asset master numbering:

- Internal assignment allows the system to assign asset master numbers.
- External assignment requires you to assign an asset master number.

The records of an asset master can be selected according to the purpose (and therefore according to the task) being carried out by the user. For example, you can associate the Real Estate view with those who need it and the Insurance view with specialists in that subject. The details of asset views generally are determined during customizing.

Identifying Time-Dependent Data

Some of the data stored in an asset master record may become inappropriate outside a particular time period. Such data is defined as time-dependent data, and the system automatically compiles the history of the changes to these particular allocations.

You can decide which fields in the asset master should be regarded as time dependent. Cost accounting allocations to cost centers, orders, or projects must be entered according to the month or other accounting period to which they apply. Another type of data that must be treated as time-dependent is that associated with shift operations and plant shutdowns. These events directly affect the values to be assigned for depreciation in the period.

Perhaps the most useful way of judging whether a data item is time dependent is to consider whether anyone would interpret the meaning of any value held there in a different way if they knew when the data was collected.

Using a Workflow to Effect Mass Changes to Asset Masters

You likely will use the mass change procedure when you must make extensive changes. For example, your company may decide to set up a new system of cost centers to monitor costs in a different way. All your asset transaction data for the year may need to be re-allocated by adding the identification codes to each of the transaction documents that will reassign the values to the new cost center system. You also must update the relevant asset masters to ensure that future transactions concerning them are correctly assigned to the new cost center plan.

The system will help you develop a work plan. You select the assets to be reassigned from an asset report and then generate a work list. When you post this work list, the system opens a workflow that defines which employees are to carry out the necessary tasks. The authorized users then manually check the automatic work list and supplement it if necessary. When the task list is fully approved, you can post it. Such a program automatically generates a work list for each employee and sends it to them by SAPmail.

The validation and substitution technique can be used in this connection to enable you to set up rules to control when and how the master records are to be altered, down to the level of specifying which fields are to receive what new data.

In mass changes of this kind, many asset master records might have to be altered, and any asset master could have a profound effect on the valuation of your company if an error exists in it. The procedure for effecting a mass change with workflow control ensures that the alterations can be planned and checked in detail on a stage-by-stage basis. Document change management ensures that all these updates are documented and therefore amenable to subsequent analysis and rectification, if necessary.

Archiving Asset Portfolios

As your company acquires and releases assets over the years, your portfolio of assets could become extensive and entail very large volumes of data. If you archive any data from the SAP R/3 system, the format is consistent, and you can retrieve and operate on the archive material without having to undergo a hiatus.

Asset accounting keeps records of archiving activities, so any request for asset evaluation data can be addressed to the online database or the archives, according to the report date of the asset evaluation required. With the assurance that you can always access archived data, you can maintain your asset portfolio by archiving the asset evaluations at year-end closing. If you eliminate an asset from your portfolio by selling or disposing of it, you have the choice of clearing the information from your online database or retaining it for a specified period as a deactivated asset record. You can use such information, for example, to assist in establishing the records of a similar or replacement asset.

Access to asset masters can be controlled by additional authorization to limit an employee's scope for updating master records to specific assets or classes of assets. You can also restrict the display of particular data fields and prevent the update of others on an individual user basis. Classification of authorization can be arranged to cover any combination of the following asset master data structures:

- Company code
- Business area
- Plant
- Asset class

Although you can design and store a workflow with extensive logical conditions to manage a complex mass change to asset masters, you cannot execute this change unless you have access to the special authorization object. This check prevents unwanted mass changes to the asset master data set.

 TIP By using the authorization facilities, you ensure that the only people who make changes to the data about your assets are those who are responsible and qualified to do so properly.

Using Valuation Techniques

You might like to think of depreciation as an amount of money that will be taken out of your company each accounting period on behalf of each of your assets. If you have a valuable asset, you can perhaps sell it. The price you could realize might be more than you paid for it, in which case your company would enjoy negative depreciation. Often, your operational assets wear out from productive use, and their values decline. Eventually, these will be scrap and will perhaps cost a great deal to eliminate.

The following sections discuss some computations that can be applied to compute values for depreciation.

Using Depreciation and Value Types in Asset Accounting

A scheduled calculation is applied to determine the amounts that are recorded as depreciation to estimate the decline in value of the operating funds. Negative values of depreciation represent increases in value. A depreciation key is established as a master record that can be evoked to control the valuation calculations.

The valuation of an asset can be carried out in various ways. Some of these techniques are acceptable for legal purposes, but others may be confined to internal uses, perhaps in some regions of legal force but not others. The FI-AA module makes available the following valuation types by providing access to the data and the methods of using that data:

- Acquisition and production costs
- Investment support measures
- Transfer of reserves in accordance with tax guidelines
- Revaluation using indexed replacement values
- Revaluation using manual entries
- Ordinary depreciation
- Scheduled depreciation
- Unplanned depreciation based on current value depreciation
- Special tax depreciation
- Interest by asset
- Interest by depreciation area

These value adjustments can be classified by depreciation type, as follows:

- Ordinary depreciation that records the decline in value of an asset by normal wear and tear over its useful life
- Special tax depreciation
- Non-scheduled depreciation
- Transfer of reserves
- Interest

Understanding Other Types of Depreciation

For tax purposes, depreciation can be calculated as a percentage over a tax concession period without reference to the actual wear and tear of the asset. This can differ from the depreciation calculation approved by the commercial law in force. The difference must be recorded as a special item on the liabilities side of the balance sheet. You are allowed to form open tax-free reserves from untaxed profits based on tax law provisions if you show them as a special item. Tax will become due on special items during later periods.

Two familiar reasons for unplanned (non-scheduled) depreciation are fire and natural disasters. Falling out of date as a result of technological progress can also be a non-scheduled depreciation. You may have to base your depreciation calculation on the current value of the asset rather than on a value computed as a percentage of the cost distributed over the predicted useful life.

Transferring Reserves

When an asset is sold, the amount realized is regarded as a hidden asset. This amount can be transferred during the year of disclosure to newly acquired assets that are replacements for the asset sold.

This transfer of hidden reserves diminishes the acquisition and production costs recorded for the newly acquired assets. If no transfer takes place (perhaps because no new asset is acquired), the amount that arises from the sale must be assigned as a reserve to be set against profit for the year. If assets are acquired in subsequent years, this reserve must be transferred to them in the period in which they are acquired.

Using Depreciation Areas

When you post an asset transaction, you may take the opportunity to update some accounts set up for purposes not strictly required for legal financial accounting. It may be convenient to define depreciation areas that accumulate asset transaction data to enable you to analyze and compare different areas. You could define separate depreciation areas that represent the valuation of assets for different purposes, such as the following:

- Valuation of assets within a corporate group
- Valuation for a commercial balance sheet
- Valuation for a tax balance sheet
- Valuation for costing purposes
- Valuation of net assets
- Valuation of assets defined on the basis of any geographical attribute
- Valuation of assets defined on the basis of any commercial attribute
- Areas defined on the basis of any logical combination of other areas or the values already calculated for them

The combination of asset valuation methods can be used for internal controlling, for example, to compile valuation data for a special group within an enterprise using a particular currency conversion.

A depreciation area is specified as an entity of type 3007, Asset Valuation Category. A depreciation area need not correspond to any business area that your company may have delineated for internal purposes. You can establish depreciation areas to evaluate your assets from several points of view. Each area must be defined by specifying the following information:

- The depreciation types required
- The valuation rates to be used, such as the costs of acquisition or production, the replacement costs, and investment support measures
- Other special rules to be applied, such as depreciation below zero and currency handling rules

Part

Ch

4

The system calculates the necessary values for all your depreciation areas and maintains them in parallel so that you can readily switch from one to another when reviewing the reported data.

A depreciation area can be co-extensive with a business area, but it is sometimes convenient to make it independent of the business area system. Entity type 2009, Business Area, is a non-independent unit in Financial Accounting for which a balance sheet and a profit and loss statement can be prepared purely for the purpose of internal reporting. This type forms no part of legal balance sheet obligations. However, a set of business areas under a client code together include all the General Ledger accounts required for the financial documents.

Using the Book Depreciation Area

The concept of applying a book depreciation to an asset is used when it is convenient to ignore any variations of individual assets and to compute a value based on some form of aggregated or summarized information. Insurance, for example, can be based on a book depreciation area calculation of value. The following standard computation functions can be applied to yield data for a book depreciation area:

- Ordinary depreciation, allowing for wear and tear
- Unplanned depreciation
- Special depreciation, disregarding actual wear and tear
- Investment support
- Indexing based on inflation rates or rates computed on the basis of collated statistics that indicate the change in value of similar assets

The following special rules can be applied in the book depreciation area:

- Cutoff values below which the asset is treated differently for depreciation purposes
- A multiple shift under which the computation to be applied for depreciation purposes can differ according to the value of a parameter (such as the number of shifts worked in a plant in the period) that is accepted as a valid index used to influence the depreciation formula

Using the Tax Depreciation Area

The following standard functions can be applied to yield data for a tax depreciation area:

- Ordinary depreciation
- Unplanned depreciation
- Special depreciation
- Investment support
- Indexing

The following special rules can be applied in a tax depreciation area:

- Cutoff values
- Multiple shift

Using the Cost Accounting Depreciation Area

The following standard functions can be applied to yield data for a cost accounting depreciation area:

- Ordinary depreciation
- Unplanned depreciation
- Investment support
- Interest
- Indexing
- Below-zero depreciation

The following special rules can be applied in the cost accounting depreciation area:

- Fixed or variable depreciation
- Multiple shift
- Suspension of depreciation for one or more accounting periods

Using the Reporting Valuation Depreciation Area

The following standard arithmetic functions can be applied to yield data for a reporting valuation depreciation area:

- Ordinary depreciation
- Unplanned depreciation
- Special depreciation
- Investment support
- Indexing
- Foreign currency

Using the Net Asset Depreciation Area

The following standard functions can be applied to yield data for a net asset depreciation area:

- Ordinary depreciation
- Unplanned depreciation
- Indexing

Part

I

Ch

4

The following special rules can be applied in a net asset depreciation area:

- Cutoff values
- Multiple shift

Creating a Chart of Depreciation

If you declare depreciation areas, you can assemble a set of them to be displayed in a chart of depreciation. You can also assign them a common set of parameters. A company code can be assigned to only one chart of depreciation, but several company codes can use the same chart. For example, you may want all companies in a country or economic area to use the same chart of depreciation.

N O T E   The depreciation parameters defined in the chart of depreciation are applied to all asset depreciation areas in the chart.

Maintaining the Depreciation Area Data

A business transaction in asset accounting is a one-time posting. The FI-AA module carries out automatic updates of asset values using the defined valuation rules for each depreciation area. In this way, the valuation data under the different sets of rules is maintained in parallel.

You can post values and depreciation parameters to all depreciation areas or to selections of areas. The reference technique enables you to nominate a depreciation area and use its values as the basis for the values of another area. You can also specify valuation and depreciation parameters for particular depreciation areas and for individual economic units within them.

Developing Derived Depreciation Areas

You can generate a derived depreciation area by adding or subtracting the values of one area from those of another. For instance, you could keep a derived area to record the difference between book value and net value of a set of assets. You can add area values or take the average of two or more. For example, the standard U.S. chart of depreciation maintains a derived area to compute the valuation differences due to different tax regulations, such as Primary Federal Tax Book and Alternative Minimum Tax. In Germany, a derived depreciation area is used to determine the difference between the total tax depreciation and the book depreciation. This difference is indicated as a reserve for special depreciation.

As a function of its interface with FI-Financial Accounting, the Asset Accounting module can post the values of one or several depreciation areas to suitable accounts in the General Ledger. These accounts can then be used to prepare in parallel such additional balance sheet versions as the following:

- Commercial balance sheet
- Tax balance sheet
- Group commercial balance sheet

Applying Special Valuation to Fixed Assets

The special valuation features of FI-AA are available as enhancements of the basic functions for handling the three main depreciation types:

- Ordinary depreciation
- Special depreciation related to country-specific tax laws
- Unplanned depreciation

The main group of special valuation functions are designed to provide the information needed by specific company accounting areas set up for internal purposes such as cost accounting. However, several special valuation techniques can be managed in connection with the depreciation area system.

Using Investment Support Measures

Some government authorities award subsidies or grants to a company for investments in certain industries or regions. The FI-AA system can show these amounts either as reductions in acquisition values on the assets side or as value adjustments on the liabilities side of the balance sheet.

You can treat an investment support measure as a reduction in the depreciation base in a depreciation area. If several investment assistance grants are to be managed for the same asset, it may be best to create a depreciation area for each investment support measure. The amount drawn on each subsidy or grant can then be shown separately.

Using Indexed Replacement Value Depreciation

The base for ordinary depreciation is often the historical acquisition costs, or the costs of producing the asset in-house. In addition to this baseline, you can calculate depreciation on the basis of the replacement value of the asset, indexed to reflect changes in value.

Two reasons exist for indexing the replacement value of an asset:

- The replacement value changes because of inflation.
- Technological progress will probably affect the price that would have to be paid for an adequate replacement.

Either or both of these indexing factors may be positive or negative. The system enables you to define two index series for each asset class that used to adjust the replacement value for assets in the class. These two series can be used as numerical models for inflation and obsolescence. After defining an index series, you can assign a point number to any accounting period so that the calculation for that period adopts the correct value in the index series and then adjusts the depreciation to allow for the anticipated changes in replacement value.

Using Backlog Calculation of Depreciation

You may find it helpful to recalculate the depreciation values you have been using to figure depreciation for balance sheet or internal purposes. This process of backlog depreciation calculation helps you to ensure that the indexing is applied to both the historical acquisition or production costs and the current net book value.

The system enables you to combine backlog calculation with any depreciation method, but your legal environment may not.

Using One-Time Revaluation

Every few years, you might want to offset inflation and carry out a so-called one-time revaluation of your fixed assets. Exactly how a company does this is a matter for management decision, but the system has an interface that accepts individual revaluation rules to prepare for applying them to the asset database.

Using Imputed Interest in Cost Accounting Depreciation

If you have a fixed asset, you could sell it and raise capital. Therefore, the asset represents capital in use. This amount of money could depreciate or attract interest if it were suitably invested.

It has become an acceptable accounting practice to post an amount to the appropriate cost accounting object that represents the imputed interest or the (imputed) depreciation of the capital in use in each fixed asset. Therefore, an order or a cost center is appraised of the change in value of the associated fixed assets that could have accrued as the result of depreciation and interest charges or earnings.

Using Valuation for Insurance Purposes

The FI-AA module can store insurance data for each asset on insurance masters that record two values:

- Current market value
- Value as if new

You can set up a depreciation area to calculate values for current market value for insurance. This uses the same techniques as the depreciation and revaluation areas.

The current value for insurance purposes based on the value as new do not need to be calculated as a specific depreciation area—you can record in the asset master an index series to represent the changes over accounting periods of the value as if new. These index series values are referenced automatically to calculate the current insurable value as if new.

Using Valuation of Net Assets

If your company operates in a country that requires a separate statement of net assets, you can define a depreciation area in the FI-AA module for this purpose. A net asset depreciation area typically operates valuation rules to achieve the following conditions:

- Values take inflation into account.
- Depreciation is carried out only down to a specified cutoff value.
- Depreciation values are also calculated as an average of several depreciation methods.

Simulating the Effects of Depreciation

Applying a set of calculations based upon depreciation area formulations can be carried out in simulation mode in which the results are available for display. No changes are posted to the balance sheet ledgers.

A simulation depreciation area can be defined and used to try the effects of different parameters.

Using Tax-Based Depreciation as Special Valuation Reserves

Depreciation for tax purposes can be calculated as a percentage over a tax concession period without referring to the actual wear and tear of the asset. In some countries, the legal provisions enable you to copy the tax valuation rates for depreciation and then use them to form the commercial balance sheet.

This could differ from the depreciation calculation approved by the commercial law in force. For most users of a commercial balance sheet, it is important to be able to see how each asset is valued in commercial terms, whatever the tax valuation rates may be.

The FI-AA module enables you to show the book depreciation of a fixed asset on the asset side of the balance sheet. If this depreciation is not the same as the value allowed under the tax regime in force, the difference must be recorded as a special item on the liabilities side of the balance sheet. The item is then classed as a reserve for special depreciation and acts as a value adjustment on the liabilities side of the balance sheet. These calculations are carried out as a derived depreciation area, which ensures that these valuation reserve postings are transferred to Financial Accounting and the General Ledger.

You are allowed to form open tax-free reserves from untaxed profits, based on tax law provisions of this kind, if you show them as a special item. Tax may become due on special items during later periods, depending on their depreciation over this time.

Using Group Valuation for Consolidation

The fixed assets in some of the company code balance sheets of a corporate enterprise might not be treated for depreciation purposes in the same way as the fixed assets of the parent company responsible for consolidating the accounts. To accommodate these differences, you can set up a depreciation area in each company code that computes the asset depreciation in exactly the same manner as the consolidating parent. These depreciation areas use the same methods and currency so that the consolidated results are compatible.

SAP R/3 FI-LC Consolidation is a module specialized for the creation of group balance sheets. In particular, this module represents correctly the value movement of any asset transactions between affiliated organizations.

Using Individual Special Depreciation Areas

The standard SAP depreciation areas provide a flexible method of valuation for fixed assets, as well as for reporting their value changes from different points of view and in a variety of aggregating structures. However, you can also create any number of special depreciation areas and assign them individual parameters.

If you have already run FI-AA to assemble cumulative depreciation reports, the module retroactively determines the depreciation using any new special depreciation areas you create.

Calculating Depreciation

The calculation procedures for fixed asset depreciation accounting are governed by their purposes:

- Legal requirements that are country specific
- Accounting techniques that include public (external) accounting and the internal accounting for company-specific purposes

A comprehensive set of country-specific depreciation keys is provided in SAP R/3. These keys serve to trigger the calculation procedures for all depreciation types, such as ordinary depreciation, special depreciation, and so on.

Defining User-Specific Depreciation Keys

If you cannot initiate the precise depreciation computation you require by using one of the standard depreciation keys, you can define a procedure of your own. If your legal environment initiates a new procedure, you may need to create a fresh depreciation and assign it the necessary data processing functions. The basic calculation elements are available in the system, but you must specify the following parameters or accept the defaults offered:

- Depreciation method, such as straight line depreciation
- Reference value, such as the acquisition value
- First-year convention, such as the half-year rule
- Method of determining the depreciation percentage, such as a useful life distribution
- Periods for calculation, such as calendar months

Understanding Standard Depreciation Methods in SAP R/3 FI-AA

Any or all of the available standard depreciation methods can be used in parallel for each fixed asset. The basic method involves applying a straight-line depreciation calculation to the reference value that distributes the loss of value evenly over the useful life of the asset. If the asset is acquired at some point after the beginning of this useful life, the depreciation must be based on the remaining useful life. The depreciation calculations in use worldwide are essentially variants of the straight-line useful life model. They include the following methods:

- Declining balance method of depreciation
- Declining multiphase depreciation
- Sum-of-the-years digits method
- Depreciation based on the number of items and the number of times they are used
- Depreciation of equipment based on the number of Units of Production (UOP), as used by mining and extraction companies
- The average of two or more depreciation methods
- Special depreciation calculation mandated by an accounting authority
- Special depreciation type, such as the percentage during the tax concession period

Ending the Depreciation Calculation

If you are using a depreciation area designed to serve cost accounting, it may be useful to continue to depreciate an asset beyond the point at which its book value has become zero. You can continue to calculate depreciation at a reduced percentage after an asset has reached the end of its useful life. The following possibilities are supported by FI-AA:

- Depreciation continues until the end of the asset's useful life.
- Depreciation stops when an asset's book value becomes zero.
- An asset can be depreciated below zero value.

Allowing for Cutoff Values and Scrap Values

Some countries apply an asset accounting rule that stipulates that an asset cannot be depreciated below a certain value for balance sheet purposes. This rule assumes that an asset always has at least a scrap value. The FI-AA module enables you to specify this cutoff as a percentage of the asset value or as an absolute value.

If you know the cutoff percentage or the cutoff absolute value, you can subtract this amount from the depreciation base amount before the depreciation calculation begins. In this case, the figure would be entered as scrap value. Alternatively, you could operate the scrap value as a cutoff value in the depreciation calculation.

Relating Depreciation to Usage

If your plant depreciates regardless of whether you use it, you might be content to use a fixed rate of depreciation. However, a plant receives much more wear and tear if it works than if it remains idle.

You can model a depreciation rate that is proportional to some index of usage, such as the number of shifts worked in the period. Perhaps some assets retain their value if they are shut down. In practice, variations of value arise for many different reasons, and the best calculation model may be a combination of a fixed rate plus a variable depreciation rate related to usage.

Defining Asset Accounting Periods

Financial accounting and asset accounting can define without restriction the fiscal year and the accounting periods within it. You can have more than 12 months in a fiscal year, and your accounting year need not last 365 days.

 N O T E   If you decide to run a computation using a shortened fiscal year, the FI-AA module automatically adjusts the corresponding depreciation values.

Each national accounting authority can decide to implement a particular set of rules for applying depreciation. The SAP R/3 system contains functions that support all the known regulations.

When a company acquires, retires, or transfers a fixed asset, there must be a method of calculating how much of the value should be assigned as depreciation to each of the periods in the fiscal year in which the change of asset took place. For example, the mid-quarter convention assumes that an asset will have been acquired, retired, or transferred completely on the mid-quarter date.

Another possible country-specific or company-specific rule might set a particular value as a maximum that can be taken as the reference value for the purpose of calculating depreciation. This maximum may have no relation to the acquisition value of the asset, to its replacement value, or to any characteristic of the asset apart from the fact that it has attracted the stipulated maximum.

Handling Currencies in Depreciation Calculations

Many companies operate in international markets in which it is optional or mandatory to establish independent economic units. In SAP R/3, such affiliates are assigned a company code under a consolidating parent at the client code level.

Any or all affiliated companies can function in a different local currency, yet the corporate balance sheet must be readable in a single currency. Group consolidation in these circumstances requires currency conversion.

Using a Special Group Currency Depreciation Area

The FI-AA is provided with a special depreciation area designed to report depreciation in the group currency. This area, however, is separated into the individual company code organizations and is computed by using the value of each posting at the time the business transaction was first posted. The AA module directly converts all acquisitions into group currency at the time of the transaction by using the exchange rate then prevalent.

Using this calculation results in an acquisition cost of the asset that accounts for the prevailing currency exchange rate between the currency of the business transaction and the group reporting currency. The subsequent depreciation can be calculated based on this one-time assessment of historical acquisition cost. The system automatically determines retirements of assets and transfers on the basis of a percentage of book depreciation values.

By using a historical acquisition cost value that takes account of the exchange rate at the time, the AA system prevents currency fluctuations from influencing the cumulative computation of depreciation. If depreciation were to be calculated in a step-wise manner, a temporary high or low currency valuation in one period could have a disproportionate effect on the value to be assigned to the asset in the future.

Applying Differentiated Capitalization Rules

Some regions of legal force use particular rules for treating some assets as capital. For example, differences exist as to whether freight can be valued in the same way as other assets. There may be different rules about who owns a delivery in transit. This could affect balance sheet calculations if the group rules differ from the rules of the affiliated company.

In such cases, you can enter values for the acquisition or production of a fixed asset that are differentiated with respect to depreciation areas and that take into account the time of the posting transaction.

Allowing for Currency and Valuation Differences

Fixed assets are depreciated in a procedure defined as a foreign currency depreciation area for the group. Another depreciation area for the group uses the local currency of each individual organization.

By comparing valuations from both depreciation areas, the system can distinguish the differences that arise from currency conversion. The system can also identify the differences caused by divergent valuation rules.

Using Parallel Currencies in the General Ledger

SAP R/3 FI supports the maintenance of all General Ledger values pertaining to a company code in up to three currencies in parallel. Three local currencies can be defined at the customizing stage.

Part

II

Ch

4

Each currency has a corresponding depreciation area. This enables you to post the value of a fixed asset to the General Ledger in three currencies in parallel. Therefore, you can transfer asset values in local currency to the FI-LC Consolidation system, where they are converted at an exchange rate that can be specified when the consolidation is reported.

If you have no special consolidation requirements and report only in foreign currencies, you do not need to set up special foreign currency depreciation areas. As an alternative, you can designate specific currency conversions to be used for all standard reports through the SAP R/3 . Financial Information System.

Simulating Depreciation for Planning Purposes

The main reason that you would simulate depreciation is to help you prepare a plan of acquisitions and retirements. For example, you may be running CO-CCA Cost Center Accounting, to which you would want to assign planned values for depreciation based on a simulation. The following factors can make this a difficult task unless some form of simulation is available:

- Different depreciation methods can make appreciable differences to the year-end closing situation.
- The depreciation method used can influence the management case for planned acquisitions and retirements.
- The anticipated or forecast changes in the values of fixed assets over future fiscal years could indicate opportunities for strategic planning that should begin soon.
- There may be opportunities to take advantage of special tax-related depreciation that can be optimized by precise and selective amount distribution across accounting periods.

The concept of asset transaction simulation can be portrayed as a what-if exercise in which the asset accounting system is used in a testing mode that has no effect on the actual asset transaction database. However, the full function set is available to demonstrate the effect on the balance sheet of any planned patterns of acquisitions and retirements. You can use data from your existing or historical assets, and you can acquire data on assets that are likely to be available. You can also generate hypothetical assets that help focus your long-term asset strategy by applying the FI-AA module to asset data that is realistic and that can be manipulated to refine the simulation. The structure of a simulation of asset depreciation follows the standard SAP convention of always identifying a plan as a specific version. This ensures that you encounter no confusion between the results of one planning or simulation run and another that was carried out with one or more parameters changed.

The simulation specification typically designates the following data objects and invites you to specify values or accept the suggested defaults:

- The simulation version that you intend to edit to become a new version, or a new simulation specification for which you will enter or select the details
- The asset class for which the simulation will be run
- The depreciation key to be used to control the depreciation calculations

- The useful life, or formula to be used to compute it
- The indexing arrangements to be applied, if any
- The validity period for the simulation, defined as starting and finishing dates or accounting periods

As part of the simulation, you may also want to test the effects of some asset acquisitions, retirements, and transfers.

After you initiate a simulation, you can call on any of the standard reporting and display functions to process the simulated data in the same way as if they resulted from actual asset transactions. The following options illustrate the useful analyses that can come out of a simulation of asset depreciation:

- Displays of the effects on the profit and loss operating results, with and without special depreciation
- Superimposed graphs of the changes in the value of an asset class, given various assumed values for the length of the useful life
- Graphs of the depreciation of individual assets that have been depreciated over the simulation period, using different depreciation calculation procedures

In any of these simulated activities, you can use your existing parameters, such as depreciation keys. You can also generate new depreciation procedures to which you assign temporary keys so that they can take part in the simulation. Each different simulation specification is stored as a version so that you can use it again on different data or edit it to generate new versions.

Changes to rules used for depreciation are not made very often. Accounting standards dictate that for comparison purposes, asset depreciation methods should generally remain constant. Any changes must be highlighted in the notes to the accounts, together with the reason for change. It is typically also required that you show what the depreciation impact would have been under the previous provision.

Previewing the External Rendering of Accounts

When you must prepare the balance sheet and the profit and loss statement for an economic unit in your corporate enterprise, there may be scope for presenting these accounts in different ways within the legal framework. For example, you may be at liberty to use special depreciation over some or all your assets.

T I P A simulation using each of the various legal options can help you identify the best combination.

The process of depreciation through wear and tear and gradual market fluctuations is usually assumed to be a continuous one and is said to be subject to the principle of continuity. The calculations do not allow any sudden changes in the value of individual assets. However, you may want to explore the effects of modifying the depreciation parameters for your current assets in certain asset classes. In particular, you will want to know how these changes are likely to affect the operating result shown in the profit and loss account.

If you are allowed a range of depreciation methods, you may want to see how each one affects the net book values. The FI-AA module provides functions for the following simulation analyses:

☐ Depreciation for selected individual assets

☐ Depreciation for selected asset classes

☐ Depreciation for any time periods

☐ Depreciation for any combination of existing or temporary parameter values

N O T E Different simulation dimensions can be combined. ☐

Previewing the Depreciation of Planned Investments

The depreciation preview facilities of the FI-AA module are fully integrated with SAP R/3 IM-Investment Management, which is also referred to as TR-IM-Treasury, Investment Management. The effect of this integration is to enable you to include in your simulation any of the investment structures, such as the following:

☐ Capital investment orders

☐ Capital investment projects

☐ Investment programs

The IM- Investment Management module is discussed in Chapter 11.

Simulating Asset Transactions

The SAP R/3 system of master records for assets enables an asset to acquire or retire other assets during the course of a fiscal year. In fact, you may have defined an asset as a stock of material that functions as a buffer from which quantities are drawn and to which deliveries are made throughout the year. Similarly, a building can acquire additional assets as plant items are installed.

The simulation functions of FI-AA enable you to test out the changes in value of an asset as it becomes subject to different patterns of purchase or sales decisions. You can plot the depreciation profile under the various simulation versions you have defined.

Representing and Displaying Depreciation Values

The life of an asset can be characterized by an extensive sequence of business transactions and many different calculations of its value from various points of view. The records of this life comprise many individual values. You will need help to filter this database and to present the information in a manner that can be easily understood.

The following online displays of depreciation data are available for single assets or classes of assets:

- Listing of line items for transactions and depreciation for a particular depreciation area
- Notification of the changes in a particular depreciation area, such as book depreciation, over the course of one year
- Display of the changes in a particular depreciation area over several years
- Comparison over one year of the values computed by up to three different depreciation areas
- Comparison over several years of the values computed by up to three different depreciation areas
- Retracing a derived area to the real area on which it is based, such as a reserve for special depreciation

The display of changes in values usually includes the opening balance and the changes in the current year. You can alternate between posted depreciation values and planned depreciation values. The acquisition values and the value adjustments are shown together with the resulting book values.

If you need to see the background data, you can access the following sources:

- Asset transaction posting records
- Depreciation parameters
- General master data

Displays for comparing values usually offer up to three value areas on different lines from such options as the following:

- Acquisition costs
- Production costs
- Depreciation
- Net book value

You can display all the records posted to the asset over the current year.

Displaying the Depreciation Calculation Procedure

The SAP technique of drill-down is applied to the depreciation displays to provide the user with pathways through the calculation that can be traversed in various ways to arrive at a display made up from any combination of the following data sets:

- Each depreciation area
- Each depreciation type
- Each asset transaction

You can look at the results of a single asset transaction in terms of any depreciation area and any depreciation type.

Integrating Asset Transactions

The business transactions associated with assets can be differentiated by one important characteristic: whether they affect profit. Some transactions affect only the balance sheet.

In the first class come the transactions that record the acquisition and production costs of a fixed asset. The other transactions are depreciation value adjustments that appear only in the balance sheet.

To supplement the asset transactions for acquisition, production, and depreciation, the FI-AA module recognizes several different transaction types and treats each transaction differently with respect to any or all of the following data:

- Accounts to be included in the scope of an account assignment
- Depreciation areas to be active
- Value fields to be updated

Using Standard Business Transaction Types in FI-AA

The transaction type groups available for asset accounting are as follows:

- Acquisitions
- Retirements to sales, those to scrap, and those unplanned
- Transfers
- Manual depreciation
- Write-ups
- Transfers of reserves
- Down payments
- Revaluations

Although you can create customized transaction types, the advantage of using one of the standard types is that the associated transactions are simply processed in a uniform manner across all applications. For each transaction type group, you can define validation conditions in addition to the standard checks.

If you post an asset transaction, a posting document is created. The transaction can be reversed in the FI-AA module or in SAP R/3 FI.

Applying Account Allocation

The General Ledger accounts that are updated when you post an asset transaction are determined by the account allocation you have prescribed for transactions of this class. The accounts to be used for each depreciation area can be freely assigned for all types of transaction by means of the account allocation for each asset class.

If you have an integrated system with FI-Financial Accounting and CO-Controlling linked to your FI-AA Asset Accounting module, you can extend the range of account types available for inclusion in the account allocation defined for an asset class. In particular, you can assign a transaction to the following additional accounts:

- Internal order or project for in-house production
- Cost center
- Profit center
- Quantities and text

All these additional accounts keep records for purely internal purposes and form no part of the external accounting system directed toward the balance sheet and the profit and loss statement.

Using Collective Assets

Assets can be managed using quantities and quantity units. For example, goods of small value are usually carried and depreciated as collective assets. During transaction processing, the quantities are updated with the appropriate sign according to the debits/credits indicator of the asset transaction.

Acquiring Fixed Assets

The Integrated Asset Accounting module supports all types of process sequence through which assets can be acquired and retired. If the systems are integrated, it is not necessary to post asset acquisition individually in asset accounting. For example, the following source modules can automatically provide the capitalization values of the assets concerned:

- Accounts Payable
- Purchasing
- Inventory and Warehouse Management
- Job Order Settlement
- Plant Maintenance
- Project Settlement

When an asset is retired, Accounts Receivable is posted with the amount realized as sales revenue and automatically determines the profit or loss generated by the sale. Accounts Receivable then posts this amount to the profit and loss statement, with appropriate identification, and also to cost accounting if you have installed and configured this component.

Understanding Procedures for Acquiring Assets

An incoming supplier invoice for a fixed asset can be sent to a suitable accounts person, who opens an asset master record with the appropriate account allocation and valuation parameters. The Accounts Payable department then records the acquisition and verifies the posting document, created with the input taxes and discounts entered automatically.

When the acquisition document is posted, the values are recorded in the master records of the following applications:

- FI-GL
- FI-AP, where an open item is created
- FI-AA, where depreciation is computed and various totals are updated

Purchasing an Asset in Materials Management

The R/3 Purchasing component of the MM-Materials Management application can be used to purchase an asset. In this case, the asset can be assigned to an asset master record when the order or purchase requisition is first posted. The details are then automatically entered into subsequent documents, such as a goods receipt or an invoice receipt. The actual value of the asset can be posted when the invoice is received or when the goods are received.

The usual source of materials for in-house production is to use parts from stock. The asset transactions must be posted in MM by specifying each material number and the asset number to which it is assigned. The asset history sheet can represent this as a transfer posting from current assets to fixed assets.

Acquiring Assets Through Capital Investment Projects

The costs of a large capital investment project as an asset produced in-house are accumulated on an order or a project maintained by R/3 IM-Investment Management. Some or all of these costs can be capitalized and settled internally on a corresponding asset under construction, which is a data object maintained in FI-AA. Therefore, a company can build for itself a fixed asset and thereby increase its capital.

When the construction of the asset is complete, a final settlement occurs and the asset is transferred to the Assets in Service account. At the same time, the relevant cost accounts and the balance sheet accounts in Financial Accounting are updated to record the capitalization. The new fixed asset is acquired through project settlement in the IM-Investment Management module.

Acquiring Assets Through Plant Maintenance

A major overhaul and refit of a manufacturing plant can be managed through the PM-Plant Maintenance application. The expenditure gives the company a much-improved plant, and the plant, as a fixed asset, acquires additional assets. These new assets can be capitalized directly from the maintenance order to the corresponding asset.

Using FI-AA in Isolation

The Asset Accounting functionality can be installed as a separated system that operates through clearing accounts. The asset acquisition and retirement transactions can be entered exclusively in FI-AA as a standalone module. The period closing results then must be posted to the clearing accounts before their effects can be seen in the General Ledger.

Using Periodic Depreciation Posting

Depreciation must be calculated and posted to the relevant income statement accounts of finance accounting. This can be accomplished manually or automatically by means of the system of depreciation keys that affect the periodic calculations.

An asset transaction in the FI-AA module causes a change in the total forecast depreciation. This module does not immediately correct the value adjustment accounts and the depreciation accounts in Financial Accounting. These are not updated until a transfer is effected by the posting of the scheduled depreciation to the corresponding accounts in financial accounting. FI-AA and FI-GL are only in agreement after the FI posting run has been performed. When your system is set up, you must designate which depreciation areas are to be used to calculate the depreciation amounts that will be accumulated in the General Ledger. Then for each of these areas, you must detail the following parameters:

- ☐ The additional accounts to which the depreciation must be posted, such as company code, cost center, or order
- ☐ The period rate at which each depreciation area amount must be posted

Using Manual Depreciation Posting

If you must manually enter the asset base amount and instruct the system to calculate the depreciation automatically, the corresponding General Ledger accounts will not be posted immediately. The FI-AA module transfers the base amount and the depreciation to Financial Accounting during periodic depreciation posting.

Using Write-ups to Cancel Depreciation

If the calculated depreciation in a period exceeds the amount allowable, you may have to use a write-up of the difference to correct the value of the fixed asset. You may also need to write up the value of an asset that has been subject to unplanned depreciation if the reason for this unexpected loss of value no longer exists. For example, an idle and unwanted plant may have been heavily depreciated and then be reinstated because of an unexpected demand for its products. It might be appropriate to write up its value to cancel some of the former depreciation.

You can manually post write-ups in the FI-AA module. This increases the book value of the corresponding asset and corrects the depreciation values according to the method of calculation used for them.

Part

II

Ch

4

Retiring a Fixed Asset

The following standard transaction types can be used to record the retirement of a fixed asset:

- Retirement by way of sale with proceeds
- Retirement by way of sale without proceeds
- Retirement to scrap
- Retirement to an affiliated organization
- Retirement due to unforeseen events

When an asset is retired, the system operates according to the gross principle and closes out acquisition and production costs separately from the value adjustments. Retirement lists of various kinds are used to analyze the asset retirements for a given period so that a decision can be taken whether to allocate any book profits arising from the retirements to reserves for the procurement of replacements.

An asset can be retired in part or completely. To post a complete retirement, you enter the asset number, the retirement date, and the transaction type. The system calculates automatically all the amounts to be closed out. Partial retirements must be entered with the following parameters:

- The value of the asset at retirement, in terms of acquisition and production costs
- The quantity or the percentage of the asset being retired

N O T E If you specify a quantity of the asset being partially retired, the system calculates the percentage value from the acquisition and production costs for that quantity.

Retiring an Asset to a Customer

If you sell a fixed asset to a customer, the transaction document can be used to post the receivable from the customer, the proceeds from the sale, and the notification of the asset retirement. If you are operating a fully integrated system, the R/3 FI application ensures the continuity of information across all these postings.

The system also automatically compares the proceeds from the sale with the book value and so calculates the book profit or the book loss. This entails an income statement posting. You can have the income debited to a clearing cost center. If the asset master record was assigned to a cost center, you can have the income debited directly to this cost center.

Posting Mass Retirements

If your company sells a large and complex fixed asset such as a manufacturing plant or a building, there may be many subassets to be retired. The FI-AA module can manage a mass retirement posting.

The assets to be retired must be selected and assigned through a work list procedure that is processed as a workflow similar to a mass change of master data. Suitable people are tasked with processing the details of the mass retirements.

The total proceeds from the economic units sold in a mass posting can be divided and coded so that the amounts can be distributed under your control. Three ways exist for coding the proceeds from the sale of a fixed asset:

- Proportionally to the book value
- Proportionally to the acquisition and production costs
- To a distribution scheme created when you use a program block in the ABAP/4 language

Posting Gross Value Transfers

You can use the FI-AA module to transfer values from one asset to another in the following circumstances:

- Transfers from assets under construction to assets in service
- Transfers between items of the active fixed assets
- Transfers between affiliated organizations

The module always applies the gross method for asset retirements and transfers so that the acquisition and production costs are processed separately from any value adjustments such as depreciation and write-ups.

Recording Transfers to Affiliates

When two organizational units in a corporate group effect a transfer of a fixed asset, the event must be recorded in Asset Accounting as a retirement from one and an acquisition for the other. From the group's point of view, however, the transaction must be represented in Financial Accounting by a balance of zero because there is no change to the value of the fixed assets held by the group. This requirement is organized by FI-AA by using separate transaction types that can represent the event correctly in both the asset history sheet of the individual asset and the asset history sheet of the corporate group.

When your system is customized, you can set up the following conditions to define separate affiliate transfer transaction types for each depreciation area you intend to use:

- The proceeds of the seller will be transferred within the group as a gross transfer addition valued at historical acquisition costs.
- The transfer will be valued at historical acquisition costs with value adjustments applied.

The second transaction type takes account of changes in value and is appropriate for transfers between those departments in your company that are not independent because their transactions are posted to the same company code.

Part
I

Ch
4

Managing Assets Under Construction

Many countries stipulate similar functions for both assets in service and assets under construction (AuC), usually with the following reservations:

- Scheduled depreciation is seldom permitted for assets under construction.
- Assets under construction must be shown separately in the balance sheet.

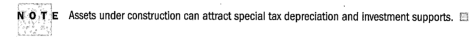 **NOTE**   Assets under construction can attract special tax depreciation and investment supports.

Because of their similarities, both assets under construction and assets in service are managed by R/3 FI-AA in the same way, using asset master records and assigned balance sheet accounts. This ensures that transactions concerning an asset under construction are automatically posted to the assets under construction account, even before this asset becomes operational. The same masters collect the transaction data after startup.

Understanding Capitalization of an Asset Under Construction

The Asset Accounting system provides a special transaction type to control transfer postings for assets under construction. A summary transfer posting of the value of the asset under construction is made to one or more master records of the assets already in service. This type of summary transfer posting continues each year until the year in which the asset is completed. In the year of completion, the new asset is balanced by reversals that correspond to the summary transfer postings made to the other assets already in service.

The asset history sheet of the newly completed asset then shows the value acquisitions of previous fiscal years as transfers and the acquisitions of the current year as reversals. The assets already in service have their summary transfer postings balanced as acquisitions in the year the new asset came into service.

This procedure may not be necessary if an existing asset does not have to take account of any related assets under construction. Open item management may be more convenient.

Using Open Item Management

The principal data to be assembled while an asset is under construction can be extracted from the following sources:

- External activities by contractors
- Internal activities by the company
- Withdrawals from stock

It is customary to account for the materials used to construct an asset as withdrawals from stock rather than to initiate special purchases of them.

The FI-AA module can manage all aspects of a capital investment measure as open items in a single asset under construction master. Each line item, such as a down payment made and acquisitions of subassets, must be cleared. This ensures that the details are recorded as posting documents where they are available for subsequent analysis, even after the asset goes into service.

It may be convenient to run a collective management of several economic units under development by posting the transactions as open items to a single asset under construction master. When the work is completed, the values of the individual line items can be allocated to various recipients and then further distributed if it is necessary to refine the valuation of subassets.

Making Down Payments for Assets Under Construction

A down payment must be initiated by a down payment request that is assigned to the corresponding asset. The building or assembly of the asset need not be finished. When the actual down payment is posted, R/3 FI automatically generates the corresponding line items and posts them to the master of the asset under construction.

This procedure ensures that the balance sheet items of the fixed assets include proof of any down payments made. The corresponding final settlement is posted to the asset under construction as if it were a standard acquisition. The final settlement amount eventually is offset by the down payments.

A down payment on an asset under construction represents an investment and can therefore be the recipient of an investment support measure. The down payment can also be subjected to depreciation calculations, even though it is not usually permissible to apply scheduled depreciation to a down payment on an asset under construction.

When an asset under construction is finally capitalized, the financial documents can show the payment amounts in the current year as acquisitions to the asset. Down payments from closed fiscal years are represented as transfers because they will have been capitalized in the year they were made.

Using R/3 FI-AA for Capital Investment Projects and Orders

Large fixed asset investments can be managed as internal orders or as projects. The R/3 IM application (also known as Treasury-Investment Management) is designed to support the cost accounting and the project planning and control essential for large investment programs that run over several years.

However, the functions used by IM are also available to the FI-AA module, although the continuity does not extend beyond year-end closing unless the IM application is installed and configured. This application supports the following business processes:

- Capital spending requests
- Capital investment measures
- Capital investment programs
- Simulation and depreciation forecasting

Part
I

Ch
4

Chapter 11 develops the topics of investing in financial assets and covers the strategies for managing their acquisition and disposal.

Using FI-AA with CO-OPA Order and Project Accounting

If you manage fixed assets such as buildings and machines, the settlement of capital spending orders is of crucial importance. The SAP R/3 system offers detailed settlement rules and a close integration between the FI-AA Asset Accounting component and the Controlling application through the OPA-Order and Project Accounting module. The following arrangements can be utilized:

- Settlement of costs to the appropriate balance sheet accounts under the heading of Assets Under Construction while the capital spending order is ongoing
- Order-based display of special depreciations for Assets Under Construction
- Recognition of subsidies, grants, and down payments
- Settlement of partial orders over a hierarchy of orders

Because all costs are based on unified posting and settlement rules in the SAP R/3 system, you can allocate costs from orders and projects to the various target objects using either the same rules or rules you have specified separately. You can keep track of complex overhead costs using maintenance and capital spending orders.

Operating to Planned Cost Schedules

When dealing with costs and deadlines on orders and projects that take a long time to complete, you have to recognize the financial facts of life. Money is not always available when you need it. When performing financial and liquidity planning, you need to know what costs are expected on the orders and projects. It helps to have some idea of how the costs are likely to be incurred in detail over the first few accounting periods, and in broader terms up to the date of completion.

A cost schedule is a plan extending the length of an order or project, showing the values expected to be allocated to costs. The schedule has a key date. Until this date is known and entered into the plan, the forecast of costs must be moved ahead to the best estimated date.

The SAP R/3 system provides support in the following ways:

- The system automatically determines the tasks from the planned start and finish dates for the order.
- Cost distribution across the schedule can be suited to the specific order.
- Graphical representations of the data model are readily available online and in print.

The following manipulations of the cost schedules and the task plans are automatically available:

- Shifting the start date, retaining the duration
- Compressing the duration, retaining the finish date
- Expanding the duration

If you have carried out cost element planning or created a unit costing for the order, the system can use this information to develop a cost schedule.

Using Fixed Asset Special Transactions

An asset is subject to the normal business transactions, such as acquisitions, retirements, and transfers. However, a few events of importance do not lend themselves to management by these functions. In most cases, a special transaction has been designed to handle each situation.

Using Investment Support Measures

One of the special transactions applicable to a fixed asset is the investment support measure. For example, a regional subsidy can be available to pay for a percentage of the acquisition cost of certain types of assets if the transaction is settled within a specified period.

The FI-AA module accepts a definition of an investment support measure and stores it on a master record if the following information is entered:

- Time period over which the investment support will be available
- Percentage of the acquisition and production costs that can be claimed
- Maximum amount available
- Required period of retention of the supported assets before a penalty is incurred

An asset support measure can also be confined by the awarding authority or by the receiving company to particular company codes, plants, cost centers, and asset classes. This information is also stored on the investment support measure master held by the FI-AA module.

Part

I

Ch

4

Posting Subsequent Acquisitions

You have the choice of posting a subsequent acquisition to the fixed asset master itself or of creating a subnumber master record to receive the new acquisition without losing the connection to the main asset. You can also generate super-number masters to become virtual parents of a set of main assets.

The subnumber technique is useful because it includes a method that preserves the details of the acquisition and production costs of a subasset. The year of acquisition is recorded so that the proportionate value adjustments of the main asset can be subsequently analyzed throughout its lifecycle.

If you have a main asset and a set of subassets, you can effect mass changes by addressing only the parent. Doing so results in uniform depreciation.

Performing Post-Capitalization Corrections

A special fixed asset transaction is sometimes needed to make up in later years for acquisitions that were omitted when the accounts were closed. The FI-AA module applies the gross principle and posts the acquisition and production costs of an asset omitted from previous fiscal years. This provides for the calculation of any value adjustments theoretically accrued to the asset in the interim.

Transferring Hidden Reserves

When an asset is sold, it may turn out to be worth more than the value of it computed by the depreciation procedures. This difference in value can be treated as a hidden reserve that can now be assigned elsewhere. No asset is acquired, only a value that must be correctly placed in the financial accounts.

A set of special transaction types is available to transfer the hidden reserves to one or more of the current year acquisitions. According to the depreciation valuation method used, one of two procedures is applied:

- The hidden reserves amount is used to reduce the value of the depreciation base in the book depreciation area.
- The hidden reserves amount is posted to the liabilities side as a reserve for special depreciation.

Capitalizing Leased Assets

Two methods exist for accounting for leased fixed assets:

- Capitalize the leased asset according to its present value.
- Apply the capital lease method so as to treat the leased asset as a costing-based acquisition.

A leased fixed asset is subject to a lease agreement from which the system can calculate the net present value of the payment debits scheduled for the future.

As soon as a leased asset is acquired, the system posts all the anticipated payment installments, with their due dates, to the account of the vendor from whom the asset is leased. These payments can be reduced to a net present value, and their total can be compared to the present value of the leased asset based on acquisition or production costs. The difference between the present value and the amount that will actually be paid is shown separately as interest, and this amount is cleared periodically when depreciation is posted.

Reporting Assets Through the FIS

The Financial Information System (FIS) can display reports selectively on fixed assets using the asset history sheet format together with standard and customized reports.

Performing Year-End Closing of Fixed Asset Accounts

At the center of the Asset Accounting system is the asset history sheet report. Year-end closing includes the task of checking all asset history sheets. It may be necessary to consider alternative closing valuations that can arise as the result of using different depreciation methods. You may find that a simulation that compares these methods is the most useful way of arriving at the best valuation.

At year-end closing, you may have to make some adjustment postings to account for inventory differences that arise when the planned quantities do not correspond with the actual quantities of materials as determined by the physical inventory. When all the necessary manual adjustments have been made in connection with the fixed assets, any depreciation values that have not already been posted must be transferred to Financial Accounting so that they can contribute to the balance sheet and the profit and loss statement.

Finally, a special year-end program is called to carry out all the necessary checks that answer such questions as the following:

- Does the General Ledger contain all the asset values and the depreciation?
- Have the procedures for dealing with residual values been carried out?

Until these checks have been carried out and the fixed asset accounts have been corrected (if necessary), the year-end closing cannot proceed to the last activity, which is to block the asset account areas of the General Ledger against any further postings or changes for the current fiscal year.

Two year-end programs exist for FI-AA:

- The fiscal year change program allows postings into a new fiscal year while the old year remains available for processing.
- The fiscal year change program closes the old fiscal year against changes to assets.

Manipulating the Asset History Sheet

Each of the companies in your corporate group can operate under a different accounting regime that obliges them to maintain a particular format for asset year-end closing reports. The FI-AA module enables you to set up alternative asset history sheet formats that can be used in parallel to meet the requirements of your affiliated organizations.

The first step in creating a custom variant of the asset history sheet is to determine the titles of the cells that eventually receive the data. The next step is to choose which transaction types contribute to the data in each cell.

Maintaining a Report Selection Tree

A report system can contain many different standard and custom reports. You would not want to design a report if there was one already available to do what you require. On the other hand, each user may have a different set of priorities for accessing data. The database system also has preferences. Some assemblies of data can take a long time if diverse records must be accessed. A structured reporting system tries to ensure that subsequent report calls do not cause the system to carry out the same task needlessly.

A report tree for an individual user is built from a list of evaluations and reports provided by the INFOSYSTEM of Asset Accounting. This list includes such items as the following on the first level:

- General reports
- Depreciation lists
- Transaction lists
- Master data directory
- Change lists
- Special reports
- Application log

The second level of the list provided optionally expands the items nominated at the first level.

The depreciation lists include the following variants as options:

- Depreciation
- Depreciation/interest
- Depreciation comparison
- Depreciation simulation
- Manual depreciation
- Depreciation posted

The reports of the master data directory include the following:

- Asset history
- Property list
- Insurance list

You have the choice of creating a user report tree from a reference file that you specify or creating a tree on the basis of a standard application report tree, such as the Asset Accounting tree.

Activating History Management

If you have signified in the fixed asset master record that a particular asset is currently active, the system generates an asset chart. The content and structure of this chart can be defined for each asset class.

The function of the asset chart is to report all the information relevant to the history of an asset over any number of fiscal years.

Manipulating Asset Reports

Your varied assets may well demand varied treatments to give you the information you require. The FI-AA module enables you to define a report solely in terms of the records used to compile it. When you display the data, you have control over how the source data elements are sorted and how the summations are carried out. You do not have to make any changes to the definition program for the report in order to carry out the following procedures online:

- You can break out any set of asset records represented as a summation line on a report by double-clicking on that line.
- You can have the depreciation of an asset computed by any depreciation area formula analyzed to show how the value of the fixed asset changes according to the procedure defined for that area.
- You can nominate depreciation areas to generate comparisons of value changes according to the depreciation area calculation applied.
- You can call for versions of the sorting procedures to be carried out before the evaluation is computed, and you can instruct the system to display the summations at each stage of the sort as a hierarchy.
- You can build hierarchies of evaluation for any desired time period.
- You can specify sorts according to depreciation amounts and then selectively summarize the highest group by defining them by number or by a percentage.

Generating Alternative Reports Interactively

If you start with a list display of a report and select one line, the system assumes that you are interested in the detailed records used to compile the values in that particular line. By clicking on a line of a listing report, you automatically select a particular set of records. You can then call for a specific type of report and the system will go ahead and produce it using the assumed set of data.

This is a perfectly standard SAP facility, so you can call for similar interactive analysis of data in associated applications. For example, if you are running a cost accounting application in your SAP R/3 system, you can select a cost center and choose the value assigned to it at year-end closing. This automatically assumes that your next request for a report will be targeted at the elements used to compile that cost center valuation. These elements are likely to include the fixed assets and their depreciation as it has been computed from a cost accounting point of view.

There are many ways of looking at a portfolio of assets. The system is very flexible, in that you can nominate any field or any combination of the fields in an asset master record as the basis for a search specification in preparation for a session of interactive reporting.

Customizing Ad Hoc Reports

The ABAP/4 programming language can integrate any custom report you require with the rest of your R/3 system. However, the first step should be to check that a standard SAP R/3

Part
II
Ch
4

has not already been designed that could have its display edited to yield what you require. The next option is to use the standard report facilities to see whether you can design the report you need by using the available facilities. When you have the report you require, you can save the logical pathway used to compile it so that a similar report can be generated on other compilations of data.

If what you require is a one-off evaluation of a set of fixed assets, and if you do not expect the situation to arise again, then you can use a standard R/3 system query that is often referred to as an ad hoc query. Ad hoc queries are structured to suit the unique circumstances and are not needed again in precisely that form. Your SAP R/3 implementation was most likely supplied with some examples of ad hoc queries that are suitable for your industry and that need very little editing. Asset evaluations and inventory list reports are often supplied as model examples.

If you must design what you need, the procedure begins by nominating the tables that define the databases you will access. The system enables you to arrange all the fields available from these databases as columns for a list-format report. You can rearrange or omit columns and specify the titles, line length, display column width, and the output length of the fields.

Developing an International Asset Management Capability

The SAP R/3 system is designed as a potentially worldwide support for a global organization that carries out business in several industrial sectors and across many national boundaries. This kind of international business data processing cannot be achieved by any single software mechanism. At least the following factors must be accommodated:

- Automatic multilingual operation must be possible.
- Language-independent graphic symbols must accompany translations into each language.
- The structure of an organization must be represented in such a way that the accounts can be attributed to the unit responsible by a reliable structure at various levels (such as group, company, company code, and business area).
- Currencies must be handled in a flexible manner that can reflect the differences in the acceptable business practices of the various host nations.
- Data must be available and verifiable to meet the legal accounting requirements of different nations and their tax laws.
- Consolidation of accounts at all levels of a global enterprise must be a standard facility.

The FI-AA module is supplied in a form that is neutral with respect to country, legal requirements, and currency. Default settings are evoked to customize the module to suit the location of the implementation. Depreciation is customized by nominating from standard computation procedures and creating new depreciation logic if circumstances change. Standard charts of depreciation are provided with the appropriate depreciation keys for the following countries:

- Austria
- France
- Germany
- Great Britain
- Italy
- Japan
- The Netherlands
- Spain
- Switzerland
- The United States

Currency functions are standard throughout the SAP R/3 system and are applied consistently throughout the separate organizations of a corporate group. In particular, the Asset Accounting operations adopt the following conventions as standard:

- Any procedures defined as depreciation areas in the chart of depreciation can be applied in any currency.
- Asset accounts are maintained in parallel currencies in the General Ledger and in the depreciation area accounts that support it.
- All standard reports can be compiled in any currency using definable currency conversion procedures.

Each host nation may be operating under a different business climate. This would necessitate special functions to meet the local legal requirements and still permit meaningful legal consolidation at any level within the corporate structure. The following examples of special functions illustrate the diversity of the facilities available:

- Named depreciation types for tax purposes, such as ARCS, MACRS, and ADR in the United States
- Capital lease methods for leased assets, such as those allowed in the United States and Spain
- Depreciation exact to the day, as in France
- Revaluation for countries with high inflation
- Controls at special periods, such as the mid-quarter convention used in the United States
- Transfer of reserves, as in Germany
- Special depreciation procedures defined as they come into force
- IFB investment incentives, as in Austria
- Investment support measures, as in Germany
- Investment support grants

Part

Ch

4

Consolidating Company Accounts

In this chapter

Combining Financial Statements

Legal consolidation is the process of combining the financial statements of two or more individual companies to produce a consolidated financial statement that complies with legal requirements. The process can include the following operations.

- Reclassification
- Reappraisal
- Consolidation

Any or all of these processes can be carried out on any or all of the following data objects.

- Equity
- Receivables
- Obligations
- Profits
- Sales revenues

The numerical values stored in these data objects encapsulate the monetary values assigned to the assets and contracts associated with the company at the moment when the period accounts were closed. What a company is worth is a matter of opinion, but the legal convention of the host country defines how the business community computes values to represent this worth. Consolidation must reconcile potentially different points of view on the value of a company if the balance sheet of the corporate group is to be created.

There is a tendency to regard the consolidation process as a difficult and time-consuming process that must be accomplished quickly as soon as the year is closed and that is best kept in the accounting department. Fully integrated enterprise systems must have a powerful consolidation system to compete with this viewpoint.

Consolidation involves more than summing the individual company balance sheets. This process can express the balance sheet policy of the corporate group in relation to the balance sheet policies of the individual organizational units.

This chapter sets out the various functions that can be called from the SAP R/3 FI-LC module, entitled Legal Consolidation (or more often referred to simply as Consolidation) because it can be used to conduct parallel consolidation operations that suit the corporate group without necessarily complying with the legal requirements of any particular nation. For example, this chapter helps answer the following questions.

- How does SAP R/3 cope with the changing requirements suggested by the European Union guidelines?
- How can assets be reported when different nations place different values on them?
- How can a corporate group summarize the business activities of many affiliates when they each operate under different tax laws?

Using the FI-LC Consolidation Module

The principles behind consolidation are based on the theory that the legal entity of a corporate group should be portrayed as if it were a single company. This entails reporting on the assets and the financial and revenue position. It may be necessary to carry out any or all of the following operations as preparation for rendering the external accounts of a corporation.

- Elimination of investments
- Elimination of intercompany payables and receivables
- Elimination of intercompany profits and losses
- Elimination of intercompany expenses and revenues
- Elimination of investment income
- Reclassification

This SAP component is also referred to as FI-LC Legal Consolidation. A legal consolidated financial statement can also be supplemented and used for internal information purposes.

N O T E   An internal consolidation report does not have to comply with legal requirements.

Consolidated financial statements are often required promptly, yet they usually must be assembled from incompatible data communication protocols in a software environment that is, to say the least, heterogeneous. Extra details may be required, and there will be a need to validate the data.

The purpose of the SAP FI-LC Consolidation module is to optimize and automate the consolidation process. The module offers the following additional functionality.

- Integration with the accounting software used by individual companies
- Automatic and reliable transfer of data from the individual financial statements
- Integration of internal and external group reporting
- Multinational accounting functions
- Standards for processing representations of organizational structures

The method of FI-LC Consolidation is first to prepare the financial data in each individual company and then to affect computer integration.

Interfacing by Design

The consolidation software has always been designed with the expectation that the data from the constituent companies will be stored in different accounting systems that are possibly legacy and third-party implementations. As such, a system of interfaces has always been necessary. If the affiliated organizations already use SAP R/3 software or mainframe R/2 software, the consolidation process can be fully integrated.

Part

Ch

5

In addition to the design of efficient interface systems, the need for speedy consolidation at year-end closing has resulted in many detailed improvements to the design of the data objects themselves. For example, the entity type 2001, Chart of Accounts, is designed to be uniform across all companies so that diverse charts of accounts can be processed by the same consolidation software.

Changes in the international business environment are increasing the importance of group accounting and are enlarging its scope. The following factors are salient in this respect:

- Many companies have been restructured without regard to national boundaries.
- The rule of instituting a separate company code for each national business unit in a corporation is no longer applied universally.
- Communities of nations, such as the European Union, may change legal consolidation norms.
- International companies might have to prepare worldwide financial statements that include all their affiliated subsidiaries.
- The cost of processing data for consolidation increases if entries must be standardized across companies, and if the values must be converted to a common reporting currency.
- The consolidation process may have to eliminate intercompany profit and loss before rendering external public accounts.
- Asset accounting may have to include an extra depreciation area to arrive at a standard valuation that can be referenced at the corporate level.

The FI-AA Asset Accounting module, for example, makes provision for the following computations in preparation for group consolidation.

- Maintaining, parallel to local ledger depreciation, a special depreciation area according to the rules for the corporate depreciation area
- Maintaining information, such as exchange rate variations, for a central historical currency conversion, or maintaining a local depreciation area database in historic group currency

It may also be necessary to maintain information that properly represents the changing values of fixed assets transferred to other group companies in the fiscal year and in following years. It is important to know which company owns each part of an asset during the transition period so that individual accounts can be closed properly and can contribute to the consolidated financial statements.

The functions of group-wide planning and controlling must meet the traditional legal and regional requirements. In addition, the system must be capable of reporting on the basis of products or services. The system must also support a very wide range of reporting and display demands. The following questions illustrate the type of questions that can be asked over and above the legal financial requirements.

- How do the values of particular assets or asset classes change in the different organizations within the group?

How does the group distribute the total investment, and how is it budgeted?

How are the various asset areas within the group ranked with respect to the relative cost of maintaining them?

Reviewing the Benefits of Enterprise Consolidation Software

One of the sensitive measures of the quality of consolidation software is the time saved in closing the books. The SAP R/3 FI-LC module saves time in the following ways.

Faster collection of financial data from subsidiary companies

Minimization of manual entries

Automatic reconciliation of intercompany transactions (except for queries)

Minimal manual entry to consolidate investment transactions

These time-saving advantages are greatly increased by having a database of financial transactions in the General Ledger that can be copied to the consolidation database online. You can then view your group data at any time during the period without waiting for closing.

Using the Trading Partner Concept

A trading partner is defined from the point of view of a consolidated company. In this sense, a trading partner is a company engaged in a business relationship.

When a posting of an intercompany transaction occurs, the system applies a special posting procedure that uses a trading partner value taken from the document to initiate an intercompany reconciliation at the document level. As a result, there is no need to effect this reconciliation as of the reconciliation closing date.

Preparing for Consolidation

Although a fully integrated financial accounting system can benefit from automatic functions of various kinds, the principles of consolidation are essentially those based on manual accounting. Before consolidation, preparation must take place.

You or your system must carry out the following operations.

Match the individual company chart of accounts to the group chart of accounts

Eliminate intercompany Payables and Receivables, and revenue and expenses that arise because individual companies in a group enjoy a variety of sender-recipient relationships

Record the acquisition years of assets for historical currency conversion

Consolidate investments

Computer integration is relatively straightforward if every individual company has installed and configured only SAP applications. In this case the companies share a common environment of standard documents and data objects controlled by SAP standard business process software.

If one or more individual company has been in the habit of using only paper forms and ledgers for accounting, there obviously must be a stage of data input to at least a personal computer with a means to convert the data to a medium suitable for transfer to the SAP FI-LC Consolidation system. The alternative of last resort is probably a conventional mailing of the data to the host company's head office where a SAP R/3 workstation can be used to re-enter the data.

N O T E If one or more individual companies uses a software system that can communicate with one of the interfaces supported by SAP, you can use specific programs to facilitate the transfer of financial data.

Standardizing Entries

If the accounting practices of an individual company do not agree completely with the format chosen for presenting the consolidated financial statements, it is possible to account for the differences in amounts by posting a standardizing entry to a head office account designated for this purpose. These entries are stored in a separate file.

Eliminating Intercompany Payables and Receivables

FI-Financial Accounting eliminates intercompany balances by open item only if each trading partner has been marked in the vendor master record. You must also ensure that the reporting procedures inform the consolidating department of the numbers of these trading partners; at least on the items that relate to intercompany Payables and Receivables, revenues and expenses.

The law requires that all intercompany balances be eliminated before presenting the balance sheet and the profit and loss statement. All possible pairs of individual companies must be investigated for evidence that they have been trading with each other.

In practice, significant differences between the way individual companies keep their records can make complete elimination impractical. The most frequent causes of discrepancies in elimination are as follows:

- Currency translation differences
- Differences in the timing of entries for goods in transit between individual companies
- Specific reserves set aside for doubtful accounts
- Liabilities that are not acknowledged in the records

The cause that is most difficult to handle is currency translation; the others can usually be resolved by thoroughly applying corporate policies.

If the individual companies have installed and configured SAP accounting applications, automatic dual currency accounting will occur, in which every transaction is documented in both the local currency and the currency designated for all transactions in the group. The FI-LC component enables you to trace any currency translation differences between the local currency at the prevailing rate of exchange and the transaction currency. A corrected exchange rate can then be posted in the balance sheet account designated for this purpose and later brought into the consolidated financial statement.

Problems in currency can also arise when not all companies involved in the consolidation are part of a SAP system. This is especially true if currency translation takes place in two company code organizations, where one uses the reciprocal exchange rate of the other. Intercompany loans, in particular (which can run into hundreds of millions of units), can result in exchange rate differences in the hundreds of thousands of units.

Preparing for Consolidation of Investments

When you use FI-LC Consolidation, you can specify which consolidation methods are to be used for subgroups of individual companies. For example, step consolidation first consolidates each accounting unit within every subgroup separately. Subgroups at the same level of the organization are then consolidated with each other, and so on until the final consolidation yields the financial information for the group as a whole—the top level.

You can specify what should happen if different methods yield differing results. Likewise, you can use these methods and options in parallel. The system can carry out simultaneous consolidation using each of the methods chosen to calculate equity shares that represent the values of the individual holdings. This is known as the matrix method.

NOTE   Simultaneous consolidation treats all accounting units as equals under the head office and performs the whole consolidation in one step.

FI-LC takes account of any minority interests in investments and any hidden reserves as it performs any of the following procedures. In most instances, these procedures are performed automatically.

- First consolidation
- Subsequent consolidation
- Step acquisition and indirect changes in ownership
- Increase and decrease in capital
- Write-down of investment
- Complete divestiture or partial disposal
- Transfer of investment to a new owner

The balance sheet and the profit and loss accounts are corrected in parallel by the system. Goodwill and hidden reserves are amortized. Auxiliary records are updated. Every elimination entry is explained clearly, concisely, or in detail, at your command.

NOTE   The system meets the legal requirements for an asset history sheet and the special situation of equity consolidations.

Part

Ch

5

Using What-if Versions and Forecast Simulations of Consolidation

The system enables you to copy the consolidation data to a new version of the consolidated financial statement. You can then edit certain control tables for the new version so that a different method of consolidation is used. For example, you might want to see what would happen if valuation were done differently, or if exchange rate differences were handled in another way.

You can also create a simulation of the consolidation process by using forecast data in place of actual financial statements data. All the same manipulations can be carried out on plan data just as on actual data.

Meeting Annual Reporting Requirements of Complex Companies

The SAP FI-LC Consolidation component is the application of choice for analyzing and reporting for large and complex groups. The following types of reports are usually required, at least annually, but they can be performed on an ad hoc basis at any time.

- Asset history sheet, reserves, and special items
- Summaries of Payables and Receivables
- Detailed information on selected items
- Group or parent company comparisons
- Sales by region or by product line

SAP standard product FI-LC Consolidation includes predefined report specifications that serve most of these reporting needs.

Using Special Report Designs

Small-volume reports can be generated to view online, to print, or to store using the standard display control and item selection functions of the R/3 Basis component. This flexible type of interactive reporting is a specific SAP technique.

Extensive consolidation reports and audit trails can be sent to a printer or a transfer medium. For example, preconsolidated financial statement data for a subgroup can be sent by electronic means or can be transferred to a tape or a disk so it can be passed to the next level in the group.

 TIP   Consolidated financial statement information can be directed to word processing and spreadsheet facilities, where it can be attached to letters and prepared for presentation.

Reporting Interactively

The process of interactive reporting starts with a display of data that appears on that screen as part of a warning or an advisory message from some other part of the system. Such a warning also could appear because you specifically asked for it by calling for a search based on a range of parameters to narrow the possibilities. You might ask for items over a certain amount, for instance.

When you see an interesting data object on the screen, you can find out more about it if you place the cursor on it and use one of the function keys to locate what you want to know. You might want to perform a what-if analysis using a value or other parameter in place of the actual value used to compute the item.

The following types of query can be readily initiated.

- Details of specific items, moving to ever-finer detail as you repeat your query action
- Comparisons
- Investments in companies
- Transaction types
- Standardized and consolidated entries
- Graphical presentations of selected data

If your system is integrated with other SAP application modules, you can gain access to the data they record. For example, you can inspect account balances and documents in the SAP FI-Financial Accounting system if your FI-LC Consolidation component is integrated with it. If your installation uses the SAP FI-AA Asset Accounting module, you can see and use in reports the information in the acquisition and retirement records.

Your finished report can be readily drafted to show whatever combination of detail and summary information best serves your purpose.

Using Ratio Analysis

One of the important benefits of having an up-to-date accounting system with a flexible reporting facility on a powerful computer is the speed with which complex business calculations can be provided with the information necessary to ensure that they are valid. A frequently studied outcome of business calculation is the ratio, which is a comparison between two numerical values obtained by dividing one by the other.

A ratio that compares one production period with another can be a useful indicator to guide internal management. The financial position of the company can be compared with that of a rival by means of one or more ratios. Ratios between individual company performance and consolidated financial statement amounts can be used to explain or amplify the annual report.

The FI-LC facilities enable you to define the same mathematical procedure for all these ratio calculations, but the actual variables and data depend on the purpose and the version number of the ratio calculation you specify when you call for the result.

Suppose you define your ratio calculation in two stages:

- You specify where the information is to come from.
- You specify how the information is to take part in the calculation.

Part

I

Ch

5

Suppose, for example, that you are interested in calculating the equity ratio, which you have agreed to define as the ratio of equity to total assets. The information could be gathered from three sources, but only one will give you exactly what you want.

- Equity(1) = Paid-in Capital + Reserves + Retained Earnings
- Equity(2) = Paid-in Capital + Required Adjustments + Pension Reserves
- Equity(3) = Total Assets - Total Liabilities

Equity(1) is defined in the language of a business report, and Equity(2) appears by law on the balance sheet. Equity(3) is expressed in the terms used in cost accounting. Your definition of the ratio you want corresponds to Equity(3). This is what the system will use to calculate the ratio for whatever time periods or organizational units you specify.

If you select an element on your display, the system shows you how it computed this element; the system displays the individual values that took part in the calculation on a split screen. You can also call for a 3D display of the information you have isolated for your calculations.

Using Interim Periodic Financial Statements

Unlike the annual consolidated financial statement, interim periodic financial statements can be selective in the information they report. You can flag each individual company to indicate its reporting category, and you can adopt the suggestions of the system based on the following ratio thresholds.

- Individual company information required will be provided.
- Data will be derived from prior periods (as plan data).
- This company will be omitted from the periodic report.

Consolidation intervals, such as the following, must be defined for each subgroup of companies.

- Yearly
- Half-yearly
- Quarterly
- Monthly

Different companies tend to post entries to accounts at different times of the accounting period. The system eliminates intercompany Payables and Receivables, which balances the unavoidable timing differences.

T I P Intercompany profits and losses can be eliminated by using information from the previous year's financial statements.

N O T E The system automatically posts depreciation accrued during the periods of the periodic consolidated financial statement.

Understanding Options for Consolidation

In the format for any account balance (external or internal), some fields can be used to eliminate intercompany balances. You can extend this format and use it to eliminate transactions between companies and business areas with sender-recipient relationships. This feature can also be used for detailed internal group reporting.

Because the SAP system uses central data administration, simple validation ensures that external and internal reports use the same data.

Performing Positive Auditing with the SAP R/3 Auditor Workstation

The SAP R/3 Auditor Workstation is a module that can operate with individual companies and on a global enterprise basis. This feature can operate as a stand-alone module and can interface with the data sources through standard SAP interfaces. The module operates online with the SAP R/3 system. The auditors work in the operational system and must be authorized to read the current data set.

This workstation focuses on more positive auditing activities and consulting, although the standard processes of compiling evaluation documents and reports are fully supported. The Generally Accepted Accounting Principles (GAAP) remain the guiding standards, but the workstation is optimized for the benefit of internal and external auditors, system auditors, and cost accounting personnel. The module was first developed for the German auditing environment and is being enhanced with the capability of recognizing other auditing conventions.

The R/3 Audit Information System is also available to the auditor workstation. This information system can construct an audit report tree from which the user can call individual reports and evaluation programs that can work with pre-closing interim lists, such as Assets, Receivables, Balance Confirmation, Balance List, Domestic Customers, and so on.

Part

Ch

5

Customizing the Consolidation Software

Two standard methods exist for changing the way SAP software operates. Most variations can be accomplished by altering the parameters of the standard functions. However, if you have the necessary authorization, you can alter the sensitive settings of the consolidation software—if you choose to do so, however, you risk moving your system away from one of the preconfigured legal consolidation procedures.

The following facilities are offered to assist you in customization.

- You have the option to define new currency translation methods.
- You have the option to define additional methods for the consolidation of investments.
- You have the option to alter the Financial Statement items catalog in the FS Items file.

If you exercise any of these options, your activities are recorded in the table modification audit reports.

The SAP R/3 FI-LC module is provided with preconfigured consolidation plans and FS Items suggestions that require very little customizing. For example, the following industries are offered a range of different plans for the FS Items catalog.

- Commercial businesses
- Banks and insurance companies

The module also comes with the following facilities.

- Entry forms in numerous languages
- Currency translation definitions and formulas
- Consolidation method definitions

Any of these items can be edited to suit your company.

The SAP R/3 FI-LC module is an integral part of the FI-Financial Accounting system, so no separate system need be installed. However, you may want to run consolidation from a computer separate from your main system for either or both of the following reasons.

- Year-end closing can be conducted without disrupting the production system.
- Data is directly posted to consolidation at the transaction document level rather than being transferred periodically from the operative systems.

The SAP ALE Application Link Enabling system is used to connect the operative computers and the consolidation computer.

Applying Step Consolidation

If you have a corporate system that comprises two or more independent computers running your financial accounting, and if your corporate structure is such that each subgroup of affiliates holds its financial data in a separate computer, several computers will be used to perform consolidation. In this case, you can apply step consolidation to each subgroup computer in isolation and later consolidate the results.

If all your affiliates share the same computer system or network, step consolidation is performed internally. First, you define subgroups that are subjected to consolidation from the bottom of the hierarchy upwards. If you then initiate the consolidation function, the system compresses the completely consolidated subgroups from the bottom to the top of your consolidation structure. The results of step consolidation may well differ from those achieved by simultaneous consolidation because the details of any subgroup can be obscured when the subgroup is combined with the next layer.

Applying Management Consolidation

The SAP R/3 systems from 1996 have the capability of supporting additional types of consolidation. For example, the user can define management-consolidation procedures that assemble data on the basis of any structure using the standard SAP organization of client and company code, together with any logical combination using such user-defined transaction data collectors as the following:

- Business area
- Profit center
- Product group
- Any consolidation unit that can be defined from the data stored in the transaction documents

This extension of the standard consolidation functions that support management consolidation is provided with an automatic reconciliation function that ensures that the control accounts of the management consolidation function are always maintained up to the latest transaction posting. The concept of special ledger accounting has been extended by providing a set of additional ledgers in a special format that cannot be modified.

These facilities are installed as the EC-MC Enterprise Controlling - Management Consolidation package. The management consolidation system uses the same techniques as the Executive Information System (EIS), to which it can transmit compressed summary data.

Consolidating with FI-SL Special Ledgers

The Special Ledgers component of the FI system provides a method of defining data structures according to the special purposes and business needs of the user. A system of Special Ledger accounts can be defined to accumulate totals and line items that can be updated from any source. All SAP system business transactions can contribute, or there could be a selection condition for posting to any Special Ledger account.

Using Special Ledgers to Extend FI-LC The FI-LC module has three 10-digit user fields that can be used to receive the results of consolidation performed by the FI-SL module using additional account assignment terms stored in the Special Ledger.

Using Special Ledgers Without FI-LC Your company may not need to consolidate using automated processes. The FI-SL module is used when the following operations can be performed manually, as necessary, and the results posted manually.

- Elimination of intercompany Receivables and Payables
- Elimination of intercompany profits and losses
- Investment consolidation

In the FI-SL module, you can perform simple elimination by ignoring totals records in the reporting module that were added by related companies. No automatic adjustment postings, no difference postings, and no computations of proportions take place.

Consolidating with the Executive Information System

Although the Executive Information System (EIS) is essentially a decision support information provider, it can handle external data input, currency translation, and financial reporting. The EIS also can manage user-defined data structures. At the reporting stage, you can manually eliminate intercompany sales by permitting a user to update transaction data records by editing the displayed values.

Part
I

Ch
5

Exploring Consolidation Master Data

A financial statement produced by the consolidation procedure refers to reporting entities using a six-digit alphanumeric key, which is referred to as the company ID. Each company ID is recorded in a company master record. A reporting company can be one of the following entities.

- A subsidiary company that is fully consolidated
- A joint venture to be partially consolidated
- An associated company to be treated as an equity holding
- An external company that should not be consolidated
- A business area within a separate legal entity

Master records can be maintained in the system for companies that are not included in the external consolidated financial statements. You may want to add to such records the reason why the company is not included in the external consolidation. This function is used for internal accounting and auditing.

Using the Business Area Concept

A business area is an organizational unit used in financial accounting, although it does not necessarily form part of the legal financial statements. A business area represents an internal accounting or reporting object that is legally non-independent, even though it has a balance sheet and a profit and loss statement as if it were an independent organizational unit. A business area is a subdivision of a client, but it may not extend across more than one client.

One advantage of compiling transaction data for a business area is that this data can be used to depict areas of activity that are not reported through the company code system. Some national systems may require that data be collected on specific business areas that are then consolidated across regions or industry structures.

In the SAP scheme, business areas are set out by assigning predefined categories. The following categories of entities can be receivers for subsequent postings of transaction data.

- Plant
- Division
- Cost center
- Order
- Sales area
- Event defined by a manual entry

These business areas can each generate a reconciled balance sheet. They can also be used in conjunction with the company code to define a business area in addition to a company code consolidation unit.

If you want to compile financial statements for similar business areas in different company codes, you can define a subgroup so that it includes precisely the organizational units you require. For reporting purposes, a subgroup is a set of companies defined on any convenient basis. The consolidation system processes the data as if the subgroup defines a legal company.

Defining the Items in a Financial Statement

If you have different charts of accounts in use within your corporate group, you must assign all the accounts to a single catalog, called The Consolidation Financial Statement Items catalog, or the FS Items catalog.

Each item in the individual financial statements must be assigned to only one item in the unified FS Items catalog. The assignment of individual accounts to FS Items is made in the General Ledger account master records in the FI-Financial Accounting module. When consolidation takes place, the items are condensed to the values of the line items when the balances are transferred.

Information about a line item is conveyed by a system of additional account assignments that can be displayed in the line. Four categories of additional assignments have been defined, and you can add three more to your own specification. The predefined additional account assignment categories used for information are as follows:

- Transaction types
- Partner companies
- Currencies
- Acquisition years

The predefined transaction types are as follows:

- Fixed assets
- Special items with reserve
- Provisions
- Appropriations, Equity

The predefined partner company FS Items are as follows:

- Loans to members of the consolidation group
- Payables/Receivables to/from members of the consolidation group
- Investments or shares in members of the consolidation group
- Expenses or income with members of the consolidation group

The predefined currency FS Items are as follows:

- Payables/Receivables to/from members of the consolidation group
- Loans to members of the consolidation group

Part
1

Ch

5

The predefined acquisition years category includes fixed asset items with historical currency conversions.

Each account assignment combination that receives a line item value is stored as a single record. Data can be added directly at this level as further values that have been assigned to the combination are posted. Data can also be added at a global level and can be broken down into more detail later by signifying the appropriate assignment combinations.

Using Statistical Line Items

The items in a unified FS Items catalog are numbered, and this number is used as an ID code for all reported or derived numerical information. This data is regarded as statistical, in that it does not directly represent original transaction values. Statistical lines are used in the following circumstances.

- Balance sheet and profit and loss statement items
- Quantitative statistical information, such as sales quantities
- Nominal statistical information, such as the number of employees
- Definitions of how ratios are to be computed

Extensive reporting facilities are available so that you can selectively access all types of consolidation line items.

Understanding Methods of Consolidation

The purpose of consolidating the financial statements of the members of a corporate entity is to render a set of external accounts as if the group was a single company. Because groups can differ widely in their internal structures, several methods exist for organizing the consolidation process and the data preparation that it entails.

Defining Types of Companies

A company can be defined in any way you choose for internal accounting or management purposes. But for the legal rendering of the external accounts, strict definitions govern what may be defined in the consolidated financial statements as autonomous entities.

A subsidiary company must be fully consolidated because the direct parent company can exert a controlling influence. This is because the parent company shares the same management or because it has an equity holding of more than 50%.

A joint venture company must be consolidated proportionally to the share of the investment. The investment shares of the independent direct parent companies in a joint venture are usually the same, such as 50% or 33.3%, and so on, according to the number of investing parent companies.

An associated company is a company in which you have an equity holding.

An affiliated company is a consolidated company in which you have an equity holding of between 20% and 50% so that you can be said to exert considerable influence.

Performing the First Consolidation

When a subsidiary, a joint venture, or an associated company is represented in the consolidated financial statements of a corporate group for the first time, the process is the same for all consolidation methods. The investment book values of the direct parent companies of the new acquisitions are compared with the equity of each investee. If any differences exist, they are allocated to goodwill or to fair value adjustments. The minority interest values are also calculated at this first consolidation.

The example in Table 5.1 demonstrates the type of display available for the results of the first consolidation of an asset in which the consolidation group holds 75%.

Table 5.1 First Consolidation in the Year of Acquisition

Asset ID	Total	Consolidation group's share	Share held by external companies
75% Investment		2,400	
- Capital	2,000	1,600 -	400 -
Difference		800	
- Hidden reserves	400	300 -	100 -
+ Hidden encumbrances	200	150 +	50 +
Goodwill or reserve allocation		1,450	450

Performing Subsequent Consolidations

Although it is common practice to name all consolidations after the first as "subsequent consolidations," the term can also be reserved for the process of consolidating for investments. The main operations of subsequent consolidations are as follows:

- Correction of external companies' shares, based on changes to capital and reserves
- Depreciation of hidden reserves
- Depreciation of goodwill
- New first-time consolidation if the step acquisition method is in operation
- Increase or decrease in capitalization
- Divestiture procedure, if the asset is sold

The system automatically posts documents to eliminate investment values and records items such as goodwill and minority interest.

Using Step Consolidation   Step consolidation is applicable to a hierarchy of companies in a multitiered corporate group. The lowest-level companies are consolidated first, then these accounts are consolidated at the next level, and so on.

Extra preparation for consolidation may be required if any lower level company is not fully integrated with your SAP R/3 system. This may be the situation with a company that has recently been incorporated into the group.

Using Simultaneous Consolidation   Simultaneous consolidation is a procedure that takes into account in a single step all the existing investments of an investee within a subgroup and the resulting minority interests. One characteristic feature of simultaneous consolidation is the opportunity it affords for calculating the difference that arises from the consolidation of investments between the following entities.

- The corporate group investments for the direct parent company
- The investee's equity weighted by the group share

The simultaneous consolidation procedure is useful when the investment structure is not in the form of a hierarchy because it can report an exact analysis of the share attributable to each individual company.

Using Proportional Consolidation   Proportional consolidation is a method used for consolidating investments in joint venture companies. The financial statement data from the individual joint venture companies is incorporated in your consolidated financial statements only in proportion to your share of investment in the joint venture.

Using the Equity Method of Consolidation   If an associated company (or a subsidiary or joint venture company) is not fully consolidated, or if it is only proportionally consolidated, the equity method of consolidation is applied. The individual financial statement data for a company included "at equity" does not have to be entered into the SAP R/3 FI-LC system because only changes in equity are reported for consolidation. The method adjusts the shareholding reported in the consolidated balance sheet.

Using the Purchase Method of Consolidation   When the parent company within a subgroup exercises a controlling influence over a consolidated subsidiary company, the purchase method of consolidation is used. It is assumed that a controlling degree of influence can be exerted over a subsidiary if the management is identical, or if the investment by the parent in the subsidiary is more than 50%.

Using the Revaluation Method of Consolidation   The revaluation method has features of both the purchase method of consolidation and the proportional method. This method is used when minority interests have a share of silent reserves as well as the corporate group. Both types of shares are all dissolved during the first consolidation. This effectively revalues for first consolidation purposes all the assets and liabilities of the investee company.

N O T E   The book value method of consolidation is an alternative to the revaluation method of consolidation. ▢

Using Consolidation Reporting Subgroups

Any two or more companies, selected in any way you choose, can be associated as a subgroup for reporting purposes, although you cannot change the structure of subgroups after the first consolidation takes place. A company can be assigned to more than one subgroup.

A subgroup usually is not defined in a hierarchical corporate group, unless for internal reporting requirements.

Preparing Data at the Subsidiary Level

Preparing data for consolidation at the subsidiary level entails applying the same logic as corporate consolidation. Inventory valuation must take place for the balance sheet and consolidation closing dates. The perspective of this valuation can be local, commercial, tax law, or corporate group. The methods can vary for each viewpoint.

Furthermore, the valuations most useful for the periodic financial statements need not be the same as those required for external accounting. The software programs can be passed using different parameters.

The results of valuations are based on individual subledger values and are posted as totals figures in a separate account. You can therefore maintain these accounts in parallel in local currency and the corporate reporting currency.

A financial statement can be prepared in various versions generated according to how you assign the various balance sheet and profit and loss accounts. The consolidation display identifies the separate versions and shows the total of the differences between local and corporate group valuations as a corporate valuation adjustment posting.

Eliminating Intercompany Posting Transactions

If individual financial statements are to be successfully used to produce a consolidated group balance sheet and a profit and loss statement, then the intercompany posting transactions must be clearly identified. The sender-receiver relationship must be clear. You could achieve this clarity by maintaining separate accounts for all possible intercompany transactions. But even for small companies, this would waste system resources.

The SAP method involves logging the relationship in the transaction document, where it can be used as a retrieval key to prepare the data for consolidation. Intercompany postings incorporate the trading partner company ID in all document lines by copying it from the customer or vendor master record, or by requesting that the user enter it manually.

With this code in place, you can arrange for automated reconciliation activities at the level of the individual financial statement. This prepares the data for eliminating intercompany Payables and Receivables and for revenue against expense elimination.

Using Valuation Areas for Consolidating Fixed Assets

Various systems of statutory consolidation rules preclude any procedure designed to apply central or global rules to fixed assets. It is mandated that fixed assets should be valued according to the single valuation principle, under which each asset is to be assigned only one value.

The SAP solution maintains parallel valuation areas that each record the results of a different calculation. Therefore, you can set up a valuation area purely for internal accounting purposes. That valuation area can be used in consolidation across any structure of organizational units without corrupting the valuation data that must be maintained in the local books. This is done using the currency and legal valuation methods of the region of legal force in which the fixed asset is located.

Chapter 4, "Accounting for Assets," includes a discussion of the methods of maintaining asset histories using the appropriate currencies and exchange rates. The FI-AA module can provide the following facilities.

- Maintaining separate valuation areas
- Preparing for centralized historical currency translations based on the year of acquisition
- Maintaining decentralized valuations of corporate group value areas in the corporate group currency
- Tracing the value changes from the corporate and individual company viewpoints on a year-by-year basis as assets are transferred to other members of the corporate group
- Calculating and eliminating intercompany profits and losses as part of the process of preparing for consolidation

Transferring Data

To be able to produce consolidated financial statements every year, it is necessary to transfer reported data quickly and without errors. In addition, if your group operates under active corporate management, there is a requirement that management consolidation usually must follow a reporting cycle much shorter than the fiscal year. Demands for different viewpoints and data selections often also are present, to enable management to focus on opportunities for improvement.

It is not good enough for subsidiary companies to mail their operating results to the head office once a year. The ideal requirement is perhaps a networked consolidation using an intermediate storage medium, if necessary, and direct links from workstations in the smaller affiliates. This can be seen as an internal consolidation system that does not replace the statutory global consolidation process but rather provides a more active management-consolidation function. This function can be run on a satellite system to conserve central resources, with application link enabling (ALE) posting transaction data automatically (where justified) because it affords a more timely summary of the true trading position across the group.

NOTE   The ultimate in integrated global system management is to automatically post the data of
        each transaction to the consolidation database. ▢

Using Consolidation Groups

A convenient way to set up the interface between financial accounting and the consolidation system is to define one or more consolidation groups. When an affiliated organizational unit sets up the procedures for data integration, various parameters can be assigned in the "sender" system. For example, the fiscal year may be the accounting period, but a variant of the fiscal year can be designated for the purpose of internal accounting. You can decide on a four-week period for internal consolidation.

The choice of consolidation types usually ranges as follows:

- Company consolidation
- Consolidation of business areas
- Profit center consolidation

The source of data to be used can be direct posting from the transaction, or you can apply a scheme of data roll-up to assemble batches of data for the consolidation database. Another possibility is to arrange for the data to be extracted from the FI Financial Accounting database.

Using a PC to Enter Consolidation Data

A consolidation system running SAP R/3 FI-LC could receive data from a personal computer. Two SAP applications are available to run in the PC environment—one is based on DBASE, and the other uses Microsoft Access. In each case, the rules for data entry and validation checking are defined in the consolidation module and are downloaded to the PC, where they support the standard functions of entry, print, check, export, and import. The DBASE and Microsoft Access applications can be used to define entry formats and reports.

The import functions enable the PC to accept data from subsidiary applications that may be third-party systems. Export to the consolidation coordinator can take place only if the data passes the validation checks. The transfer can take place via disks or directly through remote function call (RFC) operations.

Standard forms are available in all the languages supported by SAP. These forms have the normal SAP design, in which the presentation of the form and the active fields are determined by parameters held in tables that the user can edit without disturbing the underlying software. The user can also add new language sets to be assigned to the fields when they are displayed for entry or reporting. How a particular form is used in your company and the language are matters that are assigned in the company master record.

The following examples of online operations illustrate the versatility of the consolidation module.

- Calling up the balance sheet and the profit and loss accounts to display one value per item

Part

I

Ch

5

- Calling up selected asset items
- Printing out comparable figures from the previous year as a guide for the person entering the data

Asset items can be selected on the basis of any logical combination of the following attributes.

- Transaction type
- Trading partner
- Currency
- Year of acquisition

Developing a Validation Rule Language

Any value that is entered into a key field is automatically checked for validity so that company ID, line item number, and transaction type are not allowed unless they fall within the permitted ranges. The consolidation module also enables the user to define the validation procedures to be applied by recognizing a code that identifies a specific validation version. For example, the critical values that define the boundaries of an acceptable entry to a data field can be changed from one accounting period to the next. At the level of consolidation, the data objects of interest are concerned with the operating results of the individual companies being consolidated.

A step-wise status management system is available to control the application of the checks specified in the validation version rule set. If any particular company fails to satisfy the assigned validation rules, then the status management system holds up the consolidation until the error is resolved. The following types of logical checks can be applied under control of the validation rule language and its status management system.

- Are corresponding line items, such as profits according to the balance sheet and the profit and loss statement, compatible with the depreciation values recorded in the asset history sheet and the profit and loss statement?
- Do the line item totals, such as assets and liabilities, balance?
- What period values have changed more than a certain percentage from the values of prior periods with which they can reasonably be compared?
- How do line item values compare with specified baseline or target figures?

If any checking process detects a suspect condition, a warning message can be issued. If an error is detected, a suitable report is generated. The status management system is set up so that each level of proving validity produces a status update only when all errors are removed and all warnings are acknowledged.

Changing the Balance Sheet from Local to Consolidated

Each independent organizational unit at the company code level produces its own financial documents, the balance sheet, and the profit and loss statement. These must be approved by local auditors, who ensure that the statutory requirements are met for the region of legal force in which the company is located.

Exactly how these external accounts are rendered can be subject to group guidelines, provided they are compatible with the local regulations. For example, certain assets can be reclassified and assigned value adjustments that place them in accord with the valuations used in other affiliated companies. In these instances, some of the preparation for consolidation has been decentralized.

However, cases do arise in which the consolidated corporate accounts must report additional company-specific corrections to the data reported from the local accounts. The local accounting function may not be aware of this corporate requirement, so the adjustment might not have been made under the group guidelines arrangement.

The following items can appear in consolidated accounts as a result of this type of adjustment.

- Changes in local valuation of assets
- Adjustment postings to corporate valuation
- Postings to corporate group values as a result of elimination of intercompany profit and loss accounts
- Postings to corporate group values as a result of subgroup-related consolidation postings if a multistep preparation for consolidation is being operated

This type of centrally posted adjustment to the accounts of a specific company are known as adjustment postings and are identified as such so that they can be analyzed separately from the reported data.

The sequence of preparation for consolidation can take the following form.

1. GL1, the first General Ledger financial statement produced by an individual company, is audited locally.
2. Local adjustments, reclassifications, and individual asset revaluations are posted in accordance with the valuation guidelines of the group.
3. GL2, the second General Ledger financial statement produced by an individual company, is audited locally.
4. The parent company receives all the individual GL2 financial statements and collates them.
5. The parent company applies central adjustment postings to effect global corrections, if necessary.
6. The parent company applies cross-company consolidation postings to GL3 (the summarized financial statements) to produce the consolidated financial statements, which are then inspected by auditors.

Using Centralized Adjustment Postings

Adjustment transactions are stored in a separate line item database in the SAP R/3 FI-LC module. A single type of posting is used to enter both company-specific adjustment postings and multicompany consolidation postings.

A system of document type codes is interpreted to control the assignment of document numbers automatically and to ensure that various validation checks are carried out. Balance sheet profit and loss corrections can be posted, and allowances can be entered for deferred taxes.

You can deduce how the account is to be assigned from the FS Item, as defined in the catalog of financial statement item types. The trading partner and the type of transaction can also influence the account assignment.

Standard data entry assistance is provided by the system's capability of referring to earlier posted documents. A certain facility can automatically reverse a posting document, and you can sort transaction documents and display the posting data from various points of view.

Using Currency Conversion for Consolidation

A variety of technical methods exist for carrying out currency conversion in preparation for consolidation. The following methods are the most widely used.

- Closing date method
- Modified closing date method
- Temporal method
- FASB 52: U.S. Dollar Perspective
- FASB 52: Foreign Currency Perspective

Groups of FS items in the balance sheet and the profit and loss statement are converted at one of three exchange rates.

- Current rate at the closing date
- Average rate
- Historical rate

FI-LC Consolidation can translate any line items at any rate and can use any method for any of the individual companies. This program provides solutions for several problems.

- Exchange differences can exist between the date of the transaction and the date of the currency conversion.
- Rounding differences can exist.
- The assets history sheet uses rates current on the reporting date.
- If a transaction difference is posted, the previous translation differences must be reversed.
- Translation differences can be treated so that they either have no impact or have a positive impact on profits. This might have to depend on the currency and the trading partner.

If line items from the balance sheet and the profit and loss statement are not translated at the same exchange rate, differences can arise between two accounting periods that will affect the totals when the individual items are summarized.

You can initiate a sensitivity analysis to discern the impact of currency translation on the overall results. In cases in which a translation difference is detected, you can display the line item groups that contributed to this difference. You may also want to discriminate the relative magnitude of such factors as the following:

- Proportion of foreign currency volume compared with total corporate volume
- Variation of translation differences with changes in key financial statement amounts, such as balance sheet totals and net income
- Differences arising due to historical, key date, and average exchange rate calculation methods
- Effects of exchange rate fluctuations during the fiscal year

The SAP R/3 FI-LC module provides a versatile array of functions for carrying out consolidation over all types of corporate structures and for analyzing the results and detecting any anomalies present.

Eliminating Intercompany Profit and Loss

The SAP method of reconciling accounts across a corporate group depends on the use of trading partner ID codes. When these are recognized, they cause automatic reconciliation at the line item level. When the data is presented for consolidation, the trading partner ID is used to identify candidate items for the process of eliminating intercompany Payables and Receivables and for eliminating intercompany revenue and expense items.

When the system searches for possible intercompany items that could be eliminated, it takes all constituent companies on a two-by-two basis and seeks items that fall into the following types of elimination sets.

- Intercompany sales
- Intercompany interest gain or loss
- Intercompany Payables and Receivables
- Intercompany loans

The search for balancing items is not always successful. The following are common reasons for differences.

- Currency translation differences
- Differences in the timing of postings, such as when goods are in transit
- Incorrect intercompany account assignments

It is customary to define the handling of goods in transit and the intercompany account assignments in the corporate guidelines. If all members of a corporate group use the standard SAP practice of reporting their balances in the transaction currency in addition to the local currency, then the system can display the differences due to currency translation.

NOTE   One of the most important benefits of using the SAP R/3 FI-LC module is that it can analyze the sources of elimination differences that arise between any pair of affiliated companies.

The reconciliation and elimination of intercompany Payables and Receivables between trading partners can often be executed with precision at the balance sheet item level. However, the profit and loss statement can embrace many revenue and expense items, which consequently makes it more difficult to reconcile.

The system accepts user-defined sets of accounts that can be allowed to engage in mutual offsetting. For example, you could perhaps offset the sales revenue and materials expense accounts with one another. Interest expense and interest revenue represent another compatible pair.

If you specify that the revenue item for a partner relationship is to be reported by group, the system attempts to match it by amount with an expense for the partner. The other option involves instructing the system to report all revenue and expense items in the partner relationship.

Reclassifying Capitalized Assets

If you use consolidated profit and loss statements in period accounting, sales revenue must be reclassified as other capitalized internal activities or as changes to inventory.

The transaction type code on the balance sheet documents identifies the reclassification, and the system automatically reposts the amounts if the receiving trading partner has capitalized assets supplied within the company.

Reclassifying Intercompany Profits to Inventory

Intercompany profit and loss elimination can be carried out on the basis of documents selected as follows:

- Inventory management records classified by product group and corporate group vendor
- Vendor records classified by product group and corporate group customer

It is necessary to obtain the book value and possibly the quantity of the inventory items used to eliminate intercompany profit and loss during consolidation. Allowance must be made for incidental costs and value adjustments. The vendor partner can provide detailed information about sales revenues and production costs or summarize this as an intercompany profit and loss percentage rate.

The retroactive calculation method first eliminates the book values of incidental costs and value adjustments for the inventory items. Then the system computes the difference this makes to the production costs for the same items. Alternatively, you can instruct the system to calculate a global percentage share. The final step is to deduce the change in intercompany profits from the prior accounting period and then post this amount to the profit and loss statement.

Accounting for Intercompany Fixed Asset Transfers

The company in the group issuing a fixed asset has records of the associated data, which includes the following:

- Acquisition costs
- Cumulative depreciation
- Depreciation method used
- Sales revenues
- Asset history sheet showing opening balance, acquisitions, divestitures, revaluations, and closing balance

The elimination process yields records that detail the following types of information, as appropriate for each asset transferred.

- Profit eliminated in the transfer year, calculated as acquisition value minus residual book value
- Details of the elimination of the acquisitions and divestitures from the asset history sheet
- Depreciation correction for the years before the transfer year
- Details of divestiture to external companies
- Details of resale within the company

The receiving company in the group maintains records containing the following types of information about each fixed asset transferred.

- Acquisition amount
- Depreciation method to be applied
- Asset history sheet, showing opening balance, acquisitions, divestitures, revaluations, and closing balance

The transfer of a fixed asset may have to be represented in the consolidated financial statements by the following actions.

- Eliminating the acquisition and divestiture from the asset history sheet in the year of transfer
- Making an appropriate adjustment to the profit and loss statement revenues
- Posting corrections to depreciation and intercompany profits for consolidations in years before the year of transfer
- Continuing making corrections each year until the asset is fully depreciated, or until it is sold to a company outside the corporate consolidation group

The full benefits of the SAP system in relation to the consolidation of fixed assets are best appreciated by installing and configuring both FI-AA and FI-LC.

Part
I

Ch
5

Consolidating Investments

The practice of consolidating investments is aimed at offsetting the investments of a direct parent company against the appropriate assets of the subsidiary. This ensures that there is no double reporting of the same asset in the consolidated financial statements. The basic method is to distribute the investment among the subsidiary, joint venture, and associated companies according to their proportional equity. The main procedures are step consolidation and simultaneous consolidation.

The methods for consolidation investments are assigned to individual companies without regard to any subgroup to which they may have been assigned. A methods table is compiled to record your decisions on which consolidation methods and variants are to be applied. Different methods can be used simultaneously.

Using Automatic Investment Consolidation

The FI-LC module processes the following types of investment transactions automatically.

- First consolidation
- Subsequent consolidation
- Successive acquisition and indirect changes in ownership
- Capital increases and decreases
- Complete divestiture
- Reporting

Using Fair Value Adjustment Postings

A fair value adjustment is a difference between the value of a balance sheet item on the consolidation date and the value in the investee's balance sheet. A lower value appears on the asset side, and a higher value appears on the liability side.

The FI-LC module automatically takes into account any fair value adjustments made. If an asset is partially owned by a company outside the consolidation group, this factor is also taken into account. The balance sheet and income statement are corrected at the same time that any of these factors are taken into consideration.

N O T E Goodwill and fair value adjustments are amortized by automatic postings and can be analyzed by a separate calculation.

Defining Goodwill

Goodwill is the difference derived from consolidating investments. It is capitalized as an intangible asset and is written off over the useful life of this asset, which has been prescribed by the legal authorities or by the company guidelines.

At the first consolidation, the goodwill value of an investment is computed by calculating the difference between the following entities.

- The corporate group's proportional share of the book value of the investment for the direct parent companies
- The proportional equity of the company to be consolidated

Silent reserves of equity holdings that exert no controlling influence are taken into account in calculating these proportions.

As an example, goodwill could be calculated as the difference between the value as a going concern and the breakup value of a purchased company. If additional benefits accrue, such as knowledge transfers and customer contacts, these would be valued as goodwill. Another example of goodwill could be the value of a purchased company that arises by eliminating this particular company as a competitor.

Badwill arises from the consolidation of investments as an accrued liability. It appears on the liability side of the balance sheet as a separate item. The badwill value arises when the acquisition costs for the investment in a company are less than the proportional present value or book value of the company's net assets.

Using the Consolidation Report Tree

The reporting tree is a standard SAP facility that displays the reports available as standards together with any reports you have defined for use in your company. Any particular types of report needed for the region of legal force in which you operate can also appear on the reporting tree. You can edit the display of the reporting tree.

In accordance with normal SAP practice, the consolidation reports are designed to collate the necessary records and then offer you the opportunity to direct your inquiry. You can do so by selecting and sorting subsets of the collated records and by adjusting the manner in which the totals are computed and displayed. By selecting an item in a report tree, you call up either the report itself or a screen in which you can select further details to refine the scope of the report. Standard drill-down facilities are provided so that you can access the records used to compile any data element that you select from your screen. A drill-down sequence is usually set up as a standard or customized feature when your system is first installed.

The top level of the consolidation reporting tree offers the following options.

- Master data
- Financial reporting data
- Control parameters
- Journal entries
- Totals report
- Report writer
- EIS drill-down reports

The report writer option points to a user-defined selection of standard and custom reports. The following list illustrates a typical user's report tree from the report writer branch.

- U.S. balance sheet and income statement
- U.S. income statement, level development
- U.S. industry segment information (with sublevel report choices)
- U.S. geographic region information (with sublevel report choices)
- U.S. cash flow statement
- Standard SAP reports (with sublevel report choices)
- Comparison reports
- Changes in value
- Changes in value by document types
- Group asset history sheet
- Receivables and Payables aging report
- Group quarterly income statement
- Income statements by quarters and by divisions

Many of the reports enable you to work interactively by using such options as the following:

- Branching to other reports
- Displaying break-down values by company or trading partner
- Displaying break-down values by subgroup or business area
- Displaying in the same report the comparable data for several years
- Calling upon predefined variants of the same report and displaying the results in a single report for comparison
- Calculating the variances between nominated columns of a displayed report

Two tools are available for designing reports or customizing standard reports.

- The consolidation database report function
- The Report Writer/Report Painter standard SAP tool for designing any report, and the display screens for presenting the results

Designing Custom Consolidation Reports

All reports must be designed on the basis of the values presented and the format to be displayed in print or on the screen. The format is defined by specifying three elements in the form of tables that can be edited by a user with suitable authorization.

- Page header
- Row construction
- Column layout

The header definition includes the text to be presented as titles and the names used to label the variables. Row construction specifies which FS item numbers are to be used. Each row construction specification is annotated to signify whether it is to be a text row, a value row, or a totals row.

The column layout table is responsible for defining the information that is to appear in the report. The following parameters are specified in the column layout table.

- Report version ID
- Range of periods to be considered
- Year
- Level of data

The level of the data is defined according to the particular report and the structure of the consolidation group, which interact with the methods of consolidation available. The level of data definition can include such levels as the following:

- Local values
- Corporate values
- Consolidated values

After you designate the data to be subject to valuation and the format of the report, you can direct the valuation program according to a further series of parameters.

- Whether the report will await a unique call from the user
- Whether the report will be bundled in a sequence of reports called by a single bundle identifier
- Whether the report will appear in various language versions
- Whether the displayed data will be scaled

Most reports can be directed at any of a variety of output media, such as the following:

- A menu-based display with programmed function keys
- A Windows display with standard scrolling functions
- A departmental or system printer
- A special purpose display to present a predesigned extract of the report results
- Output to a word-processor file that can be displayed under control of the user
- Output to a spreadsheet package

Using Active Excel

The totals held in the consolidation system database can be accessed directly from Microsoft Excel. If you have installed and configured additional software components, you can also access master data and transaction data to contribute to an Excel report. These add-ins also enable you to create a spreadsheet column by copying the profit and loss statement structure with the correct FS item numbers.

Part

I

Ch

5

If you opt for the active function, Microsoft Excel can access your R/3 system using RFC methodology and can retrieve the current values to go into your Excel report. When consolidation data is changed in R/3, the Excel spreadsheet is updated automatically.

The Excel spreadsheet report procedure offers additional facilities for calculating, formatting, and printing group reports. Once the format is specified, fresh data and subsequent period data can be displayed without additional report design.

The standard snapshot function enables you to capture the data at a particular instant. Extra flexibility is available by using pivot tables to effectively define pathways to the data of interest.

One of the advantages of accessing R/3 from Active Excel is that you can work in spreadsheet format, not only to see the results but also to adjust the tables of the parameters that control how R/3 retrieves information for the cells of the report.

Using Drill-down and Accessing Other Reports

The standard drill-down function makes use of re-keying rules that refocus a display, for instance, from the account level to the line item, or from the company code level to the parent company. These facilities are available in most reports.

An extension of the drill-down procedure is developing what can be called a report-to-report interface in which it should be possible to call virtually any report from any application integrated in your system, even if it is across a network. For example, you could obtain the line item value for a company for all its associated account balances and their constituent documents by calling upon the relevant report from FI-Financial Accounting after select the company from a display in your FI-LC module.

As an illustration, the following sequence could be initiated from the EIS.

1. Consolidated profit and loss statement
2. Individual company profit and loss statement
3. Reconciliation ledger
4. Project list from the R/3 PS Project System
5. Single project
6. Cost elements
7. Line item

This illustrative pathway to the line item of an individual project cost element is but one of many such pathways available from a report-to-report interface set up in an R/3 system of integrated applications.

Analyzing with Key Figures

A key figure is as a formula applied to specified variables or base factors. A key figure can be used in analysis for any of the following purposes.

- To clarify individual company and consolidated financial statements
- To support comparison with competing companies
- To support internal company control

Defined key figures can be displayed in any of three types of presentations.

- Chronological order
- External hierarchical comparison
- Internal hierarchical comparison

If one or more key figures yield markedly different results over time or over one of the structural divisions, then an explanation could be warranted because there may be an error, a change of business, or a change of market. Any of these events detected in time can trigger a useful improvement of profitability.

TIP When you are looking at a key figure display, you can arrange a split screen to reveal how the base factors relate to the results.

The following are useful key figures that are available as standard formulas and that could be presented over a range of fiscal years.

- Sales, and sales per employee
- Equity capital amount, also specified as a percentage of the balance sheet total
- Balance sheet total
- Employees at year end
- Investment in tangible assets
- Depreciation
- Cashflow amount, also specified as a percentage of sales
- Research and development costs

Trends in key figure results can be displayed in tabular format or as graphical presentations.

Using Simplified Schemes in Periodic Consolidation

Interim financial statements need not be particularly precise when compared to the year-end closing. Some consolidation simplifications can help reduce the costs of processing interim reports.

For example, a more global item line number can be selected for an interim report. In addition, there may be ways of allowing for unavoidable timing differences when eliminating intercompany Payables and Receivables. When investments must be consolidated on an interim basis, the system can post the profit and loss results from depreciation posting as accruals.

Using Consolidation Simulation

Each specification of a consolidation scheme is treated as a version. If you edit a version, the system automatically creates a new version number and stores the version you started with in its original form. With this mechanism, you can set up a simulation comprising any number of consolidation versions computed in parallel and from which your displays can select the factors in which you are interested.

For example, you could begin with the actual financial statement of an individual company and make a copy that would be automatically differentiated as a version of the actual. In the simulation copy, you can modify any of the consolidation methods because these are defined in the control tables and do not affect the base data or the standard software. For a comparative report, you could display the actual financial statement alongside the version you modified for the purposes of simulating the effect of a change in one or more parameters. ◉

Planning and Controlling

6

Controlling by Cost Management

In this chapter

Recognizing the Aims of Controlling

The prime aim of controlling is to hit the target. In business, the objective is a profit target related to the capital and other resources deployed—controlling relates to how these resources might realize more profit if they were otherwise engaged. From a business data processing standpoint, the act of controlling is defined as a set of management accounting tasks performed within a company. These management accounting operations are supplementary to legal requirements to produce the balance sheet and the profit and loss statement.

Defining Management Accounting

Management accounting, or controlling, can be defined as a set of phases or subobjectives with such titles as the following:

- Planning the value movements over a series of accounting periods
- Monitoring the relations between the planned value movements and the actual values achieved in the respective accounting periods
- Reporting the planned and the actual value movements
- Advising financial management and production management of reported discrepancies and anomalies in the reported data
- Advising financial management and production management of forecast discrepancies and anomalies in the anticipated value movements that might warrant preventive, precautionary, or palliative actions
- Informing all kinds of management of the relationships between planned and actual data in such a way as to make this information immediately intelligible and preferably indicative of the options for future activities

The method of controlling involves conceptualizing the company as a set of functional areas in which cost centers can be present. By definition, a cost center is an area in which costs are incurred. A cost center can be a unit within a company distinguished by area of responsibility, location, or accounting method. Departments such as Procurement, Production, Sales, and Marketing can be treated as cost centers, or particular items of productive resource can be nominated as the focal points to which costs are attributed in the cost center procedure.

If you have decided how to structure your company for the purpose of controlling and have produced a scheme or plan showing the cost centers, your next conceptual task is to arrive at a method of tracking the expenses and revenues so that these value changes can be assigned to the cost centers in your plan. A simple scheme is to send each invoice to one of the departments that holds the necessary funds. You can then see from the financial accounting records where your costs are incurred. However, several weaknesses arise in this plan. For instance, not all departments may have a budget. Furthermore, some departments may carry out a very wide range of diverse activities, which should really be differentiated by assigning at least some of them to specific cost centers so that management can consider the wisdom or profitability of that part of the enterprise.

A different approach involves noting every item of expense and every element of revenue. If you do this, you can later sort your notes in various ways to build up costs and revenues according to any particular scheme. As another option, you could use the SAP R/3 CO-Controlling module to make copies of all your transaction document details and hold them in a separate database. From this database, you could call for the values to be totaled in various ways to show how your costs and revenues have changed in successive periods.

If you wish to be prudent in the matter of spending, you must look to your cash flows. You can plan expenditures for some time ahead by assigning values to future accounting periods.

The scope of the controlling activities can and should cover all the various ways in which a company can increase or decrease its value. In particular, the controlling disciplines should be applied to the following business areas:

- Funds to manage the procurement, use, and creation of funds in all functional areas
- Financial and liquidity management, by planning and monitoring scheduled payments for projects and orders
- Capital investment controlling, to transfer activities to be capitalized so that depreciation and operating profits can be computed
- Cost and profitability accounting, to monitor the costs of all company activities

If your company is to be profitable, you must exercise planning and control over all its activities. In particular, you will want to use the established techniques in the following functional areas:

- Human resources
- Procurement controlling
- Logistics controlling
- Inventory controlling
- Sales controlling
- Asset controlling

Reviewing the Techniques of Overhead Cost Management

The function of overhead cost management is to plan, allocate, control, and monitor secondary costs. Several overlapping sets of techniques are available in the technical literature and are fully supported by SAP R/3 in the form of the modules comprising the CO-Controlling application. This section introduces the main techniques and points out some of their similarities and differences.

Using Cost and Revenue Element Accounting   This branch of cost accounting begins by identifying costs and revenues. It delimits the costing-based outlay costs and the opportunity costs by assigning them to cost elements (both primary and secondary) recognized by the financial accounting system as items in the chart of accounts.

Using Cost Center Accounting A cost center is an area or a virtual section of the enterprise in which costs are incurred and revenues are earned. The costs are allocated to the departments responsible for controlling them. Cost origins are identified in the cost centers.

Using Internal Activity Accounting Secondary costs can be allocated in proportion to the activities produced by the cost centers. These costs can be distributed on the basis of the activities in which several cost centers may be involved. See Chapter 7, "Costing on the Basis of Activities," for more details.

Using Overhead Cost Orders and Projects An operational order is created in a cost center for a concrete task or function. This order must be planned, controlled, and settled in detail. Complex orders are controlled by the PS-Project system, which is described in Chapter 8, "Controlling by the PS-Project System."

Assigning the Procedures of Cost Accounting

The SAP Business Navigator is a component of R/3 that is used to access the R/3 Reference model where all the available software is documented. If you select the overhead cost accounting area, you can access a matrix display of the standard processes and techniques available. On this matrix, you can signify which processes you intend to use to build a customized overhead cost accounting procedure for each of your cost accounting control areas. This section summarizes the principle costing tasks represented in the SAP R/3 system.

Completing the Assessment Procedure

The assessment method entails allocating all costs to a cost recipient or product. The primary costs and overhead costs must be associated with the product or service that has incurred them. Although the assessment procedure accumulates separate information on primary and secondary costs, they are combined to compute full costs. This procedure does not identify fixed and proportional components. The cost receivers are products or other units, and the secondary costs are allocated to them under the control of key codes. Planned and actual data can be compared.

Performing Overhead Surcharge Calculations

The overhead surcharge is similar to the assessment procedure, in that full costing is applied to the planned and actual values. No splitting of costs into fixed and proportional components occurs. However, cost center planning will have determined an hourly rate for each activity in the activity structure, and this rate is used to calculate the labor costs assigned to particular cost recipients or products. The remaining secondary costs are distributed as overheads.

Using Static Standard Costing

The cost center structure that is to use static standard costing is first divided into allocation bases, and activity types are defined so that quantities of activity can be allocated to them. These allocations of activities form the basis for costing. No splitting of costs into fixed and proportional components occurs. From the work plan, the calculated full activity prices are transferred to the activity quantity structure to compute the cost values.

Product costing on this basis can be used to compute the costs of goods manufactured and so provide values for the products sold. The value of the products sold, which is based on full costing, can then be used in cost-of-sales accounting. From the cost of sales, the profitability analysis for these products or services can then proceed.

Using Flexible Standard Costing Based on Marginal Costs

Costs are first split into fixed and proportional components based on dividing the cost center structure into activity types. Activity price calculation using planned activity prices then occurs to value the activity quantity structure.

The results enable you to improve decision making on marginal costs and help you determine short-term price floors because you can exercise analytical cost planning to calculate proportional costs. Cost object controlling yields the cost of goods manufactured using the full costs basis.

Using Profitability Analysis

Product costing based on the costs of goods manufactured can be used in cost of sales accounting to value sold products on the basis of full or marginal costing. Contribution margins can be calculated on the basis of marginal costs in profitability analysis because you have determined both the fixed and proportional costs.

Defining Cost Objects and Cost Centers

A *cost center* is an organizational unit that embraces a unique set of cost origins. Activity types or primary and secondary cost elements are regarded as *cost origins*.

A cost center can coincide with an operational department, or it can be defined in terms of its functional area. Geographical characteristics can be used to specify a cost center. Yet another way of dividing up your company for the purposes of controlling is to recognize ownership or the location of responsibility. You can define some cost centers in terms of how the transactions are to be settled.

The main criterion for judging the quality of a scheme of cost centers is how well you can use it for the following related tasks:

- To allocate secondary costs to sales activities in a meaningful manner that calculates the costs of sales
- To control in detail how costs are incurred within the enterprise

Using Cost Objects

The basis of computer support for business controlling is the *cost object*, which is an account assignment term that points to a database record structure in which actual data can be stored. A cost object can hold the details of costs, budgets, sales revenues, and other data objects that represent value.

The cost object section of the database is identified with a cost object that is recognized by the employees of your company, such as an individual product or a product group. The defining feature of a cost object is that you must be able to identify a quantity of at least one activity that is associated with the object, such as a manufacturing process or the warehousing of a quantity of material. A cost object can be inactive in an accounting period because no work is being done there, but it will still incur costs in terms of maintenance and investment.

You can also associate a cost object with a physical place or a section of a physical place that is differentiated by its use. In a production plant, you can classify groups of resources using industry-specific criteria. For instance, you could define some cost objects in terms of recognized shop floor areas in which certain types of work is performed. After assigning a shop floor area number, you could then post the costs incurred there to a cost object data structure associated with this number.

Defining Cost Objects

A cost object is an activity unit represented by a Controlling Object–Costs data object. The function of a cost object is to collect costs or sales revenues and the data that identifies their origins. A cost object can be specialized according to the type of object for which it collects costs or sales revenues, such as a production order.

A cost object represents a concept that is particularly important when using the CO-Controlling application. A cost object is the main data object of preliminary costing, simultaneous costing, and final costing. Other entities from the integrated logistics modules can also be used as specializations of the Controlling Object–Costs object. The following entities can function as specialized cost objects:

- Procurement or requisition order
- Material as a finished product
- Production order
- Assembly order
- Run schedule header
- Process order
- Network
- Sales order
- Work breakdown structure element

A cost object can be one of several objects that contribute costs and revenues to a business area. In addition, a cost object can be one of several objects that post costs and revenues to a company code.

NOTE A cost object is always assigned to exactly one cost accounting area in which there is a common method of cost accounting using the same business year division.

Developing Overhead Cost Management

The function of overhead cost management is to plan, allocate, control, and monitor secondary costs. The secondary costs are expenses for which one single receiving data object cannot be directly and fully identified according to the cost-by-cause principle. Consider these examples:

- Secondary expenses, such as building insurance
- Secondary labor costs, such as supervisor wages
- Secondary materials costs, such as coolant cleaning materials

Secondary costs that cannot be allocated directly and completely to operational activity units, such as products and services, must be assigned to subareas within a cost accounting area. A cost center for each subarea must receive the costs or revenues and then distribute them to the operational activity units, such as products.

The SAP R/3 approach to controlling is elaborated in the CO application and therefore is integrated with both the FI-Financial Accounting application and also with any other application that has been installed and configured. The following components comprise the SAP CO-Controlling module and constitute an integrated system for overhead cost controlling:

- CO-CCA Cost Center Accounting
- CO-ABC Activity-Based Cost Accounting
- CO-OPA Order and Project Accounting
- CO-PA Profitability Analysis
- CO-PCA Profit Center Accounting

The FI-SL Special Purpose Ledger module uses accounts that are based on a range of subledgers that enable overhead cost analyses from different points of view. For example, accounts can focus on cost centers, product costs, or activities. These facilities are provided so that the SAP R/3 CO-Controlling application can be used as an internal accounting system that is fully integrated with financial accounting.

The implementation of a controlling function in an organization is carried out in an SAP R/3 system in the following phases:

- Defining the structure of the organization in terms of units to be controlled
- Setting up information flows that can monitor the performance of the controllable units
- Running the controlling system through cycles of the controlling tasks, which are repeated at a frequency suited to the type of business process

The R/3 system integrates all these phases by offering standard business programs that are fully integrated with each other. If you install the system in your company, the SAP Customizing procedures prompt you to select the functions that match your requirements. You are also invited to provide such details as the specific terms and names of work units so that the system is an accurate representation of your company.

Placing Cost Centers in a Structure

The structure of a business organization can be seen from different points of view. One company might see itself as a group of complete and self-sufficient units reporting to a head office; another might think of the main functional areas, such as Procurement, Production, Sales, and Marketing.

To make use of a fully integrated system and exploit the value-adding functions available in a modern, computer-based installation, it is necessary to define an organization in terms of a detailed structure of cost centers with specified relationships between them.

The SAP R/3 system with the CO-Controlling component gives you the functionality you need to capture the structure of your company in the form of a comprehensive cost center plan that clearly defines the responsibility structure of your company. When you have such a structure, the system uses it to run all the controlling functions.

This structure must be rich enough in features to capture any type of organization and express it in a form that can be used by the computer system to carry out automatically as many of the necessary operations as possible. When automatic operation is not possible or required, the system should be capable of providing as much support and guidance as possible, and should make the work as efficient and effective as circumstances allow.

Adapting the R/3 Organizational Structure

The structure of an organization from an accounting point of view must be formally defined if it is to be used by a computing system. SAP R/3 defines a multilevel structure in terms of nested classifications, known collectively as the Enterprise Data Model (EDM). The EDM model is outlined as follows:

- *Client* is a name attached to a data set that cannot overlap any other client data set. For example, TEST and TRAINING could be clients with separate data sets. Standard SAP R/3 works with only one client at a time.
- *Company code* is the identification number of an independent accounting unit that can generate its own financial statements. It is a legal requirement that a group operating in several countries must establish a separate company code unit for each country. The system must record all the transaction data necessary to compile the balance sheet and the profit and loss statement for a company code. A company can comprise one or more company codes.
- *Business area* is a subdivision of a client that further classifies the value movements posted to the General Ledger of a parent company code. The business area is not an independent business unit, although it manages the transaction information and the financial results shown in the company code balance sheet and the profit and loss statement, insofar as they concern that particular business area.
- *Controlling area* takes into cost accounting both the accounting units, such as company codes and business areas, and the logistics units, such as plant and sales organization. A controlling area can embrace several company codes, provided that they all share a common chart of accounts. All internal allocation transactions must refer only to objects within the same controlling area.

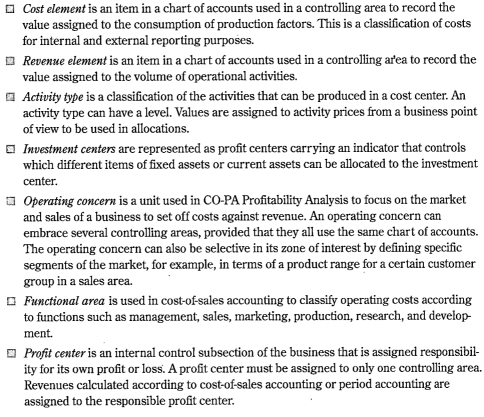

- *Cost element* is an item in a chart of accounts used in a controlling area to record the value assigned to the consumption of production factors. This is a classification of costs for internal and external reporting purposes.

- *Revenue element* is an item in a chart of accounts used in a controlling area to record the value assigned to the volume of operational activities.

- *Activity type* is a classification of the activities that can be produced in a cost center. An activity type can have a level. Values are assigned to activity prices from a business point of view to be used in allocations.

- *Investment centers* are represented as profit centers carrying an indicator that controls which different items of fixed assets or current assets can be allocated to the investment center.

- *Operating concern* is a unit used in CO-PA Profitability Analysis to focus on the market and sales of a business to set off costs against revenue. An operating concern can embrace several controlling areas, provided that they all use the same chart of accounts. The operating concern can also be selective in its zone of interest by defining specific segments of the market, for example, in terms of a product range for a certain customer group in a sales area.

- *Functional area* is used in cost-of-sales accounting to classify operating costs according to functions such as management, sales, marketing, production, research, and development.

- *Profit center* is an internal control subsection of the business that is assigned responsibility for its own profit or loss. A profit center must be assigned to only one controlling area. Revenues calculated according to cost-of-sales accounting or period accounting are assigned to the responsible profit center.

The software of the SAP R/3 system is designed so that you can use the standard functions on the data objects as defined in the system. This initial structure is defined as the R/3 Reference Model. Any of the structures in this model can be replicated and linked to completely match the structure of your company. None of these copying and linking activities disturb the underlying software, so the enterprise data model that you construct works perfectly when you use it in production. This model also works perfectly if you populate the enterprise data model with planned data as part of your controlling endeavors.

Part
II

Ch
6

Planning and Controlling a Business with R/3

In accordance with the basic divide-and-measure approach to business control, it is useful to differentiate the operational controlling systems from the functional controlling systems. The operational controlling systems are provided with SAP R/3 components to support the following four operational tasks:

- Capital investment controlling, which transfers activities to be capitalized and used to calculate depreciation and operating profits

- Financial controlling, which monitors and plans scheduled payments from projects and orders

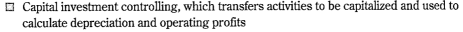

☐ Funds controlling, which oversees the procurement, use, and creation of funds in all areas

☐ Cost and profit controlling, which monitors the costs of all company activities

Controlling with Job Orders

Each SAP R/3 application can process various types of orders that represent simple jobs within a controlling area. An order can be used for planning, monitoring, and allocating costs. The following types of orders are distinguished by their business significance in the SAP R/3 application indicated:

☐ Imputed cost (CO-Controlling)

☐ Overhead cost order (CO-Controlling)

☐ Capital investment order (CO-Controlling)

☐ Orders with revenue (CO-Controlling)

☐ Maintenance order (PM-Plant Maintenance)

☐ Production order (PP-Production Planning)

☐ Assembly order (PP-Production Planning)

☐ Run schedule header (PP-Production Planning)

☐ Process order (PP-Production Planning)

Job orders tend to focus particularly on the activities needed to achieve a business result.

Using Projects as Control Structures

A project is a data structure used to represent a complex structured job taking place within a controlling area. The project is used to plan, control, and monitor the schedule, resources, capacities, costs, revenues, and availability of funds. A project cannot be assigned to a General Ledger account or to a special purpose ledger account.

A work breakdown structure (WBS) element is a concrete task or subtask that can be further subdivided. A WBS element can be costed and assigned to an account.

For more information about projects, see Chapter 8, "Controlling by the PS-Project System."

Accounting with Cost Elements

The SAP R/3 standard business functions provide all the functionality needed to support most modern cost accounting systems.

The main differences between costing concepts arise in connection with the scope of the costs they include and the structure of these costs with respect to the organization structure. Variations in the use of standard versus actual costs exist, and other variations affect the allocation of costs directly to the products or services, in contrast to allocating them to overhead. Methods can also differ in the relationships between cost center activities, such as in the use of primary costs, cost components, and secondary cost breakdown.

Operating Cost Element Accounting

Cost element accounting demands organized recording so that the costs incurred during a particular settlement period are accurately recorded and sorted. When you operate the SAP R/3 integrated system, each business event relevant to cost accounting generates a document that bears information about the cost element and the account assignment of its posting.

Cost element accounting is a standard approach that is integral to the R/3 system. Functions are predefined to create and maintain cost element master data and to calculate imputed cost elements. The R/3 system can mediate the importing and incorporation of posting data from external systems. Full reporting occurs on cost elements. Individual business transactions are structured, recorded, assigned, and reported using the FI-GL General Ledger profit and loss account structure.

Defining the Cost and Revenue Element

There is a legal requirement to distinguish between costs that arise in a company code, as follows:

- Primary cost and revenue elements for goods and services procured externally
- Secondary cost elements attributable to internal activities

A cost element is a classification code. This is a mandatory data field on transactions that involve costs arising in a company code. A cost element is used to label and differentiate the types of cost, which affects how each is posted.

Primary cost elements are maintained in the General Ledger master records. Secondary cost elements have no counterpart in the financial accounts and are maintained exclusively in cost accounting.

It has always been the case that the proportion of secondary to total costs is high in a service industry compared to manufacturing. However, this proportion is increasing rapidly as, for example, automation takes a larger share of secondary costs in relation to the production costs that can be allocated directly to materials and procured services.

Cost elements are formally classified according to their use or origin, such as material cost elements, settlement cost elements for orders, and cost elements for internal cost allocations. A primary cost element is an item in the chart of accounts in which the values are recorded to represent the consumption of production factors such as raw materials and energy.

Part
II

Ch
6

A cost element is also used to maintain a collection of information, in particular, the transaction documents that bear the code of the cost element and that have been selected, for example, for a specific accounting period. The cost element concept ensures that each business transaction posted under a particular cost element in the CO-Controlling system is properly assigned to the relevant cost centers, orders, projects, cost objects, and so on.

Each material issue in MM-Materials Management, each invoice recorded in SD-Sales and Distribution, and each external invoice in MM-IV Invoice Verification flows via the FI-GL General Ledger account to the appropriate cost or profit object. The expense accounts of the FI-GL General Ledger chart of accounts are automatically adopted by the CO-Controlling system as primary cost elements. Additional primary cost elements must be added to the financial chart of accounts to accommodate accruals and imputed costs. The aim is to ensure that all the costs incurred in a particular accounting period and documented in the CO-Controlling system are properly reconciled with the General Ledger. It is also possible to establish a default coding block (cost center) for a particular cost element.

Secondary cost elements are created and managed only in CO-Controlling. They represent value flows such as the following:

- Internal cost allocation
- Surcharge allocation
- Settlement transactions

Using Cost Element Parameters

The CO-Controlling system carries an extensive set of standard cost elements that you can adopt and edit for your own installation. A matchcode search facility helps locate the one you want on the basis of a specific name or label that you have assigned. The matchcode search can also include values such as order number ranges and dates to narrow the field of your search. You can strike out those you are unlikely to need.

The standard cost elements begin with certain established parameters,. such as the following:

- Default coding block assignment
- Whether quantities are recorded in addition to values
- How costs are displayed in reports

N O T E The system logs any changes you make to the cost element masters.

Classifying Cost Elements

The following cost element types are recognized by the SAP R/3 system because their documents bear a key code:

- Primary cost elements
- Imputed cost elements
- Revenue elements
- Sales deductions
- Cost elements for external order settlement
- Cost elements for internal order settlement
- Assessment cost elements
- Cost elements for internal activity allocation

Reporting on Cost Element Group Structures

A cost element group is a technical term for a set of cost elements, such as salaries and bonuses. The cost element group can be used to define lines and columns in reports that use the appropriate records. The cost element groups can be used for planning purposes. No constraints govern how you combine and structure cost elements in a cost element group. You can display a cost element group in the form of a tree diagram. The hierarchies and subhierarchies of a cost element group can be deployed without constraint. You can use cost element groups to arrange the structure, or you can use cost objects (such as personnel costs) or function-oriented criteria (such as purchasing and sales).

One task of planning for secondary costs is to define standards that help control these costs and assign reasonable values to the internal activity costs. Secondary costs are charged to the cost centers where they were incurred, or to the jobs that led to their occurrence. Secondary costs therefore can be charged according to their origin defined by the location where the work takes place or the activities are involved.

Planning occurs using target costs that can adjust the plan account for operating rate changes. At the end of the accounting period, the target and the actual costs can be compared, and the results can be used to modify appropriate controls.

Checking Posting Data in Cost Accounting

Each posting from cost accounting to an account assignment object is controlled by a reference check that first confirms that the cost object exists and then locks the entry. Validation is the process of applying individual checks in addition to the reference check. The user can define logical rules and conditions that can refer to any data held by R/3 at the time. You can specify whether a query should lead to a warning or an error message.

When the posting occurs, the system checks to see whether the account assigned for the relevant cost center is also allocated to a profit center. In such a case, an automatic extra posting occurs. This is a so-called statistical posting that does not cause a false value movement by posting the same amount twice. *Substitution* is the name given to the process of changing posting data characteristics. As with validation, this automatic process depends on the outcome of a logical conditional checking procedure that can be set up by the user.

Posting to an Auxiliary or Statistical Cost Accounting Assignment

The CO module receives the primary data as a General Ledger posting from financial accounting. However, the account assignment term in this posting document can be expanded by adding assignments to various auxiliary or statistical cost accounting objects. For example, you might have a statistical order to accumulate cost data about a specific job.

The system always makes sure that only one cost accounting object acts as the cost object and is posted with costs. All the others are treated to a statistical posting that is identified as such so that it is used only for statistical purposes, never for totaling costs.

Using Imputed Costs Accruals

Some data posted to cost accounting is necessarily the same as in financial accounting. However, some costs are incurred without a corresponding expense posting in financial accounting. Furthermore, some business expenses are posted differently in financial accounting and cost accounting because a different quantity unit or different valuation rates are used. The accounting period most useful when controlling a business is seldom the same period used for financial accounting.

These kinds of discrepancies must be reposted in financial accounting as imputed costs so that the true value of the resources consumed in production in the period can be totaled. To effect this reconciliation, it is necessary to use accruals that assign imputed costs to the financial accounting periods under an account heading that indicates their cause.

Two sources of data exist for calculating imputed costs:

☐ Imputed costs are computed in financial accounting, are posted as a recurring entry in financial accounting, and are passed to cost accounting.

☐ Imputed costs are computed in cost accounting by using the costs already posted there.

Three methods of calculating imputed costs exist in cost accounting:

☐ Cost element percentage surcharge

☐ Planned = actual allocation

☐ Target = actual allocation

Imputing Costs as a Percentage Surcharge

If you know the cost elements, you can build up a database from which to calculate the imputed costs for each financial period by allocating a percentage surcharge to each period. You can do this for both planned data and actual costs, by period and by cause. For example, you might accrue a Christmas bonus as if it were a monthly cost throughout the year by posting it to a cost element in the General Ledger titled Imputed Christmas Bonus.

 TIP Any number of cost elements can be linked by a tracing factor, from which a value is calculated by applying an overhead percentage rate.

Imputing Costs by the Planned = Actual Procedure

If no relevant historical values or quantities are available to enter into your base cost elements, you can make a plan or estimate of them across the relevant time periods and by cause. Then you can instruct the system to post the planned values as imputed costs and later, if necessary, post an adjustment when the actual cost data becomes available. You might accrue insurance charges by assuming that the actual costs will equal the planned and distributed-as-planned across the periods.

Imputing Costs by the Target = Actual Procedure

If you expect your costs to be directly related to the operating output, you can use the techniques of activity-based cost accounting to arrive at target values. The more activity that takes place, the greater the imputed cost.

The system posts the target activity costs as imputed costs to the relevant financial accounting periods and causes as represented by the cost objects. Again, you must instruct the system to make an adjustment posting when the actual values can be obtained.

The Role of Imputed Cost Calculation Objects

An imputed cost calculation object is one of a number of results analysis objects used to reconcile balances between financial accounting and other applications. Financial accounting must remain reconciled with cost accounting. This means that no balance should emerge as a cost that is not identified in financial accounting.

To achieve this, an imputed cost calculation object is created that is credited every time a cost center is debited for an imputed cost calculation. When the expense is actually posted, the appropriate imputed cost calculation object is debited by a corresponding amount. At the end of the year, the user must transfer any remaining balance to profitability analysis or reallocate it by distributing it to cost centers or by reposting it to some other account.

Allowing for Price Variances

The CO-Controlling system can calculate the influence of price fluctuations for each posting transaction. The difference is displayed as a variance in the SAP document that records the transaction.

The SAP MM-Materials Management application can provide the difference between the standard price of a material and the moving average price. These price variances can affect the difference between target and actual values, for example.

Differences can be computed between the actual cost to the cost center and the value posted to it from FI-Financial Accounting. The difference as a percentage share of the actual value can be distributed across a number of cost centers.

Using the Reconciliation Ledger

The reconciliation ledger is maintained by a group of functions with the aim of integrating the internal and external accounting systems. The reconciliation ledger must provide facilities to overview and reconcile any value flows arising within cost accounting that affect the balance sheet and the profit and loss statement of the enterprise.

The data in the reconciliation ledger is summarized, compressed, and evaluated. Allocations in cost accounting can cross company code boundaries, or functional areas or business areas. If any of these cross allocations occur, they are registered in the reconciliation ledger, from where they can be automatically or manually assigned to appropriate accounts.

The reconciliation ledger consolidates the data from company code and business area controlling cost objects according to a user-selected set of controlling object types. These are related to the cost elements of the General Ledger to which they are posted.

Transactions between company codes and across business or functional areas must be reconciled by clearing accounts in the reconciliation ledger. This way, the value flows finally reported in the consolidated balance sheet and the profit and loss statement are accurate reflections of the net value flows in the corporate group.

An additional service performed by the reconciliation ledger is to offer a navigation aid through the controlling accounts, starting with the profit and loss accounts of the General Ledger. It is always possible to drill down through the reconciliation ledger structure to the cost controlling objects of the constituent company codes.

The flexible SAP R/3 reporting system enables you to analyze cost elements from any point of view:

- By individual cost elements, cost element groups, or subgroups
- By other cost objects, such as cost centers, orders, and projects

Implementing Cost and Profit Controlling

The modular structure of SAP R/3 applications is designed to enable you to implement progressively according to the developments and requirements of your company. The application modules are discussed in a sequence that is in accordance with this concept of progressive implementation.

CO-CCA Cost Center Accounting is specialized to help you plan, monitor, control, and settle all business activities and responsibilities. This module has functions to create and maintain cost center master data and to accept or modify definitions of statistical key figures. Cost center postings and transfers have their specialized functions, as have distribution, assessment, and allocation between cost centers. Primary cost elements can be used in the planning functions for cost centers. The user can define the screen and printed report layout formats from the cost center reporting system. Planning functional dependencies and the detailed planning of cost centers are supported by the CO-CCA Cost Center Accounting component.

Activity-based cost accounting is used to cost the internal flow of activities with functions to plan, evaluate, and allocate. CO-OPA Order and Project Accounting is specialized in the tasks of planning, monitoring, and settling the activities, services, and processes that take place as the result of internal orders and projects. These two modules are covered in Chapter 7, "Costing on the Basics of Activities."

CO-PA Profitability Analysis is required to report on the business viability of complex sales organizations and complex product hierarchies. See Chapter 9, "Analyzing Profitability," for more information.

Applying the Controlling Area Concept

Navigating through the details of a controlling system involves using the Business Navigator component. This improves the presentation of a structure made up of units and links that can also be accessed directly. This structure is stored in the SAP R/3 system and can be inspected in various ways, including by a graphical representation. The structure can be the same topological network as the management structure, with each level of managers reporting to more senior managers on the level above.

Traditional business organizations tend to have a pyramid structure, rising to the owner on the pinnacle. Government and military organizations are notorious for having very tall pyramids. Modern, small companies in the high-tech domain are notorious for having very flat structures, very few layers of management, and a boss who is ready to speak to anyone at almost any time. The logical justification for any type of structure is based on the demands placed on it by external circumstances and by the owner's need to exert some control over it.

The controlling area of the owner is perhaps limited to the managing director or the chief executive officer. This person has a controlling area of the whole company. The department heads have controlling areas defined by the territory of their departments—or perhaps their controlling areas are better specified by the activities for which they are responsible.

The SAP R/3 CO-Controlling module holds master data on the controlling areas that you establish for your company. These can correspond exactly with the departments that exist already, but if you are looking for a method of adding value to information and material as they pass through your company, it would be prudent to at least consider other ways of setting up controlling areas.

What you should look for are profit centers that can be controlled on the basis of the measured profit they contribute to the company. One or more of these profit centers constitute an area of responsibility that is a proper subject for the application of controlling area discipline.

The conceptual tools of area controlling include the following types of cost objects:

- The *cost center* is defined as a place in which costs are incurred. The cost center may be a unit within a company distinguished by area of responsibility, location, or accounting method.

- The *order* is an instrument for planning and controlling costs of what can be considered a relatively simple job. In a business environment, the order is represented by a document. In the SAP environment, the order is an SAP document, which has a standard set of constituent parts and is subject to strict internal control by the computer system. This ensures that the system can follow the legal requirements of an audit trail.

- The *project* is an instrument for planning and controlling costs during a complex job. The defining characteristic of a project is that it must achieve a certain result in a specified time without exceeding its budget. Many types of projects exist, including capital-spending, research and development, engineer-to-order manufacturing, investment program, and data processing and customer project.

The individual cost object is also an instrument for planning and controlling costs. Whatever work is undertaken (whether planning, controlling, informing, and so on), certain features can be used to focus the computation of costs. The cost object need not be a real object, and it doesn't really have to engage in any activity that consumes resources or generates revenue. The cost object can be just a convenient conceptual destination that can appear in the accounts with accrued costs or revenues. On the other hand, the accounts might be easier to interpret if most cost objects represent tangible units of products or resources that are recognized as such by the people who work with them.

Defining Profitability Segments

The control of a business could be improved if information is collected separately about part of it. For example, a calculation of profitability entails comparing costs and revenues. It might make sense to compute profitability over some aggregate of your business activities. You can define this sector or segment of your business by using any combination of data terms that already exist in your system.

You could create a master record for a market or a business segment structure based on the sales of certain products, in a specified market area, over a range of accounting periods. Another example of a segment would be the value of the raw materials in each possible location in which there exists spare capacity for additional production. This defines a segment in a dynamic fashion because different locations could be chosen each time on the basis of spare production capacity.

In logical terms, a controlling area is defined as a set of accounting units within an organization that all use the same cost accounting configuration. Usually, the controlling area is coextensive with the company code, which usually stands for an individual company in a corporate structure. For cross-company cost accounting, one controlling area can be assigned to cover the areas of responsibility of more than one company code.

These conceptual tools have been efficiently programmed into the SAP standard business processes in the most useful of forms, the generic form. You can customize the generic form to fit your particular circumstance. For example, you can record in the master data how you want to define the business segments and how you want to select which cost objects to monitor. You also can determine how orders and projects are assigned to cost centers.

The CO-Controlling module accepts your requirements and delivers a flexible controlling system that fits your company.

Understanding the Flow of Control Data

CO-Controlling uses transaction data from the FI-GL General Ledger accounts to maintain its own set of records. Overhead costs are posted to a cost center according to their source of origin. The CO-Controlling system uses additional postings to assign the primary costs to other cost objects, such as orders, processes, other cost objects, and business segments.

CO-Controlling shares both primary costs and overhead costs among the assignment objects according to their use. The CO module also allocates the values to other cost objects for the purposes of control and analysis.

Revenue and sales deductions are posted directly to the relevant business segment or profit center. The cost objects either remain in inventory or are posted to profitability analysis. As a result, you can conduct period accounting at the profit center level, taking into account changes in inventory. You also can call for cost of sales accounting in each business segment.

CO-Controlling operates a system that is parallel to the FI-Financial Accounting system but separate from it. You can display a business-oriented profit and loss analysis because all the data objects that have a bearing on the computation of value added are represented in the analysis and can therefore be scrutinized down to the details of the individual transactions from which the data is drawn. The cost data is allocated according to rules under your control. You should encounter no obscurity in interpreting the analysis reports.

Customer quotations and sales orders produce the information that CO-PA Profitability Analysis needs:

- Billing documents
- Sales quantities
- Revenues
- Sales deductions

Goods that are issued, received, or manufactured produce the information necessary for the calculation of the following:

- Manufacturing costs
- Standard costs
- Moving average price
- Transfer prices

External activities carried out by contractors, for example, are either posted directly to CO-PA Profitability Analysis from FI-Financial Accounting, or they are settled from the orders and projects, which also input to CO-PA Profitability Analysis.

Analysis for separate business segments can be conducted because cost and revenue data can be posted directly to a business segment, just as they can be posted to any cost center. Any of the following systems can carry out direct postings automatically:

- FI-Financial Accounting
- CO-Controlling
- MM-Materials Management
- SD-Sales and Distribution

In contrast, a profit center is not a separate account assignment object. The values held by it are derived from the master data assignments of the cost objects in the CO-Controlling system.

The postings are treated as statistical values because they do not contribute to the balance sheet and the profit and loss statement—their values have already been recorded in the General Ledger. Posting these values to a profit center occurs automatically under the supervision of the CO-PCA Profit Center Accounting standard business functions.

Connecting Financial Accounting with Controlling

At the heart of every accounting system must be the General Ledger, and the SAP system is no exception. The FI-Financial Accounting module serves the FI-GL General Ledger.

The chart of accounts contains all the accounts available to a company. Every company, and therefore every unit identified by a company code, must be assigned to the same chart of accounts if cost accounting is to be applied to the whole organization.

The concept of the controlling area is integral to the internal controlling functions. In simple company structures, only one controlling area can exist, and it will therefore be co-extensive with the company code. Complex corporate structures can distribute the constituent company codes among several controlling areas.

Each controlling area is assigned a chart of accounts. This ensures that every transaction in each area is posted to an account in the chart of accounts. Therefore, every transaction is reconciled and participates in the financial accounting that provides the balance sheet and the profit and loss accounts required by law. Different controlling areas can operate with different charts of accounts, either because this is more convenient or because the local legal authority requires it.

The CO-Controlling system uses the FI-GL General Ledger accounts directly. In particular, this system uses the FI-GL General Ledger profit and loss accounts as primary cost and revenue elements.

With certain exceptions, the CO-Controlling system needs no separate reconciliation with the FI-GL General Ledger and its subledger accounting systems. The exceptions arise if you use the special feature of CO-Controlling that manages imputed costs or accruals. CO-Controlling enables you to create imputed costs at a level of detail other than that used in financial accounting—you can record costs that have no equivalent, or that have an equivalent with a different value, in the accounts of financial accounting. These intentional differences can be reconciled and cleared by using the CO-Controlling functions provided for this purpose.

Secondary cost elements are maintained by CO-Controlling in addition to the primary accounts of the FI-GL General Ledger. This constitutes a two-level system of accounts—each level can record accounting data using a different degree of detail.

However, the extra details maintained by CO-Controlling in the secondary cost elements are integrated with the FI-GL General Ledger accounts by means of the controlling areas, which are represented in the common chart of accounts. In accordance with Generally Accepted Accounting Principles (GAAP) standards, it is possible to trace any transaction posted on the General Ledger down through the controlling area to the cost center, which holds all the details of the cost elements used to compute it.

The value flow in the subledgers of the FI-GL General Ledger is always reconciled via special reconciliation accounts. You can always analyze data into summaries using these accounts, which provide you with such reports as monthly debits and credits, account balances, and so on. You can inspect individual business transactions as well. With this kind of functionality, you can substantiate any value shown in your trial balance.

If you have installed and configured an SAP application such as CO-Controlling, you have an additional and parallel way of looking at the value flows in your organization. But because the system is fully integrated, you know that the values and value flows revealed by the external accounting documents, the balance sheet, and the profit and loss statement are fully reconciled with the value flows uncovered by your parallel internal accounting system (implemented using the standard business functions of the SAP CO-Controlling module). You have a fresh way of looking at how the values change by doing business.

Understanding the Value-Adding Process and the Role of Cost Objects

In simple terms, a *cost object* is something that incurs costs. Two cost objects cost twice as much, and 10 of them cost 10 times as much. A cost object can represent a product.

You can declare that a particular cost object exists in a market segment by entering it in the master record of that segment. This cost object could also be identified in the processes of inventory accounting.

A cost center is charged overhead because that is where the costs originated. Overhead posted to that cost center then is transferred to the cost objects that are the responsibilities of that cost center. The proportion of the overhead allocated can be determined according to the quantities of cost objects. In this way, the cost object bears a share of the overhead.

Revenues and sales deductions are reported in the relevant market segments and profit centers. You can use period accounting at the profit center level, incorporating changes to the inventory in the period. You can also use cost-of-sales accounting at the market segment level.

N O T E   The cost object method enables you to use an accurate system of accounting to help you control the value-adding business processes of your company. ☐

Using Integrated Planning and Decision Support

One important decision to be made involves the product mix. You want to make sure that you optimize the contribution of each product line to the profit margin. Your methods include tentative variations in the planned production costs, which the system develops through the work flows of your organization to arrive at the planned values in each area of interest. You can display any combination of planned values for any cost object or set of objects, right up to the planned figures for the entire company.

This is integrated planning, and it depends on the following functions programmed in the CO-Controlling system:

- Planned assessment, distribution, and accruals of imputed costs
- Planned allocation of internal activities
- Planned assessment of costs on orders and projects

These functions cannot succeed unless you provide the data or tell the system how to find them. The system supports you in this preparation by guiding you through these essential tasks and performing the necessary calculations automatically wherever possible:

- Planning of cost centers
- Planning of internal orders and projects
- Determining standard costs of products for stock production and for unit costing of customer orders
- Planning contribution margins and profits in sales management

Again, the system needs information to help you in the development of your plans. CO-Controlling provides the program support for the following preliminaries:

- Creating the activity plan, using the activities for each work center and cost center
- Integrating detailed planned sales quantities for the individual reference objects, including assigned costs and revenue, with the production plan
- Developing automatic standard cost estimates based on bills of materials and routings

Reporting in CO-Controlling

The SAP Executive Information System (EIS) and the reporting facilities of CO-Controlling are fully integrated. Within the SAP R/3 computer system, the reporting facilities are highly flexible. Reports are easy to define for *ad hoc* purposes and are also easy to maintain as needs change. The content and format are virtually unlimited and can be differentiated by user groups.

Reports can be stored, recalled, and processed by the SAP graphics presentation component. Online navigation facilities make it easy for you to switch between report formats without losing the focus of your inquiry. For example, you can select an item on a list and use the function keys to call up a more detailed report on the item selected.

Standard predefined reports are available for the following purposes:

- To compare actual values with the planned entries
- To compare the performance of different cost objects, such as cost centers, orders, and projects
- To assemble balance lists and balances of activities
- To inspect individual line items

You can select a cost center and call up all the settlement objects linked to it. You can also trace the costs on each object, back to the individual business transactions that caused them.

N O T E Reports designed in the CO-Controlling module are applicable to all CO components.

Integrating CO with R/3 Applications

All the information in all the R/3 applications installed and configured is available directly. The CO-Controlling system can call upon any of the information outputs of the system—from the annual sales and production plan to the individual planning steps, and down to the planning and processing details of individual orders.

For example, standard business functions are available for the following tasks:

- Using bills of material and routings to prepare cost estimates for products and orders
- Updating a costing as production progresses by transferring times and material valuations automatically as they become available
- Evaluating quantities used of supplies and raw materials
- Evaluating semifinished and finished products in stock
- Using cost-of-sales accounting to provide an ongoing analysis of profitability based on invoiced sales quantities

The success of a controlling function depends on the integration of planned and actual data at all stages and levels of the production process.

Establishing Cost Center Accounting

A cost center is a place in which costs are incurred because at least one activity originates there. A cost center need not correspond to a real place in the geographical sense—it can be a functional unit that makes business sense. If one person does two different types of work, you might find it helpful to place one type in one cost center and the second in another. The cost center is a unit within a company distinguished by area of responsibility, location, or special accounting method, and by activity-related aspects.

All cost centers must belong to a controlling area. If more than one FI-Financial Accounting company exists in the area, then you also must specify which cost center belongs to which company by assigning a company code to the master record for each cost center.

Using CO-CCA Cost Center Accounting

The CO-CCA Cost Center Accounting module maintains master records that represent your cost centers and organizes the storage of related data. Each cost center has a defined validity period, and all changes to the master record are related to this validity period. You decide when cost center changes take effect.

Progressive implementation of cost accounting can occur because a cost center can be created with its basic characteristics and can receive postings of auxiliary account assignments. These are simply checked on receipt. They can be reposted if full cost accounting is subsequently installed.

The cost center master record indicates by parameters which functions can be active. The following questions address these parameters:

- Will the cost center master record accept planning data?
- Is posting allowed to this cost center?
- Will the cost center maintain open items or commitments?
- Can quantities be entered on the cost center master record?
- How are commitments handled for this cost center?
- Are statistical revenue postings accepted?
- What blocking logic applies?
- What is the type of this cost center?
- What is the cost center currency? (This defaults to the area currency but can be changed.)

The cost center concept ensures that transaction data can be validated against cost center masters as soon as they are established, even if CO-CCA Cost Center Accounting is still being implemented. This module also prepares data for other cost accounting areas, such as cost object controlling.

Cost centers can be grouped in alternative configurations that can be changed at any time. The transaction data itself is always assigned to the relevant cost center. Alternative cost center groups can correspond to organizational or functional distinctions related to decision-making, departmental, or controlling requirements.

For example, your cost center hierarchy could be headed by the corporate headquarters responsible for the first level, comprising management, logistics, and affiliated cost centers. The logistics cost center group could control costs from different organizational areas, such as warehouse, energy, buildings, and fleet. Each of these, in turn, could perhaps include a set of cost centers.

N O T E A cost center master record is usually created and maintained for each fiscal year, although it can be recreated for subsequent years.

The warehouse cost center group can be used to group together the following component cost centers for reporting:

- Goods receipt checking
- Goods receipt warehouse
- Goods issue warehouse

The energy cost center group can be used to group together the following component cost centers for reporting:

- Power
- Water
- Gas

The buildings cost center group can be used to group together the following component cost centers for reporting:

- Corporate headquarters
- Warehouse buildings
- Production facilities

The fleet cost center group can be used to group together the following component cost centers for reporting:

- Executive cars
- Road transport vehicles
- Internal materials-handling vehicles
- Dedicated rail wagons

Cost centers themselves can be allocated to a business area and a profit center and therefore contribute data to them as required. The data stored in a cost center section of the database includes the following:

- Control information for planning
- Control information for settlement
- Control information used by the Controlling Information System (CIS) and the Executive Information System (EIS)

N O T E   The parent company code of a cost center can be changed from one financial year to the next. ☐

Part
II

Ch
6

Understanding Actual Costing

When primary costs are entered, you specify a cost center as the destination in the cost accounting system. SAP R/3 automatically creates an SAP document to record the transaction and posts it to the appropriate subledger of the FI-GL General Ledger. At the same time, CO-Controlling makes a second copy for itself. As a result, CO-Controlling can be self-contained, yet the audit trail remains intact.

The following SAP applications are fully integrated with CO-CCA Cost Center Accounting and can act as feeder systems sending actual cost data to specific cost centers:

- FI-Financial Accounting sends costs from external invoices and imputed cost calculations.

- FI-AM Asset Management sends imputed depreciation and interest for book values and replacement costs of fixed assets assigned to the cost center.
- MM-Materials Management sends details of the consumption of overhead materials.
- PP-Production Planning sends notification from production orders.
- HR-Human Resources Management sends payroll costs and employee benefit costs as postings to expense accounts.
- SD-Sales and Distribution sends sales data and distribution costs.

The data from these feeder systems can be used in calculating statistical key figures for the purpose of internal cost allocation and ratio analysis. The data can be formed into groups and used in the same way as cost elements and cost centers.

External data from non-SAP systems can be automatically transferred through SAP standard interfaces. A flexible and supportive interface also exists for the manual input of data. Every transaction is recorded in the standard form of a CO document, which is supplementary to the standard SAP document created by every transaction.

The actual costs transferred to a cost center can be recorded in separate accounts to identify their origins. A further distinction is maintained in the records between activity-related allocations made during the business period and those made at the end of the month or other business period. These kinds of postings can arise from direct internal cost allocations or as repostings.

A reposting in cost accounting usually occurs from one cost account assignment object (such as a cost center or job) to another when the external accounting system makes a mistake in assigning the item.

Understanding Cost Distribution Within CO-CCA

Costs can be transferred between cost centers, but the original cost element data remains unchanged. CO-CCA Cost Center Accounting sponsors two types of distribution of costs:

- A periodic transfer of primary costs in CO-Controlling, known as *distribution*
- Distribution of primary and secondary costs within CO-Controlling, known as *assessment*

The distribution method of CO-CCA Cost Center Accounting is totally flexible and remains under your control.

The sender is a cost center with access to the rules for distributing the cost elements to the receivers, which are possibly also cost centers. You have control over the allocation structures to ensure that distribution suits the needs of your company. The identity of the sender is preserved in all distribution postings, and the system keeps a log of all the relevant data.

You can simulate distributions to test the effects of the rules before you post the values. The variety of available distribution rules is illustrated by the following examples:

- Fixed specific amounts, or values calculated at the time and based on shared portions or percentages

- Actual data or planned data
- Allocation across a group of cost centers, which is defined in the distribution rule

Distributions in cost accounting can occur only within a controlling area, so sender and receiver cost centers always exist in the same controlling areas. For example, you could allocate 70 percent of a cost arising from sales evenly to the cost centers for individual sales representatives. You could then split 20 percent between the central sales organizations in proportion to the number of sales representatives working for them. This example illustrates that you do not have to distribute all the costs—the sender cost center still has 10 percent.

You can witness the effects of a distribution immediately by calling for a standard online report, available through the special functions keys. You can repeat the distribution procedures at any time.

Understanding Assessment

The function of assessment is to allocate primary and secondary cost elements. The processing logic is similar to that for the distribution method. The cost center sending cost data is credited with the total of the accounts assigned to it.

The receiver cost center is debited using a special secondary cost element signifying that the transaction is part of an assessment procedure. By looking at the appropriate secondary cost elements, you can analyze the results of the assessment.

Understanding Surcharge Calculations

One cost allocation method available in CO-Controlling that is supplementary to assessment is to use the surcharge calculation function. This calculates a supplement (usually as percentage), which is used to apply overhead in absorption costing on an individual transaction basis. For example, this occurs when a service receiver is charged for overhead incurred by the service provider.

You can call on CO-CCA Cost Center Accounting to calculate a surcharge at a percentage rate based on one or more cost elements. The system simultaneously credits and debits the relevant cost centers with the calculated surcharge, which is posted under a predefined surcharge cost element.

Understanding Cost Center Planning Procedures

The purpose of cost center planning is to anticipate the volume of costs for a particular period at each cost center you identify in your company. You can plan for one fiscal year ahead or for several. You can divide the year into parts (up to 365), or you can use a rolling system of planning.

Within your overall period of choice (say, the fiscal year), the system reallocates any planned values according to your selection from the predefined distribution keys. You can add your own distribution keys to this set.

You also must decide on a planning level, which defines the cost center where you set out your plan. If the plan is to be applied across the entire enterprise, the planning level is the SAP client that subsumes all subordinate companies. If the plan centers on a single subsidiary, the level is the company code. This code appears on all records associated with this plan.

The plan specifies details such as the following:

- Quantity-based activities
- Value-based primary and secondary cost elements
- Statistical key figures

When you settle on the planning level, the system provides detailed planning support in the form of standard texts that document the plan and formulas for calculating all the standard statistical key figures. The SAP product costing system can supply information to your plan in the form of quantity and value details of particular cost elements.

Although you can change and correct the cost center plan at any time by repeating individual sections of the overall planning sequence, you can also block your plan, version by version, to prevent any changes. Furthermore, you can use the standard R/3 authorization functions to control changes to your plan.

Your cost center plan may contain a planned value for a particular cost element that should really be subjected to more detailed attention. The system enables you to define individual items to separate what you regard as the important factors that should be subjected to detailed planning. The following influencing factors illustrate the concept:

- A material may be subject to wide fluctuations in cost due to an unstable market. Your plan could specify the code number of this material, and the SAP MM-Materials Management application would keep your plan up-to-date by posting the current price of this material to your plan.
- Some cost centers in your plan may be sensitive to employee-related wages and salaries. You could evaluate this influencing factor using price tables and cost rates, by employee group or by individual employee, if necessary.
- Some cost centers may be sensitive to the costs associated with individual activities and external services. You might highlight these as influencing factors to be actively and automatically taken into your plan.
- You may have some risks or overheads that should attract surcharges at some cost centers. These can be factored into your plan.

N O T E SAP standard business functions are available to support the concept of linking cost centers with a cost center budget. ☐

Posting Key Figures to Cost Centers

A statistical key figure is a number or a ratio used in planning. Key figures can be transferred from the Logistics Information System (LIS) to cost accounting and can be used for internal allocations to cost centers. The role of a key figure is to represent the comparative quantity of a value, such as the proportion of annual output forecast for each month in the year. Key figures can be used as the basis for internal purposes as part of representative value analysis and various simulations when the actual figures are not available or not appropriate.

Transferring Data

Data for cost centers can be automatically transferred from third-party systems through standard SAP interfaces. Manual data is supported by an extensive range of preset values and key figures, together with facilities for copying values from other periods and from other cost centers. Manual and automatic data transfers generate CO documents to which origin verification can be applied by referencing other document numbers and texts.

Performing Period-End Tasks

The scope of period closing and its timing may well depend on the completeness of data arriving from other systems, such as financial accounting. If all primary cost elements are to be processed, you must determine the sequence of the period allocations for the period-end closing. Distributions and overhead calculation must come before cost center assessment. If follow-up costs appear, the processing run can be repeated in the period involved.

The actual costs incurred in the cost centers, apart from costs allocated in inventory, can be periodically transferred into profitability analysis to be verified.

Multilevel fixed cost absorption is carried out by allocating costs to any market segment or revenue object, from which they can be assigned to any level of the contribution margin hierarchies. This accommodates both variances from the production cost centers and costs from the sales and distribution and administration cost centers to be transferred to profitability analysis.

Performing Period-End Clearing from Cost Centers

At the end of the period, all cost centers can be cleared of all costs with the following procedures:

- Activity allocation and production orders are used to settle part of the costs to inventory.
- Any production variances remaining on the production orders can be periodically transferred to profitability analysis.
- Any cost center costs remaining are distributed directly from the cost centers to revenue objects.

Using Cost Centers in Planning

A *plan* is a way of setting goals for a cost center. A *variance* is a difference between some aspect of the plan and the actual results. A variance detected and reported can lead to a beneficial change in the process flows.

If you want to use standard costing, you must set out a cost plan that includes the values and quantities for the relevant time periods, without reference to the actual values and quantities of preceding periods. You can use transfer prices based on planned costs and activity quantities to assign values to internal activities during the current period before the actual costs become available.

A cost center plan usually applies to a period of one year and is part of the enterprise plan. The components of the plan are quantities of activities and consumption. From these quantities, the value flows are computed for the cost center. If the cost center managers cooperate, these values can then be used as goals or targets if they take into account both the internal conditions of the cost center and the external market conditions. The preset goals can be adjusted as market conditions, and other factors can change during the period.

When the accounting period closes, the differences between planned and actual (or between target and actual) values and quantities can be used to trigger changes in processes intended to improve efficiency. The results of the cost center activity in relation to the plan can be used to assign values to these business activities that are not unduly influenced by unusual events that may have occurred during the period.

Integrating Cost Center Plans with Other Plans

The usual beginning of a short-term plan is the sales plan. The sales plan sets targets for the quantities that should be sold in the planning period. The planned sales volumes form the input to the production plan.

The production plan must determine the quantities of raw materials and operating supplies needed to produce the volumes called for in the sales plan. In addition, the production plan must specify the capacities needed, in terms of the people and production facilities, and the time schedule in which they must be engaged if the production targets are to be met.

The capacities identified in the production plan are passed to the available cost centers, which must make available the activity units to supply the target capacities. At the same time, the cost center managers must plan how the costs and activities needed will be transferred from the relevant cost centers.

From the planned costs and the planned sales volumes, it is possible to calculate the revenues. This information is then used to calculate a value for planned profit. Of course, the scope of production planning and cost center planning can be curtailed by financial planning, which is affected by profit planning.

Other plans in the enterprise encroach upon production and financial planning. Subplans from any or all of the following sources must be taken into account:

- Investment plan
- Procurement plan
- Inventory plan
- Personnel plan

The cost center planning module can receive planning data directly from the following integrated modules:

- Human Resources
- Asset Management
- Plant Maintenance
- Production Planning
- Logistics Information System

N O T E   The cost center accounting module can transmit planning data to the PCA Profit Center Accounting module and to the FI-SL (Special Purpose Ledger) component.

Planning Techniques with Cost Center Accounting

A planning view is a summary of the planning technique and scope. Planning periods are usually a year or a regular division of a year. Two main types of planning views exist:

- Decentralized planning, where plans are developed for individual cost centers
- Centralized planning, where the head office manager distributes the plan values

The recipients of the head office directives are special cost elements or cost element groups in the cost centers. For example, all cost centers may be given payroll plans from the head office.

Plans are automatically tagged as versions and are stored as separate versions if parameters change. For example, the previous year's actual figures may constitute the first version of the next year plan. Adjustments in the form of proportional revaluations and changes to the planning quantity numbers are recorded as versions, perhaps as several versions as different managers contribute their views.

It may be helpful to record a best-case and a worst-case version, or a least versions portraying various degrees of optimism and pessimism. Versions of a plan can be run in simulation mode and can be compared with each other in a report. Standard SAP layouts are provided for cost center planning reports, and certain facilities enable you to set up template planning screens (layouts) into which the planned data is inserted.

Developing Planner Profiles

A planner profile specifies which planning layout or screen is to be used for each planning area. The planning areas recognized by cost accounting for this purpose are as follows:

- Cost elements and activity inputs
- Activities and activity prices
- Statistical key figures

Within the planning area, you can decide which planning layout is to be used.

Planning Authorization

A planning profile can be associated with an authorization group so that access to a plan is controlled. In decentralized planning, for example, it is important that alterations to a plan are made by people in the appropriate cost center and area of responsibility. Default values can be specified for plans as a form of guidance for the local planners.

Planning locks can be set according to the following levels:

- ▣ Version
- ▢ Cost object, such as cost center or job
- ▣ Period
- ▣ Procedure, such as distribution or activity allocation

Plan copying can be used as follows:

- ▢ Entire version
- ▣ Cost centers or cost center groups
- ▣ Procedures
- ▣ Time segments within a fiscal year

Revaluing Plans

An existing version of a plan can be revalued to change planned amounts for primary cost elements proportionally. For example, payroll costs can be planned on the basis of an estimated rate of inflation and can be later revalued when a better estimate is available or when a rate increase is negotiated.

The use of plan versions with different parameters can be regarded as a form of simulation that you can use to explore what the values might be if, for example, your primary costs changed.

Transferring Planning Data from Other Systems

If one or more of your integrated systems have developed plans, the data can be transferred to cost accounting. For example, the following applications can contribute plan data:

- ▣ Planned personnel costs can be acquired from the HR-Human Resources application.
- ▢ AM-Asset Management has period depreciation and interest calculations for each asset that can be transferred to primary cost planning objects.
- ▣ PP-Production Planning has developed schedules of the services required, and these service quantities for each period can be transferred to cost center planning.
- ▢ Statistical key figures developed in the logistics information system can be copied to cost accounting.

These contributions to cost planning can be corrected at any time to ensure that the resulting plan truly represents what you want your business to achieve.

Integrating Internal Orders into a Plan

If an activity in a cost center has been planned to occur at a certain level, you may discover that the resulting capacity will not suffice. You can update a planned activity by an internal order. The sender cost center is credited in the plan, and the plan activity is updated by the same values.

A rate is assigned for converting a quantity of an activity to a value, for planning purposes and perhaps for pricing. If this rate changes, the rates applied to any planning objects that include the same activity should also change. This revaluation occurs automatically with planning integration as it is implemented in SAP R/3 and later versions.

Profit center accounting must be provided with all the costs that have been determined in the planning processes. Again, this is an automatic function of SAP R/3 if so configured.

N O T E If you run the integrated planning object regime, the planning objects are settled to the appropriate cost centers, and the settlement process automatically generates planned costs in the cost centers.

Planning with Cost Centers

There may be as many different ways of planning across cost centers as there are different companies. Each needs a custom planning scheme. However, there is a basic sequence that is almost always the most prudent way to establish the targets by cost center and by period. The following entity clusters should be assigned planning values in order:

- Statistical key figures
- Service performance
- Consumption and costs

The next step is to transfer all the activities as scheduled in production planning. You will probably have to reconcile the activity network to make sure that no cost center is assigned more activity than it can provide from its available capacities. Next comes the allocation of activities and values to the individual cost objects, followed by careful calculation of the activity prices once you know the production resources in which these activities will take place.

If you have not done so already, you should bring your plan into accordance with any other subplans approved by the board of management or their planning advisors. You will not want to publish a plan that requires more qualified employees than will be available over the periods of your plan, nor will you be popular if you plan to use high value materials over periods when they are expected to fetch premium prices.

Iteration is a mathematical technique in which a process is repeated until the result settles down to a decent compromise. Planning works like this, and the SAP R/3 functions make sure the process takes place in an orderly and traceable fashion.

Statistical key figures may be nothing more elaborate than a target number of units to be sold in each of the product divisions. On the other hand, they may comprise logically complex ratios, such as the return on capital invested in high-risk ventures in business areas of high inflation. The useful key figures enable you to build a plan with reasonable estimates of the capacities needed for each of the critical activities in each planning period. Will you have the plant idle, or should you invest in extra productive capacity?

If you can manage to accumulate the quantities of the activity types required in each period in each cost center, then you can apply primary and secondary cost allocations to these activities and their sponsoring cost centers.

Primary costs are defined as those incurred by the consumption of goods and services that come from outside the company. The following are classified as primary costs:

- Payroll costs
- External services
- Material costs
- Operating supplies
- Imputed costs

If some of your requirements can be met by calling on other cost centers, you have two ways of accounting for them in your planning. You can plan them as activity inputs and credit the sending cost centers, or you can plan them as secondary costs.

Some of your primary costs may have to be planned without reference to activities. Your shop floor manager must be paid salary regardless of how much work takes place on the shop floor.

Another scenario in which you might assign primary costs without reference to the quantity or type of activity planned arises if you do not operate activity accounting and therefore cannot relate primary costs to activities in any strict computation. See Chapter 7 for a more detailed discussion on the methods of relating primary costs to the activities in your company.

Planning Secondary Costs

An input of secondary costs must be posted when a cost center calls upon another cost center to provide goods or services. If the amount of this hired activity depends upon the amount of some activity in the hiring cost center, then the planning process must take this into account. On the other hand, if the service provided by the sending cost center is not related to the activity in the receiving cost center, then the plan must assign a value to this service that is not related to activities.

Planning Functional Dependencies

When activities are used to plan activity prices, a calculation of a planned sum could be distributed across all the cost elements. It is recognized that the cost of a cost element, such as a unit of the product, is functionally dependent on the costs incurred by the cost center, in relation to the number of units produced in the period. This is referred to as detail planning of a primary cost element.

This technique can be applied recursively; that is, the costs can be planned on the basis of the costing of the goods and services that make each unit of product. You can apply the same technique to these goods and services themselves.

Budgeting a Cost Center

A *budget* is an amount assigned to a time period. You can set a budget and compare the actual postings to a cost center with the budget. If the postings do not balance, you have the option of changing the budget or changing the activities.

The cost accounting information system is provided with reporting tools to enable you to compare actual costs, commitments, and the budget for any or all cost centers.

A budget profile can be specified so that the amounts are spread over a range of accounting periods according to any distribution function you care to impose. ◉

Costing on the Basis of Activities

In this chapter

Determining the Profitability of Product Lines

The traditional method of controlling a business has often been a matter of keeping careful records of what has been spent and what has been sold. At the end of the financial year, the balance sheet and the profit and loss statement should reveal whether the business has been profitable and whether it owns any assets of value or is responsible for outstanding obligations.

Cost-of-sales accounting and period accounting are formal methods of tracking revenues and expenses on a monthly basis to detect poor operating results in time to do something about the business processes.

If your business has more than one product or service, you probably want to know how each of your product lines is performing so that you can make at least an informal judgment of how profitable they are in case you decide to alter the effort and resources you devote to them. The formal method of product costing is designed to set out all the ways in which each product consumes value and how each product can earn revenue. The formal method of activity-based costing is designed to refine product costing by assigning a value to every activity in your company so that any changes you make in resource allocation can be represented as a plan. Such a plan produces a series of period value targets built by adding the values of all the activities intended for each period. Of course, you can compare target values with actual values as soon as the period operating figures are available.

Introducing Cost Object Controlling

The purpose of product cost accounting is to determine the unit cost of whatever product units your company handles. These units are referred to as cost objects, with one cost object for each product, or one distribution package for each product. The context is a technical production system customized to a particular company; the outcome is a company-specific costing system that integrates the flow of cost information from its origins.

There is a core technical discipline based on the principle that costs should be accurately allocated to the processes that incur them. Several costing systems embody this principle.

Product cost accounting addresses two types of costing:

- Production order costing
- Inventory costing

Four types of cost object controlling are differentiated because they offer particular clusters of benefits according to their type of business:

- Make-to-stock production
- Process manufacturing
- Make-to-order production
- Plant construction

All these types of product cost accounting are supported by the CO-Controlling module by the flexible use of cost objects.

Identifying Costing Requirements of Different Types of Companies

Modern controlling methods have been developed to support technical manufacturing processes and service industries. The methods must match the needs of the individual company. The SAP approach is to establish a core of standard business functions that can be controlled by the implementor through the medium of parameters to yield a customized system finely tuned to the requirements of the different user classes in the specific company.

Manufacturers require a costing system that shows where and by how much their manufacturing processes add value to their raw materials. They differ in their style of manufacturing according to whether they make to a production order or make to replace stock on their inventory. Their processes differ over a range, from discrete one-off production to repetitive production to continuous flow production.

Trading companies need a method of costing to enable them to apply overhead and surcharges to the cost prices of their goods, which they often must keep to set final selling prices.

Service companies tend to adopt the principles of process costing, which revolves around the concept of cost drivers—in this case, service activities. The companies must have the means to define, measure, plan, and pass on costs incurred by their cost drivers, service calls, and other activities.

Understanding Make-to-Order, Make-to-Stock, and Continuous Flow Costing

The manufacturing industry has a polished costing method based on routings of work units and bills of materials. Manufacturers need to know what processes the product must undergo, the costs of materials and resources, and the quantities required. This is referred to as the *quantity structure* for this product. If you have this information, you can begin to cost the product by assembling the costing components.

In the make-to-order company, the customer order sets off costing. Because each order is unique, there may be a shortage of routings and bills of materials that can be applied without editing. Yet it is of the utmost importance to be able to arrive quickly at a cost prediction for this one-off product so that the company can issue a quotation and take part in competitive tendering for the work. An effective costing system for this sort of company would have to make this approach to one-off tendering a high priority, for all future business may depend on its speed and accuracy.

Those manufacturers who make to stock apply standard bills of materials and routings about which they may well have copious actual data. Products and orders for them can be costed from this database.

When the manufacturing process is continuous (such as in repetitive manufacturing), it is probably not amenable to much in the way of variation. This process probably works at its best only if the rate of flow falls within narrow limits. Nevertheless, management and shareholders still hold an interest in the contribution of the various cost components to the cost of the finished product. It is important to understand how and why costs vary if the flow rate and quality are allowed to move out of the normal operating ranges. This might happen because of variations in the raw materials or in the environmental conditions at the manufacturing plant.

Understanding Product Costing Techniques

A costing system uses a set of costing objects, which are the different products, production orders, resources, and so on. The only qualification for a costing object is that it can be allocated costs that mean something when they are totaled under that costing object. The costing objects can be conceptual or tangible, organizational or geographical.

The pivotal concept in costing centers on a structure of cost drivers customized to a specific company. These cost drivers are cost objects onto which the actual costs are settled according to how they were incurred. SAP R/3 CO-Controlling provides a range of model structures on which you can base a structure specific to the needs of your company.

Three types of costing values can be settled on a cost structure:

- Planned values
- Target values
- Actual costs

Two ways exist for applying cost data to arrive at a specific costing:

- Allocating the full costing to the cost objects
- Allocating only the variable costs to the cost objects, and applying overhead or surcharge

These ideas are discussed in Chapter 6, "Controlling by Cost Management."

An integrated costing system must have at least the following capabilities:

- Calculating alternative cost plans using different versions and timings
- Controlling the activities and the value added by each operation
- Settling actual costs, according to how they occurred, on a specific cost structure

Understanding Unit Costing

If your company makes unique products only to customer orders, you need unit costing. You have very little choice but to cost each individual order by deciding which unitary components you must put together. You also must determine what other costs will be incurred as you do so.

The relevant database is a set of reference unit cost estimates. CO-PC Product Cost Accounting helps you locate which elements you need, and you can transfer them in blocks to the relevant quotes and sales order items or to the cost accounting objects (which are orders and projects).

This builds the planned costs of the quote, which can be compared to the actual costs as the order proceeds toward completion. Materials that are consumed have their quantities or values assigned to the accounts under the correct cost element headings as data is collected on the activities that consume them. Overhead is applied, and charges for external activities add to the cost.

The sales order is documented with a continuous comparison between planned and actual costs for its lifetime. From this data, a simultaneous calculation of the contribution margin can be computed, and the results are recorded on the sales order document.

Understanding Order Costing

In make-to-stock production, it is useful to combine order and unit costing methods because order lots and batches of products are usually produced in response to production orders. Different cost estimates are prepared as alternative versions that take part in simultaneous costing to ensure exact control of the actual costs incurred by the relevant cost elements, sender cost centers and their activities, materials used, and so on.

The system supports settlement of some or all the costs to stock an automatic calculation to support inventory control over finished and semi-finished products. The value of stocks of unfinished goods and works in progress can be calculated automatically.

Process manufacturing includes production processes that have a step-by-step structure and those that entail a cyclical input of materials. Continuous flow production, such as in repetitive manufacturing, is characterized by long processing runs of a single basic material. Many types of manufacturing plants perform more efficiently if the raw materials and the process cycles are not subject to undue perturbations.

The control document for continuous flow processing is the period production order. Comparisons are made between target and actual costs, planned output for a period, and actual output, including cost use from backflushing surplus material or summarized confirmations of production. The costs are charged to individual cost elements of the production structure in relation to the quantities produced.

Backflushing occurs in the chemical industry, for instance, when some of the output can be returned to the process as a semi-finished product. There may be by-products and co-products with alternative uses to the main product, and some products may bypass some of the production stages in the process cycle. The production order documents these variations.

Trading companies need a costing system that can provide accurate valuations of the costs and the prices, taking into account the individual costing and pricing structures that prevail in the type of business and under the market conditions at the time. The basic method involves applying overhead to cost prices. Costing the overhead enables you to apply the overhead according to cost elements, or in relation to the overhead you have already calculated. The system enables you to use different levels of sales prices, such as net sales price or gross sales price, to compute additional overhead or surcharge, such as discounts or cash discounts. These factors differ in wholesaling and retailing.

Part

Ch

7

Service companies use the functions and elements of process costing. The service operations must be defined in terms of individual activities that can be measured. If these activities can each be measured, then they are subject to planning. When the work is done, the actual amount of each activity component can be entered in quantitative terms. In this type of situation, the measured activity is the cost driver. The valuation process can cost each activity using predetermined rates and allocate the costs to the service cost structure under the appropriate cost element headings. From this point on, the flexible reporting system of SAP R/3 can be used to collate the information and present it for the benefit of the decision makers in your company. In particular, the actual data compiled after a plan has been developed on the basis of activities can be used to refine the values assigned as rates for given quantities of each costed activity. In this way, the estimates for the next plan that involves these activities can become progressively more accurate. An accurate plan can be of great value because it enables the materials supervisor to purchase the right amount of raw materials and consumable stores. The plan also ensures that the key resource, the personnel, is planned with precision.

Assigning Costs to Cost Objects

A cost object exists for SAP R/3 if there is a master record for it. The function of a cost object is to control the allocation, analysis, and settlement of costs related to the object it represents. A cost object can relate directly to a production unit; it can be an organizational structure component that is useful in reporting value flows. In essence, a cost object is an identification number and a set of master record data fields that can be accessed in connection with that number.

N O T E Unit costs of all cost objects serve as the basis for arriving at all costing values. □

The cost object could be an entity that is quite independent of any particular SAP application, a convenient peg on which to hang information relevant to the specific costing procedures of your company. A cost object can collect the costs of two or more other cost objects. This constitutes a cost object hierarchy, which can branch down any number of layers and extend to any number of cost objects on each level. Most cost structures exist in the form of cost object hierarchies of this inverted tree shape if plotted, for instance, through the SAP R/3 online reporting system using the graphical interface.

If you run projects or production lines, you might find it informative to have certain cost information gathered by cost objects, in parallel to the normal product costing. One way of achieving this is to define unique cost objects for each project or production line of interest.

If your installation has other SAP modules installed and configured, you will find it convenient to use the cost objects from these applications to define your own unique cost objects by copying some or all of the data structures from these predefined SAP cost objects. For example, the following application modules use particular cost object types:

- PS-Project System (network and project item)
- CO-Controlling (internal order)
- SD-Sales and Distribution (sales order)

- MM-Materials Management (material number)
- PP-Production Planning (production order and routing)
- PM-Plant Maintenance (maintenance order)

If you have the unit costs for all your cost objects, you can display inventory costings and call for profitability analyses using the full set of fixed and variable costs. You can use any combination of the costing systems current in your company.

The SAP R/3 system carries the definitions, in the form of master data, for all the cost object controlling functions of the SAP integrated system. Any transaction that bears data relevant to costing is processed according to these definitions.

Using Results from Costing a Cost Object

Costing results are stored by version so that different methods and different periods can be compared. Each assembly is itemized in a costing created from a cost object. The data used can be planned or actual and can be expressed as valuations or as quantities to which standard rates can be applied by the system at the time. The results of a costing comprise information on each of 40 cost components for each cost object, itemized for each assembly, and the whole is replicated for each version of the costing structure, if required.

Legal analysis demands that the origins of cost estimates be identifiable. This, in turn, requires that details be kept for the cost origins of all the contributors to the values recorded as the cost object components. A cost origin must be a document that identifies a transaction by such means as follows:

- The vendor number for external procurement and the provision of external activities
- The operation number, the identification of the sender cost center, and the activity type for each internal activity
- The material number or material group code, if stock movements or the consumption of goods occurred
- The cost center for charging overhead

The SAP R/3 system running CO-PC Product Cost Accounting can carry out the following procedures using cost origins to associate posted movements with cost elements:

- Conducting valuation using individual cost structures or cost rates
- Assigning costs to standard cost elements
- Establishing the costing basis for overhead
- Accepting planning and account assignment directives at any level of the costing structures
- Preparing reports at any analysis level to display planned or actual resource-usage variances

Part
II

Ch
7

Understanding Valuation Methods

The following costing systems are available in the CO-Controlling module of the SAP R/3 system and can be used in any combination:

- Unit costing
- Product costing
- Production order costing
- Cost object controlling for make-to-stock production
- Cost object controlling for process manufacturing
- Cost object controlling for make-to-order production
- Cost object controlling for plant construction

The valuation of input factors and the presentation of this data for costing analysis are carried out by a uniform valuation method across all costing systems. The source of the data differentiates the methods, insofar as different methods exist for costing when technical quantities are involved (such as when using bills of materials and routings). Variations also occur when existing cost estimates must be copied or referenced. Manual entry of cost estimates is supported, and the R/3 system offers suggested default values whenever possible for editing.

The valuation process extends to the following calculations:

- Planned input quantities with planned allocation rates and planned prices
- Actual input quantities with standard prices and standard activity prices
- Actual input quantities with actual prices and actual activity prices
- Partial or total output quantities
- Scrap quantities
- Order-specific cost settlement according to the quantities delivered
- Calculation of all types of variance
- Profitability analyses to different layout formats

Input quantities can be evaluated by any of a range of methods. The method chosen is recorded as the valuation variant. These variants are listed below:

- Standard prices and current prices, both future or previous
- Moving average prices
- Tax-based and commercial or "political" prices
- Standard activity prices
- Actual activity prices
- Applying variances on standard or actual prices adjusted to match changes in planning or historical amounts

In the service sector, it is possible to instruct the system to split the costs into fixed and variable components. This enables you to carry out marginal and absorption costing in parallel. You can take any point of view of output to evaluate services rendered.

By having the required functionality available online, the system can offer a modern control system covering products and the analysis of results. The following outcomes are supported:

- The cost of goods manufactured and the cost of goods sold are displayed on efficient and informative cost structures that are understandable from a business point of view and are accurate from a product cost accounting perspective.
- The company can see the effects of using different valuation techniques on the financial accounts and year-end closing. This ensures that choices can be made on the basis of correct information.
- Not all the divisions of a corporate group must use the same valuation methods; each can use the ones most suitable for that division.
- Detailed costing records can be made available for each alternative or parallel valuation of variances between planned and actual costs for each business segment.
- The costing methods throughout the group do not necessarily depend on the costing documentation requirements of the logistics operations.

Understanding the Role of Flexible Analysis and Reporting in Product Cost Accounting

The structure of a report can be made to suit your requirements. The standard system contains many predefined standard reports, which you can modify and extend, often in the online mode. Both the format and the data are under your control.

Orders can be grouped by order type, for instance, and line items can be selected based on their connection to a specific cost object. Summaries and graphical representations are available at all stages of analysis and reporting.

Cost objects can be compared, and the variances can be computed using any dimensions for comparison, such as between orders, between periods, between similar cost objects, and between cost objects of very different kinds.

Planning and Simulation from Unit Costing

You can apply unit costing regardless of the status of an order. This is because unit costing is based on a quantity structure that you define manually. Some of the uses of a comprehensive system of unit costing are as follows:

- Price determination.
- Costing to make quotes and tenders.
- Costing to support the processing of orders.
- Planning of costs and resources to prepare order and project cost estimates.
- Making sample cost estimates for new or existing products using an existing estimate as a reference model to be edited and updated.
- Defining sales prices for sales orders.

Part
II

Ch
7

- Preparing, planning, controlling, and settling investments by means of orders and projects.
- Preparing cost estimates for base planning objects, which can range from a single-level assembly to a multilevel structure that includes other base planning objects. A base planning object can also be an instrument for integrating information from other non-SAP applications.

You can display the costing information before, during, and after production or project activities, as well as before, during, and after sales activities.

In the activities of sales and distribution, you can use unit costing to good advantage in the following ways:

- To transfer unit cost estimates at any time to reference objects such as orders, projects, and sales orders
- To cost and check quickly the feasibility of extra sales orders (or alternative or modified product components or characteristics) and any changes in the activities involved

Organizing Product Cost Controlling

The role of product cost accounting is to control the costs that accrue as a result of producing a product or performing a service. The accounting disciplines involved in product cost controlling serve as supports to the following operational functions:

- Pricing policy elaboration
- Pricing calculation control
- Production cost management
- Inventory valuation
- Profitability analysis

The basic software functions for all these tasks are integrated in the SAP R/3 Basis system. Additional functions are provided by the integrated FI-Financial Accounting, CO-Controlling, PP-Production Planning, and MM-Materials Management applications. Just how much functionality must be configured from each of these applications depends on the structure of your company and the extent to which you intend to operate product cost controlling.

The focus of product costing is the order-neutral costs of producing tangible or intangible goods, such as services. Computing product costs independently of any specific order ensures you can arrive at a standard cost estimate for each product. This amount is often specified at the beginning of the fiscal year and then is subjected to various adjustments that arise from profit planning to yield the planned prices. The invoice price is the result of applying discounts or surcharges according to the customer and the order.

The output results of product costing should include values for each product for each of the following parameters:

- ☐ The order-neutral cost of goods manufactured
- ☐ The order-neutral cost of goods sold
- ☐ The product cost of manufacturing optimized by comparative costing
- ☐ The product price floor

Order-neutral product costing also assembles the data needed by the following operations:

- ☐ Calculating the cost of manufacturing each product for the purpose of inventory valuation
- ☐ Calculating the variances between target costs and actual costs for the purposes of cost object controlling
- ☐ Analyzing profitability with contribution margin accounting

Understanding Cost Object Controlling

All the various costs incurred as the result of manufacturing are collected and collated so that they can be associated with a suitable cost object. The nature of this object depends on the product and the company. The choice of object must provide for the following considerations:

- ☐ It must be possible to assemble sets of cost objects, or use a single cost object, to determine the actual costs of each product or service.
- ☐ The cost objects must have a means to show and explain why variances exist between the planned product costing and the actual manufacturing cost.
- ☐ The set of cost objects must be capable of yielding meaningful and legal values when the work is still in progress.
- ☐ It must be possible to associate the revenue arising from the sale of the product with a relevant cost object or set of cost objects.
- ☐ It must be possible to compare the revenues that accrue to a cost object with the actual and planned costs of manufacturing the product it represents.

Using Cost Objects in Different Industries

All companies may at times use any of the standard or customized cost objects in the SAP R/3 system. However, some types of enterprise tend to have preferred cost objects.

For example, service industries tend to use general cost objects, such as orders and contracts. Large-scale engineering companies accustomed to collating costs on cost object hierarchies that are complex orders and that may well be managed by projects and task networks. These are discussed in Chapter 8, "Controlling by the PS-Project System."

If your company specializes in products made to order, then the natural cost objects are the sales order or the production order.

The SAP R/3 system can treat a single material as a cost object. This is not as restrictive as it sounds because a *material* can be a finished product, a semi-finished product, or even a defined unit of a service. The material as a cost object can be found in the continuous process industry,

Part

II

Ch

7

in repetitive manufacturing, and in order-related manufacturing, where there is perhaps a mixture of make-to-order and make-to-stock production. The production order is a useful cost object in such cases where an executive decision must be made on the amount to be manufactured to cover firm orders, anticipated orders, and perhaps a reserve.

When the manufacturing process is complex and subject to many variant specifications, the bill of materials and process routing can be represented as master records that can then function as cost objects. The values to be assigned as the costs of the material components of an order can be copied from the materials master records, where they are represented as materials prices. Services are usually valued according to the sum of the separate activities, each priced at a standard rate that is specific to the particular cost center providing the necessary activity capacity.

If you accept that a product costing system must be capable of assigning a value to any product at any stage in its manufacturing process, then you must be prepared to migrate values from one cost center to another as the work progresses. The system integrates these value movements by means of simultaneous costing so that the value of each cost center is accounted as the actual costs accrued in the cost objects for which it is currently responsible.

Planning Product Cost

All product costing systems must begin by being assigned costing items. The SAP R/3 automatically identifies any suitable items from the logistics modules. Material consumption items are found in bills of material, for example. Activity consumption is recorded in routings.

If they have been assigned quantities, the items are converted to corresponding costing items. You can also define costing items from a batch input or as a result of manual input, such as when you enter an estimate for a new order.

When you or the system identify the costing items, values must be assigned to them. Material usage must be costed at current prices, and activity usage must be valued according to cost center rates.

If your manufacturing takes place in several phases, the costing is carried out separately for each stage. Unit costs at one stage are used as transfer prices to become part of the input costs of the next step. This process is referred to as a BOM explosion because the system treats each unit of a bill of materials as a separate costing object that may itself contain a bill of materials to be expanded through all the various stages of the associated routing.

Automatic costing runs are executed by the system for multistep processes. At customizing, you determine when and how you wish to be informed of any problems in the automatic costing process.

Understanding Costing Transfer Options

When the quantity structure of a hierarchical cost object is exploded, each cost object might have to supply partly finished goods to the next step valued at transfer prices. The sequence of steps can cross company boundaries. The following possibilities are supported by the SAP R/3 system:

- A partial cost estimate can be devised, in which the semi-finished constituents are transferred at standard prices.
- Cross-plant costing can be conducted using the existing costing of the sending organizational unit.
- The quantity structure can be exploded and recosted across company boundaries, as necessary.
- Cross-company transfers can be treated as purchases and handled as external procurement.

Understanding Product Costing Variants

The various forms of costing have been developed for good commercial reasons. They can be applied at the user's discretion.

All products kept in stock are assigned a standard cost estimate that is valid for a specified planning period, such as a fiscal year. This period yields a planned cost of goods manufactured and a planned cost of goods sold. These unit values are the same, regardless of how often they must be included in the production program or how many are ordered by customers.

A costing lot size of the product is specified for a standard cost estimate. A planned price for the material is associated with each costing lot size. An order estimate computes the appropriate number of material lots needed, as well as the planned material price. Surcharges are applied to provide for the material overhead allocated for this amount of material.

The costs of production are calculated on the basis of the amount of activity needed per costing lot size and the planned activity price for all operations needed to set up and manufacture the costing lot. The production costs are often stored on the routing document for the process.

Indirect costs can be included in activity prices, or they can be added as a surcharge percentage of production costs. Costs of administration, transportation, and insurance are calculated as planned charge rates using percentages, usually of production costs.

N O T E   When the costs of manufactured goods are determined through the standard cost estimate procedure, they are stored as standard prices in the material master records. ▣

Using Target Costing

The bill of material and the routing for the complex production network for a product can undergo changes as the product specification develops or as different raw materials are used. The standard cost estimate can be updated by adopting the previous costings and recomputing the altered elements, such as the variable costs. This process is referred to as the target costing, and it can be compared to the standard cost estimate to yield a variance report.

Part
II

Ch
7

Using Current Costing by Key Dates

Goods forming part of a product can be costed using the quantity structure associated with the product and its components. The price is obtained on a specified key date so that the costing reflects the most up-to-date prices. Inventory costing is an example of key date costing.

If you have been able to order the materials you need for a batch of products at very favorable prices, you may not wish to pass on this advantage to your customer. On the other hand, you may decide to operate with a competitive price by specifying a key date that ensures that your key date costing calculation takes into account your purchase of materials at favorable prices.

Some industries have established the practice of costing materials at a particular date in the year that represents a compromise between periods when the seasonal price of materials is higher or lower than the average for the year.

Viewing Product Costing Results

A product is often a structure made up of various levels that represent sub-assemblies or sub-processes, all of which must be costed to obtain a true product cost estimate. When you view the costing of a product, you might want to inspect the data at various levels and from different viewpoints. For example, cost components can be examined from the following points of view:

- ☐ Costs of goods sold
- ▩ Valuation of selected cost components for tax purposes
- ☐ Commercial inventory valuation
- ☐ Legal procedure for inventory valuation

Using Cost Itemization

If you want to look at the individual items in the quantity structure of a product, the itemization function enables you to focus on cost elements and on cost origins, such as the manufacturing operations that generated those costs. The database from which you can draw includes for every manufacturing level all the costing items identified in the quantity structure. This database also holds information on the surcharge calculations and the values and parameters used by them.

If a particular manufacturing level includes a complex assembly, you can interactively explore the costing of this structure. If you call for a cost element itemization report, you receive a summary sorted and totaled by costing item.

If you ask for a cost component split, you can define how the summarization should assemble the calculated costs. Up to 40 cost components can be defined. The details of the cost origins that contribute to the cost components are maintained so that you can inspect them for any manufacturing level.

Using Manual Input for Unit Costing

Unit costing takes place if you enter a quantity structure manually rather than calling up a bill of material and routing. In unit costing, you develop an individual costing spreadsheet detailing such items as the following:

- Materials
- Internal activities
- Variable items
- Surcharges

Any of the variants of product costing can be applied to a costing sheet. You can edit the document table structure and use word-processing and spreadsheet facilities to develop your own format for unit costing. You could use a unit costing sheet to plan costs for orders for which there is no defined quantity structure suitable for automatic costing.

Reference costing is a technique used in unit costing to nominate predefined base unit costing objects. This technique enables you to carry out material explosions when elaborating your unit costing sheet. For example, you may have a predefined base object comprising some materials and activities, each with a quantity and a resulting value. If you assemble a unit costing sheet and enter a line item that is a reference for this base object, the system inserts its details in your unit costing. A base object can itself refer to other base objects, and so on, to any level of complexity.

If you use the Microsoft Excel interface, the results are stored in the R/3 system as an Excel session. Through this interface, you can enter costing items and set up calculations. If you are online with the R/3 system, you can retrieve material masters and the standard cost estimates that they carry.

Controlling by Cost Objects

Cost objects are used for controlling purposes in three main activities:

- Preliminary costing
- Simultaneous costing
- Period-end closing, that includes final costing

Each of these activities is discussed in the following sections.

Using Preliminary Costing

If you have an order for a product for which your system carries a defined lot size master record, you can conduct order-related preliminary costing to determine the planned costs of the order. As soon as you identify the product, the system provides a copy of the quantity structure of materials and activities needed to produce it. Preliminary costing can use these quantities to assign a value to the order.

Part
II

Ch
7

You can also enter costing items manually or through batch processing, perhaps through one of the dedicated costing interfaces such as the CPIC. In all cases, the system automatically performs preliminary costing, from which you can select cost elements or itemization for display and update.

Using Simultaneous Costing

The function of simultaneous costing is to assign values to all material and activity use that has been confirmed as completed. This data comprises the actual costs on the cost object and can be compared with the planned costs.

If you produce to stock and only partial deliveries have been made to stock, you can apply the simultaneous costing procedure. This ensures that the standard cost estimate or the planned costs of the order are applied to the amount delivered to stock. In this way, you can calculate a value for the costs of the partial delivery. These costs are referred to as target costs and can be compared to the actual costs of the order when the full delivery to stock has been completed.

Using Period-End Closing for Order-Related Production

When a cost object is the focal point of controlling, the accounting period must be closed according to a strict sequence. The sequence for order-related production, and for repetitive and process manufacturing that is not directly related to a sales order, is as follows:

1. Calculate the overhead on the cost object.
2. Calculate the work in process.
3. Calculate the variances.
4. Carry out settlement.

A *variance* is a difference between the number expected and the number obtained from the data. For example, a variance can exist between the planned delivery date and the actual delivery date. A production batch can include items that have slightly different dimensions, although they all fall within the specification. A more serious variance is the delivery of items outside the tolerances, or a delivery of fewer items than the quantity desired. The variances must be calculated separately for the following origins:

- Scrap
- Price
- Quantity
- Use of reserves
- Lot size variance
- Output price

Settlement is an accounting process that ensures that the value of the work done and the work in process is credited to the proper account so that this value appears in the financial documents. If you operate control accounts that are supplementary to the legal requirements, the values are also posted to these accounts so that your management can refer to them when looking for opportunities to improve the profitability of your business. The settlement process entails simultaneous posting, as follows:

- The work in process is posted to financial accounting.
- The work in process is posted to a profit center.
- Variance and scrap values are settled to profitability analysis.
- Variance and scrap values are settled to material or price difference account.

Settlement can be in full or periodic. The full settlement method allows for the total variances to be determined and settled for the corresponding cost object only if the work associated with that cost object reaches a specified stage in its life cycle. For example, if there is a short lead time in order-related production, it may be sensible to delay the final determination of variances until after final delivery, when the actual costs can be compared with the target costs of the movement into stock. Before final delivery, the difference between actual costs and the credits that arise from the partial deliveries is shown as work in process.

Periodic settlement entails calculating the work in process, scrap, and variances and settling these for the corresponding cost object. This method is appropriate when there are long-term orders in repetitive and process manufacturing. Each period, the actual costs are adjusted by work in process and scrap costs. Then the target costs for the movement into stock for that period can be compared with the actual costs for the period.

Postings for work in process can be made automatically to financial accounting. Scrap and variances are settled to inventory or price difference accounts. Standard cost accounting ensures a statistical posting of the period costs to profitability analysis, where the standard cost of goods manufactured and the production efficiency are calculated on the basis of the standard cost estimate.

Using Period-End Closing for Sales-Order-Related Production

If you manufacture specifically for a particular sales order, the sequence of closing accounts at period end follows a different logic from that applied when you manufacture to stock in anticipation of future orders.

Results analysis for a sales order is carried out at period-end closing to show sales revenues, costs of sales, reserves, and work in process. The sequence is as follows:

1. Post the direct costs.
2. Calculate the overhead on the cost object.
3. Calculate the work in process.
4. Calculate the costs of sales.
5. Calculate the provisions.
6. Carry out the settlement.

Part

II

Ch

7

The settlement comprises the following postings:

- The work in process is booked in financial accounting.
- The provisions are booked in financial accounting.
- The sales costs are booked in financial accounting.
- The sales revenues are booked in invoice.
- The sales costs are booked in invoice.
- The work in process is booked in the profit center.
- The provisions are booked in the profit center.
- The sales costs are booked in the profit center.

N O T E   The revenues and costs of sales are periodically settled in profitability analysis.

Calculating Overhead Surcharges

The calculation of overhead charges begins with a reading of the direct costs of the orders that have been previously posted. A calculation base must be defined. This could be the production costs or the direct material costs of a specific origin group. The calculation base can be split between fixed and variable costs.

The surcharge for overhead is calculated either as a percentage of the calculation base or as a choice from values related to quantity. Different surcharges can be allocated to different types of products. When the surcharge is allocated to the product, the cost center specified on the line item of the costing sheet is simultaneously credited, perhaps with separate values for fixed and variable costs.

Accounting for Work in Process

If the full settlement procedure is in use, work in process is assigned a value that depends on the status reached by the order. If the order is released, the work in process is shown as the difference between the actual costs and any credits assigned because some of the work has been delivered. If the work extends over several periods, the changes to stock are accounted periodically. When the order is a final delivery, the work in process is written off.

Target costs can be involved that take account of the amount of work that has been costed, up to the moment when the period accounting is closed. These targets are based on the product's standard cost estimate to which the pertaining overhead charges have been added.

Interpreting Production Variance

Cost center accounting often reveals problems or variances of the following kinds:

- Planning over-estimated or under-estimated the actual values.
- The actual costs of a cost center do not agree with the target costs.
- The cost center is absorbing too much or too little of the overhead.

It is possible to view a cost center report showing these kinds of detail. However, it may be very difficult to explain the variances. The following questions illustrate the analytical gaps:

- Have wages increased, or have more wage hours been used?
- Was more spent on energy because more units were consumed or because the price increased?
- How were the fixed costs allocated to activity receivers in the cost center?
- In which activity types in the cost center were the largest variances detected?

Almost all cost centers will show variances between planned or target and actual costs. The problem is to identify the instances that should be regarded as opportunities to make improvements.

One differentiation that you may have to recognize is the difference between cost center input variances and cost center output variances. For example, variances can arise from the difference between planned and actual values that appear on the input side, such as costs and consumption quantities representing the resources needed to produce activity. These include wages, salaries, energy, and plant maintenance.

Understanding Standard Variance Categories

The system calculates and saves the values for the standard variance categories for each cost element and each cost origin as part of the final costing of an order. The following are the standard variance categories:

- Price variance
- Quantity variance
- Structure variance
- Input variance
- Lot-size variance
- Transfer price variance

A factor used in the costing process can change in price after the standard cost estimate has been calculated. Price variance is shown as the difference in price multiplied by the actual input quantity.

Part
II

Ch
7

If the quantity of a factor used changes with respect to the standard cost estimate, a quantity variance is calculated. This is the difference in quantity multiplied by the price used for the standard cost estimate. The standard price is usually chosen for the standard cost estimate. Quantity differences can arise because of inefficiency in creating the activities in the cost centers so that the work is less than planned. Activity additional to that planned can also arise if the cost center employs processes that are less effective than planned.

When resource-usage variance occurs, such as the kind that occurs when the activities are created by a different mix of human and plant resources from that planned, or some other production factor is completely replaced by another, a variance of the actual cost can arise. This is identified as a structure variance.

If overhead surcharges differ from those planned, or if there are any residual differences that cannot be attributed to any other input variance category, the differences are shown as general input variances.

On the output side of a cost center, quantity variances can arise if actual lot sizes differ from the fixed lot sizes entered in the standard cost estimate. Differences arising in this way are shown as lot-size variances.

Perhaps the cost center should be credited with a different amount because the planned or manual allocation prices used in the standard cost estimate do not reflect the value of the result achieved. The cost center therefore can deliver the finished material at a transfer price different from the price established in the standard cost estimate.

Calculating Variance Category Results

In a typical production plant, the variance calculation begins with the confirmation of the scrap quantities and the work in process. The standard cost estimates are applied to the scrap quantities to yield the scrap costs, which are related to the operations in which the scrap materials were produced. Quantities are planned for scrap for each operation, so the unplanned scrap costs can be calculated for each cost element and for each cost origin.

Developing Target Costs

Target costs are calculated by multiplying the planned costs by the quotient or ratio of planned to actual activity as it occurs in a cost center. Target costs therefore equal planned costs only if the planned activities are the same as the actual activities, in both quantity and type of activity. An alternative way of calculating target costs is to multiply the planned costs by the quotient or ratio of the planned quantity of goods to the actual quantity of goods manufactured in orders.

Both methods of calculating target costs use the planned costs and modulate this figure by a factor that represents the magnitude of the changes that were not anticipated by the planning process. One method bases the factor on activities in cost centers; the other uses quantity of goods manufactured.

The purpose of calculating variance is to measure and explain the differences between actual costs and target costs. Two methods exist for working out target costs, and they can be set up as alternative target cost versions to be applied and compared as required.

One method of calculating target costs is to apply the standard cost estimate to the quantities of material delivered under the order. The other method is to apply the price of the materials as used in the preliminary costing of the order and then adjust for the quantities actually delivered.

The standard cost estimate simultaneously determines the standard price of a material. If there is a difference between the standard cost estimate calculation for an order and the actual costs of this order, this indicates that there is a difference between the standard price and the actual costs. Perhaps the standard cost estimate should be revised, or perhaps the difference is attributable to transient factors that are expected to return to normal in the near future.

The other target costing version that uses the preliminary costing of the order can also be used by noting the variance between preliminary costs and actual costs. These variances represent the differences that arise during production because the preliminary costing was carried out when the order was first opened, and the actual costs are calculated when it has been settled. This target version is used to identify variances and inefficiencies within the production process itself.

Yet another target costing version can be designed to use the standard cost estimate for materials. This version adjusts the cost estimate to the costing lot size of the order. Target costs calculated in this way can be compared with the planned costs taken from the preliminary production order costing. Variances that arise from this calculation represent the changes that have taken place between the estimates used in planning and the estimates applicable when the order was released. This target version is used to identify variances resulting from the scheduling of the order, not those from production inefficiencies.

Using Settlement

The outcomes of settlement as a conclusion to final order costing and at period-end closing are as follows:

☐ Inventory changes in the period are posted to financial accounting and profit center accounting.

☐ Production order variances are settled.

Two ways exist for carrying materials in accounting to portray the value flows in your organization:

☐ Materials are valued at transfer prices.

☐ Materials are valued at standard prices.

There are two corresponding ways of settling production variances. If the material is carried at transfer price, any production variances are debited to material stock unless there is insufficient stock. In such a case, the variance posting is made to a price difference account. If the material is carried at the standard price, the variance posting is made to a price difference account, regardless of the stock position.

Part
II

Ch
7

If you operate profitability analysis, production variances can be differentiated by materials and variance categories and then shown as period costs. These values reflect the efficiency of the cost center in handling the particular material in the reporting period. The cost center profitability calculations are usually aggregated to a division or business area level. See Chapter 9, "Analyzing Profitability," for more details.

Using Cost Objects in a Hierarchy

Cost object controlling is designed to focus on the costing of products. If you plan the cost of your products going into stock, you can arrive at a system of target costs for these materials. You can manufacture these products on receipt of an order. If your production orders are per product, you can enter inward stock movements on the same basis. You can set up activity completion confirmations and material consumption confirmations to enable you to post the actual costs of these inward stock movements on the basis of individual products. These products form natural cost objects for your planning and costing systems.

Suppose that you manufacture products not in response to external orders from customers, but in response to internal orders that maintain certain levels of stocks in anticipation of future orders. This type of manufacturing is recognized as a make-to-stock process.

A similar situation exists in continuous process industries, where the products are managed as production lots, runs, or even campaigns. In this type of plant, there might have to be a delay in posting the actual consumption of materials until after the manufacturing has finished. Inventory differences might arise because the actual output differs in quantity and specification from that planned. One production line may be producing several products between which it is impossible to allocate some of the costs. For instance, the costs of setting up and taking down a production line of this type are very difficult to allocate if the products are to be the receiving cost objects.

In these circumstances where the product is not really a convenient entity to treat as a cost object, a different system must be used to associate certain actual overhead costs with cost objects. A hierarchy of cost objects can provide a solution to the problem of allocating actual costs meaningfully.

For example, you could have a plant that had two production lines. Suppose each line could produce Product A. Suppose Line 1 could also produce Product B, but Line 2 could not. You might therefore have three possibilities:

- Product A made on Line 1
- Product B made on Line 1
- Product A made on Line 2

Now Product A will not always be the same in its costing because it can come from either of two different production lines. You must have two costing versions for Product A. One version is to be applied to the Product A from Line 1, and the other is for the same product made on Line 2.

A convenient cost object in this kind of situation is the run schedule header. The production order sequence specifies the program of production order operations needed to plan and control the production processes. It is to these activities that the work in process and scrap data is related by the accounting procedure.

The cost object hierarchy for this illustration has the structure shown in Figure 7.1. There are two production lines: Line 1 carries only Product 1, which is designated as Version 1 because this product can also be manufactured by Line 2. If Product 1 is made by Line 2, it could have slightly different characteristics and may have to be costed separately because it is manufactured in a different plant. For example, there may be a cost entailed by switching Plant 2 from one product to another. For these reasons, Product 1 is designated as Version 2 if it is produced by Line 2.

FIGURE 7.1

Building a cost object hierarchy.

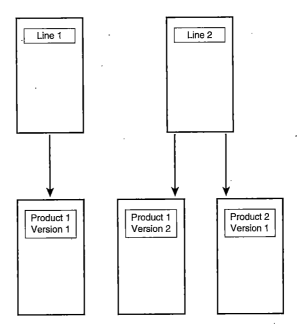

Figure 7.1 represents only the outline of a cost object hierarchy. Each product version has its own data objects to collect the information needed for accounting purposes and for planning and controlling the production plant.

For example, the following processes are active in this kind of production facility:

- Raw materials management
- Overhead accounting
- Delivery control and logistics
- Work in process monitoring
- Accounting for scrap and energy waste

- Product costing
- Profitability analysis

Using Responsibility-Related Controlling

If you have established a cost object hierarchy, the costs can be posted to the levels of the hierarchy for which a responsible person can be identified. Each operation can be controlled by a different person, or a section of a production sequence can be the unit of responsibility. The costs are posted to the level at which a person can be identified who is potentially able to make a difference in the profitability of the cost object. Different costs therefore are posted to different levels. The plant manager is responsible for different costs to the production operator.

Using Product-Related Controlling

A hierarchy of cost objects is used in controlling based on the product. Costs are again posted to different levels as convenient, but they are then distributed down the cost object hierarchy to the individual cost objects at the lowest level. The allocation of costs is governed by the relative values of target costs summarized across each level. The actual costs are distributed among the cost objects in proportion to the target costs calculated for them.

Using Activity-Based Cost Accounting

In cost accounting terms, an activity is a process that can be counted and that attracts costs. In business terms, a production process is achieved by a network of activities. If you want to find out the cost of a process, you must know the activities and the quantities of work done by each.

The purpose of the SAP R/3 CO-Controlling module is to help you plan, monitor, and settle activity types in the accounts of cost centers.

N O T E Activity types serve as allocation bases and are used as cost drivers to determine and send incurred costs to receivers.

The system enables you to develop fully integrated activity costing in a controlled, step-by-step fashion. There is an inevitable logical sequence, as follows:

1. Define the activity types of interest to your company because they add value, attract costs, or both.
2. Specify how each activity type will be measured and what units should be used.
3. Create a plan using your activity types and their quantities.
4. Extend the plan to include the costs that are dependent on activities and the rates to be applied.
5. Allocate, or set up rules to allocate, activity costs for both planned and actual data.
6. Predistribute the fixed costs, and attach a value to each activity type that cannot be measured.
7. Determine the variances over the period, and allocate them to activities or cost centers.

Using Activity Types and Allocation Bases

The measurement of productivity must start with a measurement, or at least a quantitative assessment of activity. In a production cost center, there are measurements of time required; number, weight or volume of each product; and units finished and semi-finished. The service cost centers have records of jobs, hours worked by each skilled trade, energy, and materials used.

Sales and administrative tasks are also becoming subject to measurement of a nominal kind, where something that can be counted (such as the number of calls made) is used as an index of activity. Each call entails an amount of work that can be assessed and evaluated, at least in average terms. Depending on the type, data on an activity typically includes information on the planned activity quantity, the capacity, and the output quantity. Activities can be assigned to activity groups so that you can carry out some operations on all the members of the group simultaneously. This might be useful as you change your controlling task from planning to allocation, to determination of cost rates, and so on. No limit in CO-Controlling governs the number and scope of the activity groups you use.

The master record of an activity group contains parameters that you can use to define how the group is handled. There are parameters to define the settlement cost elements to be used in the direct allocation of planned and actual values. You can flag particular activities as statistical, which ensures that the system adopts a standard procedure for calculations according to the needs of the moment, including assessment, distribution, and computing ratios for use in reporting.

Applying Internal Activity Allocation Methods

The system provides for allocating overhead costs to cost centers and business processes. Two methods are available:

- ☐ Costs posted to cost centers are distributed to business processes.
- ☐ Costs posted to business processes are allocated to cost objects.

Using Value Accounting The characteristic of value accounting is that costs are simply allocated from sender to receiver without showing the underlying relationships between the activities involved. The method is easy to implement, but it permits only limited forms of analysis. The areas of application of this method are in cost center distribution, cost center assessment, and process assessment.

The sending cost object does not reveal its operating rate or the extent to which its capacity has been utilized when merely the full costs of production are posted. Variance calculations are limited to straightforward comparisons of planned costs and actual costs.

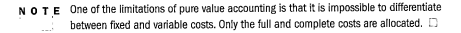

N O T E   One of the limitations of pure value accounting is that it is impossible to differentiate between fixed and variable costs. Only the full and complete costs are allocated. ☐

Part II
Ch 7

Using Quantity Accounting The process of quantity accounting is more costly than value accounting because there are more calculations to be performed and more records to be kept. Cost centers and processes must be capable of reporting the quantities of their various activities and the prices they are charging for them individually. This entails detailed planning and measurement of the actual quantities. First, a quantity structure is built to show how much of each activity is transferred between cost centers. Then a standardized price list is applied to convert the quantity flows to value flows.

Understanding Activity Planning and the Flow of Activities

For each cost center, you must arrive at a planned value for each activity. You must reconcile this amount of activity with the amount of activity planned in the logistics system. The system can assist you with this.

The CO-ABC Activity-Based Cost Accounting module differentiates three types of planning:

- Planning statistical key figures
- Planning activity quantities
- Planning primary and secondary cost elements

A statistical key figure in planning can be simply a number for each posting period, or it can be a cumulative number computed for each period on the basis of data. If the cost center produces activities that are quantified, the planned or actual quantity of output can be the basis for planning the primary and secondary cost elements. This is because the output quantity of the cost center can be converted to values.

Given the input of primary and secondary costs to a cost center·and the output in terms of evaluated quantities of activities, you can instruct the system to compute the efficiency of the cost center in each of its activities. The same method is used to plan the activities to be produced and consumed in the flow of internal activities. You then have the basis for planning secondary costs.

Understanding Simulation and the Reconciliation of Activities

The logistics plan and the controlling plan may be inconsistent, but bottlenecks and idle production capacity can be foreseen.

Interactive activity analysis enables you to look at several activities at once to see which have spare capacity and which are destined to be subjected to demands beyond their capacity. You may be able to initiate a displacement of work or resources or to replace one activity by another. The system immediately simulates the cost effects of your tentative change of plan, which you can either confirm when you are satisfied or store as a separate version of the plan.

Starting at any cost center, you can command a display of the activity types received from or sent to an adjacent cost center level. This enables you to trace the functional dependencies between individual activity types.

Using Activity-Based Cost Planning

Each activity type and each cost center can be given as many cost elements as necessary. You can enter the planned cost elements as values or as values to be computed at the time based on the quantities and the rates prevailing. The cost element can be given a planned overall value or a planned quantity.

Both procedures can be carried out as full or marginal costs and can direct a split into fixed and variable components. The system provides formulas, formal specifications, texts, and report characteristics.

The CO-Controlling system distributes the planned values for the variable primary cost elements for the year. You can see the effects on costs of any fluctuations in planned activity levels. You can call for the fixed costs to be distributed using standard rules or your own rules.

The internal exchange of activities also causes secondary costs to be incurred. These are computed by valuing the amounts of the allocated activity quantities at the appropriate standard rates defined in the sender cost centers. The receivers of internal activity costs include the following:

- Cost centers
- Orders for cost centers that are overhead cost orders
- Production orders for semi-finished and finished products
- Capital spending orders for fixed assets
- Sales orders or sales cost objects

After planning values for internal orders, you might want to allocate the planned costs to the receiver cost centers. The original producing cost centers retain the information.

Using Political Prices

Standard prices and standard rates at which cost centers activities should be charged are among the important results to come out of any planning exercise. The total cost is divided by the total quantity in each case.

You may be in a business that prefers not to use the actual or historical standard price computed as an average based on total cost and total quantity. You may have to set rates that are determined by political factors rather than by computation.

You must enter political rates manually. You can then use them to evaluate planned and actual quantities. The system retains an accurate representation of internal activity cost flows and cost allocations, even if the rates are not the strictly determined product of formal business planning.

Understanding Indirect Allocation of Costs to Non-Measurable Activities

The system has indirect cost allocation functions that you can use to allocate costs accurately to the objects that caused them. You may be able to apply standard methods if you can derive an index of activity to serve as a quantity to which you can apply a rate. But the indirect allocation functions are available for times when the most reasonable method is to assess costs and allocate them to their causes.

For example, you could set up a master record and name a cost center as Quality Control. You could determine an hourly rate for inspection and then estimate how many hours of inspecting could be made available from the quality control cost center. From the logistics information system, you could obtain an estimate for the number of items to be inspected in the reporting period, both for incoming and for outgoing goods. The actual cost of inspection could be calculated from the hourly rate for inspection based on using the full capacity of the quality control cost center. You would have to modify this total by applying the ratio of the total capacity of the center to the amount of inspecting actually needed in the period. If you could not measure the number of items inspected, you would have to use an estimate based on some reference quantities, such as the consumption in the period of some measured resource thought to be proportional to the number of items inspected.

Understanding Cost Center Variances

Variance analysis is a method of monitoring business activity. A variance is defined as the computed difference between actual costs and planned costs, using the following formula:

Actual cost = Planned cost plus or minus the variance

Variances can be calculated at any level:

- ☐ Cost center
- ☐ Cost element
- ☐ Activity type

Four variance factors explain why actual costs can differ from planned costs:

- ☐ Price variance, caused by differences between the actual and the planned prices of the goods and services used.
- ☐ Usage variance, arising from uneconomical working practices in the production process.
- ☐ Volume variance, which occurs when the planned volume is not reached or is exceeded. This gives rise to fixed costs that are under- or over-absorbed by the actual volume of product.
- ☐ Cost center over- or under-absorption of fixed costs, as a result of using standard rates in the plan that differ from those applied in the posting of actual activities, the so-called political rates. The same effects can occur if the cost center plans have not been reconciled.

The total of these variances for all cost elements and activity types within a cost center provides the overall variance for that cost center.

For each combination of cost element and activity type on each cost center, the system maintains a value structure for controlling. Each of these values is split into a fixed part and a variable part:

- Planned costs
- Target costs
- Variance types
- Actual costs
- Planned/actual usage

You can have the variances calculated and included as part of the cost components. The formulas follow:

- Actual Cost = Planned Cost plus or minus Cost Variance
- Actual Price = Planned Price plus or minus Price Variance
- Target Costs = Actual Volume times Planned Rates
- Usage Variance = Actual Costs minus Target Costs minus Price Variance
- Volume Variance = Target Costs plus or minus Actual Activity times Planned Price
- Over- or Under-absorption = Target Costs minus Allocated Costs minus Volume Variance

Charging Variances

The CO-Controlling system evaluates each activity by applying the planned rate to the activity quantity. If you have the historical variances, or if your system can get them for you, you have the possibility of using them in a fresh version of your plan. Similarly, if you have some way of anticipating future variances, or if you want to conduct a what-if simulation exercise, you can create a fresh plan version.

You may want to use anticipated variances in the cost allocation process. To represent accurately the value flow in your company, it is essential to allocate cost center variances periodically. You can specify whether to use historical, standard, or anticipated variances for the subsequent charging process. In this way, you can transfer all variances directly to your profitability analysis system.

An alternative approach is to pass on usage variances to the receivers but keep as a charge on the producing cost center the variances resulting from too little output. These variances go to the profitability analysis system from there.

You can charge variances periodically to the following types of receivers:

- Individual cost centers
- Internal orders or projects
- Production orders, and so to the finished and semi-finished product inventory

- Cost objects in profitability analysis
- Fixed assets

If you arrange for actual variances to be charged to cost objects in CO-PA Profitability Analysis, you will be on the way toward creating the detailed cost structures necessary for a system of contribution margin accounting.

Variances are posted under the system using the rules and procedures of direct cost allocation. The system specifies the allocation cost element by its identification code and by whether the value is fixed or variable on either the sender or receiver object. The system also ensures that identical variance types are in use.

The effect of all these procedures is to accurately allocate all actual costs to the precise area of the company where they were caused. This serves both the legal requirement of external accounting and the need for comprehensive internal reporting as a basis for controlling the company.

Using Alternative Activity Rates in Parallel

The method described in the previous section can be regarded as an imputed allocation approach: Cost centers accrue costs because of the activities they undertake and the overheads they enjoy. The CO-Controlling system also operates a system of parallel activity rates that can provide a family of alternative evaluations relevant to various accounting purposes.

At the cost element level, you can put together a portfolio of costs to be included in an alternative activity rate for each cost element. If these rates are used when calculating internal activity flows, you can produce cost estimates that conform to all legal and tax regulations for which your portfolio is correct.

These calculations lead to the derivation of the balance sheet and profitability analysis. You can compare costs of sales and total costs of production, both estimated and as they appear in the external financial documents.

Using Activities and Services Costing

By looking more closely at the way they produce their goods and services, companies have made extensive improvements. The need exists for a system of structured overhead costing. The first thing to do is to identify and define the cost drivers, which are the factors that can be used to influence how activity costs are allocated to the cost centers that generate them.

The cost driver is a subprocess that can be measured for individual cost center activities, such as the following:

- Number of purchase order items successfully processed
- Number of quotation items
- Delivery items in sales
- Dunning operations and payment differences handled

Subprocesses are grouped together into primary processes that can be addressed by the product costing system to determine the costs of administrative and service activities. You will discover what each subprocess costs and can initiate an activity-based profitability analysis.

Planning and Simulating the Subprocesses

The basic disciplines of activity-based accounting must be applied to ensure that the activities at a cost center are integrated with the accounting and controlling systems. However, there is a further level of detail to be considered if activities are to be analyzed into their constituent subprocesses.

A business process can be represented by a chain of activities and products or a network of such chains. In the SAP R/3 system, this chain or network is managed by a process sequence structure, which can be of any complexity. The process sequence structure can be used to simulate the flow of material through a sequence of activities that create perhaps a series of semi-finished products and that terminate with the finished product. The SAP PP-Production Planning module specializes in this work.

The system of costing based on a process sequence structure requires that all the processes and subprocesses be quantified in terms of quantity and value flow. This is so that analysis and reporting can occur at a level of detail that yields a balance of activities. Such a process documents the ways in which the activity level of the parent cost center exerts influence on the costs of the primary processes and their subprocesses. How do support costs alter when business gets better or worse?

Using Process Cost Rates

The purpose of applying the methods of activity-based costing to the detailed processes and subprocesses of a production company is to compute process cost rates. How much does it cost to put one invoice item through the office? How much to move one pallet from production to warehouse?

If you have process cost rates at this level of detail, you can take a standard costing based on a bill of materials and routings, for example, and cost each of the processes entailed. You can also have the SAP system do it for you.

If you have these process cost rates for all the subprocesses in each activity type, you can transfer the process costs from CO-CCA Cost Center Accounting directly to CO-PA Profitability Analysis.

Because you have the process costs associated with each activity embraced by CO-CCA Cost Center Accounting, you can include these process costs in the value flow patterns that are identified by both Product Costing and Period Costing.

Part

II

Ch

7

Using Internal Order Accounting

The CO-OPA Order and Project Accounting module is specialized in the tasks of planning, monitoring, and settling the activities, services, and processes that take place as the result of internal orders and projects.

The distinguishing feature of CO-OPA is its capability of settling in detail the actual costs according to rules particular to each item. The system also has the following important capabilities:

- ☐ Planning is available for all resources and costs required, in quantity and value.
- ☐ Charges can be computed from prices at the time, with imputed allocations of overhead and actual costs.
- ☐ Open items (commitment items) for purchase requisitions, purchase orders, and material reservations are closely monitored.
- ☐ All cash-related procedures, such as down payment requests and down payments, are displayed.
- ☐ Order reports are evaluated and analyzed concurrently.

The purpose of internal orders is to monitor costs to assist in decision making and to manage the allocation and settlement of activity costs to target objects, including FI-GL General Ledger accounts. Projects can also be used for these purposes. Complex projects are discussed in Chapter 8.

Internal orders are usually defined for a particular task, event, or internal change measure that must be planned, monitored, and settled in great detail. These orders are distinguished by their origin and by the time allocated for their completion. They vary in their settlement arrangements and in how they appear in the reporting functions.

SAP R/3 classifies internal orders as follows:

- ☐ Production-related orders used in Logistics
- ☐ Sales orders used in SD-Sales and Distribution
- ☐ Internal orders used in CO-Controlling

Although the internal orders of the Logistics modules and the SD-Sales and Distribution component serve mainly to monitor resources used and sales achieved, they also document estimated costs, actual costs, and revenues. In the PP-Production Planning and Control modules, the order has the job of annexing information on the latest estimate of costs until the actual costs replace them when the order is complete.

Sales orders that document costs and revenues are accessed by the CO-PA Profitability Analysis system. These sales orders also carry the information needed by CO-Controlling and PP-Production Planning and Control, for example. The orders for processing and settling internal costs usually support the integration of different business systems with the ways the particular company likes to do business and settle the costs.

Internal orders in CO-Controlling are differentiated by the following characteristics:

- ☐ Whether logistical, controlling, or settlement is the main function
- ☐ The content of the order, such as product or project
- ☐ Whether the item is an individual order or a standing order

☐ The significance of the values on the order, such as plan costs, actual costs, or variances

☐ The settlement receiver for the order, such as fixed asset account, cost center, cost object, project, stock, business segment, sales order, or FI-GL General Ledger account

An important feature of the CO-OPA Order and Project Accounting component is that you can assign the relevant costs on each of the orders and projects to the various receivers, split by period and allocated accurately by cause. The costs can be used for both overhead cost controlling and production controlling.

If you wish to have an internal order that is a simple single-level project used only in the CO-Controlling system, the system invites you to specify how you want to monitor it and settle the costs incurred.

Integrating Order and Project Accounting with Asset Accounting

If you are managing fixed assets such as buildings and machines, the settlement of capital spending orders is of crucial importance. The CO-OPA Order and Project Accounting module offers detailed settlement rules and a close integration with the FI-AA Asset Accounting system to yield the following advantages:

☐ Settlement of costs to the appropriate balance sheet accounts under the heading of Assets Under Construction (AuC) while the capital spending order is ongoing

☐ Order-based display of special depreciation for AuC

☐ Recognition of subsidies, grants, and down payments

☐ Partial orders settled over a hierarchy of orders

Because all costs are based on unified posting and settlement rules in the SAP R/3 system, you can allocate costs from orders and projects to the various target objects using the same rules or rules that you specify separately. You can keep track of complex overhead costs with maintenance and capital spending orders.

The distinguishing feature of the SAP module CO-OPA Order and Project Accounting is its capability of settling in detail the actual costs according to the individual rules for each item. The following must be specified:

☐ The target object(s) defined as one or more fixed assets in FI-AA Asset Management

☐ The date of the settlement

☐ The scope of the costs to be settled

☐ The settlement cost element heading

☐ The supplementary information

The system also has the following important capabilities:

☐ Planning is available for all resources and costs required, in quantity and value.

☐ Charges can be computed from prices at the time, with imputed allocations of overhead and actual costs.

- ☐ Open items (commitment items) for purchase requisitions, purchase orders, and material reservations are closely monitored.
- ☐ Display is possible for all cash-related procedures, such as down payment requests and down payments.
- ☐ Concurrent evaluation and analysis of order reports can be performed.

Using Planned Cost Schedules

Costs and deadlines on orders and projects that take a long time to complete are constrained by the financial facts of life. Money is not always available when you need it. Financial and liquidity planning must know what costs are expected on the orders and projects. It helps to have some idea of how the costs are likely to be incurred over the first few accounting periods in detail—and in broader terms thereafter up to the date of completion.

A cost schedule is a plan, extending the length of an order or project, that shows the values expected to be allocated to costs. The schedule has a key date. Until this date is known and entered on the plan, the forecast of costs must be moved ahead to the best estimated date.

The SAP R/3 system provides support to the EC-Enterprise Controller in the following ways:

- ☐ The system automatically determines the tasks from the planned start and finish dates for the order.
- ☐ Cost distribution across the schedule can be suited to the specific order.
- ☐ Graphical representations of the data model are readily available online and in print.

If you have carried out cost element planning or created a unit costing for the order, the system can use this information to develop a cost schedule.

A costing system uses a set of costing objects, which are the different products, production and other orders, resources, and so on. The only qualification for a costing object is that it can be allocated costs that mean something when they are totaled under the heading of that costing object. The costing objects can be conceptual or tangible, organizational or geographical.

The pivotal concept in costing is the structure of cost drivers, or cost objects onto which the actual costs are settled according to how they were incurred. SAP R/3 CO-Controlling provides a range of model structures on which you can base a structure specific to the needs of your company.

Understanding Order Data Formats

The master data record for an order comprises the order number and the parameters for controlling the business and technical system functions that deal with it. You are authorized to use a certain range of order numbers; otherwise, the system assigns the number.

The order master bears control data to signify the transaction groups in which it can take part. For example, an order type Planning allows the entry of information such as primary costs and overhead costs for planning purposes only.

The order master also includes parameter fields to organize overhead components and to control the settlement functions. Some orders have the function of monitoring all open purchase orders, for example; others are intended for the detailed settlement of individual cost items.

This system of order parameters set into the master records enables you to establish a suite of order types. These order types can be used to nominate the manner in which each order directs the value flow in your company along the lines already defined by your organizational structure and the way in which your company chooses to group its business functions.

Managing the Status of Orders

The status of an order is the stage it has reached in its life cycle. The SAP CO-OPA Order and Project Accounting system is particularly flexible because it enables you to decide what should happen at each stage and, indeed, through which stages a particular type of order should proceed through its life cycle on its way to completion. For example, you can choose where to have the system plan primary or secondary costs for each order.

The typical status sequence for an order encounters the following stages:

- Order opened, basic data identified
- Planning primary and secondary costs
- Released for posting
- Execution
- Technical completion
- Accounting completion

Some of these business functions can operate across more than one status. You can permit planning information to be added to an order while it is being executed, for example.

Classifying Orders by Content

Because they are treated differently, orders are classified by their content and controlling objectives into various types. Job orders collect and analyze the planned and actual costs for a commodity or operational event that will not be capitalized, such as minor repairs or staff training. These orders are settled on the objects that caused them, by means of the periodic cost center accounting procedures.

Capital spending orders on the fixed assets produced in-house and on maintenance costs serve to manage the planning and allocation of costs over the lifetime of the order, which can be an open order.

Production orders are used to gather primary costs from FI-Financial Accounting and secondary costs from overhead assessment. Activity costs come from internal allocation. Issues of raw materials and semi-finished materials are notified from MM-Materials Management. Production orders in Logistics use bills of materials, routings, and cost centers. They are fully integrated into the overall capacity planning and monitoring functions.

Sales orders can have posted to them any type of cost and revenue items taken directly from SD-Sales and Distribution. These can be transferred directly to the appropriate business segments in CO-PA Profitability Analysis.

An individual order is typically unique and of long duration. The quantity structures are seldom fully known at the start, so planning is carried out in stages. Where an individual order entails multilevel production processing and a complex web of activities, partial orders can be created. The SAP R/3 Project System is specialized for this kind of work in make-to-order production.

Standing orders are used when cost centers must be split into smaller activity units, such as small repairs, minor maintenance, or individual vehicles in a company fleet.

Statistical orders are used to receive additional account assignments for the purpose of summarizing, sorting, and displaying cost objects according to specific criteria. The amount posted appears under the original cost element heading on the appropriate account and again on the statistical order. Revenues can also be collated by a statistical order.

Planning Orders

You can plan the overall value of an order. You can also plan according to the cost elements and activity types, either on the specific order or by transferring the values from a unit you have already costed. The following cost elements and activity types are amenable to planning on orders:

- Primary costs by cost element or cost element group, in values or in quantities to which the system applies cost rates at the time
- Cost center activities as the secondary costs, planned down to the level of individual operations if necessary
- Overhead, planned using the overhead application functions
- Statistical key figures, to be used to form business ratios when reporting

Distribution keys provide a choice between planning orders on a yearly basis with a standard distribution across months, and planning for each month separately. Order groups can be assembled for overhead calculation, planning, and reporting.

The functionality and screens used in CO-CCA Cost Center Accounting can give planning views of your flexible combinations of planning objects and planning content. For example, you can call for planning views on all or any of the following situations:

- Many cost elements on a single order
- Many cost element groups on a single order
- Many cost elements on an order group
- Many cost element groups on an order group

Whatever planning steps you take, you can store in the system a choice of standard explanatory texts with additional information to document your decisions.

If a long time elapses before the order is executed after planning, the assumptions on which the plan was built could become out-of-date. Each plan is noted as a new version whenever you change something so that subsequent analysis presents an accurate picture.

If a plan has already been released and changes must be made, you can instruct the system to document the entry of the modified order plan and the changes made to it, in the form of a copy of the plan line items that have been altered.

Using Open Items

If you want to place a reservation on a certain quantity of material, or if you still have a commitment to pay for an external service on a specific order, then you enter an open item. In the display, open items appear as values and quantities under the appropriate cost element heading in the correct fiscal year and in the period that includes the planned supply date.

Open items can arise through purchasing in the MM-Materials Management system. If the invoice has been received, the open item can be evaluated from the actual prices; if not, the anticipated price must be used. Delivery costs are displayed separately so they can be evaluated in the appropriate currency for the place where each cost element was incurred.

Material reservation in MM-IM Materials Management, Inventory Management creates an open item that is evaluated at the carrying price. You can also generate an open item manually in the form of a funds reservation.

As you reduce an open item, the system helps you manage it using the original currency. Analysis and posting can take place under the system rules for foreign currency and its exchange.

The aim is to replace each open item on an order with the corresponding actual costs. If an open item concerns external services, the system reduces the purchase order by value using the invoiced amount, whether full or partial. The system identifies any price differences by account and by order.

If an open item is a goods purchase order, the system automatically reduces the quantity and the value for the open purchase item as soon as the goods are received. If the invoice is received before the goods, the system adjusts the open purchase order by adopting the invoice value in place of the purchase order value. If any amounts on the invoice or on the services received remain unsettled, the order stays open until they are finally cleared completely.

The order number and the posting details are retained when an order progresses from one business transaction to the next. As a result, the system can document the purchase order history, which enables you to trace a partial delivery or a partial invoice to the purchase order and then back to the original purchase requisition.

N O T E Open item management illustrates the close integration of Logistics and Accounting in the SAP system. ☐

Part
II

Ch
7

Using Actual Cost Accounting Transactions

Every SAP transaction generates an SAP document. If the document contains a posting to an order number, the CO-OPA Order and Project Accounting system charges the amount to the order under the relevant cost element heading and with that order number. You can trace the history of origin of each line item throughout the lifetime of the order.

Activities must take place so that production orders, maintenance orders, and job orders are fulfilled. These activities are the responsibility of one or more cost centers. For each of these activities, the responsible cost center demands payment in the form of an internal cost allocation.

The CO-Controlling system evaluates the activity quantity at the appropriate rate. At the same time, line items are created to document the flow of value from the producing sender objects to the receiving objects. These take the form of a credit to the sending cost center and a debit to the receiving order. This is the process of direct internal cost allocation.

If the activity is not amenable to quantification—if you cannot say exactly how much of the item is needed for the order—you must use indirect cost allocation, in which a periodic total is shared in some way between the receiving cost centers or orders.

Overhead is a charge that should be allocated as accurately as possible to the items that must share its burden. This distribution is discussed in the section on CO-CCA Cost Center Accounting.

Settling Orders

Order settlement is the process of passing costs from the originating order to other cost objects. Two groups of these target objects exist: internal postings within CO-Controlling, and external postings to the accounts managed by FI-Financial Accounting and other applications.

Internal postings settle orders automatically using CO-CEA Cost Element Accounting. This component creates the necessary credit and debit line items for any of the following objects:

- Cost centers
- Internal orders
- Projects
- Business segments
- Sales orders

Orders can be settled by postings to external objects using the following functions:

- FI-AA Asset Accounting, for assets under construction or capitalized assets
- MM-Materials Management, which settles any product manufactured in-house to inventory under the material number for a warehouse
- FI-Financial Accounting, which can settle orders to the appropriate FI-GL General Ledger account

Knowing Settlement Rules

Each order master includes a data element that determines the settlement rule to be applied to that order. The rule includes the following control parameters:

- Period of validity for the settlement rule.
- Target object or objects to which the costs are to be sent—for example, if part of the costs of the order will be capitalized and the rest distributed between certain cost centers.
- The cost element or elements under which the order value is to be credited. Using cost element groups results in a debit to the receiver under each element.
- Settlement of costs to a cost element within the CO-Controlling system.

The settlement rule can be a defined debit to the receiver. Several receivers can be targeted in proportions calculated from equivalence numbers or percentages. Absolute amounts can be settled, or costs can be based on quantity—the system uses the rate current when the settlement is performed.

If the order includes information on a suitable target object for settlement, such as a responsible cost center or a related project identification, the system operates a default distribution rule generated on the basis of this information. Orders that allocate costs to cost centers tend to be settled periodically; capital spending orders are settled at period-end after the project has been completed.

Orders to be settled can be grouped according to the following criteria:

- Order type
- Date when the settlement is to be performed
- Receiver of the settlement
- Corporate or company code
- Settlement to internal or external accounting system

You can create a settlement simulation list in the CO-OPA Order and Project Accounting system using the allocation groups to check that the orders are both correct and complete. When the simulation is correct, you can use the list to execute the settlement. You can reverse a settlement made previously and repeat it at any time.

The system calculates the total settlement and the individual amounts debited to each receiver in the controlling area currency, from which you can convert if necessary. The settlement function differentiates between debiting the full costs of an order and debiting only direct costs. You can have previously distributed fixed costs in CO-CCA Cost Center Accounting, in which case this is provided for in the value flow.

N O T E The order reporting system shows you the settlement history, which comprises the dates and details of the amounts already settled, any reversals performed, and the balance remaining on the order. □

Using Order Summary Evaluations

If you want to compare two or more orders in detail, you may find it helpful to have the system classify orders using a hierarchy. The CO-Controlling system enables you to put any criterion at the top of your hierarchy and any other criteria at each level below. You might ask these sorts of questions:

- How do the various companies in this group compare across these functions: repairs, advertising special campaigns, and so on?
- How do the various companies in this group compare, for all departments and all production orders?

These criteria together create a hierarchy over which the system can collate the data, in this example, for all production orders. The SAP R/3 flexible reporting functions enable you to view this data at any level of your hierarchy and to switch readily from one viewpoint to another.

In fact, the system offers a complete system of order reporting, from line item up to order, cost center, controlling area, and company. The online reporting techniques enable you to take any summary and drill down to the details of the order items that contribute to it.

Using Cost of Sales Accounting

The cost of sales accounting method using standard costs to produce interim reports enables you to look at any market segment immediately, without waiting for the actual data to arrive.

The market-driven needs of sales management dictate that the system be capable of estimating profits in the short term by using interim reports based on standard values and imputed costs. These interim values are derived from standard manufacturing costs with cash discounts and rebates because the actual data is not available at the time the billing document must be issued.

When the actual data arrives, the interim reports are usually reconciled with it on a period basis to yield the cost of sales accounting using actual costs (reconciled reports). Because of the lag in time, these reports are not so useful for managing the sales activities; their function is more to document and summarize. ●

8

Controlling by the PS-Project System

In this chapter

Defining Projects

In the context of business data processing, a project is a complicated plan to accomplish something that cannot be managed as a single order. (Sometimes single-level projects can exist, however.) Project management includes monitoring the progress of the work and settling the costs when the procedure is finished. A successful project is distinguished by carefully planned objectives, efficient execution of the plan, and a prudent control of resources.

N O T E   When a project lasts across several accounting periods, the costs are settled in each accounting period for those elements of the work that reached a certain milestone stage. □

The purpose of the R/3 PS-Project System module is to manage efficiently all the stages of a project, from planning to completion. The efficiency comes from having the right information available when it is needed, as well as implementing an automated data processing routine to deal with it.

Five types of projects contribute to the definition of what functionality is required of a project system. Though each of the following project types are specialized, they are not specific to any one industry or field of business:

- ☐ Research and development
- ☐ Engineer-to-order manufacturing
- ☐ Investment programs
- ☐ Maintenance projects
- ☐ Information technology projects

Each project proceeds along a trajectory, a path of activities that consume resources, until the purpose of the project is achieved and reported. At each stage, SAP R/3 standard business functions are organized in support by the R/3 PS-Project System. The system is fully integrated with all other SAP R/3 applications.

Setting the Project Trajectory

A project plan can be developed in detail at any time after a master record is created to identify the project. You can begin with a simple list of key events, or you can copy a project structure from one already in your implementation.

Although some the stages of a project can be abbreviated (and some extended) according to the nature and complexity of the endeavor, it is usually possible to discern phases or groups of tasks, especially if the R/3 PS-Project System is at work. The following sections indicate what is achieved at each phase. Later sections discuss the individual functions.

Performing General Planning

Rough-cut general cost planning usually begins a project and aims to set times and values against a work breakdown structure, or at least a listing of what must be done. The first draft of a work breakdown structure (WBS) can be arranging the list of what must be done so that the elements are arranged in sequence (if that is how they must be performed). If some elements can be performed in any order as long they are all completed before a particular task begins, then this can be shown in logical or tree diagram form. The PS-Project System provides graphical help for this purpose.

Each task in a work breakdown structure is represented in the SAP R/3 system as one or more of the following types of WBS elements:

- A planning WBS element that contains the planned values for the actual costs
- An account assignment WBS element to which actual costs are posted
- A billing WBS element to which revenues are posted

A WBS element can be associated with a specific organizational unit, such as a plant or business area. If you do not explicitly make this assignment, the PS system uses the organization data from the project definition.

If a WBS element is associated with a particular piece of equipment or a functional location, such as a workplace, you can record this as an assignment to the element. This could then be used for plant maintenance according to the scheduled time or work quantity performed at the location.

As soon as a plant is identified, the person responsible is identified. But you can also define the areas of responsibility and the responsible people for the elements of a work breakdown structure. The system also provides user-defined fields in each WBS element record that you can use for your own purposes.

Performing Detailed Planning

The details of a project are subject to fine planning, which may utilize cost element planning or unit costing methods. You may use manual entries for critical dates, although the system may be able to carry out automatic detailing of activities if they have been used previously. The R/3 system will look after scheduling and highlighting of time-critical activities as soon as the requisite data is available.

Coordinating Resources

System support for coordinating resources is provided by the following:

- Purchase requisitions and materials reservation plans produced automatically under control of the MRP-Material Requirements Planning module.
- Inventory management.

❏ Network planning of capacities, materials, operating resources, and services. Particular people defined by their experience or qualifications can be located through the HR-Human Resources application.

N O T E   R/3 Release 4.0 provides you with the facility to specify a dynamic agent. This agent is specified in a master record as an organizational object that is authorized to execute a particular workflow task. Depending on the task, the agent can be an organizational unit, a user, a job, a position, or a named employee. ❏

Supervising Projects

System monitoring of materials, capacities, and funds takes place as the project is approved and executed. Material availability is checked as soon as your customer places an order. Capacity planning is supported by a capacity planning table that displays any schedule delays, bottle-necks, or overloads. You can initiate corrective measures interactively with this display.

A budget management component supports approved and released project budgets, funds commitments, and assignments to projects. This component checks the availability of funds and transmits an alarm to the project manager if any problem is foreseen.

SAP Workflow is integrated with the Project System so that you can keep all departments in touch with the progress of the project and any changes made to it. The actual values from Accounting, Purchasing, Inventory, and Productions are written directly to the project records. You can arrange for the values to be assigned to the appropriate WBS element and to the net-work display records for such transactions as the following:

❏ Postings
❏ Purchase orders
❏ Material movements
❏ Production orders
❏ Plant maintenance orders

Closing Projects

Project closing entails the following actions:

❏ Revenues from sales orders are automatically written to the project from the SD-Sales and Distribution application when they occur. The interest is calculated as part of the closing procedure.
❏ Results are analyzed up to a specified date.
❏ Settlement takes place by settling all or some of the incurred costs to one or more receivers, such as cost centers, fixed assets, or objects in the financial statement.

During the results analysis, the realized revenues are compared with the accrued costs up to a specified date. The outcome of the results analysis can be written automatically to the profit-ability analysis. At this time, the system posts values to the appropriate balance sheet accounts for works in process, bad debt provisions, and any other provisions you have specified.

The control panel for the project system is really the Project Planning Board display, which the user can configure for each project. The control panel adopts the standard planning board graphical symbols and is virtually unlimited in the number of elements and the time periods represented.

The PS information system is provided with open interfaces to Microsoft Word for Windows and Excel to enable you to perform word processing and spreadsheet operations to analyze project results. You can also manage projects in conjunction with Microsoft Project and with communication links that can confirm actual project data.

Using Different Project Views

Within an organization, each functional department looks at a project from a different point of view. Each specialty may need a different selection from the project information. However, with an integrated system, when somebody enters data, everyone else may utilize it. The project system can filter out data to suit each type of user.

Using Sales View

The sales staff focuses on the customer order and the sales cycle, from inquiry to quotation to sales order, billing, and delivery notes. Values, dates, and quantities are obviously important. The customer is the object of attention. Technical documents and specifications could be as important as costings, prices, revenues, and cost elements in accounting. Commercial practice controls inquiry processing, quotations, order processing, delivery documents, and invoicing. These events can be seen in the sales view.

The work breakdown structure and the networks can easily portray the internal and external structure of a sales order and can provide you with data objects to which you can assign planned values as and when they become available. All the pieces can fall into place automatically as soon as the customer places an order, even if the details must be added later. You can check the availability of materials immediately and make plans against which to monitor material requirements and stock levels. The system enables you to conduct materials requirements planning and inventory control for individual sales orders, if necessary.

Using Manufacturing View

Manufacturing operates with planned orders and production orders in conjunction with bills of materials, plants, work center hierarchies, and production schedules. These are the entities of the PP-Production Planning and Control application with which the project system is fully integrated.

You can allocate planned orders and production orders to specific WBS elements or to network-level activities, as appropriate. You then have two options. You can analyze data from a project view using the project hierarchy and network activity cost objects, or you can take a manufacturing approach to analyzing data.

The cost objects of the manufacturing view are taken from the logistics applications. They include plants, work center hierarchies, and production schedules. Costs and dates are important, but so is the availability of production resources according to the scheduled requirements. External resources may have to be employed.

The production manager can call for a different format for the project planning board display. The analysis of results might also take a different layout from the analysis used by the sales view because inputs capacity planning and costing arise.

Capacities represent the capability of a work center to perform a specific task. They are differentiated into capacity categories and are arranged hierarchically. The same capacity can be available from more than one work center.

When the project system is in operation, the work capacities needed by projects must be scheduled in addition to the other work going on in the plant. This integrated function is an important part of production capacity planning activities.

Using Materials Management View

The materials manager must manage vendors and manage inventory. The project manager must meet target dates and stay within budget. The PS can support both interests in the following ways:

- Materials with long lead times can be ordered by preliminary orders.
- Materials requirements can be processed with strict dates.
- Stock required in the project can be monitored at appropriate intervals independently of the main inventory management.
- Costs can be subject to continuous updates to maintain accurate values for the commitment of funds.

Linkage occurs through the materials elements of a project to the functions of the MM-Material Management application. These include material requirements planning, inventory management, and purchasing. In particular, the MM functions can support the project system by carrying out the following tasks:

- Processing inquiries and requests for quotations
- Processing quotations by vendors
- Assigning prices to vendor quotations
- Selecting vendors on price and delivery performance
- Processing purchase orders
- Processing goods receipts
- Verifying vendor invoices
- Managing the project inventory or the general inventory

The standard Material Management functions enable you to inspect the values assigned to the project elements, so you can selectively focus, for example, on the MRP controller, the purchasing organization, or even on the specific storage locations holding the project materials.

It may be the practice to manage your supply chain through electronic data interchange to include suppliers of your materials outside your company. In such cases, your project identifies the contracts and scheduling agreements and has them built into the work breakdown structure and the networks so that proper control can be exercised.

Using Finance View

The control of cash flow is important in project work because large gains or losses accruing on interest payments can seriously affect the profitability of the project. Incoming and outgoing payments can be planned manually because purchase orders assigned to projects or down payments negotiated with the customer are documented in the master records to indicate the payment dates.

The CO-Controlling application maintains a system of commitments that is the equivalent of the General Ledger accounting in financial accounting. A commitment represents a contract or schedule that is in the planning stage but is not yet represented in financial accounting. The commitment provides a method of recording activities that will lead to actual expenditures in the future. These anticipated expenditures can be analyzed for their effects on cost and for their implication on the future financial situation. For example, a purchase order that is intended to replenish materials at a cost center can be managed as a commitment in the CO system. If you have materials reserved for a specific order or project, they too represent a commitment and can be managed as such.

Incoming payments can be fed automatically to the commitment items, but outgoing payments must be planned manually. The project system derives such expected payments automatically and writes them to the project on the expected date. You can include interest calculations in the project plan. The PS posts the values to the Cash Management and Forecast module of the financial accounting system.

Actual payments and down payments from the customer are recorded in the project records. You have the option of including the imputed interest value directly in the project result calculation.

Using Controlling View

The CO-Controlling application maintains a database for controlling purposes that is shared by all the applications integrated with it. The controlling database holds planning and actual data that originates in the CO, FI, SD, PP, MM, and PS applications. The controller can view the latest information on such key activities as the following:

- Down payments
- Payments
- Material requirements

- Reservations of stock
- External processing

In accordance with standard SAP practice, the controlling view of a project can activate filtering to focus on different areas of responsibility in the organization, such as controlling departments, controlling areas, overhead allocation structures, and cost center hierarchies. Of course, the controller can also focus on project specifics by referring to the work breakdown structures.

Using Capital Investment View

A project can be seen as a scheme of work and as a controlled consumption of resources. You may prefer to look upon it as an investment of capital on which you are looking for a profit. Each phase of the project can be treated as a capital investment in its own right.

The management of capital investments is discussed in Chapter 11, "Managing Investments." If you have established a capital investment program, you can use the PS to total planned values for new projects and then direct them to suitable places in the program.

The capital investment program assigns budgets to appropriate accounting periods. These budgets can then be distributed top-down to projects awaiting approval. The system automatically ensures that the budget framework as approved in the capital investment program is not exceeded.

The annual plan values for projects that have been applied for and for projects already running can be totaled to create an annual expenditure budget. If you are operating with annual budgets from the capital investment program, the system automatically allocates them to the individual projects.

 One way to monitor current expenditures is to compare the programmed budgets with the project's actual costs in a standard report designed for this purpose.

Your project may attract investment subsidies. These can be entered as project preliminaries. Support work for pre-investment management decision-making generally makes use of the following system faculties:

- Document management
- Personnel management for the assignment of project staff from SAP R/3 Release 4.0
- Pre-investment analysis
- Project control by status key definition
- Workflow links with work centers and accounting
- Workflow links with project approval management

Before a project is approved, it may probably be helpful to consider how the assets created will depreciate over their anticipated life cycle. The first simulation of depreciation can start as soon as you have a project cost estimate and a planned start-up date. The result may well influence the assessment of the economic feasibility of the project.

If you are running the FI-AA Asset Accounting module, you can review approved capital spending projects in the depreciation forecast list. These planned depreciation values are automatically transferred to cost center accounting.

Assets under construction can be displayed in the balance sheet accounts through the project system. The following facilities are available:

- [ ] Displaying the asset history sheet
- [ ] Calculating special depreciation for tax purposes
- [ ] Displaying the status of capital investment grants
- [ ] Computing valuation amounts, using different valuation rates as defined in the valuation areas of AA-Asset Accounting
- [ ] Excluding from valuations those costs or cost portions that cannot be capitalized
- [ ] Transferring assets while still under construction
- [ ] Retiring assets while still under construction

The project system enables you to analyze the origin of any cost element of a completed asset back to the original project document. The capitalization of completed assets can be partial or complete, and you can control this at the summary level or on a line-item basis.

Using Profitability View

Current customer projects can be subjected to profitability analysis so that you can inspect a concurrent profitability forecast. This is based on the expected time series values for costs of sales or works in process. With this feature, you can determine how the values are derived for the billing plan, for example, or you can reference a plan of how the costs are expected to be incurred. You can also construct a forecast to show the development of costs as the project progresses through various percentage-completed stages.

N O T E Alternative profitability analysis versions can use planned and actual values.

The concurrent profitability forecast using actual values usually occurs at period-end closing and can use any of the following procedures:

- [ ] Completion based on actual costs
- [ ] Completion based on calculated percentage of completion
- [ ] Revenue-based results analysis
- [ ] Manual completion based on actual line items

The results of concurrent profitability analysis can be stored in any degree of detail. You can maintain financial statement versions for a project so that you can compare different accounting procedures. This could be useful if you need to differentiate the effects of including or excluding internal fixed price agreements, for example.

Using Enterprise Controlling View

The project system can support higher-level enterprise controlling by posting data to accounts that monitor market segments, profit centers, or the business as a whole. Incoming orders for a project can update the totals in profitability analysis, and the system can keep track of any changes to these orders.

Profit planning for future periods is supported by data from the project system forecasts. The profitability analysis system automatically records the values as soon as transaction data is posted, such as costs of sales in the income statement or as work in process in the balance sheets. Chapter 9, "Analyzing Profitability," discusses the control and forecasting of profitability.

Because it can adopt any or all of these viewpoints, the R/3 PS-Project System is the embodiment of integrated business accounting. Not only can a specific project take advantage of the functions of the separate applications, but the PS-Project System itself can also serve as the main executive controller for the entire business.

The PS-IS Information System is an efficient project analysis tool that is undergoing continuous program development to increase the depth of its analytical penetration and the clarity and pertinence of its presentation methods. The following additional functions are in development to enable you to better assess the progress of a project:

- Milestone trend analysis will detect and compare schedule deviations and trends.
- Earned value calculation will provide another internal progress check and an activity confirmation for the customer by comparing various methods of measuring earned value during the progress of an activity.

Placing the PS in the Organizational Structure

The R/3 Basis system has a comprehensive suite of data structures on which it is possible to map in detail the structure of your company, no matter what business or industry you operate in and no matter how individual your organizational structure is.

To help you become aware of the data architecture of the R/3 system, an information model shows the information objects of all the integrated application software. This is referred to as the R/3 Reference Model, and it can be accessed directly or through the Business Navigator presentation tool. This model not only shows you what data objects are available in the R/3 system, but it also reveals clearly how these data objects relate to each other.

You can see how your specific business can be accurately represented in the R/3 data objects. If you choose to make a decision on which functions will be required, the R/3 Basis system annotates the reference model so that you can see what you have selected. This annotated structure is then referred to as the Enterprise Data Model (EDM) of your implementation and is the principal instrument for controlling how your system is built. The standard R/3 Reference Model is available for inspection without any annotations that are specific to your implementation.

When you have identified the processes and business control instruments of your company in the Reference Model, you can be certain that they will be fully integrated when the time comes to run the finished system.

Understanding How the PS Module Is Presented

The PS-Project System is delivered ready to be configured and customized to fit your particular situation. An implementation guide (IMG) introduces the business functions, and a customizing menu provides access to the standard settings and technical recommendations. You set up the R/3 PS-Project System in the IMG-Implementation Guide itself.

The R/3 PS-Project System makes extensive use of the SAP Enterprise Data Model to support you in the definition and management of your projects. For example, the standard organizational structures in the FI-Financial Accounting module have a strict logical form. *Client* in an SAP system refers to the highest level of the organizational structure. The owner of the entire corporation is identified as the Client and is assigned a client code between 002 and 999. Client codes 000 and 001 are reserved for use by SAP. Client 001 probably is a client created for testing purposes. You can also reserve a client for training purposes. The transaction data associated with one client cannot be transferred to the transaction records of another. However, the particular design of your implementation as developed in the customizing process is represented as customizing data, and this can be transported from one client to another.

Although the R/3 Reference Model contains only one definitive example of each data structure, a company can build any number of replications into its EDM to represent all the working elements that exist.

The R/3 Reference Model is presented through the R/3 Business Navigator, which is an information model that can show you the software elements of the R/3 system and explain their purpose. The R/3 Business Navigator offers a component view that details the static structure and functional capabilities of all the software modules. The process flow views comprise a selection of different process flow configurations that you can study and copy.

For example, if you are looking at the PS-Project System with the R/3 Business Navigator, you can see how various types of projects can be graphically represented and executed under control of the standard R/3 software. The displays can be presented in any language for which your implementation has been configured.

 TIP When you have drafted an operational project in the PS format and have stored it in your system, you can use the R/3 Business Navigator to explore and document it.

Logistics organizational structures, for example, follow strict logical definitions. The modules in the logistics group are as follows:

- SD-Sales and Distribution
- PP-Production Planning
- MM-Materials Management

- PM-Plant Maintenance
- QM-Quality Management

Because all applications are integrated with the FI-Financial Accounting module, the logistics structures must map to the financial structures. The financial statements must be prepared up to the client level. In the applications modules, the data structures must extend to a great depth of detail to encompass the operational entities that add value to the business through the activities in which they engage. If managers care about an activity, then the system has a place for it.

A client can have any number of the following:

- Controlling areas
- Business areas

A controlling area can have any number of the following:

- Profit centers
- Cost centers
- Company codes (how subsidiary companies are identified)

A company code can have any number of the following:

- Purchasing organizations
- Plants

The plant is the main organizational element for Materials Management. A purchasing organization can have any number of purchasing groups.

A plant can have any number of the following:

- Functional locations or pieces of equipment
- Storage locations
- Work centers

A storage location has a separate inventory maintained for it. This is defined as a physical location or group of locations in which stock can be held.

A work center is defined as an organizational unit where a work step is carried out to produce an output. The activities performed at or by a work center are valuated by charge rates that can vary according to the cost center and activity type. Work centers can be defined on any convenient basis and do not have to coincide with physical locations. Work centers can be machines, people, production lines, or groups of skilled people. They can be narrowly defined or can encompass an entire geographical location.

Each work center master record has a cost center assigned to it. For planning and reporting purposes, work centers can be arranged in work center hierarchies. The output from any work center can be assigned to any number of work center hierarchies for the purpose of planning and reporting.

A work center can have any number of the following:

- Activities
- Machines, plant, pieces of equipment, and production resources and tools
- Persons

A person is defined as a natural person in whom an enterprise-internal interest exists. A business partner is defined as legal or natural person, or a group of legal or natural persons, in whom or in which a business interest exists. A work center cannot include a business partner.

Associating Structures in a Project

A project can be concerned with any combination of entities in the company. The project system itself illustrates how the data objects of the R/3 system are used to monitor and control the costs and revenues of the work done in your company. Each element points to the responsible organizational unit represented by a data object. These data objects can attract not only the costs and revenues information but also any technical information relevant to the operations of the accounting system or the other functions of your company.

The master data records used by the PS-Project System are formally structured. A "project" is represented by a master record with a predefined structure of data fields. One of these fields contains the unique identification code of the project, which is then associated with all the elements attached to this data structure, such as WBS elements, profit centers, and so on.

A project has the following components:

- One project definition
- One or more WBS elements
- One or more networks or subnetworks

NOTE   In practice, networks and work breakdown structures can be used independently. It is common to used the term "project" to refer only to a work breakdown structure.

A project definition has the following components:

- One project identification
- One controlling area
- One company code
- One cost center

A WBS element has the following components:

- One profit center
- One business area, if this facility is operative
- One company code
- One cost center

- One jurisdiction code (optional)
- One plant
- One or more activities
- One or more functional locations and pieces of equipment (optional)

The functional location is a place where plant maintenance activities occur. The equipment refers to the objects upon which the maintenance is carried out.

A network has the following components:

- One profit center
- One business area
- One jurisdiction code
- One plant
- One or more activities

A network is recursively defined so that any element in a network can itself be a network, and so on. Therefore, the term "project" may refer to an element of a larger project, and so on. However, it has become the convention to define a project by specifying a work breakdown structure. A network is used to specify what must be done in terms of activities and their relationships, such as timing and sequence.

An activity has the following components:

- One activity type
- One or more material components

An activity type is one of the following:

- An activity processed internally
- An activity processed externally, via a purchasing organization and a purchasing group
- A general costs activity assigned to a plant

A material component has the following components:

- A purchasing organization
- A purchasing group
- A plant
- A storage location

Establishing the Project Definition

The project definition is a data object requiring certain fields to contain valid entries, such as those that relate the project to the company organization. The project definition also includes text to describe the project goals or mission. You can add a reference to the settlement rule to cover all the objects in the project.

N O T E It is not necessary to define any activities or networks to establish a project definition. These can be added later. ☐

Using Basic Data

The basic data repository of the PS includes templates for project management entities. The following are the most important standard structures:

☐ Standard work breakdown structures

☐ Standard networks

☐ Standard milestones

☐ Standard texts

Using Standard Work Breakdown Structures

The work breakdown structure (WBS) defines a project in terms of the tasks and subtasks that must be completed. A standard WBS is a template for creating a new project. It creates a model project that is fully integrated with the rest of your system as soon as you assign it an ID code and save it. You can define several model projects and arrange for the system to use them as appropriate to generate projects, for example, in response to any of the following events:

☐ Customer inquiry posted in the SD–Sales and Distribution module

☐ Quotation posted in the SD-Sales and Distribution module

☐ Sales order posted in the SD-Sales and Distribution module

Project organization and coordination are managed through the WBS, which is defined as a master record structure that can store the work, time, and cost data associated with a project.

A WBS can be used to track costs incurred in a network. It comprises a hierarchy of tasks and subtasks to any number of levels and can be represented by a tree diagram.

If you do not have a model project already defined as a standard WBS, the individual tasks must be entered to generate valid WBS elements. The level of detail can be increased at any stage of a project.

The WBS elements can also be used to plan dates, costs, and budget, before and during a project. Each element is assigned an operative indicator, which determines its properties for the duration of the project:

☐ Planning elements for actual costs

☐ Account assignment elements to which you want to post costs

☐ Billing elements to which you want to post revenues

Existing organizational units in your company's enterprise data model, such as a plant or a business area, can be associated with specific WBS elements. The default assignment for a WBS element links to the organizational structure specified in the project definition.

WBS elements already in existence can be referenced during data entry, as can portions of the hierarchy from other projects. For plant maintenance purposes, for instance, you can assign a piece of equipment or a functional location to an element in a WBS.

Each WBS element can be assigned to an area of responsibility and to a responsible person within that area who is accountable for the work of this element of the project. The WBS element master record also contains data fields that can be defined by the user to carry additional information.

Using Standard Networks

In general terms, a network is a connected structure of nodes and links that signify relationships between the nodes, such as "Must be completed before_ ." The nodes represent activities. The nodes in a network can also be networks. A subnetwork is part of a network.

In the R/3 system, a network is defined formally as an activity-on-node structure containing instructions on how to carry out activities in a specific way, in a specific order, and in a specific time period. The project system provides graphical displays of networks upon which all maintenance operations can be conducted by selecting a displayed node icon and initiating an appropriate function.

Three types of activities can be represented by WBS elements:

- Activities internal to your company that may require a capacity of a machine or a person
- Activities performed outside your company or by outsiders
- General costs activities

The third type of activity element is defined as a general costs activity because it is used for planning costs when you do not want to refer to any other data object in the system. You can also use a general costs activity to accumulate incurred costs, such as insurance, that are not directly attributable to any one activity.

Activity elements can be used to represent the components of a complex activity. Each activity in an activity hierarchy can be broken down into internal, external, and general costs activity elements.

N O T E You can assign to a WBS activity element the production resources and tools (PRTs) needed to perform the work. [ ]

The system can create a purchase requisition for all activities classified for external processing by running the MRP-Material Requirements Planning module. You can refer to the associated purchasing information record to obtain prices and delivery times for external activities.

Using Relationships Between Activities   A standard network is a template that creates a new network that you can save under a unique ID code. You can connect several standard networks with logical and temporal relationships to build an overall network for a project. Subnetworks are treated the same as networks by the project system.

You can assign a network to a WBS element and instruct the system to roll up the data from all the constituent networks and assign to the relevant WBS element the costs, schedule data, and capacity data.

Within a network, the activities can be restricted by the time available or for technical reasons. Some activities take a long time, some cannot begin until others have finished, and so on. The PS module makes use of four types of relationship between activities, as follows:

- Finish-Start, where the second activity cannot begin until the first has completed
- Start-Start, where the second activity cannot start until the first has started
- Finish-Finish, where the second activity cannot finish until the first has completed
- Start-Finish, where the second activity cannot finish until the first has started

Using Network Types   A complex project uses both a WBS and an activity network. The R/3 Network Library can be augmented by user-specified neutral network structures for the commonly used processes that can be copied into your project. The network type distinguishes networks by their use. The network type controls are as follows:

- Costing variants for planned and actual costs
- Number ranges permitted
- Status profile

Using Standard Milestones   A milestone is an event that can occur during the life cycle of a project. In the SAP R/3 system, an event is a particular set of data that is recognized for its significance. When the predefined data situation is detected, the system registers an event by creating a record and perhaps also triggering a sequence of functions.

In project management, a milestone is usually defined to mark the transition between one phase to the next, or between one cost center and another. You can assign a milestone to a network activity or to a WBS element.

A standard milestone is a template that generates a new milestone in an existing network or WBS element. You can group standard milestones to report on them as a set.

Using Predefined Milestone Functions in Networks   The PS module includes standard milestone functions that can be predefined to perform the following tasks for specific business processes:

- Releasing activities
- Starting workflow tasks

One use of milestones in engineer-to-order manufacturing is to trigger customer billing. A billing plan is created using the defined milestones. When the milestone is reached, the system automatically copies the actual date when the milestone event conditions were satisfied to the billing plan, which then releases the billing block. The invoice is produced the next time that the billing due list is run.

Identifying Production Resources

A WBS can include elements that need documents to support the activities. These documents can include drawings and technical specifications and other matter from word-processing or multimedia sources. The documents can be treated as production resources and can be managed along with the production resources and tools (PRTs). Alternatively, documents can be allocated directly to WBS elements from a document management system, even if this is not the one installed in R/3.

The R/3 PS-Project System recognizes and maintains three categories of PRTs:

☐ PRTs with a material master record that are stock items on inventory

☐ PRTs with a document information record that are part of the R/3 document management system

☐ PRTs with their own PRT master record that can be allocated in network activities

Document management under R/3 for WBS elements maintains the following information about each document:

☐ Storage location of the document, such as CAD system, PC file, or filing cabinet. Generally, the advantages of document management are only realized if the documents are in electronic form.

☐ Object status.

☐ Location of the original data.

☐ Person responsible for the data.

Checking Resource Availability

Availability checks by the R/3 PS-Project System cover capacities, materials, production resources, and tools. When you customize your R/3 PS-Project System, you tell the system whether and how checks are to be made on material availability, and whether scheduled receipts or only the on-hand inventory should be scanned.

N O T E   A complete workflow for missing parts is provided to manage the shortage through to goods receipt and backorder updating. ☐

The system determines whether each PRT is available according to its status and refers to the PS information system to compare the available capacity with the capacity load per work center. The system then calculates the capacity utilization.

Capacity leveling is available, and simulations can be performed to see how the capacity available might be affected by such procedures and events as the following:

☐ Orders

☐ Midpoint scheduling

☐ Rescheduling

☐ Out-sourcing

☐ Work center changes

Planning in the PS

A successful project plan is characterized by its major contribution to completing the project on time and within budget. Project planning can be a process that spans the life cycle of the project and extends down to the details required.

Using the Project Planning Board

One way of planning a project is to carry out all planning activities in the main transaction documents of the project. A better way is to use the project planning board. This gives a graphical presentation of the entire project at a level of detail that is under your control.

By pointing and calling functions, you can carry out the following activities from the project planning board:

- Create activity master records
- Create WBS elements and insert them in the project
- Define milestones
- Exercise the planning functions
- Exercise the resource scheduling functions
- Perform capacity leveling
- Calculate costs

The project planning board comprises two display areas. In the table area, you can create and maintain activity masters, WBS elements, and milestones. In the Gantt Chart area, you can point and drag to change the schedule of activities and WBS elements, set milestones, and set up the relationship links between activities. The display format of the Gantt Chart falls under the user's control.

Using Calendars

The R/3 system recognizes the following calendar types, all of which can be used in project planning:

- Gregorian calendars
- Factory calendars (any number)
- Work center-specific operating calendars, with shifts if appropriate

The following types of dates are accepted:

- Basic dates entered manually for the work breakdown structure valid at the time of entry
- Forecast dates entered manually
- Actual dates to show the progress of the project
- System-calculated dates created during network scheduling

The dates you use for scheduling can be fixed dates or dates obtained from a forecast and used as a basis for developing more accurate plans.

Developing Project Schedules

The system can automatically assign project dates if they're connected to a scheduled network. Alternatively, you can plan project dates manually in the work breakdown structure. Planning dates can be entered on the lists and overviews, in the hierarchy display, or in the Gantt Chart of the project planning board. Three methods or planning forms are available:

- ☐ Top-down, beginning with the start and end dates for the highest WBS element in the project hierarchy, within which all other dates must fall
- ☐ Bottom-up, starting with the subordinate WBS elements and applying system functions to transfer dates up the hierarchy
- ☐ Open, in which you plan without reference to hierarchical dependencies but check dates before using system functions to transfer them up the hierarchy

It is characteristic of the R/3 PS-Project System that checking and automatic updating are not carried out automatically. You must total, check, and reconcile repeatedly until your project is correctly specified. In the individual WBS elements, you can compare, reconcile, or extrapolate dates. You can schedule the whole project or only part of the hierarchy, together with the associated activities.

If it is necessary to make parts of the schedule more detailed, you can create new activities and assign them to existing WBS elements. Dates from these new activities can be transferred to the WBS element, and you can link activities to develop a network local to this element. You can offset a new activity to the start or finish of an existing activity.

It is often necessary to apply constraints to a project schedule. These can be dates recognized by your implementation, such as annual plant shutdown.

Using Floats and Reduction

A slack time between activities is a float, so called because it is possible to allow either activity to extend into this time without disrupting the overall schedule. The project system has various strategies available to reduce the activity durations in a WBS if the constraints demand it.

Using Network Scheduling

You can link both networks with relationships and individual activities in different networks in the same manner. By this means, you can generate an overall network for your whole project and then apply network scheduling.

Four types of network scheduling are available. Each is discussed in the following sections.

Using Forward Scheduling   In forward scheduling, you set the start date and instruct the system to use any scheduled dates already assigned to the WBS elements. This procedure then reports the end date to you.

Using Backward Scheduling   In backward scheduling, you set the finish dates and the PS tells you when the project should start.

Scheduling to Current Date   In scheduling to current date, the system schedules forward from the current start date for the network, and then you can check whether the project will finish on or before the required date. You can use the floats along the critical path to estimate the discrepancy. In SAP usage, there is a critical path within a project if the total float is zero or negative. In general, you should be concerned if there is a sequence of tasks in which each must await the completion of the previous, and where the estimated duration of this sequence approaches the time available. Although these tasks may not have zero floats, their position in the sequence can make them vulnerable. One advantage of a formal system of network planning is that it obliges the user to specify all the links and to assign time values to them. If any delay is anticipated, the effect on the network as a whole can be simulated.

Using Today Scheduling   In today scheduling, the system schedules forward from today's date. For example, if the scheduled start of a network is between today's date and the planned start date, the system first reduces the lead time. If the finish date calculated by the system is still not acceptable, you can ask for the earliest possible finish date if the network were to begin today.

Understanding Project Cost Planning

The success of many projects depends on the costs incurred. There are a few projects in which the quality of the outcome is arguably more important than the costs incurred. Your company may want to be the first, and only on repeat orders seek to reduce the costs. Some of these costs will be excessive if they are improperly planned. Some costs will be excessive because the plan was not updated with fresh information as it became available. The project system must support continuous editing and updating of project plans.

At the conceptual and rough-cut planning stage, the planning of costs suggests the costs you expect the project to incur. At the approval stage, planning indicates the way ahead for budget allocation. During project execution, the role of the planned dates and costs is to monitor variances between planned and actual values.

The system offers the following forms of cost planning:

- Structure planning that is independent of cost elements
- Detailed planning of direct costs by quantity and value
- Detailed planning of secondary costs, using planned activity quantity and the standard CO-Controlling rate for the sender activity
- Unit costing, using data and methods from CO-CEA Cost Element Accounting, and Purchasing in MM-Materials Management, if required
- Cost planning in the network, in which the network activities are used as cost elements in the unit costing technique

Copying of work breakdown structures and parts of them can be used where projects entail the same processes. Different versions of a project plan can be saved and maintained in parallel, for example, in the best-case and the worst-case scenarios.

Using Structure Planning   At an early stage in planning, you may have just an outline WBS structure in which some or all of the elements have been designated as planning elements. You could estimate the cost for each WBS element, or you could adjust the cost taken from similar reference objects. The characteristic of structure planning is that it is independent of cost elements. You nominate or create a WBS and allocate costs for top-down distribution or to the lower levels for bottom-up totaling.

You can plan overall costs and then distribute them over the expected duration of the project, or you can define plan values for costs for individual years. The PS totals work breakdown structure values for each year.

As information becomes available the structure plan can be refined and elaborated toward detailed cost element planning and unit costing, for example.

Using Detailed Planning to Cost Elements   A cost element is an account item in the chart of accounts that is used in the cost controlling area. Cost elements of this kind are used in cost accounting to enter, classify, and assign values to the consumption of production resources.

When costs are posted (if you're using CO), they must be assigned to a specific cost element, which is either a primary cost element for goods and services procured externally, or a secondary cost element for goods and services created by internal activities.

When costs are entered, they must be identified with a controlling area and a cost element. They must also be assigned to an additional account assignment object that is offset with the cost element posting to complete the settlement procedure. This additional account assignment object must be one of the following:

- A cost center
- A network
- A WBS element
- A cost object
- A revenue object

Detailed cost element planning of this type requires planning primary costs and secondary or indirect costs.

Planning primary costs can be carried out in terms of both quantity and value. If you plan for quantities, you enter the planned consumption and then value it using the planned prices per quantity unit. Planning by value does not require the entry of planned use quantities. You enter the planned costs for each cost element.

Cost center activities can be planned as indirect costs on a quantity basis. The activity required is planned by quantity and is multiplied by the rate charged by the sender cost object. This yields a value that is stored in a secondary cost element as an internal activity allocation.

Using Detailed Planning by Unit Costing It may be the case that you can access all the information you need for costing from the integrated applications of your SAP R/3 system. You need the information on the sources of supply, the quantities, and the prices so that you can apply unit costing for project cost planning purposes. Into your plan you enter the quantities of the units for each origin, such as each material and each relevant activity defined in the CO module. The system then computes the values using the standard prices for these resources.

Using Cost Planning in Networks If you have built a network that schedules the activities and carries planned values of the intended resource use, you can have the project system calculate the costs of your plan in terms of the objects in your network. Primary costs are derived from your entries for external activities, materials, and general costs activities. Activity input is defined by your internal activity planning values.

The user can allocate materials to activities. The system then generates stock reservations for all the materials held as stock. The prices are available from the materials masters. Non-stock material is allocated by purchase requisitions, for which the plan values can be obtained from the purchasing system.

The general costs activity is an instrument for accumulating costs that cannot be assigned directly to a cost center activity or to a material. These costs can be assigned to any suitable cost element.

Planning Capacity Requirements

For internal activities in each work center, you define available capacities and specify formulas for calculating them. You can operate capacity splits, which serve to allocate capacity data to individual capacities such as specific machines or individual people. As you enter the quantity of work to be performed, you indicate the required capacity units. The system uses this information automatically when scheduling capacity requirements.

You can plan external activities by referencing a purchasing information record for a contractor, which shows the prices and delivery times. If your system is integrated with the PP-Production Planning application, the project system can initiate the creation of a purchase requisition by the MRP module from this information. When the activity is released, the user must convert the purchase requisition to a purchase order.

If you want to inspect the capacity utilization of the work centers, you can do this from the time scheduling and structure planning functions at the project planning board. The capacity evaluations display the accumulated capacity loads per period. This is the kind of information that can foretell backlogs and bottlenecks.

Using Capacity Leveling

The display and control interface of choice for capacity leveling is the R/3 Graphic Planning Table. The idea is to reconcile all your capacity demands to amounts of activities that will be available at the time. You have a range of tactical procedures at your disposal that you can compare through simulations of your plan. For example, you can see what differences you could make to the capacity availability position by any or all of the following:

- Order manipulation
- Midpoint scheduling
- Rescheduling
- Outsourcing
- Work center changes

You can perform most of the rearranging from the R/3 Graphics Planning Table. Here are some options:

- Change the sequence of activities in a network
- Split activities across work centers
- Split activities across time periods
- Change the structure of work centers
- Change the available capacity of work centers

The consequences of any changes you propose can be explored at the planning table. You have two areas on the table: One shows the work centers and available capacities, and the other shows the activities with requirements that have not yet been dispatched. You can select an activity on the graphic planning table and drag it to an available time period in a suitable work center.

Using Personnel Planning

When you install and configure the PD-Personnel Planning and Development system, you effectively extend planning in another dimension. The personnel system depends on definitions available for all the work positions in your company. These definitions use standard qualification descriptors that specify what experience, qualifications, and authorization levels are needed for each work position. Your personnel system also represents all your employees in the SAP R/3 database. These appear as master records using entity type 7005, which is reserved for natural persons in whom your company has an enterprise-internal interest rather than a business interest. Such persons can be current employees or retired employees still on the pension payroll—or at least still in the database in case they might be invited to rejoin your company.

You can use the integrated personnel system to find a person to whom a task could be assigned. You can specify the time period as well as the qualifications required. Therefore, you can conduct personnel planning over the same periods you use for your other types of planning.

The system offers you a list in rank order of all the persons suitable for a task on the basis of their availability in the appropriate work center, their available time, and the attributes needed to perform the activity. You can arrange to view rankings with different sort codes.

Using Materials Planning

The natural source of planning support for materials is the MM-Materials Management module, which can provide integrated functions for the following activities:

- Purchasing
- Inventory management
- Materials requirements planning, if your system is also integrated with the PP-Production Planning application

If you allocate a material from stock from the project system, an automatic reservation of the required quantity occurs so that it is no longer available to promise to another project or order. If the material you allocate is not a stock item, the MRP system can create a purchase requisition for the required quantity; this is submitted for approval and release for purchasing action.

If that particular MM workflow is enabled when the material is received, the receipt confirmation is associated with the relevant object in the project system so that the project manager can be informed when the material arrives.

Some materials needed for a project can be obtained on time only if they are ordered well in advance. If you know the lead time, you can place a preliminary order in the materials purchasing system. Such a preliminary order can be assigned for accounting purposes to a sales order as part of the project, or to the project account itself. The assignment serves as a purchase requisition.

If you use the project system to assign a material to an activity, and if there will be a long lead time before this material is delivered, the project system uses this planned delivery time to automatically adjust the duration of the activity. The idea is that the activity begins by ordering the material and then lasts at least as long as the time necessary for delivery.

You may decide that the stock needed for your projects should be managed separately from the inventory used for other work in your company. You can designate the materials and quantities to be managed as project stock or sales order stock so that these materials will not be available to promise to any other orders.

Using Availability Checking

If your project plan has reached the stage of assigning milestone dates or activity durations, the project system automatically checks that all the materials, production resources, tools, and activity capacities will be available at the planned start dates for the relevant activities.

Before you release a network, you should conduct an availability check. The project system enables you to specify when and how availability checks are to be conducted. For instance, you can arrange that materials needed by your project are not considered to be available unless they have been confirmed as on-hand inventory. If you are confident in your suppliers, you can permit scheduled receipts to be considered if their planned delivery times are compatible with your network.

The R/3 Workflow system can be set up to take action automatically if any material is missing. This is referred to as missing parts management. This type of management can respond to initial shortages, discrepancies in goods receipts, and updates to back orders.

Checking PRTs must take account of the planned time schedule and the capacities required. Any particular PRT is identified in the master records and is associated with a status code. This reveals whether the resource is being used by another activity, whether it is unsuitable for service until repaired, or whether it will be withdrawn from service. You have a customized status structure according to the type of PRTs used in your industry.

N O T E   You can check the availability of PRTs and activity capacities with the graphical planning table and the project information system. ☐

Understanding Project Budgeting

If your project has a budget, your management must have approved a plan that sets out the expected development of costs over the intended duration of the project. The better the planned cost development, the better chance you have of bringing in your project within budget. On the other hand, your management may not approve your plan in its entirety. You may not get a budget sufficient to cover your planned costs.

A budget for a project is created formally when planning is completed and project approval is granted. A cost plan is an estimate. A budget is a fixed amount that can be allocated to the WBS elements. You may be permitted to keep some of your budget in reserve for contingencies. You can allocate funds either by adopting the values produced by detailed planning, or by distributing the budget manually as values entered directly in the WBS elements.

Your finance director may not actually release all the funds for your approved budget. The R/3 PS-Project System recognizes the following two types of budgets:

☐ A current budget is the original budget that may have been amended by supplements, transfers, and returns

☐ A released budget is limited by the original budget total but is released in stages, perhaps in relation to WBS elements or milestones.

Changes in a budget can be accommodated by the following instruments, all of which are reversible:

☐ Supplements that you can process from the top-down in the WBS

☐ Returns of excess funds that you can process from the bottom-up in the WBS

☐ Transfers of funds that you can move from one WBS element with a budget to another, which also must have a budget, although it need not belong to the same project

N O T E   The project system displays project budgets in hierarchical format, if necessary, and checks that no release or assignment would exceed the original budget amount. ☐

Using Project Budget Management Support

The following support functions are available in budget management support:

- Logging all budget updates in an approval history
- Selecting WBS elements and increasing their budget allocation by a percentage or by an amount
- Reassigning individual WBS elements or project branches, along with their budget values, to any existing budget

Managing Budget Funds

A funds overview is provided to display what funds have been assigned in a project. If you operate passive availability control, the system reports fund commitments in a project, even if they are in excess of the funds available at the time.

However, you can specify active availability control. A tolerance level is defined per WBS element or for the project as a whole. The business transactions that trigger active availability checking must be defined in the configuration of your implementation. If you post a business transaction to create a purchase order for a WBS element, for instance, the project system checks whether the available project budget or the released funds are enough to cover it within the tolerance level. You can specify what action should occur if such an event is detected. For example, you can specify a warning to the user, plus a message to the person responsible for the project.

The following availability control parameters can be specified:

- Whether the target for comparison is the amount of released funds or the current budget
- Whether the budget to be considered is the annual budget or the overall budget for the project
- Which types of business transactions should be subject to availability control (such as purchase orders or postings in CO-CEA Cost Element Accounting)
- Whether the tolerance of an intended transaction is to be based on a percentage use or an absolute value of the variance of the budget overrun
- What actions should be triggered by a transaction that will create a budget overrun according to the parameters defined

In the event of an intended transaction triggering availability control conditions, the project manager can respond to the warning by using a special function key. This automatically displays the funds overview for the WBS element that is about to run over budget. The display gives the amount of the excess, the details of its origin, and the item in the transaction where the overrun conditions were triggered.

The tolerance limits can be configured to respond with different actions according to the amount of the budget excess in the following sequence:

- Warning alone
- Warning plus electronic message to the project manager
- Error message and rejection of the intended posting

The budget availability control function can provide an automatic system for giving early warning of those project commitments likely to exceed budget funds.

Executing a Project

If you manage your projects by the method of budgeting and releases, execution begins with project release. Many activities needed in a project are initiated from the project system. However, some activities are executed outside the project unless you make provision for them to be under direct control of the project system. For example, a purchase requisition is usually submitted to the purchasing department. A sales order is created and processed by the sales department.

For a business process to be assigned to a project and processed there, you must allocate an account assignment to a specific network activity or to a WBS element. As the project proceeds, funds assignments are generated by it. They are represented as funds commitments, open items, and actual values.

Variances arise between planned and actual values. Prices of purchased goods may change. Vendor deliveries may fall outside their planned periods. Your plant may not be capable of manufacturing or processing as much as you had planned. Unplanned events such as these require planning updates from you to supply the fresh information used in planning subsequent activities. As you update your project with new planning information, you will become aware of the more obvious trends in the data. You will probably notice when the project plan looks like it will exceed budget or come in late.

Using Activity Confirmations

Each activity must be confirmed in the system. This could be done in many different ways. You may have a data link installed, or you may have to manually enter data from an activity confirmation slip, for example. These confirmations update the capacity load of the work center and record the actual costs. The remaining duration and work to finish the network are also updated by these confirmations. A confirmation can be canceled as well.

You must enter the following information either manually or automatically into your activity and network completion confirmations:

- ☐ Degree of processing (optional)
- ☐ Work center
- ☐ Dates
- ☐ Duration
- ☐ Forecast values (optional)

The network and the work breakdown structure work together; changes in one are reflected in the other.

Confirmations to the network can be directed to the PS information system and can be downloaded to there from external systems such as plant data collection systems, Microsoft Project, or Microsoft Excel. Confirmed data can be copied to the network.

The project system enables you to confirm many activities at the same time with the Collective Confirmation Screen. Each member of the project staff can define a unique user screen that displays only those confirmations that fall within their area of responsibility. The user can define column widths and the sequence of fields and can selectively filter out unnecessary information. The user can also individualize the act of confirmation by setting default values, such as their personnel number, to be written into every activity confirmation.

N O T E Any confirmation of an activity can be subsequently canceled. ⌷

Using Actual Dates   Each WBS element in a project is associated with planned dates. Actual dates can be either entered manually to each WBS element or copied automatically from activity completion confirmation documents. Two basic schemes exist for recording actual dates; you can also apply a combination of these two schemes:

- ☐ If your plan is developed top-down or bottom-up, the project system will copy actual dates from the lower-level WBS elements to the higher-level elements to which they belong.
- ☐ If your plan is developed by any other procedure than top-down or bottom-up, the project system will update with the actual dates only those WBS elements that have a network assigned to them.

As soon as an activity has been confirmed and you have actual dates for network activities, the project system uses them in the schedule forward procedure to calculate a new finish date. The system then automatically schedules backward from the basic or fixed dates to determine the floats.

CAUTION
A negative float suggests that your project has fallen behind schedule.

Using Actual Costs and Commitments   Business transactions in the project and in the various feeder systems incur actual costs and commit funds to meet future needs. These are automatically associated with the WBS element responsible. The following transaction documents record activities likely to create commitments of funds:

- ☐ Activity allocations and confirmations
- ☐ Material issues
- ☐ Deliveries
- ☐ External invoices
- ☐ Purchase orders

- Purchase requisitions
- Manual funds reservations

Using Actual Revenues   For revenue to appear as an actual value in the project system, one of the following commercial transactions must be posted:

- Posting in FI-Financial Accounting
- Invoicing in SD-Sales and Distribution

Using Actual Payments   Payments can be processed from the project system in various ways, which include the following documented transactions:

- Down-payment requests
- Down payments and down-payment clearing
- Incoming and outgoing payments

N O T E   Imputed interest can be computed in the project system to contribute to the project result calculation.

Creating Orders for a Project

If you have elaborated and planned a project in terms of WBS elements and networks, you can extend the scope of the project by adding WBS elements and by creating orders for the project. Creating an order may be the preferred option for any or all of the following reasons:

- You may be able to use an existing bill of materials and routing as the basis for a new production order to manufacture materials.
- You can create a maintenance order to plan and monitor maintenance tasks for the project.
- You can create internal orders to allocate costs and activities for cost accounting and performance analysis purposes.

One advantage shared by all types of orders is that they can be managed from the project system and yet still be kept up-to-date by automatic postings in the controlling system.

Costs that are planned in orders and later posted represent commitments against the budget of the WBS element to which the order is assigned. The same is true of planned or actual costs posted in networks. An order for a project can be assigned for settlement to the responsible WBS element or to an account assignment object, which probably is another order or a cost center.

When the system settles an order outside a project, internal business volume is eliminated in accordance with standard accounting practice. The costs settled on a receiver become the responsibility of this receiver and are displayed there. For example, if you have settled an order for a project on a cost center, the costs settled are displayed in the information system of the cost center, not in the project information system. The project is no longer responsible.

Performing Periodic Processing

It is essential to carry out periodic valuation of long-term projects so that the balance sheet accounts and the controlling accounts can be properly rendered. In particular, the project system carries out the following tasks on behalf of any of its projects:

- Overhead surcharge calculation
- Calculation of interest
- Results analysis
- Settlement

Earned value calculation can take place at any time because the date that contributes to them is updated when the report is initiated.

Costing Overheads as Surcharges

If your project needs and takes advantage of resources already provided by your company, it may be appropriate to impose surcharges to pay for a share of the costs of their initial provision and upkeep. For example, the following resources can be costed and assigned as surcharges:

- Personnel
- Buildings
- Machines
- Materials

These overhead surcharges can be directed at any level of your project. WBS elements, networks, and network elements may all attract various types and amounts of overhead surcharges.

You can use a standard overhead costing sheet, or you can edit one to make a customized form to suit your particular circumstances or the type of WBS element to which you are directing the surcharges. You might include any or all of the following surcharge procedures in different versions of your overhead costing sheet:

- Percentage overhead rates
- Absolute overhead amounts
- Quantity-based surcharge amounts
- Surcharge rates applied to mixed or variable portions of the base amounts
- Single or multilevel surcharge calculations
- Assigning overheads to credit objects and cost elements
- Assigning overheads to allocation cost elements

A base cost element that is used as a multiplier in the calculation of overhead surcharges can be treated in various ways. For example, the total, the fixed, and the variable cost portions can each be multiplied by a different surcharging rate.

The system calculates surcharges in simulation mode without posting them to a project so that you can review the amounts and correct them before charging. Surcharge calculations and simulations can be conducted online or in background processing. A surcharge log is maintained to record how the surcharges have been applied as actual costs to the cost centers or orders.

From the stored payment, the down payment, and the internal activity transaction documents, the project system maintains an up-to-date balance interest calculation that is recorded as an accounting document. The interest calculation brings in the values on dates in the past history of the project, interest rate changes, and the effects of compound interest.

Using Earned Value Analysis

The earned value analysis functions of the project system are used to present the progress of a project and its value at particular points in time, such as period end. You can call on various techniques that can be combined under the user's control to portray the progress of a project or an individual work package within a project. The following procedures are available to be applied to a base value, such as the planned costs of a task:

- ☐ Start-finish rule to calculate value at the start and finish of each WBS element
- ☐ Milestones reached
- ☐ Measurement of the degree of processing achieved in the project
- ☐ Percentage of completion (POC) based on the actual costs as a proportion of the planned costs
- ☐ Estimation of the POC
- ☐ Time proportionality used to calculate earned value from the base
- ☐ Secondary proportionality

The start-finish rule is a measurement technique in which you can specify that a percentage of the planned work on a task shall be deemed to have been completed as soon as the activity has started.

Secondary proportionality is a method of measuring the progress of a project that uses a variable, such as the quantity of a key resource or tracing factor. The proportion of the actual to the planned quantity of the tracing factor is applied to the planned costs to calculate the value of a project at the interim stage.

If you have calculated the percentage of completion of a project at an interim stage before completion, you can use this proportion for the following purposes:

- ☐ To bill the customer
- ☐ To calculate balances and reserves of funds
- ☐ To analyze the earned value of the project

Using Results Analysis

The rules of financial accounting require that projects in process be evaluated at period-end closing. To achieve periodic valuation of long-term orders, the results analysis function compares the calculated costs and the actual costs of an order as it progresses towards completion. This method calculates either inventory (if actual costs are greater than calculated costs) or reserves (if actual costs are less than calculated costs).

The data calculated during results analysis is stored in the following account items:

- Cost of sales, or a revenue figure for profitability analysis calculations
- Work in progress
- Capitalized costs
- Capitalized profit
- Reserves for unrealized costs
- Reserves for costs of complaints and commissions
- Reserves for imminent loss

When a project is settled, the data from results analysis can be passed to financial accounting, profit center accounting, and profitability analysis.

The procedure to be followed in results analysis is controlled by the results analysis key assigned to it. The key specifies such options as the following:

- Whether revenue-based, quantity-based, or manual
- Basis on which it is carried out (planned or actual results)
- How profits are to be realized
- Whether to split inventory, reserves, and cost of sales
- To which results analysis accounts should post the results
- How the life cycle of an object is to be broken down into open and closed periods

You can set up different procedures by editing a results analysis master and creating a results analysis version. You may want to do this under the following types of circumstances:

- When your corporate group operates in more than one region of legal force and therefore needs to render external accounts in accordance with various legal accounting practices
- For financial accounting purposes that require assignments that differ from project control
- For profitability analysis

You may also want to take into account the effect of operating fixed prices between different subprojects within a project. This can be arranged through a results analysis version to enable you to pass on profitability analysis data for a subproject separately. This may be necessary, for example, when you assign certain results to profit centers.

Using Balance Sheet Comparison of Costs and Revenues

If you use the project system to transfer calculated data to the balance sheet accounts on a period basis, the corresponding balances are formed and subsequently cleared. These retain evidence of their origins in a specific project so you can maintain a concurrent costing and internal valuation procedure for each project as it is executed.

The results analysis up to a key date enables you to compare costs incurred and the matching revenues.

Using Settlements

A settlement can be performed as a simulation, or it can result in the appropriate values being updated. Settlement of costs incurred in a project on one or more receivers is automatically accompanied by corresponding credit postings to the project itself. The costs settled are recorded in the relevant receiver. Debit postings assigned to the project remain on display even after settlement.

The following types of assignment account objects could accept the settlement as receivers:

- Cost center
- Project
- Asset
- General Ledger account
- Business segment

The project or the WBS element master must include a specification of the settlement rule. This can comprise several distribution rules, each defining the settlement receiver, the distribution of costs, and the settlement type.

The settlement structure determines how the process is controlled. This structure specifies the settlement cost elements, or the value fields from an operating concern, that are to be assigned to cost elements and cost element groups.

The following settlement functions are under development by SAP:

- Settlement by amount
- Settlement of line items
- Settlement in the plan
- Settlement by cost element

A separate structure for use by CO-PA Profitability Analysis is known as the PA Settlement Structure. See Chapter 9 for more information on this structure.

Billing

A sales order or a sales order item can be assigned to a project or to a WBS element. When the customer is billed, the amounts then are automatically recorded as actual revenues in the project or relevant WBS element.

Fixed-price billing can be carried out per sales item as of a single billing date. Partial billing also can take place, splitting the total amount to be billed between the dates of the billing schedule. The following splitting options are available:

- Dates for split billing are entered manually in the billing schedule.
- Partial billing is based on network milestones assigned to the sales order from the project or from a subhierarchy assigned to the sales order.

The customer is invoiced with a percentage of the total project costs or with a predefined amount as each milestone is reached.

A billing schedule can include items for down payment as well as the actual billing items. The system creates down-payment requests that are automatically posted to financial accounting.

Using Resource-Related Billing

When a customer places a unique order, prices for services may not be stored as fixed prices in the sales order master records. Instead, billing may be based on the expenditure actually incurred. Resource-related billing uses the cost information stored in the project to create items for a billing request. When the time for billing arrives, the billing request initiates the production of billing documents. The following operations are carried out prior to the release of billing documents:

- Pricing can be based on internal prices as an alternative to using cost information stored in the project.
- Resource items against contracts and warranties is a checking process that can be used to reduce individual resource items or eliminate them from billing.
- Interactive dialog functions enable the user to manually change billing requests at the resource item level to delete items or reduce the quantity to be billed.

If you create or change a billing request, the system automatically records this fact as a document history item that can be used to ensure that no item is billed twice. The history can also be used to trace the origin of individual billing items.

N O T E Billing documents provide cost information that can be used in results analysis during project evaluation.

Using Fixed Prices in Subprojects A subproject can be defined as a section of a project or work breakdown structure that has responsibility for its own budget and is therefore obliged to manage its accounting locally. Fixed prices can be used for the transfer of goods and services between subprojects. At the planning stage, fixed prices are managed under fixed-price agreements. At the execution stage, fixed-price allocations are used.

A fixed-price agreement is a document in which you enter the subprojects or WBS elements taking part. The amount appears as a plan revenue in the supplying or sending WBS element and as a commitment in the ordering WBS element.

At the execution stage, a fixed-price allocation based on a fixed-price agreement is affected. The supplying WBS element shows the allocation as an actual revenue, and the ordering WBS element shows the amount as an actual cost. The commitment is reduced by the same amount.

Interpreting Subproject Views   The overall view does not recognize subprojects and therefore does not recognize fixed-price agreements. However, fixed-price agreements can be evaluated in the subproject view, which is accessed by entering the subproject ID code.

The subproject view for decentralized project management can be upheld in the following processes and structures:

- Budgeting and availability control
- Profitability analysis
- Commercial project structures
- Cost element reports

Using the Project Information System

Many different business specialties are used in a complex project, and their providers do not all want to use the same displays and reports. Project status in relation to the various influencing factors will be of interest to many on the team. This is closely related to project progress.

The reporting system enables you to select the degree of detail and the filtering of data appropriate to your immediate purposes. The following project role displays are available to provide starting points for interactive analysis:

- Budget
- Costs and resources
- Finances
- Project structure and schedule
- Resources

The natural way to measure project process is to compare different versions of the same project. A version of a project is a snapshot of the project data at a particular time or at a particular stage, as defined by the status of the project. A project version is either time-dependent or status-dependent. Different versions are displayed in contrasting colors, and you can compare as many versions as you require on a line or column basis to evaluate trends in costs or schedules.

Using PS Information System Reporting

The data you want to inspect can be sorted to differentiate a particular point of view. The following project views are standard structures upon which reports can be deployed:

- The project structure
- A subhierarchy, such as a profit center hierarchy

- A cost center hierarchy
- A summarization hierarchy
- A sales structure, such as a sales order

A report tree function structures and displays the existing standard and custom reports. All reports can be executed interactively or in background processing.

Selecting Standard Reports   The cost information system of PS includes standard reports to compare planned and actual budgets as well as budgets and assigned funds. Any report can be edited for content and layout and can be saved as a custom version.

Defining Custom Reports   The following information is available for use in custom reports:

- Actual values
- Commitment
- Plan values
- Budget
- Sales orders
- Results analysis

Using Structure Reports   Structure reports deploy the data in accordance with work breakdown structures and can make the following comparisons:

- Planned versus actual data
- Budget versus committed funds
- One cost element and another

The scope of structure reports using these comparisons can extend across projects or can be confined to work breakdown structures or WBS elements.

Using Cost Element Reports   You may want to report on particular cost elements taken from the common chart of accounts. Cost element reports evaluate projects, WBS elements, and networks.

Using Line Item Reports   Standard line-item reports are available for the following values:

- Actual
- Planned
- Commitment
- Budget

You can apply flexible analyses and formatting to the data collected for line-item reports to show individual postings. The standard reports have a variety of options to control the document information selected for presentation in the report. You can change the display format interactively.

Part

II

Ch

8

To help you be selective, sort and summary functions can be applied to the data in the document inventory. The individual documents can be accessed directly from line-item report displays.

Using Summarization Reporting   Several projects or subprojects of the same type can be summarized by assigning them to a generic term that can be located in a project summarization hierarchy. The following information can be summarized in this way:

- Values from WBS elements
- Values from activities and activity elements
- Values related to project structure, budgets, and cost elements

The grouping of records for the purpose of summarization is controlled by characteristics that you define for individual hierarchy levels. Reference characteristics point to fields in the project master record. User-defined characteristics are specified by selecting fields and values that will be available in the system when the database is accessed to select records for a summary.

When you have a report on your screen, you can select a summarization object and switch between cost element and project levels. This enables you to move from a summarization report to the detailed information on which it was based.

T I P   Project summarization can embody or branch to standard reports and make use of the full function set of the project and cost information systems.

Viewing the Structure and Dates of a Project

The information system offers you a family of Structure/Dates views of your project. You can select from the following options:

- Show the current status or the hierarchical relationships between selected objects that are part of the project, such as WBS elements, networks, activities, material components, production orders, and maintenance orders
- Control the data aggregation and display to emphasize totals, summaries, comparisons, sorted lists, or graphics
- List all objects in a hierarchical structure
- Inspect overviews of particular types of object in a project, such as activities
- Branch to a detail screen for the object identified on the display

Manipulating Presentation   Lists and overviews are accompanied by relevant statistics and interpretations, of which the following are perhaps the most useful:

- Number of WBS elements
- Number of activities
- Critical activities
- Number of activities started ahead of planned schedule

- Number of activities begun behind schedule
- Number of objects released and partially confirmed

You can add fields to a list or overview display, and you can control presentation and layout. You can be selective by referring to such field data as the ID of a particular manager, a controlling area, or a priority level.

The following standard graphics can be applied automatically to the data on your screen or to any part of it that you choose to select or otherwise define:

- Structure graphic
- Hierarchy
- Gantt Chart
- Network
- Period drill-down graphic
- Portfolio graphic

From the standard SAP R/3 presentation graphics, you can select as appropriate from the following list:

- Histogram
- Totals curve
- Correlation
- ABC analysis
- Segmenting
- Classification

The presentation of values and the layout of the graphics can be customized and edited interactively.

Accessing Related Information Systems   The following information systems are accessible from the Project Information system:

- Costs, finances, and revenues
- Resources

The resources information system presents information about purchasing, materials planning, and capacity planning from the following data sources:

- Capacities
- Missing parts
- Stock and requirements list
- Pegged requirements
- Order reports
- Reservations

- Purchase requisitions
- Purchase orders
- Outline agreements

The resource information system can evaluate the loads on your work centers imposed by the capacity requirements of your project. You can evaluate per project or per work center for all projects. The project system automatically notifies you of problems such as backlogs or capacity overloads. You can use the evaluation facilities to analyze how networks and production orders could affect the capacity loads on your work centers.

If the existing work center hierarchies do not yield the precise information you require, it is possible to create work center groups that combine capacity evaluations across plants and even across companies. You can encapsulate whatever you decide is the most useful way of looking at the capacity situation in your company in a capacity evaluation profile. This is stored and can be called up as necessary.

Some evaluation profiles have been identified as standard capacity overviews. For example, you can select from the following views:

- The standard overview offers the capacity requirements, the available capacity of selected work centers, and the committed capacities of these work centers by period.
- The capacity detail list shows which activities are causing capacity requirements in each period.
- The variable overview shows whatever subset of capacity requirements you define, such as the requirements caused by created or released networks.

Exploring Portfolio Graphics for Project Status Analysis

The customized displays of the portfolio graphics function are designed to use summarized data to represent the costs and work activities of several projects on the screen at the same time. The basic idea is to place each project in an area of the screen that represents a characteristic of interest. A Venn diagram uses similar logic to define sets of entities. The regions can be scaled to represent time variance on the horizontal axis and cost variance vertically.

A small rectangle defines an area in which a project is depicted only if it is on time and within budget according to the tolerances in these variances. Around this central region the next rectangle indicates projects with larger variances in time and cost. In this type of portfolio graphic display, the further out from the center a project is located, the further it is from meeting planned cost and time targets.

 TIP To add more detail, each project can be labeled by an icon in the form of a pie chart depicting project status, perhaps with a radius related to the planned costs.

CHAPTER 9

Analyzing Profitability

In this chapter

Introducing the SAP R/3 Profitability Analysis Module

In this chapter, you will discern the differences between the various accounting procedures that can support the fight against unprofitability. You will be able to deploy the most effective techniques in your own particular circumstances. You will also be able, for example, to prepare answers to the following questions:

- What are the similarities and differences between account-based and costing-based profitability analysis?
- What are the similarities and differences between computing profitability by Cost-of-Sales or by Period Accounting?
- What are the similarities and differences between cost centers and profit centers?
- What is the role of key figures?
- How is data collated for the purpose of analyzing which business activities are profitable?

This section introduces the CO-Controlling modules relevant to profitability analysis and points out the very precise definitions that are applied to the concepts and the SAP R/3 data objects that represent them. The success of the PA module depends on the clarity with which these technical terms are applied in a particular company.

The CO-PA Profitability Analysis module is developed in conjunction with the CO-PCA Profit Center Accounting module. They are both elaborations of the Cost-of-Sales procedures. There is an important distinction to be made between the following aspects of profitability analysis:

- Profitability Analysis is the periodic analysis of the profit and loss made by the strategic units or by the entire company.
- Cost-of-Sales Accounting is also a form of profitability analysis that is used in the management of market-oriented activities.

They both call on the same costing information but treat it in different ways. Sales managers need to be able to estimate profits in the short term by using interim reports. These are based on standard values and imputed costs derived from standard manufacturing costs with cash discounts and rebates, because the actual data is not available at the time the billing document has to be issued. Periodic profitability analysis has to wait for the actual values to be collated.

Calculating and Analyzing Profitability

Profitability is calculated for a business segment. The SAP R/3 system is supplied with a set of criteria from which the definition of a business segment can be assembled. The most commonly used criteria are provided as lists of proposals that can be adopted or ignored when you set up your own CO-PA Profitability Analysis system. You can define fresh criteria to suit your own circumstances.

The SAP R/3 CO-PA Profitability Analysis component is designed to make available the full range of analyses covering the following requirements:

- Current sales data valued with standard costs and prices at the level of the individual product and for individual customers.
- Calculation of actual cost variances for summarized business segments on a periodic basis.
- Proportional assignment of fixed costs in order to measure net profit at the divisional level.
- Application of period profit center accounting in situations where there are large fluctuations in stock levels.

Both the periodic profit and loss statement and the interim sales report have to be able to provide the answers to similar questions, even though their answers may take different forms:

- What is the relationship between gross sales and net sales revenue?
- How were the sales deductions calculated for each market segment?
- What was the profit on this specific order?
- Which products or market segments are showing the greatest increases in sales revenue?
- Which products or market segments are making the highest contribution margin?
- What are the shifts, if any, between the main business segments?
- What are the planned contribution margins for each product?

The Cost-of-Sales Accounting method uses standard costs to produce interim reports, enabling you to look at any market segment immediately, without waiting for the actual data to arrive. If you can wait to the end of the period, then probability analysis will give you more accurate results.

Using Standard Costs with Cost-of-Sales Accounting (Interim Reports)

The market-driven needs of sales management dictate the requirement of estimating profits in the short term by using interim reports based on standard values and imputed costs. These interim values are derived from standard manufacturing costs with cash discounts and rebates because the actual data is not available at the time the billing document has to be issued.

When the actual data arrives, the interim reports are usually reconciled with them on a period basis by applying the procedure referred to as the "Cost-of-Sales Accounting Using Actual Costs (Reconciled Reports)." Because of the lag in time, these reports are not so useful for managing the day-to-day sales activities; their function is more to document and summarize.

Using Fixed Cost Absorption Accounting

Profitability accounting requires that profit and loss be calculated on the basis of both full costs and marginal costs using contribution margin accounting. The actual costs can be assigned to the business segments en bloc or in proportion to sales. Therefore, the fixed costs can be absorbed across several levels of the organization for each period.

Part
II

Ch
9

When costs are assigned to user-defined business segments, they have usually been gathered from one or more cost centers. Costs, however, may have been assigned to orders as "direct costs" so that they can be collected from the customers. These costs can also be taken into account, and direct costs can be assigned to any level of a business segment.

In practice, an SAP R/3 Controlling application may support several methods of profitability accounting in parallel so that the user may compare and contrast his findings in the search for signs of high and low profitability.

Distinguishing the Sources of Profit

It is customary for a corporate group to establish independent operating units in different countries or in different regions of legal force that are defined by the local code of accounting practice. In the SAP R/3 system, these units are identified as company code entities, and they render their own set of external accounts as well as take part in the consolidation of accounts at the head office or client level.

In order to distinguish the sources of profit, the database must be able to associate every business transaction with an accounting data object that serves to collate and summarize the relevant information that will be used to compute the profitability of each operating unit of interest. Your company may be interested in the differences in profitability of company code units, and it may also want to trace the sources of variability down to the departments. In fact, the CO-PA module is able to refine the definition of profit source down to any degree of precision that you require.

Using Charts of Accounts The balance sheet and the profit and loss statements are rendered as the external accounts by assembling business transaction data in cost elements. These are specific accounts in the General Ledger and are listed as the items in the chart of accounts, which serves as a classification plan. The chart of accounts is stored as an entity of type 2001 and belongs to only one client, but a client can have several charts of accounts.

Here are some examples of entity type 2002, "Chart of Accounts Items":

- Undeveloped real estate
- Long-term portfolio investments
- Receivables from sales and services—domestic debtors
- Receivables from sales and services—receipt uncertain
- Payables for goods and services—domestic creditors
- Interest revenue from loans to business partners
- Semi-finished products
- Raw materials
- Auxiliary materials
- Sales costs
- Sales revenue for company-produced products and services

Each cost element defined by an account listed as an item in the chart of accounts belongs to only one chart of accounts, although a similar item may appear in other charts belonging to the same client. You may use whatever titles for these accounts that suit your business, if they are acceptable to your accounting authority.

The purpose of the chart of accounts is to record values and value flows. Financial Accounting uses the chart items for the external accounts. Management Accounting uses chart items in conjunction with the controlling database to assess progress and plan for the future.

Using Company Codes   The company code is an ID number assigned to the smallest organizational unit that is allowed to compile an independent set of financial documents for external reporting. Every transaction and supporting document has to be tagged with a company code if it is to contribute to the balance sheet and the profit and loss statement of that organizational unit.

Using Companies   A company comprises one or more company code organizational units. The individual company code financial statements are consolidated to generate a company balance sheet and a profit and loss statement. It is customary to structure an international group as a series of affiliated companies. Each country usually has a separate company and is represented by an SAP R/3 company code identifier. When several countries share accounting conventions, they are coded as a single entity. Each "Region of Legal Force" is defined on the basis of the legal and accounting practices customary or, indeed, mandatory in the geographical territory. The SAP database recognizes a set of these regions according to the directions you have established by customizing. Any country or region of legal force may contain more than one company affiliated to your group.

Using Business Area   If the division of a company into company code units does not exactly match the management accounting requirements of a corporate group, business areas may be defined by assigning separate areas of operations or responsibilities, for example, for subsidiaries or specific product lines. A business area is not legally independent, although it may compile a balance sheet and profit and loss statement purely for internal purposes, such as profitability analysis. A business area is formally defined as an entity of type 2009 and has to be assigned to just one client.

N O T E   The data stored in a business area master record can be drawn from any or all company codes belonging to the same client.

Using Functional Areas   The classification of expenses in Cost-of-Sales Accounting is achieved by defining functional areas such as the following:

- Administration
- Sales and Distribution
- Marketing
- Production
- Research and Development

Part
II

Ch
9

When an expense is posted, the details are assigned to one of these functional areas. The accumulated data is then available for reporting at any time and may be used, for example, to compute the profit contribution of a product or group of products.

There also has to be a method for deciding how any particular expense shall be assigned. Your system could be customized to suggest that any invoice should be assigned in the same way as the previous invoice from that supplier. This could proceed automatically until a new supplier appears.

However, you might want to distribute some of your expenses between several accounting headings. For this purpose, you can call upon or create a distribution key to share out the expense.

Defining a Cost Accounting Controlling Area

To enable you to refine your analysis of where your balance sheet costs have incurred, a system of account assignment objects is available for constructing a cost assignment structure. Alternatively, you can access a standard structure suitable for your industry and make a copy of it to be edited to suit your specific circumstances. The main cost assignment objects are the cost center, the order, and the project. You may also define a cost object based on a convenient product unit or, indeed, on any data object that can collect costs in a way that is understood by your company.

If the SAP R/3 system is to operate cost and revenue element accounting, it must be conducted entirely within a closed unit referred to as a controlling area. More than one company code can be assigned to a controlling area, but they must all share a common chart of accounts. This configuration could arise, for instance, in a group of companies at the company code level that operates a shared centralized cost accounting facility.

CAUTION

A cost and revenue element accounting system can only work if each posting in the controlling area includes not only the cost or revenue element but also information on where the costs were incurred and the purpose of this expenditure.

Using Controlling Areas   The controlling area is formally defined as a self-contained organizational unit within a company or group that is able to perform Cost Accounting. It is created as a master record of entity type 4017, "Cost Accounting Area." A controlling area can include more than one company code, and each of them can be operating in different currencies. A master currency will be defined, however, and the companies must all share the same chart of accounts. Internal allocation transactions must be confined to objects within the same controlling area.

If a system of controlling areas is not defined, the corporate group is assumed to be the effective controlling area. A cost accounting area ledger is maintained to represent the value movements in the cost accounting area.

Using Cost Elements and Revenue Elements   The cost elements are the account items of the chart of accounts that are used for entering, classifying, and recording the values of production resources consumed in a controlling area.

Revenue elements are the account items of the controlling area chart of accounts that are used to record the value of products sold.

Using Profit Centers   Any convenient scheme of subdividing a business organization can be used to define profit centers because they are set up purely for internal management control. They have to be defined within a Cost Accounting controlling area. Their purpose is to record the value of operating profit calculated by either or both of the two methods, namely, Cost-of-Sales Accounting and period profitability analysis.

Using Investment Centers   The investment center concept is developed from the profit center by allowing a profit center to incorporate restricted asset values when calculating profit. An investment center is created in a profit center master record. The transfer of balance sheet items is performed by running the period end reports for transfer of balance sheet items to a profit center.

Using Cost Centers   A cost center is a physical place where costs arise or a conceptual entity to which it makes sense to assign costs. A system of cost centers can be established on the basis of any scheme that is useful. The following methods are often used:

- Cost centers relate to functions or functional requirements.
- Cost centers relate to the cost allocation criteria.
- Cost centers correspond to the different activities that consume costs.
- Cost centers correspond to the various services provided.
- Each geographical area is treated as a cost center.
- Each trading area is treated as a cost center.
- Each plant or group of plant resources is controlled as a cost center.
- Each area of responsibility to which a named manager is assigned is controlled as a cost center.

One of the useful roles of a system of cost centers is to enable you to apportion overhead costs to sales activities as part of the cost calculation procedure. If you wish to exercise a cost control function, the costs attracted to a specific cost center may be the first object of your attention. Where your company handles many orders of a similar nature, the continuous monitoring function of a cost center may be very informative. If your business is characterized by large individual orders, you may not wish to assign them to cost centers because each order can be usefully monitored individually.

Using Activity Types   Although a cost center can be defined as a place where costs are incurred, it may not be very informative about exactly how those costs were accumulated. If you can divide all the work of your company into different activities that take place in various quantities in your cost centers, you are in the position of being able to calculate the cost of activities in terms of the value rate per quantity. You can then predict how the costs of a cost center are

Part
II

Ch
9

likely to change if the quantities of activities performed there were to change in the future, or if some of the activities were to be abandoned altogether. You might also be able to form a view on how much it might cost if some activity is moved from one cost center to another.

To make use of activity types, you need a price list and information on exactly what factors were used when compiling this list of activity prices. If you have a system of virtual, as opposed to location-based, cost centers, you can assign activities to them without regard to the practicalities that would be taken into consideration if you wished to transfer activities from one location to another. You can do both by planning a work item in a conceptual cost center and later assigning these activities to a physical cost center with the personnel and other resources that are needed.

Using Order Types   An order is a convenient assignment object for controlling by Cost Accounting. It can describe a simple task or work package in a controlling area and is a convenient recording focus for planning, monitoring, and allocating costs in situations where the driving factors are the activities and sequence of actions needed to meet the order. An order can also represent a computation or measurement process that is carried out for accounting or controlling reasons. If you view orders in terms of their different business goals, you will recognize the following different types:

- Production orders
- Assembly orders
- Run schedule orders
- Process orders
- Plant maintenance orders
- Orders with revenue
- Capital investment orders
- Overhead cost orders
- Results analysis orders

By and large, orders are the favored control instrument for discrete events or limited series of associated events, whereas the cost center is preferred when your business operates with a continuous flow of similar orders that is likely to carry on year after year.

The list of business goals, which can be differentiated by the various types of order, can be extended by including the more complex data structures that can be used as cost assignment objects. Project and networks are in this class.

Using Projects   A project has to be assigned to only one cost controlling area because it is used to control and monitor the various aspects of a business that are needed to complete complex tasks on time and within budget. A project, for example, can serve as the cost assignment object for all the costs incurred by the following activities:

- Planning, controlling, and monitoring the schedule of work
- Allocating and valuing resources

- Planning and monitoring activity capacities
- Controlling costs and revenues
- Monitoring funds availability

Using WBS Elements The work entailed by a project can be represented by a work breakdown structure (WBS), which is formally represented as a WBS element in the SAP R/3 PS-Project System. A WBS element can be part of a task and may itself comprise a complex work structure that is best represented by a WBS, and so on. A WBS element can act as a cost assignment object. These ideas are discussed in Chapter 8, "Controlling by the PS-Project System."

Using Cost Objects A cost object is a unit that is used as a cost assignment object in Cost Accounting. You can use some types of SAP R/3 data structures as cost objects. For example, you can use instances of the following entities from the logistics modules as costs objects:

- Procurement order
- Material
- Production order
- Assembly order
- Run schedule order
- Process order
- Network

If none of the available objects is convenient to use as a cost assignment object, you can create one manually as a "cost object" entity.

Using Business Processes You may have defined your cost centers so that all your business processes are located neatly in the cost center structure. If this is not convenient, you can group tasks performed in different cost centers and assign them to a business process master record so that you can process them as if they were co-located. You may have many cost centers, for example, that each require a system update or plant maintenance function to be carried out by a specialist team. The work of this team could be associated with a business process master so that its costs and profitability could be measured.

If you name a business process and make it a cost assignment object, the reports will tell you what resources have been used in this process. You will be able to explain why these resources were used in the reporting period. On the other hand, the cost center with a physical location in a specific plant has a named manager so that the reports can tell you who managed the resources and where they were applied in your organization.

Using Profitability Segments The CO-PA Profitability Analysis module works with a specific assignment object to which costs and sales revenues may be posted in order to compute the profitability of the business entities associated with it. This assignment object is defined as a profitability segment and it may be defined in terms of any combination of cost or revenue objects available in your system.

For example, you can use customers, products, and sales organizations as the basis for a profitability segment definition. You can also define a profitability segment according to a classifiable attribute, such as the orders that are valued over a specified amount.

Using Operating Concerns If you have many profitability segments defined over one or more controlling areas, you may nevertheless wish to recognize that the sales market for part of your organization is structured in a uniform manner. You can combine the profitability analyses of the profitability segments in this uniform sales market by assigning the segments to an operating concern master record. The profitability analysis can then be conducted and reported separately for each operating concern.

Using Object Classes The CO-Controlling application supports many different types of cost assignment objects so that you may perform control and management tasks on your specific company, no matter how it is organized. These cost assignment objects are conveniently classified according to the type of controlling activity in which they take part, although some of the types of objects are to be found in many different business activities. The main object classes are as follows:

- Cost centers are typically used in overhead cost management.
- Cost objects are typically used in production cost controlling.
- Capital investment orders are typically used in investment management.
- Profitability segments are typically used in profitability analysis.

Cost assignment objects can be assigned to an object class automatically under control of the module in which the object is created. Alternatively, you can arrange for the assignment of the cost object to be controlled by a key assigned in the master record for each project or order.

Using the Processes of Profitability Analysis

The functions of SAP R/3 in the CO-PA Profitability Analysis module are designed to provide extra information to enable you to take action when you have calculated the contribution margin or the overall contribution to operating profits arising from business activities in the different parts of your company. For example, you can apply PA results in the following activities:

- Pricing
- Sales terms and sales policy elaboration
- Quantity control and allocation to productive resources
- Allocation and evaluation of distribution channels
- Marketing

The SAP R/3 functions needed for profit center accounting are located in the EC-PCA module (Enterprise Controlling-Profit Center Accounting). They can be integrated with the CO-PA functions.

The profit center concept is designed for decentralized organizations in which the units are accounted as separate entities, and operating results have to be published for these units. You can control how these profit centers are specified. For example, you could map your profit centers on products, on divisions, or on product groups. You might want to treat your main functional activities as profit centers, such as Production, Sales, and Service. On the other hand, the most useful scheme of profit centers for your company might be based on geography in terms of the location of regional distribution centers, plant locations, branch offices, and so on.

Using Methods in Parallel

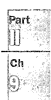

The CO-PA module enables you to compute profitability by several different procedures in parallel. The following procedures are available:

- Interim sales analysis in which the sales revenues are calculated on the basis of standard costs.
- Sales analysis based on full costs and marginal costs to yield contribution margin results.
- Fixed costs assigned to profitability segments in proportion to sales.
- Fixed costs assigned to profitability segments using a cost pool allocation sequence.
- Supplementing interim sales analysis with production and cost center variances from planned values to produce a final sales analysis that can be periodically reconciled with Financial Accounting data.

Using Variants of Profitability Accounting

The FI-Financial Accounting application is able to conduct various forms of profitability accounting without recourse to the PA application. There may be a strong case in your company, however, for installing and configuring the PA module because it enables you to follow up in detail any promising leads that are suggested by the basic PA computing conducted in the FI application. The following sections explore some of the possibilities.

Using Relative Direct Cost and Contribution Margin Accounting   If you choose to leave out indirect costs from your profitability analysis, you can assign costs and revenues to any level of your cost assignment structure. This enables you to compute the costs and profit contribution relative to any aspect or point of view of your company that is represented in your cost assignment object structure.

For example, you could have defined a profitability segment so that it collated data for a particular region and a single product. If you conduct a sales campaign in this region for this particular product, the periodic costs could be assigned directly to this segment and, thus, take part in the profitability analysis for this product. If your system already maintains a separate account for this product in this region, then there is no need to specify a profitability segment for it in the PA module. In the same way, the revenues in this region from this product appear in the calculation of its contribution margin.

Using Account-based Profitability Analysis

You can calculate profitability by comparing posted revenues and sales deductions with the imputed costs and sales deductions. However, you can leave out the imputed costs that are based on costing calculations carried out by the CO-PA application. The effect is independent of any profitability segments because the profitability results are based on the existing accounts. These results, of course, can be reconciled with the General Ledger at any time. This method is equivalent to defining your profitability segments exactly in accord with your existing accounts. That way you can show the operating results in the accounts of the General Ledger and thus ensure reconcilability with Financial Accounting at any time.

Using CO-PA and EC-PCA for Period Accounting

CO-PA uses the Cost-of-Sales approach to compute profitability. EC-PCA also uses this approach, as well as the Period Accounting approach. You can have both methods used in parallel.

Identifying Profitability Segments

CO-PA depends on your defining profitability segments as the assignment objects for cost data, quantities, and revenues. In order to prevent you from having to take up any standard point of view, the system enables you to specify any characteristic or attribute to become one of the dimensions of a reporting structure, which is stored as a profitability segment master record.

If you define one dimension to be the manufacturing plants in your company, for example, and you have four, then this dimension of the profitability segment will have four divisions. Suppose you had three product groups that were manufactured in these four production plants; then you could have a two-dimensional profitability segment of 12 cells representing the three product groups combined with the four plant units.

In another example, if you were to call for the profitability to be analyzed separately according to the distribution channel, and you had five, then the three-dimensional profitability segment would have 60 cells. Each of these 60 cells could be subjected to individual analysis of costs and revenues in order to determine its profitability. For instance, you could have the results displayed in rank order so that the first item in the list would be the most profitable cell. This cell would be computed by selecting the costs and revenues for only one of the three product groups, only if they were attributed to one specific plant, and only if they were associated with one particular distribution channel.

This example used the plant, product group, and distribution channel as the defining characteristics of the profitability segment. You could have set up other dimensions provided your system is holding the data necessary to identify when a posting should be assigned to the profitability segment in the Profitability Analysis module. You can apply logical and mathematical conditions to set up profitability segments, as in the following hypothetical definitions:

  ☐ Electronic sector product group in the company operating regions using the customers in the top sector according to credit worthiness.

  ☐ Retail customers who have not bought for over one year.

Understanding Integrated Data Flow

You can trace the flow of data for Profitability Analysis along various routes. If you post a billing document or an incoming sales order from the SD-Sales and Distribution application, the Profitability Analysis module is automatically posted with the sales quantities, the revenues, and the Cost-of-Sales deductions.

There may be direct costs that should be assigned to an intermediate level in your cost assignment structure because they are not associated with the lowest level cost objects in any straightforward manner. You can do this manually in the Profitability Analysis module.

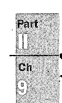

The costs of goods you have manufactured can be obtained in the form of product cost estimates or as material prices in make-to-stock production. Alternatively, you can settle costs from the customer orders or from projects.

The CO application enables you to specify in advance how Profitability Analysis shall be assigned costs in the following situations:

- When supplier invoices for wholesale or retail are received
- When costs of services are posted in Financial Accounting
- When internal activities are allocated by direct postings

If you are operating with cost centers or internal orders, you can have the overhead costs allocated to profitability segments. You can also have them subsequently updated to actual costs by transferring, as period costs, any variances from production orders and cost centers.

If you have installed and configured the SD-Sales and Distribution application, the necessary information is automatically available to the FI system. If the integrated SD application is not available, you must set up the complex interfaces into FI that acquire the data relevant to sales by extracting it from the sales documents, such as the sales inquiries, quotations, and sales orders.

Understanding Analytic Sales and Profit Planning

In order to generate a sales and profit plan, you have to call on the CO-PA facilities that provide for periodic distribution of costs, projections, valuations, and all the logical and arithmetic functions. The automatic planning functions include the following facilities:

- Copy previous year plan
- Copy previous year actual figures
- Top-down distribution of planned values
- Revaluation of existing plans
- Saving of plan data at any level of the profitability segment structure
- Multi-year planning

Semi-automatic planning in profitability segments is possible in either of the following modalities:

- You enter plan sales quantities and revenues, and the system calculates sales deductions and costs automatically.
- You enter plan sales quantities, and the system uses price list catalogs to calculate the revenues automatically.
- You enter contribution margins, and the system calculates the sales quantities necessary to realize them.

The idea of sales and profit planning is to set the processes of planning, not only for sales, production, and procurement, but also for investment, personnel, finance, and profit.

Reporting from EC-PCA and CO-PA

EC-PCA provides profit center reports in the form of listings. CO-PA uses the structure of your profitability segments to direct interactive drill-down reporting. The combined integrated system enables you to define reports in terms of the following reporting display structures:

- Layout definitions and forms
- Line or contribution margin structures
- Key figure formula definitions
- Predefined report headers

The full array of standard and custom reports is available as a standard reporting tree display that can be customized by the user.

While you have a report displayed online, the following manipulations are available:

- Drill down
- Information on the origin of the data in a line item
- Period breakdown
- Overview list
- Detail list

If you are able to specify the exception conditions or define the characteristics of the records that interest you or their data, then you can store this search procedure and use it again to focus your scrutiny of the reported Profitability Analysis results.

Decentralizing Profitability Analysis

The advantage of ALE (Application Link Enabling) is that several computers may share integration of applications. In particular, Profitability Analysis can be carried out in a central function having had all the decentralized profit-related transactions passed to it. You can carry out cost and profit planning in CO-PA from the decentralized installation and pass the data to central planning where the cost center data can be integrated with it.

One of the key distinctions to be made is between the information that can be taken directly from a sales document and the information that has to be derived from other sources of data. For example, you can add up all the quantities and prices of the products and services sold in a time period and by a particular sales team. What you cannot extract from the sales documents is a value for the materials and other resources that your company has expended in order to produce or procure these products and services. You may have set your prices to factor in some of these indirect costs, but a profitability analysis that will be of most use to you is one that can go back to basics. You may wish to explore how the PA results change if you alter the production facilities, for example.

Part
II

Ch

9

Choosing PA Classification Characteristics

The system offers you a list of proposals based on the profitability segment characteristics that users most often find convenient. You may also choose from this list and create your own. Your scheme of profitability segments is time-stamped so you can refer to it later and subject it to status control in order to ensure that the correct version is applied on each occasion. For example, you may want to rearrange your territories as markets develop, or you may need to change to a different PA structure.

Your circumstances and intentions determine what kind of Profitability Analysis structure is going to be most effective. You may elect to install several methods to be run in parallel, but several factors have to be evaluated before data structures are defined.

You may have a number of objectives in mind when designing a PA system, of which the following are but illustrations:

- Sales management aims and methods.
- Depth of detail required in the analysis, and an estimate of how this level of detail is interpreted.
- Reconciliation with Financial Accounting.
- Methods for ensuring a flow of imputed values into the Profitability Analysis, or a reliance on actual costs.
- Whether all the costs or a portion or sample are used for Profitability Analysis.
- The accounting and computation procedures to be used.

The procedures to be applied are taken from the following list, although several may be operated in parallel:

- Up-to-the-minute Cost-of-Sales Accounting per product and per customer using standard cost valuation.
- Summary level profitability segments updated by periodic calculation of actual cost variances compared with planned costs.
- Net Profitability Analysis of operating units using staggered allocation of fixed costs.
- Account-based PA using only profits that can be reconciled with balance sheet accounts in Financial Accounting.
- Period Accounting PA.

The operating results of your company can be computed in various ways according to the way you collate the data and structure the reports. Choices have to be made in three main dimensions:

- Analyze by periods or analyze by transactions.
- Apply Period Accounting or Cost-of-Sales Accounting.
- Analyze according to General Ledger accounts or analyze according to cost origins.

If you elect to analyze according to cost origins, you have the choice between the following:

- Cost-of-Sales using interim reports and standard costs.
- Cost-of-Sales using final reports and actual costs.

In the matter of computing the Cost-of-Sales, there is a further choice between the following:

- Net Profit Analysis based on full costing.
- Gross Profit Analysis based on partial costing results.

If you choose net Profit Analysis based on full costing, there are two options as follows:

- Proportional fixed costs
- Fixed cost lump sum

The reason there are so many possibilities to choose from in Profitability Analysis is that there are at least two target readerships for the results. Sales managers want to formulate plans for active marketing, while company directors want to present to shareholders a valid and favorable analysis of the entire company and be able to explain the main sources of profitability.

Making Use of Key Figures

Cost-based Profitability Analysis makes use of key figures stored in the database. The following data structures can store key figures:

- Associated quantity and value fields (duples)
- Calculated values, such as contribution margins and net profit

A *duple* is used to store quantity and value at the lowest or finest level of detail that is required in the Profitability Analysis in order to handle quantities, revenues, sales deductions, and costs for each profitability segment. Both actual and plan data can be stored in this way.

This PA database holds data that cannot be stored in Financial Accounting because it refers to objects that are more detailed than the account assignment objects needed for the balance sheet and the profit and loss statement.

The standard system provides 120 value fields that can be used to differentiate the source or purpose of the value stored. You can differentiate revenues from external customers, for example, and revenues from affiliated companies. You can also assign credit memos and discounts to separate value fields.

Costs derived in other FI and CO modules that are used in PA are also stored in value fields. Possible sources of cost data are SAP R/3 modules that have to be installed and configured in your system. Some of them are noted in the following list:

- Cost of goods manufactured from CO-PC Product Costing.
- Cost of goods manufactured and cost of goods sold from sales orders and from projects using the CO-PC and PS-Project System modules.
- Costs from overhead projects and orders using the PS or CO-OPA Order and Project Accounting modules.
- Variances from production orders derived from the PP-Production Planning application.
- Fixed costs, variances, and internal activities from the CO-CCA Cost Center Accounting module.
- External data acquired from invoice receipts via the MM-Materials Management module (MM).
- Direct postings from FI-Financial Accounting .
- Imputed costs from the CO-PA Profitability Analysis module.

Revenues, sales deductions, and costs are well represented in the key field proposals offered to you by the system when you are setting up your Profitability Analysis structure.

Planning Sales Quantities and Profits

The planning of sales quantities, revenue, and profit in the context of corporate planning is the exclusive province of the SAP R/3 CO-PA Profitability Analysis system. The business segment is the focus of this planning, and the fine details are held in the key figure section of the PA database.

The possibilities of business segment planning include the following:

- Planning the sales quantity for a business segment.
- Using the planned sales quantity and the values available to the system for revenue, discounts, rebates, and so on to compute the planned gross revenue and planned net revenue.
- Transferring the planned costs, such as manufacturing cost and cost center overheads, from the CO-Controlling system, and calculating the planned profit for a business segment.
- Planning all fixed cost allocations at different levels of the segment.

The CO-PA Profitability Analysis system enables you to plan sales quantity data for any number of business segments, defined as you wish. You can plan down to the level of the individual key figure. There is no need to specify a permanent level at which planned values and quantities are entered because each plan is treated as a version with status control and a specified period of validity. Each business can operate sales and profit planning in the most informative way and change it to meet movements in the markets.

Part
II
Ch
9

Planning in CO-PA carried out at the level of sales quantity and revenues can also be transferred to SOP (Sales and Operations Planning) in production. Thus, a sales plan created in CO-PA can be used as input to a production plan. The production plan in turn derives the costs of production from product costing CO-PC. This module in turn provides information back to CO-PA to enable it to compute the planned costs of sales for the originally planned sales. This yields a value for the planned cost contribution. This is a good example of how complex plan integration is possible using standard SAP R/3 modules.

Using Revenue Element Accounting

The Generally Accepted Accounting Principles (GAAP) require that the values recorded in the accounts of a company shall be in a permanent state of reconciliation. In order to comply with this requirement, an online accounting system has to maintain a journal, a set of account balances, and all the documents to support them. The SAP R/3 system meets these conditions and, in some respects, exceeds them.

In particular, revenue data transferred to CO-PA Profitability Analysis can be reconciled with the posted revenue in FI-Financial Accounting.

In company codes in which the sources of revenue are not readily matched to the revenue elements of the CO-PA Profitability Analysis system, it is usual to utilize the facilities of the FI-SPL Special Purpose Ledger to associate the revenue sources with the appropriate items chosen from the lists of origins recognized by this component. The additional subdivisions of revenue accounts that are supported by the FI-SPL Special Purpose Ledger remain reconciled with the FI-GL General Ledger revenue accounts. The advantage of calling on the extra analysis information available through the FI-SPL Special Purpose Ledger is that it enables accurate reconciliation with the revenue elements of the CO-PA Profitability Analysis component.

Estimating Revenue Elements

It may well happen that the billing data transferred to CO-PA Profitability Analysis is not accurate and revenue elements may have to be estimated. A sales deduction, for example, could be estimated as, say, 10 percent of domestic sales revenue, on the grounds that a previous analysis supported this as a reasonable prediction. The benefit is that the CO-PA Profitability Analysis system can provide a complete and up-to-date estimate of gross and net revenues as soon as the billing takes place.

Such estimated sales deductions are usually posted and transferred to FI-Financial Accounting, where they can be balanced with the actual sales deductions when they become available. If necessary, the CO-PA Profitability Analysis system then adjusts the calculation for future estimates.

There is a difference between account-based PA and costing-based PA:

- For account-based CO-PA, the cost of goods sold is transferred at goods issue time to ensure reconciliation with FI-GL.
- For costing-based CO-PA, the cost of the sale is only transferred at billing.

The logic is that in costing-based analysis, you never record a cost of a sale without posting the corresponding value of the sale revenue.

Developing Multiple Planning Versions

One of the applications of multiple versions of a plan for a particular time period is to be able to hold different views of the future course of business. For instance, you may have a preliminary version of a plan that is saved but also edited to become a current version, and later made up as the final version. Another classification of planning data can depend on the differing requirements of management, sales, and production. You can also maintain different plan versions to show particular content and levels of detail. You could perhaps conduct sales monitoring by comparing plan, target, and actual quantities and values.

You may copy and extrapolate data from one plan or actual data block to other time periods. If you have a suitable interface to another planning system, this data can be imported to the CO-PA module. Your draft plan may be updated by applying percentage additions or reductions. A re-evaluation function is also available to revalue a complete profitability segment or each value field separately.

The standard techniques of top-down and bottom-up planning can be used. You can enter or copy high-level planning values and have the system distribute them, or you can enter or copy the low-level figures and have them rolled up to generate planning values for higher levels of your planning structure.

Planning the Cost of Sales

You have the ability to transfer known costs from other applications and impute unknown costs. You can use the following sources of cost data, for example, in your plan:

- Special direct costs from sales orders.
- Pricing elements from Inventory Management.
- Costing results from Product Costing.
- Fixed costs planned in cost center accounting.

The plan can split costs into fixed and variable components for each profitability segment and can also identify the cost of goods manufactured and the cost of goods sold. If you have planned sales quantities across periods, you can use these values as proportions to distribute the annual planned costs. You can also create your own set of proportions to have the distribution reflect what you anticipate or intend to be the pattern of business over the time scale for which you are planning.

The sequence of planning is usually similar to the following:

- Identify the managers for whom the planning is to take place.
- Arrange the source data into convenient blocks.
- Eliminate or aggregate very small amounts or special transactions.
- Review the time sequence for the plan data objects separately for each manager.
- Adjust the plan data.

The R/3 method of transferring plan data to create alternative plan versions is applied in corporate planning so that the various business area plans can be combined to contribute to a corporate plan. In addition, the values planned at the corporate level can be used as the basis for lower-level planning.

> **N O T E** The cycle of top-down and bottom-up planning can be repeated as often as necessary to build a refined planned by iterations and adjustments. ☐

Budgeting Sales Promotions

Sales and promotion budgets are managed in PA as budget versions in the same way as other plan versions, and any profitability segment can be assigned a budget. The budget amounts are distributed according to the plan structure you have established. This structure may have an associated distribution function that automatically allocates a budget top-down to profitability segments.

A budget is subject to status control and can be adjusted and updated in a plan version before being released. After a budget has been released, there can be no changes to the planned values unless the release is canceled by a person authorized to do so.

Operating CO-PA

The Profitability Analysis module is fully engaged in the flow of data between the R/3 Logistics, Financial Accounting, and Controlling applications. Either in real-time or in periodic batch processing, the PA system acquires the following classes of profit-related data:

- ☐ Sales quantities, revenues, and sales deductions from SD-Sales and Distribution.
- ☐ Cost of sales for account-based PA from goods issued in SD.
- ☐ Cost of goods manufactured from CO-PC Product Costing or from the material prices in the materials masters of MM-Materials Management.
- ☐ Costs and revenues posted directly from invoice receipt in MM.
- ☐ Costs and revenues posted directly from FI-Financial Accounting.
- ☐ Costs and revenues in make-to-order production from sales orders and project settlement in SD and the PS-Project System.
- ☐ Cost center costs or cost center variances from CO-OM-CCA Order Management, Cost Center Accounting.
- ☐ Internal activities posted directly from CO-OM-CCA.
- ☐ Indirect costs of internal orders from CO-OM-OPA Order Management, Order and Project Accounting.
- ☐ Production variances arising from the settlement of production orders in PP-Production Planning.

If your implementation does not include the integrated sources of profit-related data, or if you are running the CO-PA module as a standalone application, you can import the necessary information through an established open interface. However, you must establish the details to customize the SAP interface in order to enable your system to acquire the sales data. Using an integrated SD system is the recommended alternative.

Calculating Gross Operating Profits

There are several accounting conventions for arriving at gross operating profits. They may all be used by posting direct costs and revenues and then allocating indirect costs to the appropriate level of the profitability segment structure. The following methods are used to value gross operating profits:

- Make-to-stock production and wholesale-retail trading may arrive at a gross operating profits valuation by applying a proportional rate.
- Production related to sales orders will compute gross profits from the order results analysis and order settlement data.
- The service industry will value gross profits by comparing direct cost postings and revenue postings.

Using Valuation by Proportional Rate

Make-to-stock production and the wholesale and retail trading industries typically process standard products. When billing occurs in the SD application, revenues and sales deductions are transferred to Profitability Analysis. If costing-based PA is being applied, the system computes costs for these sales by adjusting standard cost estimates and valuing imputed costs.

If account-based PA is being applied, the system determines the cost of sales at the time goods are issued by referring to the valuation of the change-in-stock posting that has been made to Financial Accounting. If any imputed sales deductions and costs were also posted to Financial Accounting, they will be transferred to CO-PA. Any costs or sales deductions that are not posted to a balance sheet account is not recognized by PA when account-based PA is being applied.

The use of a profitability segment depends on recognizing when a transaction is relevant to it, in the sense of having the characteristics that were used in defining the segment. The system automatically uses the sales order for customer, product, and distribution channel information. The customer master record and the material masters provide other sources of data that are needed to assign a transaction to a profitability segment. If you have specified characteristics to define a profitability segment that cannot be obtained automatically, then you can enter them manually on the order document by choosing from a list so that the transaction is attributed to the correct profitability segment.

Using Simple Margins Analysis

From a sales perspective, it is very helpful to have a continuous picture of operating results. Margins analysis uses formulas based on percentages, quotas, and specified fixed amounts. The calculations can proceed in steps, of which the following is an example sequence:

1. The posted revenue is subject to a percentage discount that is dependent on the sales total to yield the net revenue.

2. The net revenue is reduced by a profit margin defined as a specified fixed amount per unit sold and further reduced by a profit margin defined as percentage of the net revenue to yield the profits at stage one.

3. The stage one profits are reduced by another profit margin, based on a percentage of the stage one profits to yield the stage two profits.

This example uses three profit margins calculated in different ways to convert the posted revenue value in the period to a profit value. These calculations do not depend on a value for the cost of goods manufactured, but they do give an indication of the gross profit contribution margins.

Determining the Net Operating Profit

Contribution Margin Accounting has to bring in the revenues and associated cost of goods manufactured and also the other direct and indirect costs. It is usually impossible to associate these other overhead costs with specific orders, products, or customers, but they can be assigned to profitability segments. The CO-PA system enables you to calculate profits using either full costs or marginal costs.

The costs arising in a cost center are allocated to just one profitability segment. These include fixed costs from administration, sales, inventory management, and general functions. Part of the fixed costs will have been assigned in proportion to the imputed costs of goods manufactured for the product. The remainder of the fixed costs are allocated to individual profitability segments on a periodic basis. The following allocation methods are supported:

- [ ] Allocation to any combination of profitability segment characteristics
- [ ] Allocation to one or several profitability segments
- [ ] Allocation to profitability segments specified individually or by range
- [ ] Allocation in accord with predefined fixed and variable cost distribution keys that control fixed percentages or rates dependent on revenues of the destination segments

Forecasting from Incoming Orders

Data from orders coming in to the SD application can be transferred to Profitability Analysis where the date of receipt of an order is treated as if it were the settlement date. Therefore, it is valued at the rates then current. This order forecast data is maintained as a separate database and aggregated periodically.

N O T E The ad hoc forecast based on incoming orders is usefully compared with the sales and profit plan when there is only a short delay between order and billing. ☐

Analyzing Profitability Data

The reports available for Profitability Analysis are displayed in a report list or a report tree. The ad hoc report is an inquiry of a simple kind that can be interactive and use the drill-down facility, or be a predefined report focused on a form of analysis frequently required.

More complex reports are needed where there are many options at several stages of analysis. Exception reports are predefined to issue warnings when specific values do not fall within the expected range, which you can define for individual rows or columns of a report. You can also specify thresholds in terms of percentages.

The following report designs are often specified for Profitability Analysis:

- Ranking lists with threshold values to define partitions for ABC analysis in order to identify the highest and lowest percentage of instances and the "Top N" selection.
- User-defined classes for analyzing large data volumes graphically and building cumulative frequency curves.
- Detailed operating results for all the individual profitability segments in a specified controlling area.
- Detailed step-down report of the contribution margin for a profitability segment compared with another segment or period.
- Comparison of multilevel contribution margins for selected operating units.

The following display options are available for all reports:

- Actual quantities and values
- Planned quantities and values
- Comparisons of plan and actual for different periods
- Comparisons of plan and actual for any time period
- Comparisons of different plan versions

Many reporting possibilities exist. It is reasonable to assume that any format is available, provided the data is available and the characteristics needed to make a selection are accurately associated with the targeted data.

Handling Large Data Volumes

If you have a large number of profitability segments and many transactions, many items and totals will be processed. CO-PA generates a profitability segment for each combination of customer and product, for example, if you decide to make these two dimensions part of your Profitability Analysis.

If you can usefully define summarization levels in which the data elements for certain profitability segments are aggregated, then you can arrange for these summarization levels to be consulted when a report is required and, thus, save processing resources. In the meantime, they can be updated in offline batch mode when relevant data is detected.

The summarization levels can also provide up-to-date reports if the delta technique is used. This enables you to add small numbers of line items to the summarized data just before the report is compiled. The system maintains information on how efficient the existing summarization levels are in providing a data processing service to those who need the profitability reports.

Using Profit Center Accounting

A profit center is not an independent account assignment object. It derives its information from existing account assignment objects. The necessary standard software is provided as CO-PCA Profit Center Accounting. The master record of each account assignment object includes a field that identifies the responsible profit center. The profit center is defined by an organizational master record in the system and can, therefore, store descriptive information, in particular the criteria that defines which account assignment objects it is responsible for.

Profit centers can be summarized and their results combined on any number of hierarchical levels and across different hierarchies. The profit center is a way of looking at a particular selection of transaction data assigned to various accounts to see how the data affects the operating profit of that portion of business that the profit center represents.

Using Ledger-based Period Accounting at the Profit Center Level

Profit centers enable you to collate all profit-related posting information under the divisions of your organizational structure. Every posting is saved simultaneously as a line item and totals are recorded in the FI-GLX Extended General Ledger. As a consequence, CO-PCA Profit Center Accounting is functionally separate from the Cost-of-Sales Accounting used in CO-PA Profitability Analysis.

When you place an original account assignment object in the domain of a profit center, you are setting up separate data flows under control of the posting rules that are obeyed by the CO-PCA Profit Center Accounting system. Transaction data is transferred in real-time. When it comes into existence in the FI-Financial Accounting system, the CO-Controlling system sets up a copy in parallel, and the CO-PCA Profit Center Accounting system reflects this copy.

Primary cost information is reflected from

- Cost centers
- Orders
- Projects
- Product planning orders

Secondary costs may be reflected in profit centers as a result of

- Cost allocation
- Cost assessment
- Cost distribution
- Transfer postings
- Order settlement
- Accruals
- Surcharges

Revenues can appear in profit centers as the result of

- Direct account assignment from FI-Financial Accounting
- Billing documents via the interface with SD-Sales and Distribution

N O T E Values attributable to changes in inventory and work in process can also be reflected in profit centers.

Understanding the Structure of a Ledger-based Period Accounting Profitability Report

The line item of a Period Accounting profitability report represents an FI-GL General Ledger account number and its name. The line items can be selected and organized by hierarchies of profit centers.

There is continuous reconciliation at the company code level between the FI-Financial Accounting system and the CO-PCA Profit Center Accounting system. Thus, the inputs to each profit center can be any combination of the following sources of information:

- Customer orders and projects
- Cost objects
- Fixed assets
- Materials management
- Internal orders and projects
- Manufacturing orders
- Cost centers

Transaction data from any external system or SAP application may be integrated with the R/3 system.

The benefits of this integrated system include the following insights:

- The flow of the value of goods from one profit center to another is displayed, having eliminated internal transactions.
- The profitability report reveals the origins of all profit-relevant data.

Funding, Investment, and Development

Managing the Treasury

Using the Treasury Module

The scope of Treasury module functions broadly covers the management of finances so that funds can be made available to serve the business objectives of your company. Areas of interest include liquidity forecasting, market risk assessment, and portfolio planning and management. The relevant SAP R/3 functions can be accessed from the TR-Treasury module.

This chapter introduces you to the following topics:

- How liquidity is monitored
- How the treasury provides funds
- How market risks are managed

Active treasury management entails taking appropriate action as soon as the need for it can be predicted. To this end, the SAP R/3 Treasury software is capable of supporting a wide range of planning and evaluation procedures.

The purpose of the TR-Treasury module is to integrate cash management and cash forecasting both with the logistics activities in your company and with financial transactions. For example, TR enables you to apply cash-budgeting tools and commitment-accounting methods that take into consideration the allocation of responsibilities. These methods also take in the current budget positions and the sources of the relevant funds to accommodate very subtle monitoring and control.

The TR-Treasury module comprises the following components:

- TR-CM Cash Management
- TR-FM Funds Management
- TR-TM Treasury Management
- TR-MRM Market Risk Management

Applying Cash Management

The purpose of the TR-CM Cash Management module is to plan, control, and monitor the liquidity of the business and contribute to its profitability, if possible.

The key accounting distinction to be made lies between these two types of accounts:

- Cash accounts that record actual available liquid assets
- Clearing accounts that represent payments in transit

The operational concept involves taking three steps:

1. Planning all transactions that have payment advices
2. Controlling cash
3. Investing cash

N O T E A payment advice notice is a document that notifies a delivery, a payment, or the receipt of a commercial letter of credit in a connection with a foreign trade transaction. A payment notice is a document sent to a customer or an internal department to confirm a payment, to ask for clarification of any discrepancies, or to ask how the payments are to be allocated.

The Cash Management method uses SAP's fully automatic payment routines to accomplish the following two aims:

- Optimize short-term interest revenue
- Optimize money market transactions

The computer context is a closely integrated system comprising the standard functions used in SAP Cash Management, the payment program, and FI-AP Accounts Payable.

Using Cash Management Functions

The TR-CM component enables you to analyze financial transactions for a given period. Cash Management also identifies and records future developments for the purposes of financial budgeting. Payment transactions are grouped into cash holdings, cash inflows, and cash outflows. Cash Management provides information on the sources and uses of funds to secure liquidity to meet payment obligations when they become due.

Cash Management also monitors and controls incoming and outgoing payment flows. The module makes a distinction between current cash position and short-term cash management. The CM module provides the data required for managing short-term money market investments and borrowing by ensuring that all information relevant to liquidity is available to you for analysis purposes. For example, in bank account management, electronic banking and control functions provide support for managing and monitoring your bank accounts.

The liquidity forecast function additionally integrates anticipated payment flows from financial accounting, purchasing, and sales to create a liquidity outlook for medium- to long-term financial budgeting.

The cash position and liquidity forecast components generally are configured to cover both foreign currency holdings and expected foreign currency items. The functions also presented as the SAP Foreign Exchange Management component are included in TR-Treasury to enable the analysis of foreign exchange risk online with electronic banking features to enhance the integration with FI-GL General Ledger and FI-AR Accounts Receivable components.

N O T E As of Release 3.0, the SAP R/3 Treasury includes tools to analyze money markets, securities, and derivatives.

Monitoring Cash Management Procedures

The main steps needed to manage cash efficiently are as follows:

1. Store information in the form of payment advices until you receive the payments.
2. Prepare to clear open items using the information held as payment advices.

3. Process partial payments, either by open items or by account.

4. Receive bank statements by file transfer, if available.

5. Clear open items by referring to bank statements or payment advice notes.

6. Update expected cash receipts.

7. Use the payment advices to plan cash flow for a few days ahead.

Managing Cash Accounts and Clearing Accounts

Cash accounts record actual available liquidity; clearing accounts represent payments in transit. For each cash or clearing account, you can specify individually how it is to be managed. The SAP standard business functions ensure that all the items in these accounts are consistent with the balance sheet at all times.

You have five options for managing an account:

- Account to be managed on an open-item basis
- Account to be kept by value dates
- Account to be kept with various currencies in parallel
- Account to be posted automatically by the payment program
- Account to be cleared automatically by using an electronic banking function

The date in the financial year when the value of an asset is calculated can be determined by the user and can be specified in the legal requirements of the host country. For example, a specific account could be managed using the clearing date as the value date. Another business partner may be allowed to use the posting date as the value date. For some purposes, it may be convenient to use the end of the month as the value date.

Linking Cash Management and Financial Accounting

The SAP R/3 system operates on either program objects designed to carry out a business process or data objects that provide information when it is needed by the programmed business processes.

Cash management and short-term cash position forecasting depend on having transaction information made available to the various processes that will prepare data objects (such as a daily cash report) or plans to control the allocation of cash.

The TR-CM Cash Management module must be assigned transaction information from the following sources:

- FI-GL General Ledger
- FI-AR Accounts Receivable
- FI-AP Accounts Payable

If a schedule of funds is to be made available, TR-CM Cash Management must be notified so it may use this information in the forecasting. The Cash Management function should also know about recurring entries in any of the ledgers.

N O T E In addition to the integrated functions of Cash Management, this module enables you to enter expected cash outflows manually. For instance, if you do not have the payroll module of HR-Human Resources, you could anticipate payroll amounts using a manual recurring entry.

Many relationships between the parts of the SAP R/3 system will already be in place by virtue of the integrated design of the various modules. However, the precise details may have to be configured and customized to make the best use of them in an individual implementation. Naturally, this depends on which components are installed and which interfaces to outside systems are active.

Processing Payment Transactions

The payment program makes available a wide range of options for payment of individual accounts and groupings of sets of accounts. The following functions are possible under this program:

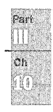

- Enter bank statements quickly
- Optionally clear open items automatically, subject to specified controls, such as the availability of cash
- Record payment advices and list them for display
- Delete payment advices
- Provide preliminary information about payment orders, checks received, bank statements, and discounted bills of exchange
- Prepare check deposit slips using default posting instructions
- Manage checks outstanding
- Control checks deposited
- Manage bills of exchange receivable and payable
- Calculate interest automatically

Throughout all these transactions, the integrity of the FI-GL General Ledger is maintained by the automatic functions of TR-CM Cash Management, FI-AR Accounts Receivable, and FI-AP Accounts Payable.

Banking with Electronic Facilities

The purpose of electronic banking is to reduce the time needed for entering data and to support the aim of timely cash management. The methods use data transfer by portable storage media such as tape or by direct communication line transfer of files. These files can contain general data or transaction data (in the form of bank statements) or transaction documents (in the SAP document format or in formats provided by other systems).

The effects of rapid file transfer include the following contributions to the goal of quicker, more secure, and more efficient processing and clearing of payments:

- Bank statements can be posted automatically.
- Bank statements can be transferred and clearing accounts can be processed automatically.

- Data can be transferred to FI-AR Accounts Receivable, and cash receipts can be processed automatically.

- Bank charges can be posted automatically.

- Exchange rate differences can be posted automatically, and foreign currency accounts can be managed more effectively.

Clearing Bank Accounts Automatically

The result of automatic bank account clearing is an improvement in your control of cash—you can process payment advices and clear bank statements on a daily basis. As a result, liquidity reserves and interest income are optimized.

You still retain the option of intervening in the automatic processes and making manual corrections. The TR-CM Cash Management position display, for example, can be arranged to separate specific accounts or groups of accounts. Furthermore, this module can split the display to differentiate checks, bank transfers, payment advices, and so on. Amounts and dates can be used to rank-order or divide into sets the items to be displayed.

Intercompany transactions and the separation into multiple levels of accounts also is facilitated. You have control over the processing of different payment methods and the minimum balance to be maintained in each bank account. The system can be primed to create all the necessary correspondence automatically.

The day-to-day management of short-term and long-term cash flows is integrated with the CO-Controlling module and its planning capabilities to ensure that fund reservations are not likely to compromise future liquidity.

Electronic banking functions are associated with payment advice note processing to enable you to make provisions for automatic adjustment of standard or custom interpretation algorithms for clearing payments.

 You can carry out a post-processing transaction to gain access to line items that could not be posted automatically.

Managing Liquidity

Reports from the system enable you to plan for liquidity because you can analyze payment dates and methods for both commitments and invoices.

Reports online enable you to compare targets, expenses, and receipts in accordance with the budget system. Down payments, invoice amounts, and final payments can be gathered into supplementary reports. An individual line item can be scrutinized, and the history of a commitment can be inspected in the form of the related transaction documents.

Analyzing Available Liquidity

Cash is money that is available, usually in currency or as a credit balance in a bank. Cash is available to make payments immediately, as compared to investments and fixed assets, which are not available to pay debts until they are converted to liquid assets.

Available liquidity represents the estimated ability of a customer or vendor to settle outstanding debts promptly. Computing this figure entails initiating two analytical tasks to gather credit and liquidity information about customers:

- Analyzing customer accounts, their credit limits, their dunning program, and payment history up to their current account balance
- Analyzing open items, both Receivables and Payables

Defining Credit Limit Control Areas

A credit control area is a set of one or more company codes and a currency for credit controlling that applies to all company codes in that area. This currency need not be the same as the currency of any of the company codes in the credit control area.

You can set a total amount as the credit limit for a group and a limit for each company in a credit control area. Several credit control areas may fall under one group.

Different customers can be assigned a shared credit limit account. Any order or invoice posted to any of these joint holders of a credit limit account causes the system to check whether the joint credit account limit has been exceeded. For example, different branches that are treated as separate customers may share a credit limit account held by the head office.

You can decide which types of transaction affect a credit limit account balance. Bills of exchange receivable, for example, are often posted to the credit limit account.

N O T E If your installation includes the SAP SD-Sales and Distribution application, an automatic check on the credit limit will take place when you enter an order.

Online customer credit control is essential if you record payments and offset paid items promptly. You can review the credit situation and the liquidity (available) of any customer at any time in terms of the following elements:

- Customer credit limit and current account balance
- Payments due
- Dunning program and dunning level in force
- Payment history

Viewing the Customer Payment History

Under your direction, the system can automatically record a payment history for any or all customers for each month (for up to three months) using the following factors:

- ☐ Number of payment transactions
- ☐ Payment amounts
- ☐ Average days in arrears for each of the three months

For the most recent period, the data is sorted by net payment and payment under each specific cash discount arrangement.

N O T E   If your business would be enhanced by having access to an extended payment history of some or all of your customers, you can set up a special-purpose ledger to have transactions posted to as many posting periods as you require for each fiscal year. You can also arrange to access the payment histories of previous years from archived records. ☐

Merely as a simulation or what-if exercise, you can ask to see how the payment history would change if this customer paid immediately all the items open on a particular date that you specify. By this means, you can simulate the payment history report, including the current open and overdue items.

The system also contributes to the payment history of a customer by recording totals of authorized and unauthorized deductions. The average discount rate is calculated, as is the interest amount based on the items paid after the due dates, including items still unpaid on the date you choose for making the calculation. A fictitious or nominal interest rate is used for these calculations, and you can set this rate to obtain a fair picture of how much interest has been lost to your company because of the late payments of this customer.

You can total the amounts outstanding on open items and also on items paid in arrears. These are sorted by number of days in arrears of the due dates for net payment or days in excess of the time limits for payments to attract a cash discount.

Tracking Items

The financial control system relies on tracking uncleared items. You can identify one or more customers or vendors and then sort their open items in whatever way is most informative for you.

Similarly, you can determine the column configuration of the report and identify the periods that interested you the most. You can instruct the system to choose open items that fall due within any range of dates. When you have found an individual account that needs your attention, you can display all the open items for that account and use the flexible line item search facilities to focus on just those lines that you require.

Controlling the Treasury

The treasurer can take action in the form of financial instruments put into effect through TR-TM Treasury Management module. To do this with wisdom requires that you first consider the results of your current liquidity, currency, and risk positions. Next you must consider the conditions prevailing in the money and capital markets. Then you can review what actions to take before implementing concrete decisions in the form of financial instruments in Treasury Management.

This module includes functions for managing financial deals and positions. It supports you in trading and transferring data to Financial Accounting. Treasury Management also provides flexible reporting and evaluation structures for analyzing financial deals, positions, and portfolios.

For short-term liquidity and risk management, you can use money market or foreign exchange transactions to even out liquidity shortages and surpluses, as well as to minimize your exposure to currency fluctuations.

In medium- and long-term financial management, your system supports you in dealing with securities and loans. Specialized functions exist for trading and settlement: There are control functions for foreign exchange and money market products, securities, loans, and derivative instruments. Derivative financial instruments facilitate active Treasury management of interest rates and currency risks.

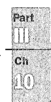

The trading area contains functions for recording financial deals, exercising rights, performing evaluations, and calculating prices (for example, the option price calculator). In back-office processing, you enter the additional data required for processing deals (such as account assignment and payment details) and generate automatic confirmations. Position management functions, such as securities account transfers or corporate actions relating to securities, are also supported in the back-office area. The general ledger is updated in the accounting area, which also offers flexible payment processing functions in addition to valuation and accrual/deferral methods.

N O T E By using common organizational elements throughout, various organizational structures, such as a central enterprise-wide treasury department or "in-house banks," can be represented in the system. This also ensures full integration of Treasury into other SAP R/3 components.

The Treasury Management component is designed to support business transactions from the trading stage to the back-office processing and then to their eventual posting in the Financial Accounting system.

The scope of TR-TM includes managing the following types of activity and financial instruments:

- Short-term cash management
- Long-term cash management
- Long-term financial budgeting
- Money market dealings
- Foreign exchange dealings, including spot dealing, forward exchange, and swap dealing
- Derivative financial instruments, including hedging transactions, swaps, caps, floors, options, and futures

- Securities management, including buying and selling, maintaining deposits and portfolios, acquiring and exercising conversion, and determining subscription and option rights
- Loan management, including fixed-term and at-notice deposits and loans, both loans granted and loans obtained
- Collateral security management, including encumbrances on real estate and guarantees

Using Treasury Reporting

The displays and functions provided by the TR-TM component include the following:

- Up-to-the-minute liquidity, currency, and risk-position data for your company and its assets
- Portfolio updates and valuations
- Option prices
- Cross rates
- Transaction data monitoring
- What-if scenario simulations in association with IS-IS, the SAP Industry Solution for insurance companies

Risk-management functions include monitoring of changes in market prices, interest rates, and exchange rates.

Sharing Functions and Tools

The central functions and tools that can be accessed from all TR-TM components include the following:

- Partner and address administration
- Investment mathematics
- Flexible instrument generator
- Status-controlled transaction processing
- Correspondence processing
- Limit monitoring
- Real-time reporting

Taking Advantage of the Data Feed Interface

The online Treasury Data Feed component of TR-TM is an Application Programming Interface (API) optimized for specific information providers. An API provides a service to your treasury for importing data on the following essential information:

- Interest rates
- Exchange rates

- Securities prices
- Stock indices

The Data Feed interface takes advantage of SAP R/3 standard data structures supported by functions that request data from the provider's interface. The formatted data is then returned to the SAP market data buffer to be used or stored for historical analysis.

You define the information you require as a request that references a standard data structure transmitted to the relevant provider for each individual instrument. You specify the instrument names that are converted to the names used by the instrument provider. Remote Function Call (RFC) initiates request through the SAP Gateway Interface.

The information provider identifies the required market data, obtains permission to quote it, and delivers it to the SAP R/3 TM module, after having priced this service and billed the recipient company.

N O T E A query log of data buffer accesses is maintained automatically by the TM component. □

Part
III

Ch
10

Managing Market Risks

One of the duties of your company's treasurer is to manage market risks as part of the task of ensuring the financial viability of your enterprise. The TR-MRM Market Risk Management module is designed to increase your company's competitiveness. The process entails continuous cycling through the following activities:

- Data collection
- Risk measurement
- Analysis of your company's exposure to the various types of risk
- Decision on the possible next actions
- Simulation of the effects of taking each of the reasonable next actions
- Active planning of financial instruments that might be needed
- Implementation of the next actions
- Continued data collection

Clearly these processes involve the other treasury and corporate financial planning functions.

The Market Risk Management module acts as an integrated central risk-control station with monitoring and management functions. MRM provides access to information on current and future cash flows, as well as on financial deals already processed.

The TR-CM Cash Management module provides the underlying support for MRM by collating all cash flows from your business sectors, such as Sales and Distribution or Purchasing. In addition, all financial transactions managed in Treasury Management can be evaluated together with the cash flows generated by the various operating divisions.

The MRM component provides various measurements for analyzing and assessing interest rate and currency risks. Market-to-market effective rate and effective yield calculations are based on up-to-the-minute market data. Such data is uploaded via SAP R/3 Data Feed, which is an open interface designed to link with standard information providers. Financial transaction and market position information can also be accessed by this route.

Managing and Forecasting Cash in the Medium Term

The purpose of a cash management and financial controlling system is to maintain liquidity to fulfill payment obligations. Short-term management consists of looking at the current liquidity position and forecasting what the situation might be in a few days, typically one working week. Medium-term cash management and forecasting has a horizon that extends to a year.

One product of medium-term financial planning is the annual cash plan. This plan must show how liquidity is to be secured over the period by exercising financial control. The annual plan can be set out at any level of detail and for any arrangement of the organizational structure that the data supports.

 TIP If you set up a simulation of market data and a flow of simulated transactions, you can explore what might happen in the worst-case scenarios. Then you can perhaps devise a strategy to hedge your market risks, or at least be aware of their magnitude.

Using an Annual Cash Flow Plan

With modern accounting systems, the financial planning period can be of any duration because the information to be reported will be assembled online when the design of the report is used to generate the presentation of the information. SAP FI-Financial Accounting supports planning in a comprehensive way:

- ☐ The fiscal year can be flexible and can comprise any number of periods.
- ☐ The multilevel dependencies between totals and subtotals, departments and subdepartments, and so on, are automatically taken into account when assessing and distributing planning data.
- ☐ Data transfers to and from other systems occur through clearly defined data interfaces, which can serve the aims of financial planning in addition to handling their other traffic.

The information sources of most interest to the financial planner are as follows:

- ☐ Accounts receivable and payable
- ☐ Planned cash expenditures and receipts
- ☐ Open orders from customers
- ☐ Purchase orders to vendors

The financial planning report must address the following issues for each period of the plan and for each of the groups within the company that are to be part of the plan:

- Overall liquidity
- Committed funds
- Types of risk

Controlling Finance

The control process comes into prominence when values set out in the financial plan are compared with the actual values achieved by the business. A quick reaction demands a short planning and accounting period so that actual and planned or budgeted amounts can be compared in time to make a correction. The SAP FI-Financial Controlling module can provide for cycles of monitoring and control that range upwards from one day. The TR-TM module can make use of these cycles.

Managing Funds Through a Budget

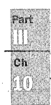

Two methods exist for managing funds for a project:

- Accept the results of project cost planning and allow extra costs to be incurred as unforeseen contingencies arise
- View the results of project cost planning and then decide on a binding budget for the project

See Chapter 8, "Controlling by the PS-Project System," for details on using the SAP R/3 project as a receiver for a budget.

Managing Decentralized Funds

Public accounting is a form of financial controlling that focuses on a budget made available to cover expenses over the fiscal year or a shorter accounting period. Recent changes to the methods of financial controlling have made the concept of public accounting equivalent to funds accounting.

The SAP R/3 FI-Financial Accounting system provides comprehensive support for two tasks:

- Preparing a budget
- Monitoring the budget by tracking the achievement of targets in each of the budget's divisions

These facilities are available to the Treasury modules and are used by TR-FM in particular.

Preparing a budget entails estimating or assigning target values for the following cash flows:

- Cash requirements for operations
- Cash requirements for capital investment projects
- Planned cash receipts

You can assign responsibility for providing, managing, and accounting for funds for each of these items separately before combining them into a total budget. Under this total, you can then prepare individual plans that set up a division between administrative and capital budgets.

TIP You can store a budget with a version number and repeat the process using some or all the parameters as a model to create a new version.

N O T E If the proposed applications of funds exceed the funds available, you can identify the funding required to balance the budget. ▢

Targeting Costs and Revenues

When a budget is translated into planned target amounts for each account subtotal that makes up the structure of the budget, each target represents the best estimate of the costs or revenues that will or should be realized.

As the period passes, fresh targets can well arise as a result of operating costs, investments, and cash receipts that were not anticipated exactly in the plan. Targets may have to be altered if the budget is not to be exceeded or underspent. The data for these adjustments may arise from any of the following causes:

- Funds released and allocated to operating areas added to the original budget
- Amendments to the budget, either in total or in allocation to subdivisions
- Internal transfers
- Commitment authorizations that can be anticipated to exceed the budget
- Unexpended balances
- Anticipated expenditures

Checking Available Funds and Paying from Funds

The funds committed are revealed by the purchase orders. The system checks that these purchase orders do not exceed the funds available.

The cash available is checked, and the vendor invoices may have to be reviewed by persons responsible for the budget.

When you post an invoice, the system updates the actual data. The system prints cash payment orders to be signed and passed to the controller.

N O T E The system can be set up to maintain a cash journal that records all cash transactions by date. ▢

Controlling Public Funds

Public accounting and the controlling of funds in the public sector tend to emphasize monitoring receipts and expenditures, that is, the sources of these funds and their applications. The efficient monitoring of payments is an important duty of public sector accounting.

The overriding principle involves ensuring that the actual expenses and payments are no greater than the budget. In some circumstances, the aim could be to have the expenses equal the budget because any underspend may not be allowed to be carried over into the next accounting period.

In contrast, organizations that seek a return on investment in financial terms might focus on budgeting for expenses. An underspend of the expense budget may be welcome. In these commercial circumstances, the cash flow statement is prepared to safeguard liquidity, to monitor financing, and to analyze investments.

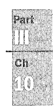

The budget uses a plan to allocate funds to each function and organization unit over a period or succession of periods. The source of funds is an organizational unit, such as Area, Division, Department, or Individual. Each source can manage the application of part of the budget to activities that are intended to add value to the information or work items passing through the company. The funds can be applied to the following areas:

- Investments, such as stocks of materials, energy, or partially completed work
- Output-related expenses, such as raw materials, supplies, or maintenance
- Serviceability costs, such as depreciation, repairs, or capital investments that affect the value of the plant

The progress of the funds through the budget period is monitored by using the ongoing business transactions. Separate records are made of the details of receipts and expenditure, using the budget structure to allocate them to fund sources (fund-holders) so that reports can show how the funds were used in relation to the budgeted targets.

NOTE   Because the structure of the budget need not coincide with the commercial or production structure of the company, the funds controlling system is capable of providing a sophisticated monitoring and control mechanism that can be aligned to whatever decision-making activities best serve the company.

Using the Funds Management Module

SAP R/3 Funds Management (TR-FM) is a Treasury component that specializes in the funds management processes. This module makes a working distinction between cash position, short-term cash management, and medium- and long-term financial budgeting. These differences represent the different time scales appropriate for your particular company. You may need to know your cash position on a continuous basis, for instance, whereas your short-term cash flow expectations can perhaps take account of anticipated receipts.

The TR-FM module provides support functions throughout the funds management cycle, from budgeting to payments. You have functions to monitor expenditures, activities, resources, and revenues.

Budgeting in TR-FM begins with an original budget that is subject to status control as it moves to approval and release. The module manages budget supplements, returns, and transfers.

Budgets are entered for areas of funds management responsibility, which can cover as many management levels as you require. You can define an area for local budgeting on the basis of any characteristics that your implementation recognizes. Funds centers and their hierarchical structure provide a base for top-down budgeting and represent responsibility areas within budget control.

As each anticipated expenditure arises, you can consult the commitment management system to determine how much of your budget has already been utilized and what funds will become available. The information system can report when and where the existing commitments of your funds were posted and tell the purpose to which they were assigned.

TIP You can identify any budget bottlenecks by calling for analyses by responsibility area and commitment items.

The TR-FM Funds Management component maintains master records that represent those budget objects that are commitment items. In this case, a budget is released in a series of stages that constitute portions of the funds that become available for commitment to expenses. Commitment items are used to split budgets by functional aspect, such as administration, production, and transportation. You can set up account assignment items to get the level of detail you need to record commitments of funds for specific purposes and to ensure that they are allocated accordingly.

The transfer of budget commitment items takes place between commitment funds centers and receiver centers for the committed funds. Again, the TR-FM module maintains master records to identify commitment funds centers that can take part in this transfer of budgeted funds.

 N O T E   Summary items are used in budgeting to emphasize the levels at which budget allocation and control take place. ▨

The structured budget data objects can be maintained and assigned to the budget commitment funds centers to provide a flexible system that can display clearly the way in which budgets are allocated to the hierarchy. The allocation of budgets can be carried out from the bottom up so that subordinate items can be committed, even if the higher-level budgets have not been allocated.

Different versions of budgets can be maintained separately, and different sources of funds can be designated for each financial management area. The utilization of these areas can be traced through the reporting system.

Budgeting in TR-FM Before a budget is approved, it is classified as a preliminary budget or merely a cost plan. At this stage the bottom-up summation of costs probably occurs. The preliminary budget is then submitted for approval, and the allocation of the approved budget can take place as top-down distribution to the budget cost objects.

You company may differentiate between funds that have been budgeted and funds that have been released. You may not be able to commit all your current approved budget in the early stages of a project or accounting period.

Using Availability Control Two styles of availability control exist:

- Passive availability control merely gives an overview of the commitment of funds, regardless of whether the budget for the period has been exceeded.
- Active availability control checks to ensure that no excessive funds commitment occurs.

The following variants of availability control fall under the specification of the user:

- Checks against the current budget or released funds
- Checks against the overall budget or annual budget for the current year
- Types of business transactions to be monitored, such as purchase orders or postings in cost accounting
- The decision of whether the availability control is conducted on the basis of absolute variances between commitment and budget or on the basis of percentage use
- The action to take place in the event that availability tolerance limits are exceeded

The availability control function has the following possible actions:

- Warning
- Warning plus message to the project manager
- Error message and a rejection of the posting that would otherwise exceed the availability control limit

Using Budget Updates Even though availability control of the active variety might be in place, a situation may arise that requires a change to the approved budget. Price increases and additional requirements from the customer or project sponsor are common contingencies, although other events may delay a work program and threaten the budget. Rolling budget planning is standard practice in some industries.

A supplement is a quantity of extra funds that can be distributed in the top-down mode to increase the current budget. Returns are excess funds that are not needed and are processed from the bottom up in the budget hierarchy. A transfer is a movement of funds within a responsibility area from one work breakdown structure or budget cost object to another.

N O T E A transfer can take place across projects, provided they all fall under the same responsibility area.

Budget updates can be made subject to status management and can be controlled through the standard system of authorization objects to limit the persons authorized to approve budget changes.

Using Funds for Specific Purposes   A cost can be classified on the basis of the purpose of the expenditure, and a budget can be split to create a separate fund for each purpose. Availability control can then be applied to constrain expenditure according to the proportions set up in the approved budget structure.

A budget can also differentiate between the sources of the funds and can maintain the origin of funds as an entry on the transaction documents.

Using Budget Planning and Monitoring   Freely definable planning horizons are a feature of the TR-FM module. The budget accounting periods do not have to coincide with the financial accounting calendar. You can even distribute budgets over several fiscal years. The monitoring of funds commitments assigned to the distributed funds can be managed on an overall global basis or by fiscal year.

Accounting transactions recorded in TR-FM keep track of down payments, invoices, bank clearing transactions, and any transactions affecting the funds, right through to final payment clearing and settlement.

Purchase orders and release orders in Materials Management automatically update funds commitments if they are identified with a budget. The module maintains a commitment management facility that can keep track of the various funds commitments. The TR-FM can show how much budget you have assigned to each CO cost assignment object, such as a cost center, an order, or a project. For example, a measurement of how much of a budget has been used can be generated by a standard budget/actual comparison report. You can also look at the differences between one plan and another, and between the commitment of funds and the actual expenditures.

You also can generate information on current assets because all purchase orders for stock items (as well as the resulting invoices and goods receipts) are recorded in TR-FM.

Using Funds Utilization History   The evidence of how, where, by whom your budget was committed is automatically assembled as the funds utilization history. With this history, you can display the analysis for each responsibility area and each commitment item. By looking at the various summarization levels in your budget structure, you can see where funds bottlenecks and shortages are likely to occur.

Introducing the SAP R/3 Industry Solution for the Public Sector

The IS-PS is a configuration of SAP R/3 in the Industry Solutions series that is optimized for use in organizations that operate wholly or mainly in the public sector. In this situation, the commercial priorities rank second behind the need to manage public funds in a responsible and accountable manner not easily monitored in terms of financial profit.

IS-PS includes an enhancement of the TR-FM module that uses the SAP R/3 business workflow system to control "budget parking." This module allocates funds across a formal system of authorization levels and authorization objects that represent the work positions in public sector organizations responsible for segments of the budget.

Using Integration with the SAP Industry Solution for Insurance

The treasury management application is integrated with the Industry Solution for Insurance and Real Estate management, IS-IS. Through this system (IS-IS), the Treasury can support the following functional areas:

- Extended management of loans
- Extended treasury management
- Real estate management
- Management of premium reserve funds and statutory reporting for insurance companies

Using Integration with the SAP Industry Solution for Banks

The TR-TM application is also integrated with the Industry Solution for Banks, IS-B, through which it can support the following functional areas:

- Back-office data pooling
- Single transaction costing
- Bank profitability analysis
- Risk management
- Statutory reporting

Using Integration with SAP R/3 Investment Management

The IM-Investment Management module includes the following components: .

- IM-FA Tangible Fixed Assets
- IM-FI Financial Investments

The TR and IM modules overlap because the functions of IM-FI Financial Investments are the same as those of TR-TM Treasury Management. The IM functions are discussed in Chapter 11, "Managing Investments." ●

Managing Investments

Controlling Investments

The standard activities of an investment department are based around the need to purchase new assets and operating equipment. The daily decision matrix includes perhaps hundreds of decisions of the following types:

- Repair this faulty asset, or replace it?
- Buy this improved equipment, or stay with the existing plant that works well although it's not the latest design?
- Snap up this resource now because it is available at bargain prices, or wait until there is a clearly defined need for it?
- How long will this plant last at the present rate of usage?
- Invest in more repair facilities to alleviate the problems with the existing equipment, or invest in new and possibly unknown equipment in the hope that it will prove more effective?

Some common-sense measures can be used to reduce the uncertainty characteristic of investment decision making. You must be prepared to search for information from such sources as the following:

- Competitors who have faced similar decisions
- Scientific disciplines with research evidence that could illuminate at least parts of your investment decisions
- In-company technical resources that may be aware of information relevant to your proposed investment
- Lessons learned from errors and equipment failures in similar activities
- Commercial knowledge gained by analyzing business activities and results in similar situations

Although the big decision might seem to be the one that initiates an investment, it may be much more difficult to abandon a project or relinquish an investment that turns out to be a failure. Worse still, it may be very difficult to cut off a project in its prime, when all is going well, just because it looks like it might fail some time in the future. But nothing in the investment manager's job specification says the work will be easy or enjoyable. Good data processing can help avoid the kind of mistakes made because the right information is not extracted and highlighted at the moment when it could be used to improve the decision-making process.

With complex and expensive investments, you have no chance to sit back and let the investment earn profit. Investment control applies throughout the life of the asset, both its useful life and its economical disposal.

The depreciation of an asset is a function of both usage and other factors that affect its value. For example, an asset could become obsolete. Chapter 4, "Accounting for Assets," concentrates on the ways in which the value of an asset can change through its lifecycle. One of the important lessons to be learned from managing buildings, for example, is that the cost of repairs and maintenance may soon add up to more than the cost of acquisition. Similarly, an inexpensive item of production machinery could cost more to run than a more expensive one.

The moral from this kind of experience is to establish a plan for the expected life of each investment and then modify this plan according to the costs of owning and operating the object. Include both preventive maintenance and the likely cost of repairs and replacements.

 You could set up a key figure report element to let you see just how much was spent on maintenance for each asset and what percentage of procurement costs this figure represents.

Managing Investments in a Corporate Group

A multinational company comprises several individual company codes, independent organizational units that render their own financial documents in the form of a balance sheet and a profit and loss statement. These company codes tend to operate in different currencies for which the SAP R/3 system can maintain parallel accounting data. Chapter 5, "Consolidating Company Accounts," discusses the procedures for legally consolidating these separate accounting structures.

Investments in a multinational corporation are represented by many records held on local computer systems. The SAP R/3 system can integrate these distributed systems by the Application Link Enabling (ALE) technology. This enables you to post and report object data structures. In particular, the capital investment programs of the affiliated companies can be reported to a central client database in R/3, even if some sending companies use other systems. External software and standard systems such as Microsoft Access can be used as sources by accessing them through the Remote Function Call (RFC) technique.

The ALE technique is applied to filter the investment documents of the distributed companies according to the requirements of the head office. For example, options exist to have investment reports at the summary level and at the level of individual investment measures and projects.

The following are the standard reporting levels applicable to capital investment management:

- Company code
- Business area
- Profit center
- Plant
- Balance sheet item
- Capital-investment program per approval year
- Capital-investment program position

The reporting dimensions for Capital Investment programs and related Capital Investment measures include the following options:

- Total and annual planned values
- Total and annual approved budget values
- Actual values
- Open item values

N O T E   The data collated at the remote systems is summarized by period as directed before it is consolidated at the head office.

Relating the SAP R/3 Investment Modules

The Treasury is the part of your organization concerned with medium- and long-term financial planning, together with the medium-term management and control of revenues and expenditures. The focus remains on the company's future financial state.

These objectives can be met to some degree by using the FI-Financial Accounting application. The modules of FI-Financial Accounting that are specifically concerned with investments are as follows:

- FI-IM Investment Management
- FI-AM Assets Management

The functions used by FI-IM are also available to the FI-AA Asset Accounting module although the continuity does not extend beyond year-end closing unless the IM application is installed and configured. The IM application supports the following investment management processes:

- Capital-spending requests
- Capital-investment measures
- Capital-investment programs
- Simulation and depreciation forecasting

Using the Investment Management Functions

The investment modules can be installed in SAP R/3 as a stand-alone system. This is referenced as the IM-Investment Management application.

Using IM-FI Financial Investments   IM-FI Financial Investments carries out the functions of TR-TM Treasury Management when the IM application is configured for investment management as a specialization.

Using IM-FA Tangible Fixed Assets   The purpose of the IM-FA Tangible Fixed Assets component is to perform analysis of capital investments and support their management. The principal functions of the component are as follows:

- Pre-investment analysis
- Capital-investment master data, planning, budgeting, and allocation

- Measurement of Capital Investment performance and integration with the CO-Controlling module CO-OPA Order and Project Accounting component
- Valuation and settlement
- Depreciation simulation
- Asset control
- Information system and connection to the EIS-Executive Information System

This component shares functionality with the FI-AM Asset Management component. The TR-Treasury module provides some enhanced functions.

Separating the Treasury Functions

As of R/3 Release 3.0, the long-term financial management functions are available in two separate but overlapping modules that can be installed independently of each other:

- TR-Treasury
- IM-Investment Management

Individual components from these modules can be installed and configured to integrate with the FI-Financial Accounting module. These components are also available in the form of integrated R/3 enhancements designed for specific sectors of business and industry and presented with an IS prefix to designate an Industry Solution.

Organizing Investment Data

The essence of complex system management involves dividing business activities into tasks and dividing data into units that can be readily retrieved and applied to the tasks as necessary. Two target readership groups exist for financial documents:

- Shareholders and legal authorities that demand the external accounts in the prescribed formats
- Internal management that must be able to freely select data to discern opportunities for improving the company

Investment control must operate with a flexible data structure that can be called upon to satisfy both types of scrutiny.

Defining an Investment Program

The highest level of investment information held in a master record is the Capital Investment program structure. An investment program is defined in SAP R/3 by a master record that specifies a hierarchical structure for all the planned and budgeted investment costs of a company for a specific period.

How you define this hierarchy is up to you. You can use the existing organizational units and also separate the reasons for the investments or the balance sheet items. If you need to, you can define investment program types that specify the objects to which investment funds can be assigned.

Understanding Capital Investment Types

An element of a Capital Investment program can be classified according to the purpose it serves by assigning it to one of a set of types that you establish. The types indicate reasons for making capital investments, of which the following are typical examples:

- Asset expansion to include new products
- Modernization
- Asset-replacement measures
- Environmental protection

Understanding Capital Investment Program Positions

A Capital Investment program position is a data object that represents a reference point within a Capital Investment program. This position refers to an organizational unit that is responsible for a well-defined stage of the project. The program position can have additional user-definable classifying characteristics, such as investment type. The object carries planned and budget values for the investment in one of the following reporting structures:

- Controlling area
- Company code
- Business area
- Profit center
- Plant

A Capital Investment program position can also be defined by additional characteristics, such as the investment type or reason. For example, a capital investment program position can be defined as an asset-replacement investment type targeted at a specific plant that belongs to a particular company code. The transaction data associated with this position is classified and posted accordingly.

A Capital Investment program is defined within a single controlling area, but there may be more than one Capital Investment program position element at any level. For example, a refurbishment project could involve several plant locations. In each plant, you can designate a technical site or other type of investment position to serve as the focal point for allocating budgets and recording costs and progress.

Each active Capital Investment program position element is represented as a Capital Investment project or an element in a project. This requires a budget, a responsible company code, and also perhaps a controlling area that can summarize the programs across more than one company code.

Any particular capital-investment order is assigned to a specific plant, a profit center, and perhaps a business area. The accounting of this capital-investment order sees to it that the costs are assigned to specific cost centers if you have installed and configured the PCA Profit Center Accounting module.

Understanding Capital Investment Measures

A Capital Investment measure is a project or an internal order that is used to carry out an asset investment. This measure is classified as a capital investment because it cannot be posted to fixed assets as direct capitalization. The usual reasons are that the project budget is very large and that it includes a considerable internal activity component.

Two types of data are stored in master records of a Capital Investment measure such as a project or an internal order. One set of data comprises the controlling information, the other is the actual data of an asset under construction. This data is used to identify the following components:

- The investment components that must be capitalized on the balance sheet
- Special depreciations that must be reported
- Capital-investment support measures needed during the construction phase

 N O T E   The Capital Investment measure can be accessed from both the financial accounting system and from the controlling system.

Analyzing Investment Proposals

A requirement for a capital-intensive investment project may be submitted for your consideration. How can you decide whether it will be wise to go ahead?

You need to know the profitability of the project at each accounting period throughout its expected life and at its final disposal. You could apply static business mathematics to compute the values invested minus the depreciation and then arrive at a trajectory of costs and revenue that provides the data for a graph of profitability over a life cycle.

Dynamic mathematics would provide a similar projection if you could define some assumptions about the interest rates and market values over a project's lifetime. For example, you could allow for predicted fluctuations by defining an internal interest rate. Alternatively, or in addition, you could compute the predicted capitalized value of your investment at each period in its lifecycle.

If you have been able to carry out similar pre-investment analyses for each capital investment program that you evaluate, then you might be able to come to a rational decision about which to choose. Your system may be able to provide actual data from previous investment projects that you can refer to as the basis for a numerical model for your proposed project. Your assumptions about future interest rates and market values can then be used to refine and update the model. As an additional facility, you could develop several versions of a pre-investment plan and associated analysis, with each variant utilizing different parameters to represent optimistic and pessimistic views of your markets and the effectiveness of your resources.

The pre-investment analysis process can be set up using data processing to enable the decision maker to choose between fully elaborated and costed plans that genuinely represent viable business alternatives. Any proposal that cannot be shown to be profitable at the planning stage, even if the assumptions are favorable, will not be considered as an option in the decision.

N O T E   In practice, determining viable projects may well turn out to be a matter of how investment resources are to be distributed among the competing claimants. Everyone can compile a wish list, but not all wishes will come true.

In accord with the common-sense procedure of subdividing complex projects into a structure of components, the SAP R/3 investment functions work with three types of values that are distributed across as many necessary units to map your investment programs to your company cost centers. Planned values, budgeted values, and distributed values are stored for the company or controlling area. Each of these three values is computed by adding the corresponding values from each of the business areas. These business areas are defined on any convenient basis and represent the budget-holding authority at a particular level under the control of a business area manager. Each business area can be further subdivided and allocated a budget in a similar fashion.

If you already have organizational units that are convenient for capital-investment budgets, you can direct the system to use them to form a suitable distribution structure automatically. You can then edit this structure manually if it does not correspond to the most convenient arrangement.

Using Cost-Planning Capital Investment Programs

The costing of an investment program, and hence the cost planning, takes place from the bottom up. You can assign the actual Capital Investment measures planned for each year to the company codes responsible for them.

The intended activities associated with a Capital Investment program must be included in the process of budgeting across the company. The controlling instruments that can be used automatically with capital investment programs are as follows:

- A project managed by the SAP R/3 project system
- An SAP internal order
- An SAP maintenance order

For each pre-investment analysis you conduct, you can specify one of these instruments. The system posts the planned and actual values that represent internal activities, external activities, down payments, and overhead to that particular instrument.

If you cannot clearly assign a certain Capital Investment measure to one company code in the investment program, you can arrange a percentage distribution of a Capital Investment measure among several program positions. If necessary, you can enter and maintain the planned values directly in the investment program structure, at any level of the hierarchy. The system checks that your manual alterations to the plan do not cause an excess in the value of the next level in the hierarchy.

Using Early Depreciation Forecast and Cost Planning

A depreciation forecast is a set of values distributed across a series of time periods. These amounts represent the best estimates of how the value of the company's assets will move as a result of depreciation. You can define a depreciation area that takes a different point of view than the actual depreciation calculated by one of the standard methods. For example, you could define a depreciation area that calculates the depreciation of fixed assets for a tax-based balance sheet. Another area may be designed to support your cost-accounting analyses by expressing the depreciation of the fixed assets in a slightly different manner.

You can include the cost plans of a Capital Investment program in your depreciation forecast. Each program position value that has been planned but not yet distributed to lower levels of the investment hierarchy can be treated as an object to be processed by a specific depreciation procedure. By this means, you can compare different depreciation calculations and capitalization programs to obtain a long-term overview of the progression of your fixed assets and the possible effects of taxes on your investments.

The R/3 line-item settlement facility enables you to use the balance sheet to trace the costing differences that arise as a result of special investment postings. Similarly, you can discern the variance between book depreciation and tax-based depreciation. Each line of every asset in your balance sheet that pertains to a Capital Investment measure bears a reference to the origin.

Your depreciation forecast can be regarded as a simulation of depreciation effects over a series of reporting periods. The values calculated can be transferred to your system of cost center planning.

Budgeting in the Capital Investment Program

A budget is distributed to the Capital Investment program positions. An individual Capital Investment measure can derive the budget directly from one of these positions. You can control just how strictly the system manages the availability of the budget funds. For instance, you can prevent any individual capital-investment budget for a measure associated with a Capital Investment program position from being assigned a value that would cause the position to exceed its allocation. On the other hand, if you do not wish to exercise strict availability control, you can monitor the situation by using current period reports.

The annual expenditure budget represents the funds that must be made available for particular investments in a given year. The IM can derive this pattern of expenditure in either of two ways:

- Aggregate the values budgeted for all the Capital Investment measures in a given year
- Use the values specified directly in the Capital Investment program

Each Capital Investment measure has an individual approved budget that is the total budget for this measure, regardless of how many years the measure may take.

The recommended procedure is to maintain approved budgets for Capital Investment programs to represent the upper limit of funds, and then to maintain in addition a continuous monitoring of the pattern of commitments made for the program's future years. The IM module provides for displays of these values in formats under control of the user.

Further subdivision of budgets is usually advised so you can distinguish budget components that must be capitalized from those that you can account for in pure cost items. You also might want to be able to display budgets divided in terms of internal and external activities.

Displaying the Budget Approval History

Each Capital Investment program position can be displayed as the original approved budget together with the following types of changes:

- Supplementary budget entries that enable extra funds to be applied in a top-down procedure from higher-level program positions to lower-level ones and to the individual Capital Investment measures, if needed
- Returns of surplus funds that are entered at the lowest level from where they are passed to a higher-level program position

Using the Research Reporting Tool

To evaluate a Capital Investment program, the Capital Investment Program Information System can be customized by using the standard reporting tool Research. For example, the following selection of standard reports can be customized:

- Capital-investment program structures, plan values, budget values, and availability
- Investment projects
- Investment order master data, order lists, and order selection
- Investment order summarization
- Depreciation simulation

Linking with the Executive Information System

The Capital Investment Program Information System is integrated with the EIS Executive Information System, from which reports can be compiled automatically using the established key figures and sorted by the existing organizational units, such as company codes, business areas, profit centers, plants, and so on. If your EIS has access to information from other affiliated companies, you may find it helpful to set up a report to make use of it.

Multinational corporations are served by the standard SAP R/3 system of maintaining currencies in parallel. The values of a Capital Investment program can be converted to the currency of the company code at the time of reporting, as well as to a currency defined as the standard for corporate Capital Investment program reporting.

N O T E The EIS is capable of interfacing with non-SAP systems carrying Capital Investment program information needed for corporate reporting.

Capitalizing Assets Directly

A large Capital Investment measure generally is budgeted. However, some assets are capitalized directly by applying the flat-rate investment procedure. For example, a general resource such as local computers and vehicle fleets is likely to be capitalized directly and then subjected to standard depreciation procedures.

If you allocate a budget for assets that will be directly capitalized, you can plan and monitor how these asset acquisitions contribute to your Capital Investment program. If you do not allocate a budget for directly capitalized assets, you risk the danger that your company will allocate resources that are not attributed to capital investment and recognized as such.

Using the Flat-Rate Investment Procedure

The flat-rate investment procedure can be used as an alternative to the Capital Investment program technique. This procedure can also be applied to individual elements in a program.

To fund assets that are to be capitalized directly, you can use the standard cost object Asset Under Construction, the SAP Internal Order, or an SAP Project. However, these instruments are not entirely satisfactory for this type of purchase because they require an intermediate step of debiting the order or project and subsequently settling it. The alternative involves recording asset acquisitions by using the SAP R/3 IM Flat-Rate Budget object as a special program item in a Capital Investment program. All the orders or projects that represent budgets for individual assets can be linked to a special program item that represents the flat-rate budget object for purchased assets.

Referencing a Capitalization Structure

A capitalization structure enables you to specify those cost component percentages of a Capital Investment measure that do not need to be capitalized for each cost element or cost element group. You also can specify these percentages for each activity type or group of activity types. If necessary, you can define different versions in the capitalization structure for the various depreciation areas of fixed assets. The capitalization structure is defined for each controlling area and is identified using a capitalization key that can be maintained in the master data of capitalization-investment measures.

Linking Budgets and Fixed-Asset Masters

In the FI-AA Asset Accounting module, master records represent the fixed assets and store all the transactions associated with them. The fixed-asset master includes a data object that records the investment account assignment to be used for any associated order or project. If you have many assets to be assigned in this way to investment accounts, you can define general replacement rules to enable your system to automatically assign assets to the appropriate investment account. For example, you could specify a logical condition to automatically assign to a designated account any asset that satisfies all the following conditions:

- Assets of a particular class, such as Vehicles
- Assets acquired in a specific business area, such as Retail Distribution in the Southwest Region
- Assets procured for an identified distribution center, such as Plant 53

Updating Open Items

An open item is a contractual or scheduled commitment that is not yet reflected in financial accounting but will lead to actual expenditures in the future. A fixed asset may be conveniently handled using open-item management. All business transactions connected with procurement of the asset are directly linked to the asset master. Purchase orders, for instance, are assigned directly to the asset number for which they are intended. The goods receipt and invoice are similarly assigned to the asset master.

When a purchase order for an asset is entered into the purchasing system, its value is used to debit the project or order to which the asset is assigned with a liability of the same amount. The liability is converted to an actual value when the goods are received or the invoice posted. If you do not want the order or project to be posted with the actual cost elements, you can specify it as a receiver for statistical values only rather than actual amounts.

Individual assets can be acquired without going through the purchasing system. They can be routed through the FI-AP accounts payable module to be posted directly to an existing asset portfolio. The additional value is then posted statistically to the order or project.

 TIP You can control the availability of additional assets by allowing them to be released to an order or project only if the corresponding budget is still available and has not been depleted for any reason.

Using the Capital Investment Information System with Flat-Rate Budgets

When the capital investment is being conducted using flat-rate budgets, the asset acquisitions are represented by investment program items and orders or projects. You can display the actual values of your asset portfolio and call for breakdowns by asset. You can readily switch between program items and their component orders and individual asset items. You can have a combined display of the total planned investment, the budgets for selected areas, and the investments that have already been implemented and contain generated fixed assets.

Creating Assets Internally by Capital Investment Measures

A Capital Investment measure is an SAP internal order or an SAP project. This measure is used to control an asset under construction within a company using the same functions used when an asset under construction is procured primarily from external sources. As a result, a Capital Investment measure is subject to external accounting rules.

Two classes of Capital Investment measures exist, as follows:

- Capital-investment order
- Capital-investment project

A project comprises a PSP project structure plan and therefore includes PSP elements, some of which can be orders.

Both classes of a Capital Investment measure have the task of managing the operational implementation of the investment plan. This includes the following activities:

- Recording primary and secondary costs
- Calculating overhead rates and interest
- Managing down payments
- Managing open purchase orders

By these means, the capital-investment order or project can provide a single data object that has collected all the costs for a Capital Investment measure. This includes both those already charged to fixed assets and those that are held in the controlling system and therefore constitute the elements of the Capital Investment program yet to be implemented.

Several reasons point to using a capital-investment order or project rather than a series of standard orders or projects. The following are probably the most significant advantages:

- Program items that have been so designated are automatically capitalized to the balance sheet account item Assets Under Construction.
- Convenient arrangements can be made to settle the Capital Investment measure at month-end closing and period closing.
- The cost of goods manufactured and the costs of acquired assets can be valued in parallel by each of the depreciation procedures.

The depreciation procedures are identified in asset accounting as depreciation areas because they are conducted for slightly different purposes. These include the following variations of the depreciation technique:

- Commercial balance sheet depreciation
- Tax-based balance sheet depreciation
- Depreciation calculated for the consolidated balance sheet

Part
III

Ch
14

Managing investments by using the technique of Capital Investment measures and their associated master record structures can be advantageous for companies that need to plan and control large individual investments, or for companies that use their own resources to create the assets.

Selecting the Type of Capital Investment Measure

Four types of cost assignment objects can take part in a Capital Investment program:

- Capital-investment project
- Capital-investment order
- Job shop order
- Asset under construction (AuC)

Understanding Capital Investment Project Structure Plans   A project structure plan (PSP) has the task of reporting a set of activities in a hierarchy that arranges the PSP elements in levels. A Capital Investment PSP element is represented by a master data record that includes information on the following entities:

- Identification of the project leader
- The requesting cost center
- The cost center responsible for implementing the Capital Investment measure
- User-defined data fields

A PSP element can be divided into lower-level elements, each of which can be subdivided, and so on. The subdivision can take place at any stage, from planning to project implementation.

The role of a PSP is to form the basis of the planning and control of a project. In particular, the PSP is specialized for the following functions:

- Display the labor, time, and cost required for a project
- Control the integration of any subsequent project's planning activities
- Plan the project costs
- Distribute the project budget

In all functions, the controlling activities extend to each level of the PSP architecture under control of the user.

A project is intended to be a structured set of activities in which the costs and the time management are planned, controlled, and monitored in as much detail as the user requires. The following logistics functions are integral to project management:

- Scheduling
- Resource and capacity management
- Network planning and cost distribution to individual activities
- Analysis of the interdependencies between activities

- Planning of optimum procedures within the project
- Scheduling of external resources
- Management of contingencies, such as resource bottlenecks and changes of requirement

Understanding Capital Investment Order Functions   Unlike a project structure, a capital-investment order is not divided into subtasks because it is a single-level structure. Most of the logistics functions that characterize project management are not needed for capital-investment orders.

Understanding Capital Investment Orders in a PSP   An order can be assigned to a PSP element in the master data records. An internal job shop order, for example, can be placed in the context of a large Capital Investment measure. If this work must be viewed or analyzed as a separate subtask, even though it is part of a large project structure plan, you can call for the order itself from the order processing system to see the progress and settlement situation. The individual order is identified in the PSP and therefore takes part in the reporting and settlement procedures of the entire project.

Understanding Asset Under Construction (AuC)   The AuC data object is used to identify assets that must be reported as capitalized assets in the balance sheet. When an order or a project structure plan is released for planning and posting, the system automatically sets up an AuC item in the balance sheet accounts. It is normal practice to set up a separate AuC balance sheet account item for each order or project structure plan element. The alternative is to identify cost elements and assign them to different AuC balance sheet account items according to their type. The system automatically creates a separate AuC record for each cost element according to its origin. Each project AuC item is then assigned to an appropriate balance sheet account AuC item.

Part
III

Ch
11

Every Capital Investment measure is associated with an AuC item in the balance sheet that represents the balance sheet value of an order or project structure plan element. This value change is reported in asset accounting, in the balance sheet reports, and in the asset history sheet. However, the system does not permit you to post any value directly to the AuC. The order or project is the primary cost object, and its value is not posted to the AuC until it is settled.

Cost Planning and Budgeting for Capital Investment Programs

Several different approaches exist in planning for capital investments, whether by orders or through projects. For example, you can draw up general plans in the form of annual amounts that take no account of cost elements or cost-element planning. You could have these annual totals broken down into individual reporting periods.

If you apply unit-costing techniques, you can plan the expected consumption of materials, constituent base objects, and materials. It may be useful to maintain a set of statistical key figures in this connection. These plans could be differentiated by organizational unit.

Using Account-Determination Keys   The primary costs of a Capital Investment measure can be planned by a cost element estimated by value or by quantity. If a cost element is to be reported according to several account-determination keys, you can apply detailed planning using these as the primary cost elements. The user can specify the account-determination key to combine quantity and value measurements. The following account-determination factors are recognized by the system:

- ☐ Material items recognized by their material numbers as defining members of an overhead area, such as Supplies Overhead Area
- ☐ Cost components arising as personnel-related wage and salary amounts valued by using costing tables and cost rates
- ☐ Activities required in support of planned external or internal activities
- ☐ Surcharges applied as percentage rates using various base quantities to compute risk surcharges and price surcharges, for example

If you have systems of cost centers and overhead rates, you can use them to plan internal activities for the Capital Investment measures in your program.

From the price of activities calculated by cost center accounting, you can work out the quantities of internal activities of the various kinds that could be performed for each Capital Investment measure. You must find some way of determining the quantities you probably need and applying the activity costs to arrive at the value that must be debited to the Capital Investment measure as secondary cost elements.

When values have been determined for primary and secondary costs, the overhead costing techniques are applied to compute flat-rate overhead surcharges for each cost element. The user has control over how much surcharge is applied and the cost element to which it is assigned.

The result of these stages is a set of planned total costs for the Capital Investment measure. This figure is then transferred directly to the Capital Investment program cost planning. The mechanism to effect this transfer automatically associates an order or project with a particular Capital Investment program position or measure.

You can view the associations between program positions and orders or projects through the availability control reports, where you can inspect the planned, actual, and assigned amounts for each Capital Investment program or individual Capital Investment measure. The source and distribution of a budget for a Capital Investment program is copied from the plan. You may wish to apply discounts to the planned amounts before you allow them to become budget amounts.

If a new Capital Investment measure begins in the current year, you can approve its total budget directly from the Capital Investment program. This total covers the entire measure, however many years it lasts. Distribution across the expected years of the program is carried out later and gives you the annual expenditure budgets, the annual slices, for each Capital Investment measure in each year.

Controlling Availability The approved total budget and the annual expenditure budgets may be subject to passive or active availability control. The passive control mode simply reports the availability of funds. Active control can be carried out directly for each activity. If your project exceeds the budget for any one item, the person responsible can be informed automatically by mail through SAP R/3 Business Workflow application. The manager can also respond through the workflow, for example, by electing to provide a budget supplement.

Goods and services required in conjunction with a Capital Investment measure can be procured through the SAP R/3 Purchasing System and FI-FA Financial Accounting. When an order for goods or services is posted, an open item is created automatically to document the commitment of funds from a Capital Investment measure or program. This document effectively plans the future costs of the Capital Investment measure. When the goods or services are delivered, or when an invoice is received, the open item is removed if the delivery is complete. If only a partial delivery takes place, the open item is reduced by a proportionate amount.

The relevant Capital Investment measure is automatically debited with the purchase order value as actual costs when the goods or services are received, or by the invoice amount when the invoice is received.

N O T E An invoice can be directly posted by financial accounting without reference to a purchase order. In these circumstances, the Capital Investment measure is directly updated by an additional account assignment annotated as Capital Investment Order or Capital Investment Project, as appropriate. ☐

Part

III

Ch

11

Documenting Internal Value Flows

Cost centers provide activities to Capital Investment measures. These activities are each specified by quantity and by value. The flow of these internal activities is recorded as direct internal activity allocation. The controlling system values the activity quantity by referring to the price determined through cost center accounting. An individual item comprising a certain quantity of a particular activity is recorded as a credit memo at the sending cost center and as a corresponding debit memo in the Capital Investment measure record, which is the receiving object.

Allocating Activity Costs Indirectly

If an activity cannot be quantified for each transaction, an indirect allocation can be performed. Allocating activity costs indirectly involves a periodic transfer posting of a proportion of the costs of providing the activity. This enables the transfer of costs between cost centers and orders.

Allocating Overhead as Surcharges on a Capital Investment Measure

In the procedures of planned cost accounting, the computation of overhead rates is used to develop a method of distributing costs. In a similar way, overhead surcharges may be applied to Capital Investment measures.

The overhead surcharges are not usually included in the cost rates for the various activities provided by cost centers. Therefore, an amount representing a proportion of the overhead surcharges must be debited to the Capital Investment measure in accord with the Cost by Cause principle.

Capitalizing Internal Activities

A percentage of internal activities can be capitalized under fixed assets. You can choose different valuation types as a basis for computing a percentage. For example, you may be able to capitalize all internal activities to fixed assets when using commercial valuation. However, for tax purposes, you may have to value your company by capitalizing only 80% of internal activities. For corporate reporting of the consolidated accounts, you may have to capitalize no more than 70%.

Posting Down Payments

It is usual for a long capital-investment project to be subject to the requirement for installments or down payments as the work proceeds. After the external activity has been completed, the invoice quotes the total invoice amount that must be posted in full. However, if you have made down payments during the course of the construction of the asset, your final payment is much less than the full invoice amount. Furthermore, the law requires balancing the accounts of AuCs so that the down payments already made are assigned as fixed assets.

The SAP R/3 solution to this complex posting requirement involves posting a down payment as such by the FI-AP Accounts Payable module. At the same time, an additional account assignment is made to the purchase order under which the down payment is made. The amount of the down payment is automatically updated in the records of the Capital Investment measure, where it is assigned to a specific cost element created for the purpose of recording down payments. At the end of the accounting period, the down payment on behalf of a Capital Investment measure is automatically prepared for capitalization by being transferred to the fixed assets account.

N O T E If your system does not have a purchase order as reference for a down payment, you can post the down payment directly to the Capital Investment measure without affecting the value flow documentation.

Using Interest During the Construction Phase

A long construction phase for an asset represents capital lockup because the value in the partially completed asset cannot be applied elsewhere in the company. Your region of legal force may permit account balancing in which the interest on capital-investment projects can be capitalized under fixed assets. In any circumstance, you may find it useful to compare the interest calculated on book depreciation versus tax-based depreciation, for example.

The system enables you to consult an interest table and determine the cost elements for which interest is to be computed. You can also specify which depreciation areas apply an interest computation, and which rates of interest are employed. Compound interest can be calculated using a time period defined by the user. The system calculates the interest at the end of the defined periods and debits the Capital Investment measure with these values.

N O T E   Within a capital-investment project, the interest on capital invested is treated as a normal cost element that can be charged to fixed assets or to the normal receivers of cost accounting assignments (the cost centers). ☐

Using Investment Support During the Construction Phase

If your Capital Investment measure attracts investment support from your host country during the construction phase, you have various ways of accounting for it. For example, you can apply any of the following techniques:

- Deduct the value of the investment support from the balance sheet values of the asset under construction. Doing so reduces the acquisition value of it.
- Treat the investment support as revenue from the asset, which does not affect its acquisition value.
- Apply the investment support as a reserve for special depreciation on the liabilities side.

If you create a special depreciation reserve for investment support subsidies, you may have to dissolve this reserve on the asset side over the useful life of the asset.

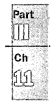

The system offers you proposal lists at each stage of planning the utilization and subsequent postings of investment-support measures. These documents are presented in formats suitable for submission to the supporting authorities.

When a capital-investment project is completed, the system must transfer Capital Investment measures to fixed assets on the asset side, with due allowance for depreciation. If the Capital Investment measure has received capital investment subsidies, the system makes a transfer posting automatically for the total subsidy amount.

Using Settlement Functions for Capital Investment Measures

Many ways exist for arranging settlement of Capital Investment measures, and many tools assist in this process. The settlement rules to be applied are stored in the master records of each capital-investment order or capital-investment project.

The display of a Capital Investment measure that includes a number of items can be settled one line at a time if you want to assign a settlement rule to each line item individually. You can assign settlement rules according to cost element so that the settlement receivers are assigned according to their origin groups. For example, external activities are usually charged to fixed assets. Internal activities are distributed on a percentage basis between fixed assets and certain cost centers.

Most items created for a Capital Investment measure are settled to an AuC account at the end of the period. However, this means that the items will be capitalized, which may not be appropriate or legal for items that should be accounted, wholly or partially, as costs. The costs should not be capitalized as fixed assets but rather settled on cost objects, including cost centers, internal orders, project structure plan elements, and profitability segments.

These cost assignments to the controlling module enable the following reports to be generated each month:

- Settlement by period to the cost-accounting receivers
- Balance sheet display of AuCs
- Asset history sheet

Customizing Final Settlement to Fixed Assets

A Capital Investment measure is intended to be used when it is completed and, perhaps to some extent, before. The following matters must be resolved before final settlement can take place:

- Shall the Capital Investment measure be represented as a single fixed asset or as several fixed assets?
- Which cost center or cost centers shall be assigned responsibility for the new assets?
- How shall the new assets be depreciated?

After you have resolved these issues, you can create master data sets for the new fixed assets and assign them to the correct asset classes. From a list of the new assets you can select line items for individual assignment, or you can settle by groups based on original cost element postings. You can also distribute a line item among several fixed asset receivers.

You may decide to settle some of the new asset items to cost centers in the controlling application. In this case, you must settle by line item to create a detailed proof of origin on the settlement receivers for controlling purposes, as well as to comply with the legal requirements for rendering the external accounts.

The final settlement process credits the AuC account with the corresponding amount. Items from previous years are shown automatically as transfer postings, and items from the current year appear as acquisitions in the final fixed assets accounts.

Reporting Internal Accounting for Capital Investment Measures

The SAP R/3 system includes a standard reporting system for Capital Investment measures. This system is used for both orders and projects. You can modify the standard reporting system to create exactly the reports that you require for your individual circumstances, and you can change them as necessary without losing the efficient collation procedures integral to the standard report.

The following are the main presentation options:

- Ongoing profitability control by budget/actual comparison
- Cost-development displays extending over several reporting periods
- Interactive drill-down report control of analyses from controlling area down to line-item level

Reporting External Accounting for Capital Investment Measures

Legal external accounting requires that Capital Investment measures show legally valid proofs of origin for the values recorded in the fixed assets accounts. An AuC automatically generates an asset history sheet and appears in the asset list as well as in any standard asset report.

To inspect this data, the following capabilities are available:

- Asset history sheets that are flexibly defined and selective in their displays of columns and lines
- Reports that are amenable to the widest range of sorting procedures
- Comparison reports that display the effects of using different depreciation area formulas

Part
III

Ch
11

Developments in Financial Management

Preparing for Open FI

Open FI consists of a network of information sources and business processes. One of the tasks of this network is to generate the data in real-time that is relevant to each decision in the commercial and financial processes. With global business being conducted between complex enterprises, it is not a simple matter to determine what data is relevant and how it should be processed. For example, you may need to assess the credit worthiness of a business partner. Your affiliated companies might have some relevant information, and you might have to access public information as well. You may have to enlist the support of the abundant computing resources of SAP R/3.

Developing Business on the Internet

Corporations are rapidly developing network software because the mechanisms are available and offer many advantages. The attractions, or at least the potential attractions, are distributed among consumer-to-business, business-to-business, and within-business applications. These applications offer the following qualities to users:

- Easy-to-use systems that can operate globally at any time
- Selective and easy access to information that is relevant at a pace and complexity the reader can control
- A low-cost marketing channel with wide market exposure and considerable penetration
- A familiar interface that can access a variety of services in depth, if required
- Immediate answers to inquiries
- The capability of asking intelligent questions because previously collected information is taken into consideration either automatically or by the operator
- The capability to control the movement of images with sound to demonstrate a product and discover which aspects interest the prospective purchaser
- Increased revenue that may arise from a low cost of sales
- Direct access, as the Internet may have become the preferred source of information for some sectors of the market
- Simple cut and paste functions that can be used to compile email purchase orders and to request other services
- Automation of standard tasks under the control of a suitable authorization profile system

Recognizing the Possibilities of Electronic Commerce with R/3

The implementation of local networks based on mainframe computers and dedicated communications has a relatively long history. Client/server configurations accommodated distributed computing, whereby the user at a workstation or simple terminal could be connected not only to databases but also to additional computing power to process the data. In simple terms, the concept entailed accessing a system through a terminal dedicated for this purpose. The extent and complexity of the system is often not apparent to the individual user, nor need it be in most applications.

However, very real limitations exist as to the number of terminals that can be operating at the same time. SAP R/3 and R/2 can adjust the allocation of computing resources to the workload on a dynamic basis. These systems also understand the provision of procedures to cope with equipment and communication channel malfunctions.

Apart from automated banking terminals, the direct conduct of commercial business by individual users is not yet widespread. But the SAP R/3 range of standard business software is anticipating a change.

Developing Electronic Delivery Channels

The customers of banking and financial services expect reduced prices and improved services. The electronic delivery channel, in any of its various forms, can be an efficient provider of the services required by the customer. But this channel can also be the means by which the customer can access competing services, sample offerings, and rapidly switch accounts to the most attractive provider.

One of the problems to be resolved centers on the inequality between low-cost self service and high-cost personal contact with a banking or financial representative. Another problem involves determining the rate to charge. Should some types of customers pay more than others?

One possible solution is to arrange the networks to recognize the customer and then deliver a service and presentation package that is finely tuned to match the needs and preferences of that individual customer. Clearly, the technology of personalized display formats and controls is available to the computer user and could be made available to the customer at a public or private terminal.

NOTE Customizing the display presented to customers using an electronic delivery channel provides an opportunity for target marketing. As a customer, you could find that each time you provide a new piece of information (perhaps by selecting from a menu), the display would become more relevant to your specific needs. ☐

Combining Components of Open FI

At each phase of a business process, certain support activities can be managed to add value to the sequence by applying information to control the process. The following sales sequence illustrates the way the SAP R/3 components can be configured:

- Marketing services
- Performing quotations
- Controlling customer credit using real-time scoring of payment history
- Processing orders
- Monitoring export credit insurance
- Processing invoices
- Factoring

- ☐ Analyzing asset-backed securities
- ☐ Dunning
- ☐ Using export credit insurance premium notification and collection
- ☐ Recording payments
- ☐ Updating customer payment history

One of the ways to make the financial systems more efficient is to link the processes into workflow sequences. A workflow sequence is initiated only by specified conditions and then proceeds automatically. The user can specify that an intermediate step shall not be taken until an authorized user inspects the relevant display and signifies approval for the next operation to take place. For example, SAP R/3 FI is used as the core application in an enhanced FI-AR, Accounts Receivable module, that is specialized to manage Asset-Backed Securities (ABS).

Cash flows expected from orders and revenues are essential components of short- and medium-term budgetary planning. You may have to take measures to protect your financial position against possible cash-flow contingencies. For example, you can create a currency exposure cover, in the form of a microhedging transaction, by allocating forward currency-exchange dealings to the order or billing document from which they originate. The effect is to automatically protect the cash flow expected from the transaction.

Focusing on Positive Auditing with the SAP R/3 Workstation

The SAP R/3 Auditor workstation module can operate with individual companies and on a global enterprise basis. The Auditor workstation can operate as a stand-alone module and can interface with the data sources through standard SAP interfaces. This module generally operates online, connected to the SAP R/3 system. The auditors work in the operational system and must be authorized to read the current data-set.

This workstation focuses on more positive auditing activities and consulting, although it fully supports the standard processes of compiling evaluation documents and reports. The Generally Accepted Accounting Principles (GAAP) remain the guiding standards, but the workstation is optimized for the benefit of internal and external auditors, system auditors, and cost accounting personnel.

N O T E Although this module was first developed for the German auditing environment, it is gaining the capability to recognize other auditing conventions. ▨

The R/3 Audit Information System is also available to the Auditor workstation. This information system can construct an audit report tree, from which the user can call individual reports and evaluation programs that work with pre-closing interim lists such as Assets, Receivables, Balance Confirmation, Balance List, Domestic Customers, and so on.

Networking Workflow

Standard Web browsers, Microsoft Exchange, Lotus Notes, and custom applications can use R/3 Workflow Wizards to automate workflow design and control the workflow via a network. Workflow status reports are made available in HTML format. The Workflow Management Coalition (WfMC) is an integrated implementation that includes the 52 published Workflow Application Programming Interfaces and provides the following components:

- ☐ Session Manager
- ☐ Distribution Architect
- ☐ Reference Model
- ☐ Computer-Aided Testing Tool (CATT)
- ☐ Organization Architect
- ☐ IMG Implementation Management Guide

Using Workflow Templates

Workflow templates are maintained as master records that can be executed and can serve as a guide for a company's own development. The individual steps of workflow templates are pre-defined as standard tasks. These contain a task description, linkage to the application logic through business objects, and prepared linkage to the company's organization structure.

The business object repository delivered in R/3 includes predefined key fields, attributes, and methods. The events associated with the business objects Workflow Definitions made from standard tasks can easily be combined and changed at any time by using the graphical editor.

Demonstrating SAP R/3 Processes

Workflow templates have been integrated into the IDES International Demonstration and Education System. This can play through the operational sequences of a sample company. The preconfigured workflow scenarios can be executed and analyzed for learning and planning purposes.

Reducing New Product Time-to-Market

If your financial operations are dedicated to a production facility, you probably are aware of the financial implications of engaging materials and the plant in production that will not generate revenue until products are sold. Your company may face additional financial pressure if it must continue to find innovate product designs and product mixes.

SAP R/3 4.0 and subsequent releases include many ways to improve value-chain management and time-to-market. The scope of these improvements to business process design must go beyond the confines of the company's production plant because the quality and timely delivery of supplies and raw materials may well be major factors that control customer satisfaction.

Altering a System Without Disruption

The Internet and intranet will change the way Receivables are dealt with. If a business is to make best use of the possibilities of electronic commerce, it is essential that the work passing through the standard business processes should be amenable to adjustment. This puts the company in a position to benefit from any change or anticipated change in market conditions.

An installed and configured SAP R/3 implementation must be capable of improvement without disruption, as you may need to reconfigure you business workflows at short notice.

Improving a Business Continuously

The Business Framework architecture includes two types of Business Application Programming Interfaces (BAPI), software standards that can be used to design ways of controlling how a business application responds to a transaction. The earlier type is used to access SAP and third-party applications from the R/3 Basis core. The most recent type of BAPI resides in the application, where it can process instructions that, in effect, reconfigure the complexities of business processes. This new BAPI is used to enable customer organizations to apply new process-control logic and to change the corresponding presentation logic. (BAPIs are discussed later in the section "Using Business Application Programming Interfaces.")

Such a process is achieved without disrupting business but, of course, occurs under the strict discipline of change management, wherein all adjustments are held in abeyance until the release date. At that point, the adjustments are recorded in the change management documentation. For example, a production company might adjust its logic from an emphasis on process control to distribution logic if the production plant became part of a different enterprise.

Selecting Components for Electronic Commerce

The work unit of SAP systems is the transaction, and the same principle applies to electronic commerce. The components available for electronic commerce are software units that can be carried in a range of operating systems and hardware devices. The idea is to make these units available for use by any system that has received the SAP certification.

Using the SAP R/3 Java User Interface

The Java Virtual Machine can be deployed into virtually any presentation device. The SAP R/3 Java User Interface can then be transmitted to any of these devices, which can be granted access to R/3. In particular, this process takes advantage of low-cost devices, such as the Network Computer (NC) and Network PC (NetPC), that need hold very little functionality locally because they are continuously in touch with the parent system over an intranet or the Internet.

The essential feature of the SAP Java BAPIs is that they use standard business objects. Therefore, the BAPIs provide a way of operating with standardized business content and logic without reference to the specific terminal device used for access.

Using Business Application Programming Interfaces

As stated previously, BAPIs are software standards that can be used to design ways of controlling how a business application responds to a transaction. In essence, the application receives a message through a BAPI, which sets up the procedures for dealing with the data that also arrives at the BAPI.

For example, a BAPI to a Human Resources database server can be configured to recognize a request for a person who has particular qualifications and is also available to carry out a task, such as processing a sales order. The server finds such a person, if possible, and returns the details to the system or person who initiated the request.

Using Internet Application Components

An Internet Application Component (IAC) is a standard business interface that is specifically designed to operate with the Internet or with an intranet. One characteristic of SAP R/3 IACs is that they are isolated from the kernel of the R/3 system. The IACs can be seen as separate components that can be developed and adapted without requiring any change in the main R/3 system.

In particular, the way an IAC reacts is determined when the Internet Web page is designed. Full multimedia facilities can be made available, and the very style of the interchange between user and system involves building on the idea that the whole supply chain responds without delay to the user's requests and requirements. Both goods and information are handled in the style of a production process in which the customer is the source of prime information.

Providing Facilities Online

The following titles indicate both the range of services that have been rapidly elaborated using the SAP R/3 IACs and their supporting BAPIs:

Part
III

Ch
12

- A product catalog with facilities to service Interactive Requests
- Employment opportunities, with reports to users on their application status
- KANBAN stock-control logic, with reporting from the SAP available-to-promise server
- Maintenance service notification
- Sales order creation, with reporting on sales order status
- Measurement and counter readings from the production plant and laboratory systems
- Quality notification and quality certificates
- Consignment stocks status
- Project data confirmation
- Collective release of purchase requisitions and purchase orders
- Staff listing
- Integrated in-box
- Internal activity allocation and workflow status

    ☐ Internal activity price list, requirement request, and requirement request status

    ☐ Asset management

Some of these are available as loosely coupled systems using the Application Link Enabling (ALE) protocol.

Protecting Electronic Commerce

The variety of processes and the very large number of users who will have access to a networked electric commerce system inevitably raise queries about the privacy of personal data and the restriction of commercially sensitive information. Malicious damage to databases and other forms of hacking are real threats.

Firewalls are interfaces that allow only the transmission of information if commands have been authorized and their sources verified. Encryption is the process of transforming a data stream according to a code, which can be used by the recipient to restore the stream to its original structure. The complexity of encryption procedures increases as code-breakers acquire the ability to decode private data.

The SAP R/3 business interfaces and Internet components are designed to implement the Secure Electronic Transaction (SET) standard, which is under development by the Internet Engineering Task Force.

Accessing Business Partner Information

The multi-service firm Dun & Bradstreet can provide real-time financial information about business partners using the D&B Access program.

Receivables management systems can be provided with online information on corporate customers, including details of the business transactions carried out with them and their affiliated companies. The collated data enables assessment of the business partner with respect to sales, accounts receivable, credit and receivables management, and the controlling areas.

The system performs customer risk management by constantly monitoring credit line usage as it processes business transactions. If a customer exceeds the limits set for outstanding debt or liquidity ratios, the system's alarm function is triggered.

The network can include information sources such as credit reporting agencies and credit sales insurance firms. For example, the D&B Access application, developed by Dun & Bradstreet Solutions in cooperation with SAP, provides a direct link between R/3 applications and the D&B database, which contains information on more than 17 million European companies.

These integrated systems provide real-time credit-worthiness scoring data, monitor insurance limits, or determine corporate group integration so that companies have comprehensive information about their customers. The full potential of this infrastructure will be reached once multilevel business processes are streamlined and automated.

Ensuring SAP R/3 Accounting Software Certification

Certificates of compliance with the Generally Accepted Accounting Principles have been awarded to the following modules:

- Financial Accounting
- Asset Accounting
- Real Estate
- Treasury Securities
- Treasure Money Market and Foreign Exchange
- Treasury Loans
- Treasury Borrower's Note Loans

Ongoing certification has been implemented for FI and MM software under development, with country-specific certification of individual functions where necessary.

Accounting Worldwide

SAP International Development is a set of models—one for each geographical area of the world. This set enables the SAP system to account for the rules and practices of the major trading communities.

INT-International Development module includes the following components:

- IN-APA Asian and Pacific area
- IN-EUR Europe
- IN-NAM North America
- IN-AFM Africa and the Middle East
- IN-SAM South America

These modules are fully integrated into the R/3 system during implementation. They are additional to the standard R/3 provision for translating screen text and currency values to suit the local language, local currency, and reference languages of the group head office system.

Confirming SAP R/3 Year 2000 Compliance

All releases of R/3 are compliant. No migration or upgrade is required for R/3 users. All date fields are four bytes, as are all related record layouts, screen layouts, matchcodes (secondary indexes), and data dictionary definitions.

Testing for Millennium Compliance   Year 2000 certification tests have been conducted on fields, transactions, and reports by using hundreds of consultants and developers who entered predefined and arbitrary data to verify software quality. Using the SAP R/3 Computer-Aided Testing Tool, many of these tests were repeated with various system dates in the range of years from several years before to several years after 2000.

Part
III

Ch
12

Checking Data Interface Compliance   Third-party data interfaces may present dates in two-digit format, but the SAP system automatically converts a two-digit year into the proper four-digit number. The input of data simulates data entry from a keyboard, so existing programs that process keyboard data entry correctly will interpret and automatically convert two-digit year dates to the proper four-digit number.

Developing the Open Information Warehouse

The purpose of an information warehouse is to provide technical, business, and statistical data for any part of a corporation. The concept of an open database includes the notion that all data is stored in tables ready to be instantly inspected and used without the need for complex data-retrieval instructions in a specific language peculiar to one vendor.

An open information warehouse suggests that all the information is readily available in a form ready for use without special access operations. The implication also exists that the inventory of the warehouse is comprehensive and up-to-date.

Selecting Data Sources

SAP information systems are available for all the main applications and are an integral part of their operation. The information systems are an obvious source of data concerning the specific areas of business activity. These systems already cooperate with one another to share master data such as supplier details and materials master data, and they are also integrated with the financial accounting modules.

If the open information warehouse is to be developed in support of the EIS-Executive Information System, a demand will arise for information from the TM-Treasury Management module, which could include online information links to the financial and materials market information systems provided by non-SAP vendors.

The following SAP sources contribute to the open information warehouse:

- ☐ Financial Information System (FIS)
- ☐ Controlling Information System (CIS)
- ☐ Purchasing Information System (PURCHIS)
- ☐ Materials Management Information System (MMIS)
- ☐ Production Information System (PPIS)
- ☐ Shop Floor Information System (SFIS)
- ☐ Plant Maintenance Information System (PMIS)
- ☐ Sales Information System (SIS)
- ☐ Human Resources Information System (HIS)

Creating Master Data Objects

One fundamental aspect of SAP standard business program design is that each data object should reside in only one location, where it is known to be the master data object. A data object may be copied but not altered without leaving a record of who altered it and when. Once a master object is updated, all subsequent calls to that object should encounter the new information.

The standard date functions in SAP have always been business objects that carry information, such as the system date and time, and processes that can transform this value to express the date and time in various time zones and in appropriate languages and formats. If you try to enter a date that is not expressed in an acceptable format, an SAP system does its best to convert it.

N O T E   SAP does not enable you to enter the time or date in a format of your own invention because this may not be understood by other users and their business processes. ⬚

Using the Document Management System

You have the resources of the DMS-Document Management System at your disposal to help you find what you require in the open information warehouse. The R/3 Classification System comprises many functions designed to help you locate information held in document form. You may search on the basis of subject matter, or you may search for an item because you know it is linked with one of the following data objects:

- Another document
- A material identified by its material number, by its name, or by part of its name
- An item of equipment, given its name or only the identification of the activity where it is used
- A project identified by its number, the person responsible for the project, the project's purpose, and so on
- A quotation
- A sales order
- A customer or a vendor identified by an attribute in the master records

Part III

Ch 12

Mining for Significant Data

The basic purpose of data mining is to look for patterns in data. The simplest pattern is one that satisfies a search query, such as all customers who have placed an order in the current financial year and who live within a specific marketing region. This type of convergent search terminates when all examples that match the pattern are found, if there are any in the database.

Data mining usually refers to more intelligent searching, which falls into the categories of supervised and unsupervised machine learning. In each case, the machine seeks to find which records in the database go together in some way because some aspects of their data can be related.

Supervision entails setting off the search by declaring some relationships in the data that must be considered, at least to start. For example, records may only be examined further if they already reveal that the customer has spent more than a certain amount in the period under consideration. Given this baseline, the supervised search can be told to look for patterns, for example, only in the type of goods purchased. You can then ask to find the purchasing patterns associated with the purchase of a particular item.

These data mining operations can tell you only which data values are associated; they can say nothing about the reasons. On the other hand, you may reasonably infer that your chances of making a sale to a prospect who has already bought a product associated with your product will be higher than if no discernible relationship exists.

The area in which the intelligent data mining engine has discerned a strong association may be the area in which to seek your objective, even if you cannot work out why some of the data values should appear as part of the significant pattern. For example, it was said that prospective air combat pilots who could list a large number of items of sporting equipment were more likely to become successful flyers than those who could name only a few. The explanations for this could be diverse: Sportsmen have better hand-eye coordination, or team players are used to doing what they are told and putting up with discomfort.

If you use a pattern discerned by data mining to guide your future activities, you must expect some disappointments. Sometimes the prediction turns out to be false for individual cases; some of the rejected candidates might have been successful. This fallibility can be demonstrated by carrying out your pattern recognition and then paying no attention to it until a large sample of data has been accumulated. How good does your prediction look now? How many successes would you have lost if you had followed the policy suggested by the pattern mined from the data? Your accountant will be able to tell you how much money you might have saved by applying the policy compared to what you actually spent by ignoring it.

For example, an unselective advertising campaign may reach some unexpected customers. That unusual data can then be used to help discern yet more significant patterns.

Some data-mining products are set up to develop a range of data models that are then applied to fresh data in a competitive manner to see which variation serves as the best predictor. By this means, it is possible to determine the relative worth of each element in the model. This may be important if the cost of obtaining the data object is high. Having to conduct an interview, for example, may entail a very high cost, which may not be worthwhile—the consequences of making a false positive prediction and the consequences of making a negative or rejected decision might not be justified. More subtle computations of probabilities can be used to steer the data-mining engine in the direction most likely to be fruitful.

Discerning Patterns of Events

One of the keys to designing useful business objects is the existence of recurring patterns that could be recognized by a system and provide business significance. The arrival of a purchase order is an event that can be detected in any of several different ways and can be checked for validity. Your business expects other purchase orders. Therefore, investment in business objects to cope with them may be worthwhile. There is a pattern to such events; purchase orders can be recognized.

If you look at a set of events that do not share any common features, you could be said to be a problem solver. You may have to create a new and unique procedure to deal with each event. But you may still find it convenient to make use of a database that contains business objects. If you are repairing a system and decide that a particular part needs replacing, it might be convenient to call up and run the maintenance object for that system. You might want to access not only system checks directly or keyed-in data, but you also might want to run the stock control module to determine the best way of acquiring the part you need and obtaining its cost and delivery information.

Operating with SAP R/3 Business Objects

An object in the language of object-oriented programming (OO) is an entity that carries a data element that signifies the state it is in, such as OFF or ON, and shows some method by which this state can be changed. More than one method of changing an object's state could be indicated, and an object may have more than two states. What matters to the user is what else happens or could happen if an object's state changes. For example, an object that has the function of recognizing when a purchase order arrives could also have the functions of checking the stock availability and the customer's credit status.

Imagine a more complicated business object that has the function of finding not only the best supplier for goods required but also other potential customers for these goods. Such a business object might behave very much like a free market enterprise. It could be allowed to search widely for both customers and suppliers. You might wish to endow such an object with rules for choosing the best buy in the context of the pool of customers available. You may also direct the object to use the profitability of each potential trading activity as one of the factors when deciding on the best course of action. Of course, it might be prudent to set limits on the scope of this free market business object and bring in a human assessor when these limits are approached.

Part
III

Ch
12

This example would not be too creative in many industrial contexts because purchasing, marketing, and sales staff carry out elements of this complex function. A standard business object, however, could add the routine widening of search horizons because the information-gathering process will not entail extra human time.

Now suppose the suppliers identified by our marketeer business object were themselves aware that a requirement for their type of product was put out to competitive tender. They might well have a similar type of business object that could find the best way of meeting the requirement. The marketeer business object could find itself being used over and over again, with each reincarnation using different particular details but still following the standard business process programmed to work as efficiently as possible.

Updating Business Objects

This chapter has illustrated the concept of business objects with examples of wide-ranging online functionality. An intermediate procedure involves holding your data as business objects that carry static information in between formal updates. A price list or a book of telephone numbers could be said to be a business object. But if you never make any updates when new information is available, your business objects are not as useful as those that are updated according to the rules programmed into them, regardless of whether you decide to update them manually.

Drawing Upon the SAP R/3 Business Object Repository

The Business Object Repository (BOR) is a database that holds reusable standard business processes that can be called upon to build a specific implementation quickly. This is but an extension of the SAP process of building standard business software elements that can be customized to suit their circumstances. Keep in mind, however, that these elements can be customized only within limits that do not compromise the functional integrity of the program. In particular, an SAP R/3 Business Object cannot be altered so that it is no longer compatible with the rest of any R/3 implementation. The object always remains a fully integrated component.

Anticipating Internet II

The next generation of Internet servers will run at many times the speed of the current devices, but much more traffic will exist on the net. Several developments are underway at the research stage, and if adopted as standards, these innovations will facilitate the setup of systems that can accommodate literally millions of users online at the same instant.

For example, the R/3 Internet Transaction Server is available to extend the three-tier SAP R/3 architecture. This server enables many users to access an SAP R/3 installation through the Internet. The Secure Electronic Transactions (SET) standard for business communications is supported, and multitasking is possible.

Raising Standards of Business Programming

The SAP R/3 Reference Model is held in the Business Repository from which each function and data object can be drawn as needed. In order to raise the standards of business programming, cooperative work is in progress to define a Unified Modeling Language (UML) that uses high-level modeling to organize and refine the components which can then take part in specific workflow sequences.

Business processes that have been defined to the UML standard can be transferred to any UML-compliant repository. For example, the Microsoft Repository has been populated from SAP R/3 and so the programmers and tool developers who use the Visual Basic language can call upon the SAP standard business processes and use them in their own environments.

Using Electronic Commerce Partner Applications

SAP has always made use of third-party development partners to accelerate the introduction of products that meet the SAP certification standards. Some more recent partner applications illustrate the widening range of business applications that has become apparent as the reliable network standards open the potential market. The cooperative products are referred to as complementary solutions.

SAP operates a certification program to ensure that complementary products interface properly with SAP, though it does not evaluate other aspects of complementary solution software.

Connecting to SAPoffice

Although the SAPoffice email system has been available from SAP R/3 Release 3.0, it illustrates the way in which a standard SAP system can be related to a variety of third-party systems. R/3 applications use SAPoffice to automatically generate electronic messages that inform users of critical business process events. Electronic messages from SAPoffice can start application processes and can be integrated with SAP Business Workflow to provide automatic messaging services for workflow processes.

SAPoffice can send and receive email messages over the Internet by means of an SMTP interface. An interface to X.500 directories is available, and you can send external messages from SAPoffice using SMTP, FAX, or X.400 interfaces. SAPoffice can receive, process, and archive incoming faxes. You can upload and download files between SAPoffice and desktop applications such as Microsoft Word, Excel, PowerPoint, Microsoft Project, AmiPro, or WordPerfect.

Accelerating Implementation with the Business Engineer

With the release of R/3 4.0, SAP significantly enhanced the R/3 Business Engineer to release 4.0. This is the support tool for Accelerated SAP (ASAP™), which is a standard worldwide methodology for rapid implementation.

The SAP R/3 Business Engineer provides an open infrastructure to help businesses shorten implementation time and optimize return on investment. As an Internet-enabled component with a release cycle separate from the R/3 releases, the R/3 Business Engineer enables you to incorporate the latest business templates and continually adopt the latest R/3 functionality to streamline your business. ●

CHAPTER 13

FICO Education and Training

In this chapter

Introducing FICO Education and Training

This section looks at the place of Financial Accounting and Controlling education and training within the life cycle of an SAP project.

In the initial stages, it helps if the reasons for opting for a system change generally, and SAP in particular, are shared with the workforce. Many companies change their core business over a period of time, change direction, or find that existing systems simply will not cope. It ought to be clearly explained to the workforce how cost benefits can be achieved in realistic timescales.

The SAP system now runs on Windows 95, is compatible with other "best-of-breed" mainframes, and is built "ready-to-go."

An expert could configure a basic system in a matter of days. It would be of little use, however, because from the top to the bottom of the company, employees have to change their routines and learn a new way of working. This takes time and costs money. It has been suggested that the ratio of software costs to hardware costs to consultancy work out at about 1:1:3. So the required commitment to this level of investment should be understood from the outset.

In order to benefit from this level of spending and potentially reduce these costs, it makes sense to focus on the transfer of skills. Financial Accounting and Controlling exists at the heart of any organization. This is partly due to the statutory nature of external financial reporting, and partly because an accurate record of financial performance is essential for the short- and long-term health of any organization.

Identifying Learning Zones

There are four learning zones, each requiring a unique and clear training approach. The following sections discuss each of these zones.

Identifying Technical Skills Candidates for this would be the employees who are going to be involved at the database management end—programmers with background knowledge of commercial applications. ABAP, UNIX, and BASIS skills and a sound knowledge of the existing company computer networks, operation systems, and systems administration would be a prerequisite.

These are the people who are going to configure and maintain the technical side of SAP. Their education would start at the SAP Training Center, using computer-based learning techniques, and would continue in the workplace under the initial guidance of consultants or in-house trainers.

Identifying Application Skills SAP is one piece of software that can be adapted to an infinite variety of businesses. The company needs staff with the skills to structure the software so that it fits the industry: oil, sugar, medical, financial, and so on. A company implementing SAP will have legacy applications and staff with a sound knowledge of the functions they perform; these staff members should be actively involved in the implementation and attend SAP applications training as a first step.

"Key users," with sound business acumen and a thorough understanding of existing applications, will need to extend their skills so that they not only operate after a satisfactory implementation, but also support and use it creatively, continuously molding it to fit their own business.

Identifying Information Skills   Information skills are critical for success in today's business environment. The rapidly changing nature of markets and competition means an organization must be able to identify and react to changing circumstances. Current thinking suggests that an organization should have a 7:3 ratio of information processing to data capture. It is important in an SAP implementation to keep in mind the information requirements of an organization and consider this in the implementation design.

Identifying Management Skills   Skills at the managerial level need to be enhanced to confront the issues that will arise as a result of system changes. Managers have to be apprised of the business risks as well as the opportunities; they need to know what to retain, what to let go, and how to formalize company policies. The SAP integration course provides good information about the impact of features, functions, and policies in an integrated business systems environment.

Change management skills are being increasingly sought. The human issues are now becoming more and more important. As the technology becomes more familiar, the need to derive a competitive edge from its use will rely on the human element. The change manager needs to work with the board and develop a *transformation* program that encompasses all aspects of change.

Companies who have developed a successful implementation, and the consultants who have supported them, will be valued for the education and training that they are able to pass on. This will further raise the profile of SAP training.

Facing the Challenges

Successful implementation of the FI and CO modules will ensure improvement of the level of financial information and control. This, in turn, should allow the company to be proactive in satisfying the needs of its markets. Commitment to these goals is a critical factor. The risks lie not so much in the technology as in the human issues; people won't accept a new idea unless they've had some part in its development or unless they feel they'll benefit from it personally. Getting people to accept new ideas is part of the educational challenge.

SAP is designed to help people do a better job, a job they can be proud of, a job providing a real sense of accomplishment. Employees seek recognition, personal benefits, and an assurance that their contribution adds value to the business.

Users who are familiar with an existing system are often able to arrive at answers quickly without having to go through all the formal steps. They may have routines memorized; they may know who must sign forms and where to distribute them. They may know where to obtain the critical information within the current systems. This knowledge makes for a comfortable way of life in which employees perform job functions efficiently without having to refer to manuals or ask for help. They have probably developed shortcuts, which they understand but which provide only very limited benefit.

The introduction of a new system requires new forms, new procedures, new disciplines, and new reporting methods. New systems may require changes in the reporting structure, and changes in job roles and functions.

This change can be threatening because users may feel that their existing skills have lost value. The commitment of management to learning within a company needs to be stressed constantly.

Points of Principle

The key messages for FICO modules users to appreciate during education and training are

- The FI module is all about getting the right information for the financial statements in an integrated manner from the business or logistics systems and direct entry.
- The CO module is all about providing useful indicators about the internal and external success of the company and a means to control company plans.
- The project team must not lose sight of the core purpose of the financial function. Performance and targets still need to be monitored carefully as staff members are released for training.
- Education and training form part of staff development on an ongoing basis, not just for the new systems implementation.
- Education provides background and contextual input—why they do things in the broader picture.
- Training is very specific—what SAP does, how it does it, and what the user must do to support the operations of the business.

Determining Impact on Business

The impact of a training program on the business is many fold. Users who are being trained are not able to simultaneously perform their current job functions. The business must continue to function while training is being conducted. Management must therefore have a full commitment to the training program. This may mean reorganizing workloads to ensure that the impact on the business is minimized. They must, above all, promote the benefit of the training for the business and also for the individual in terms of performance and flexibility.

Getting Commitment of Management   The impact of changing integrated systems in a company is not unlike replacing the nervous system of a body and will clearly raise anxieties at all levels.

Staff will look for sound leadership. There are obvious advantages to building a project team using a representative cross section of managers from key user areas. Departmental training needs can be monitored and shared.

The importance of a clear, comprehensive education and training program that is timed to address the need for new competencies is vital, particularly since the reporting requirement function remains vital to monitor the business. Frequently, education, training, and the generation of related documentation involves far more time and effort than the project team might expect early in the project.

Achieving consensus and commitment and setting the right momentum early in the project will address these issues.

Changing Job Roles, Responsibilities, and Standards   Staff job content will change. Individuals' roles may remain the same if the system is being overlaid on the current organization, but how they achieve results will be different.

Staff will need to be fully trained on the new data capture and reporting functions and will need extensive documentation to support their activities. Analysis, documentation, and training skills may need to be brought in from external sources.

Companies need to be sure that they do not loose their compliance with the companies' and various tax acts, as well as compliance with the Generally Accepted Accounting Principals (GAAP) adopted for financial reporting.

Structuring a Program

Structuring a program correctly is essential if the benefit of training is to be maximized. In broad terms, you need to focus on audience, content, and timing. You need to ensure that you identify the level of the audience for each training session. The audience will determine the requirements of the content required.

Content can refer to both the breadth and the depth of knowledge instruction required. Lastly, you need to consider the timing of the program. Training must be provided at the correct time. Too early, and the impact of the training is reduced as knowledge learned is forgotten. Too late, and you risk delaying the project or creating frustration or errors for users of the system.

Using SAP Courses

SAP courses are ideal for project team members to obtain understanding of SAP functionality. End users need to receive education and training appropriate to their environment. There is a third specific type of user who provides a key component in realizing the competitive advantage an SAP implementation provides: the information user.

Timing of attendance is all-important. A candidate returning to his work environment needs to be given the opportunity to make use of the newly acquired skills. This can be done in several of the following ways:

- Contributing to project activities
- Delivering a presentation to colleagues
- Accessing the demonstration SAP database and working through examples
- Creating discussion papers for policy development
- Analyzing current reporting requirements and future information needs
- Highlighting specific areas of concern for the project team

The point of giving structured follow-up work is to reinforce the content of the course and to make the information accessible to colleagues.

There are further benefits of attending public courses. Staff members will meet others from similar industries who are likely to be at different stages of the project cycle, and they can exchange "war" stories. It is hoped that these experiences will be of a positive nature and raise morale.

N O T E A public course will generally cover a broader scope of the SAP product and provide the trigger for thinking outside the bounds of common work practices. ◻

Designing In-House Courses

No public courses exist to meet the needs of each individual company. The project manager(s) will need to devise, plan, and deliver courses with the assistance of key users. If project managers do not have the time or specific skills to do this, they should be prepared to use the services of a training consultant who could carry out a needs analysis, devise a plan, and create the material.

At this stage, the contentious issue of the cost of training arises. Quality training can be seen to be an expensive overhead item, but it is not half as expensive as a poorly trained work force and error-ridden data.

Whether imported or home-grown, it is useful to have some idea about what characterizes quality training. The following sections provide a rough guide. Specific industries can extend this by incorporating their own unique industry requirements or features such as safety standards, confidentiality, hygiene, and so on.

Setting Goals   To be successful, an education program must have clear goals. Ideally, the following goals would be targeted:

◻ Communicate and educate at all stages, but particularly in the early stages.

◻ Gain user acceptance early.

◻ Generate high motivation.

◻ Aim for a shared understanding of the language, terminology, and functions of the system.

◻ Demonstrate a commitment to team learning in vertical groups, as well as in departments.

◻ Allow users to identify their own success and that of the system.

◻ Identify the skills users need to make the system work and acquire them.

◻ Celebrate success and progress.

If the above list looks overly optimistic, consider the alternative scenarios.

◻ Confusion and *perceived* job insecurity arising from rumors

◻ User resistance

- Poor motivation
- Interdepartmental struggles and ambiguous communication
- Users not understanding the purpose of the system
- Users ignoring the system or using it badly, corrupting or losing data

Even if this is an exaggeration, it illustrates the point that although training isn't cheap, a lack of it can be very expensive.

Getting Quality Training   Having set some high-reaching goals for the trainers, it is worth considering what goes into quality training. What will be needed to achieve these goals?

Quality training can be defined as the efficient acquisition of the knowledge, skills, and attitudes necessary to achieve and sustain specific goals.

An effective training plan should do the following:

- State the learning objectives. These should be the long-term changes in the knowledge, behavior, and skills you expect of users.
- Record and make known to the learner the success criteria used to assess learning.

  For example:

  A learning objective could be

  > The user needs to understand that the system allows for the automatic payment of supplier invoices.

  The success criteria would be

  > The user is able to request a payment proposal, execute it, and print the output for analysis and authorization.

  The terms *task* and *outcome* may be preferred; the important thing is that it must be clear to all parties concerned what is being taught and what is being learned.
- Consider the methods that will result in learning. Such methods may include computer-based learning, workshops, tutor-led sessions, consultant presentations, reading and video assignments, or practice with the system. If there are optional teaching methods, consider the candidates' preferred style of learning.
- Define the objectives before selecting a teaching method.
- Use documentation that is as good as you can possibly afford. Working with well constructed training materials will help develop the skills of less experienced members of the project team who are called upon to carry out training.

If the learning objectives or groups of learning objectives are written into the phased project planning, along with descriptors, roles, deliverables, and accountability, it is possible to deliver the training on a *just-in-time* basis. The training schedule must not be written isolated from the project plan because timing is all-important. Deliver the course at a time when the project cycle will allow the user to learn, rehearse, and then apply knowledge in a meaningful situation. It does wonders for morale.

NOTE   Within the implementation plan there should be a separate training plan that is integrated but managed separately. If it is viewed in this manner, there is less likelihood of the training dimension being underestimated or, even worse, ignored. ◻

Teaching the Adult Learner   There are other factors to take into account when dealing with adult learners in the workplace. For example, some users may be set in their ways. To effectively teach such individuals, a training program must incorporate the following attributes:

◻ Motivation—The learner must be inspired to change behavior, to respond to instruction, and to accept what is being taught.

◻ Content—The learning objectives must be presented in the context of what the learner already knows and understands.

◻ Structure—Learning must be sequenced to provide repetition, practice, and feedback of exercise results. Such structure reinforces newly acquired knowledge and skills and transfers them to real-world applications.

◻ Meaningful and relevant—The learner sees and accepts the purpose of the education as personally relevant.

◻ Immediately useful—Learning should be applied immediately, before it is forgotten.

◻ Exciting—The structure stimulates, usually through participation. Physically doing things keeps a marginally attentive learner interested.

A key to successful change management is to overcome fears that will inhibit learning at all levels. By eliminating fear or apathy, you can develop an atmosphere that will create support for your financial system. You can then make everyone want to succeed by using the system and by using it properly. This will happen if time and effort is invested to ensure that all employees understand, accept, and believe that the system will be personally beneficial, that their jobs will be better, that each department and the entire company will function more efficiently, and that resorting to informal methods to circumvent the system will be self-defeating and must be prevented. In addition, employees should achieve some degree of reward and prestige by showing that they have learned how to use the system correctly.

TIP   View the implementation of SAP as a challenge and an opportunity, not a painful problem. Each person should profit from the system, grow professionally, feel increased worth toward the company, and receive increased respect from it in return.

Managing Expectations

The expected benefits from the FICO modules may include the following:

◻ Improved recognition of cash discount

◻ Streamlining of mundane financial tasks

◻ Better management information systems

◻ Reduced costs of reporting

- Reduced clerical cost and the elimination of duplication
- Reduced headcount
- Reduction of capital costs
- Reduced cost of running old systems and associated hardware and software maintenance costs
- Increased visibility

Management needs to explain why these benefits are required and how these benefits can be achieved. This is crucial, as it justifies the replacement of old, familiar systems.

Fear of the system is usually caused because end users do not see what is in it for them; if they can see the personal benefits, they will be more likely contribute to it.

N O T E The possibilities of reduced head count will inevitably cause high anxiety and will demand some sensitive handling when developing education and training messages.

Developing Detailed Education and Training Plans

So far, the ground rules for training and education have been covered. The details of an education and training plan will vary considerably. So many factors influence it; the nature of the business, the level of existing expertise, the size of the budget, the need for speed. No two companies will be alike.

An education and training program needs to be integrated with implementation plans for multiple-phased modules. SAP is usually implemented in many different locations with different products. It is therefore important to have a structured approach.

The following sections provide a sequenced checklist that may help members of a project team, users, or managers address some of the key communication, education, and training activities to be included in a program.

Appreciating the Environment

The training program must be influenced by changes to business, any historical and current knowledge of attitudes regarding change, and skill levels. To ensure this, the following tasks should be accomplished:

- Understand the overall implementation plans and timing.
- Assess the company's communication policies.
- Review user requirements.
- Assess all areas of the business change (for example, re-engineering and business renewal).
- Assess the executive and management commitment levels to change.
- Fully appreciate the past track record of implementations.
- Assess the competencies of staff at all levels.

Management commitment levels and communication are critical items in this list. Without management commitment, employees will not show commitment. Poor communication leads to fear and suspicion.

Developing Education and Training Strategy

Consider alternative approaches to training and which approach is suitable depending on the knowledge transfer required, current skill levels, and attitudes. The following should be achieved to develop the best strategy:

- ☐ Prepare alternative approaches and a variety of teaching styles—one-on-one, workshops, modeling, self-paced, and computer-based learning.
- ☐ Recommend approaches, showing the advantages and disadvantages of each alternative.
- ☐ Secure top-level executive commitment.
- ☐ Use the senior levels of management to launch the overall program.

Launching Program

Having devised a suitable training program, you need to ensure it is launched effectively. This can be accomplished by doing the following:

- ☐ Announce overall plans in a project newsletter or similar communication vehicle.
- ☐ Address staff concerns as they arise.
- ☐ Commence the overall education program—background understanding of the project, understanding of integration issues, best practice implementation.

The importance and commitment to the training program needs to be stressed again. Any issues or concerns should be addressed prior to the start of the program.

Assessing Role Definition and Level of Expertise

In order to identify the suitability of courses for actual individuals, job roles, as they will exist in the new business, and the associated skills required need to be identified during implementation. These required skills need to be matched to existing user skills, thus identifying the skills gap. Training courses are designed to cover these skill gaps. Do the following to identify roles and the level of expertise:

- ☐ Work with the project team during FI and CO configuration and develop lists of tasks and procedures (SAP and non-SAP) that will be performed by the various units.
- ☐ The overall education and training program is developed to support change management activities—courses and how much job-release time various units require.
- ☐ When roles have been defined, these will be allocated to the new or existing positions in the departments where the FI functionality is being implemented.
- ☐ Level of expertise needs to be defined for new employees to ensure that their training requirements do not delay implementation dates.

Working with key users on the project team who are part of the organization can help foster positive attitudes for the ensuing changes.

Identifying Trainers

Identifying the correct trainers is important to the overall success of the training program. Keep the following in mind while identifying trainers:

- [ ] Trainers are identified from key users.
- [ ] Training is prepared for key users who will have to sign off policies, propose systems operation, and convert data for system implementation.
- [ ] Confirm adherence to accepted GAAP principles for the new procedures.
- [ ] Trainers are educated on how to train.
- [ ] Trainers develop the education and training material.

The skill of the trainer should not be underestimated in the effectiveness of the overall program. A trainer must be accepted by the users as having relevant business knowledge, as well as knowledge of the system. Identifying trainers from within the key users is preferable to external trainers. The train-the-trainer skills are essential, however, to ensure that the necessary transfer skills are taught.

Defining Competencies

In order to target the courses in the program effectively, it is necessary to identify existing competencies. This can be used to identify user competencies in existing job positions and the relevant competencies for new positions. The following are general guidelines for defining competencies:

- [ ] A competency measurement program is developed to assess the effectiveness of training and user competency.
- [ ] Existing staff members are assessed for existing competencies and appropriate courses are developed to improve competencies (for example, PC-use capabilities prior to starting the full FICO education and training).
- [ ] Individuals are identified for the various positions in the new/existing organization.

Because the time spent by users on courses is usually limited, it is important that existing competencies and relevant courses are identified. This maximizes the quality of the training program in the given time.

Developing Training Schedules

Having identified the training program, the trainers, and the users and their requirements, you can now consider developing individual training schedules for each user. To develop a training schedule, do the following:

- [ ] Locate and verify training facilities and equipment.
- [ ] Develop detailed training schedules for individuals.

Training schedules should be developed for each individual. Avoid the temptation to assign an entire department to a single course or series of courses. If a course is perceived as being not particularly relevant for an individual, it colors his or her perception of the entire training.

Going Live

After the training program has been finalized, a check is made to ensure that the training is ready for roll out. The following tasks are completed before going live.

☐ Assess trainers prior to the system going live.

☐ Check the accuracy of training schedule dates and locations.

CAUTION

Missing an introductory course due to incorrect schedule information can seriously affect all subsequent training.

Providing Support After Implementation

The training program does not end with the training of the initial users of the new system. It must support ongoing training, training of users for a change of role, and training for new employees. The following are guidelines for providing support after implementation.

☐ Post-implementation support programs are designed to ensure that, following education and training sessions, additional ongoing support is provided.

☐ Refresher education and training is provided after going live.

☐ Follow-up and ongoing training programs ensure that the staff uses the system correctly.

☐ Induction procedures for training new starters are formalized.

☐ The company training department adopts education and training programs.

An ongoing training program should continue to monitor the relevance of each training course. Changes in the way an organization uses the software can lead to changes in some course instruction.

Defining Scope of Education and Training

Having outlined the possible training opportunities within the project cycle, it is useful to have an idea of the range of courses that may be applied to meet the business training needs. It is possible to opt for off-the-shelf material or professionally produced courses. However, the project team must be prepared to be creative and design training courses if the need arises. The following sections suggest a range of courses and workshops generally available from SAP.

Using Overview Courses

The courses in Table 13.1 are designed mainly for orientation—orientation of the SAP product and how it relates to an organization's business, and orientation of team members roles within the project.

Table 13.1   Overview Courses

Course Name	Description
Executive overview	Focuses on business processes and information systems
SAP Integration course	Shows integration between SAP modules and impact on configuration
Team building	Establishing communication and analysis skills
FI introduction for users	Overview of features within SAP FI
CO introduction for users	Overview of features within SAP CO

SAP offers standard courses that are suitable for the overview, integration, and introduction courses. The team building course could use a standard team building scenario. This course also needs professional observers to provide constructive feedback.

Using Functional Courses

The courses in Table 13.2 are designed for project team members in the relevant functional areas and for integration team members. They are designed to teach the detailed functions of each sub-module of FI and CO. These courses are designed to provide project team members with the skills necessary to configure the SAP FI and CO systems.

Table 13.2   Functional Courses

Course Name	Description
General Ledger Accounting	Covers the detailed functions of General Ledger accounting
Accounts Payable Accounting	Covers the detailed functions of accounts payable
Accounts Receivable Accounting	Covers the detailed functions of accounts receivable
Fixed Assets Accounting and Capital Expenditure	Covers the detailed functions of fixed assets and recording of capital expenditures
Cash Management and Cash Flow Forecasting	Covers the detailed functions of cash management and cash accounting
Consolidation Accounting	Covers the detailed functions of consolidation

Part

III

Ch

13

continues

Table 13.2 Continued

Course Name	Description
Special Purpose Ledger	Covers the detailed functions of using special ledgers in financial reporting
Financial Information System	Covers the detailed functions of the Financial Information System
Cost Center Accounting	Covers the detailed functions of cost center accounting
Internal Order Accounting	Covers the detailed functions of internal order accounting
Profit Center Accounting	Covers the detailed functions of profit center accounting
Profitability Analysis	Covers the detailed functions of profitability analysis
Product Cost Planning	Covers the detailed functions of product cost planning
Product Costing	Covers the detailed functions of product costing
Report Painter/Report Writer	Covers the detailed functions of the report painter/report writer reporting tools.
Executive Information System	Covers the detailed functions of the Executive Information System
Self-paced learning programs	

Using Policy, Role, and Responsibilities

The following workshops are designed to identify and agree on the policy, sign-off, and accounting roles within an organization, and methods of assessing competency:

- Policy development and sign-off procedures
- Introduction to implementation plans
- Role of key users to support configuration, customizing, and implementation
- Defining roles and responsibilities
- Role of the General Accountant
- Role of the Accounts Payable Supervisor
- Role of the Credit Controller
- Role of the Cash and Expenses Accountant
- Role of the Asset Accountant
- Role of the Cost Accountant

- Role of the Planner
- Role of the Financial Analyst
- Role of the Departmental Manager
- Role of the Cost Allocation Accountant
- Competency assessment

These workshops are designed to agree on roles and responsibilities within the organization. The role definition workshops could start with an examination of job descriptions for these positions, but it is important to remember that SAP implementation may well change the nature of job responsibilities. Similarly, a starting point for competency assessment may be based on the required qualifications for current jobs, but will need to be modified for changing job roles.

Using Walk-Throughs and Demonstrations

The demonstrations and walk-throughs listed in Table 13.3 will be a necessary stage of acceptance testing for project sponsors. These demonstrations and walk-throughs should be tested at their conceptual design and should prove that the system can provide the standard accounting functions. The fact that this is possible should not be in question. The issue is demonstrating the integration, efficiency, and presentation of these functions.

Table 13.3   Walk-Throughs and Demonstrations

Walk-Through Name	Description
Account Cycle Simulation	Demonstration of accounts cycle: purchase-to-inventory, manufacture-to-sale, cash-in to cash-out.
Period End Closing	Demonstrate the month-end close: accruals, adjustments, period closing, and reporting.
Cost Accounting Simulation	Demonstrate the capture of costs: allocation of costs and costing of products (where applicable).
Planning Cycle Simulation	Demonstrate the planning process and any plan integration.
Period End Reporting	Demonstrate the provision of any period end reports: tax, statements, and analysis.
Policy Control	Walk-through of how the system assures compliance with company and fiscal policy.
Performance Measures	Demonstrate how key performance measures can be monitored via online interrogation or monthly reporting.

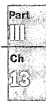

Part
III

Ch
13

Implementing

The following workshops are necessary to formalize steps for data conversion and sign-off procedures:

- Policy definition and control
- Data structuring, classification, and conversion
- Data conversion and sign-off procedures
- Performance measure seminar

Data conversion is mainly a technical issue. However, there are also business issues to consider. The timing of the project going live has an impact on the complexity of data transfer. This is much easier at year-end, but this relies on having project team members available at the same time that critical year-end processing is required.

SAP also supports standard tools to support data transfer for FI master records (general ledger, customer master records, and vendor master records.)

Providing Post-Implementation Support

The workshops in Table 13.4 support communication of procedures required to provide support to users after going live. This is necessary both to support the users and identify modifications to procedures or systems.

Table 13.4   Post-Implementation Support

Workshop Name	Description
Help Desk Procedures	Develop procedures for operation of help desk.
Issue Management	Develop procedures for issue handling, including escalation procedures and prioritization.
Responding to User Requests	Develop procedures for dealing with user requests (normally via formal help desk) and how requests are handled.

It is important to identify that any issues arising that have an impact on either system use or organizational procedures are reflected back in the procedures and courses that refer to them. This should be identified as part of the previous procedures. ●

P A R T

IV

Appendixes

SAP Glossary of Terms and Concepts

ABAP/4—Advanced Business Application Programming/4. A fourth-generation language developed by SAP in which SAP R/3 application software is written.

ABAP/4 Development Workbench—A development environment that contains all the necessary tools for creating and maintaining business applications within the R/3 system.

ABAP/4 Native SQL—A method for accessing a specific database by using its proprietary commands to implement the Structured Query Language.

ABAP/4 Open SQL—A portable method for accessing all supported databases by the Structured Query Language commands.

ABAP/4 Query—A user tool for generating special report programs without requiring any knowledge of ABAP/4.

ABAP/4 Repository—A store for all objects managed by the ABAP/4 Development Workbench.

ABAP/4 Repository Information System—A navigation aid for the ABAP/4 Repository.

ABC Activity-Based Costing—The SAP process of analyzing a company's business across organizational divisions such as cost centers.

ABC Analysis—The analysis of items such as materials can be conducted according to several criteria. These criteria could include importance or consumption value, such as the following:

- Important part or material with high consumption value
- Less important part or material with medium consumption value
- Relatively unimportant part or material with low consumption value

Account Assignment—Specification of accounts open for posting during a business transaction.

Account Assignment Element—A work breakdown structure element to which actual or commitment postings can be made.

Active SAP R/3 Repository—The directory currently in operational use that contains descriptions of all the application data of an enterprise and their interrelationships, including how they are used in programs and screen forms. During ABAP/4 program development, a separate development repository directory is maintained for versions of the program components undergoing development or modification.

Activity (Controlling)—Internal or external; a physical measure of the activity output of a cost center according to activity type.

Activity (Project System)—An instruction to perform a task within a network in a set period of time. Work, general costs, or external processing can be associated with an activity.

Activity Input—A transaction to plan the secondary cost quantities of a receiver cost center that uses activity from a sender cost center.

Activity Logs—Records of all activities in the SAP R/3 system for each transaction and for each user.

Activity Type—Classification of an activity and the data structure, for example, as follows:

- Number or quantity of units produced
- Hours
- Machine times
- Production times

Actual Costs—All the costs accruing to an object in a period.

ALE—Application Link Enabling. SAP method for using documents to carry messages that control distributed applications while maintaining integration and consistency of business data and processes across many systems.

Allocation Group—Group that defines which orders within one controlling area are to be settled together, as follows:

- By settlement timing—monthly, weekly, and so on
- By order types—repair, capital spending, and so on
- By settlement receivers—cost center, GL account, and so on

Allocation Receiver—Object to which the costs of a cost center or order are allocated.

APC—Acquisition or Production Costs. The value of an asset that is used in some types of depreciation calculations.

API—Application Programming Interface. Interface to support communication between applications of different systems.

ASCII—American Standard Code for Information Interchange.

Assessment (Controlling)—A business transaction used to allocate primary or secondary costs. The original cost elements are not retained by the receiver cost center. Instead, a secondary cost element is used to show this allocation. Information on the sender and the receiver is documented in the cost accounting document.

Asset Class—A grouping of fixed assets depreciated in a specified manner.

Asset under Construction—An asset still being produced when the balance sheet is prepared.

Asynchronous Database Updating—A method of updating a database separately from the management of the dialog part of the transaction.

Background Process—Non-interactive execution of programs, sometimes using prepared file data to replicate the user dialog to utilize the same standard functions.

Backward Scheduling—Method for scheduling a network in which the latest start and finish dates for the activities are calculated backward from the basic finish date.

App

A

Billing Element—In a work breakdown structure, a data object to which you can post invoices and revenues.

Budget—Prescribed and binding approved version of the cost plan for a project or other task over a given period.

Business Segment—Intersection of criteria to suit the relevant operating concern enabling analysis of profitability, for example, as follows:

- Country, U.S.
- Industry, farming
- Product range, animal feeds
- Customer group, wholesale

Business Segment Criterion—Chosen from SAP proposal list or existing tables, or created manually. Comprises a field name and a field value.

Business Segment Value Field—Holds a number, a code, or a string.

Business Transaction—A recorded data-processing step representing a movement of value in a business system, such as cost planning, invoice posting, and movement of goods.

Calculated Costs—An order's progress toward completion represented in value terms. Two methods exist for determining the calculated costs: calculation on a revenue base and calculation using quantity produced as a base. If planned revenue is more than planned costs for an order, there are two corresponding methods for calculating the (interim) profit realization.

Calculated Revenue—The revenue that corresponds to the actual costs incurred for an order, determined from results analysis as follows:

Actual costs * planned revenue / planned costs

Capacity (Cost Accounting)—The output of a cost center and activity that is technically possible during a specific period. Differentiated by category and arranged hierarchically.

Capacity (Production Planning)—Capability of a work center to perform a specific task. Capacities are differentiated according to capacity category and are arranged hierarchically under a work center.

Capacity Planning—Includes the following:

- Long-term rough-cut capacity planning (RCCP)
- Medium-term planning
- Short-term detailed planning (CRP)

Capital Investment Measure—A project or order that is too large or that contains too much internal activity to be posted to fixed assets as direct capitalization. The master record of a capital investment measure stores both the actual cost data and the planned values.

Capitalized Costs—The difference between the actual costs and the calculated costs of an order, calculated by results analysis. With deficit orders, this figure is reduced to allow for the loss realized.

Capitalized Profit—Calculated in results analysis by subtracting the capitalized costs from the value of the inventory from which revenue can be generated.

App
A

Cardinality—The number of lines in a dependent table to which the table under consideration, in principle, can or must relate. A line in a table may be related to another dependent line in a cardinality of one-to-one correspondence. The relationship may be one-to-many if there can be several dependent lines for any referenced line.

CCMS—Computing Center Management System.

CIM—Computer Integrated Manufacturing.

Classification—When an object is assigned to a class, values for the object are assigned to characteristics belonging to the class.

Client—The highest level in SAP R/3. Client is a self-contained unit in an R/3 system with its own master data and configuration tables, so the data of one client may not be accessed by another client. Often a training client and a testing client are present, in addition to the client code that represents your group or corporate identity and under which the SAP system runs normal business. Some data is managed at the client level because everyone in the corporate group of companies wants to refer to exactly the same information and ascertain that it has been maintained as up-to-date and correct. Vendor addresses are an example of data managed at the client level.

Client Caches—Work areas set up in the database application servers for data frequently accessed by the client's applications.

Co-Products—Products made in the same manufacturing process.

Commitment Item—A contractual or scheduled commitment that is not yet reflected in financial accounting but will lead to actual expenditures in the future. Commitment item management provides for early records and analysis for cost and financial effects. Commitment items are also referred to in SAP as open items.

Company Code—A unit within a client that maintains accounting balances independently and creates the legally required balance sheet and the profit and loss statement.

Compiler—A tool that translates source code statements written in a general programming language into statements written in a machine-oriented programming language.

Contingency Order—A results-analysis object in which the costs of complaints are collected. Reserves are created by results analysis for the expected cost of complaints and are drawn from as costs are incurred.

Control Indicator—Determines, in cost accounting, which application components are active, how certain data are stored, and what types of validation are to take place.

Control Key—Determines how an activity or activity element is to be processed in such operations as orders, costings, and capacity planning.

Controlling Area—An area within an organization that shares a cost accounting configuration; normally the same as company code. For cross-company cost accounting, one controlling area may be assigned to multiple company codes of one organization.

Controlling Area Currency—The default currency in cost accounting objects, cost centers, orders, and so on.

Conversion—Translation from one data format to another; for example, from decimal to binary code.

Cost Center—Place in which costs are incurred; a unit within a company distinguished by area of responsibility, location, or accounting method.

Cost Component—A group of cost origins.

Cost Component Layout (Product Cost Accounting and Cost Center Accounting)—A technical term. Controls how results of a product cost estimate are saved. Assigns cost elements to cost components and determines the following:

- How the costs for raw materials and finished and semi-finished products are rolled up in a multilevel assembly structure
- Which portion of the costs are treated as fixed costs
- Which costs are treated as the cost of goods manufactured
- Which are sales and administration costs
- Which are the cost of goods sold

Cost Element—Mandatory criteria for classifying costs arising in a company code to the following areas:

- Primary cost elements for goods and services procured externally
- Secondary (internal activity) cost elements

Primary cost elements are maintained in the General Ledger master records. Secondary cost elements have no counterpart in the financial accounts and are maintained exclusively in cost accounting.

N O T E   Primary costs are not necessarily always those procured externally. Similarly, secondary costs are not always those that are maintained in cost accounting. It is possible to have secondary costs, such as salaries, shown in the General Ledger. ☐

Cost Element Group—A technical term for a conjunction of cost elements used to select records for reporting and to define lines and columns in reports. These can be used for planning purposes and also in periodic allocations.

Cost Element Planning—Planning primary and secondary costs on a cost center, order, or project.

Cost Element Type—Classification of cost elements by uses or origin; for example, material cost elements, settlement cost elements for orders, and cost elements for internal cost allocations.

Cost Object—An account assignment term for individual cost objects to which actual data such as costs, budgets, and sales revenues can be assigned. For example, costs may be assigned to products, product groups, cost centers, orders, and so on.

Cost Object Hierarchy—The structure of cost objects as nodes to which actual data can be assigned.

Cost Origin—The logical category to which costs may be assigned.

N O T E Activity types and cost elements can be thought of as cost origins.

Cost Planning—Planning the costs to be incurred during a transaction.

Cost Planning Type—A technical term that indicates the purpose of a cost planning method, such as those that follow:

- Rough planning estimates of costs to be incurred for an order or for an element in a work breakdown structure
- Cost element planning
- Unit costing

Cost-Of-Sales Accounting—A form of results analysis. Sales deductions and unit costs are assigned to the sales transaction.

Costing—Calculating total production costs of individual product units, which may be a piece, a batch, a lot, or an order, for example. Costing may also take place on the provision of services.

Costing Type—A technical term used to control unit costing and product costing. The costing type determines the following:

- For which reference object a costing may be used
- Which costing object will be updated (for example, material master standard price)
- How the key of the costing file is made up
- Which costing application can use this costing type

Costing Variant—Technical term to determine criteria for a cost estimate. Comprises mainly the following:

- Costing type
- Valuation variant
- Organizational level
- Quantity structure determination, which includes the date control parameter

Costing Version—A number that differentiates between cost estimates for the same material but is calculated using different quantity structures. When production alternatives exist, more than one product cost estimate can be made for a material. Cost estimates with different production alternatives are given different version numbers.

CPI-C—Common Programming Interface-Communications. A set of standardized definitions for communications between programs.

Current Cost Estimate—A costing type that uses the value structure (prices) that has changed during the planning period to recalculate the cost of goods manufactured for a product.

Customizing—An SAP tool, provided as part of the SAP R/3 system, comprising two components: implementation guides and customizing menus with the associated functions. It does not change the program coding. This tool provides support for all the activities necessary for the following:

- Initial configuration of the SAP system before going into production
- Adjustment of the system during production
- Implementation of additional SAP applications

Data Element of a Field—A description of the contents of a record or field in terms of their business significance.

Database Interface—A work area to receive data from ABAP/4 Data Dictionary tables, and from which any data that is changed may be passed to the database.

DBMS—Database Management System. A software system used to set up and maintain a database. It includes SQL facilities.

DDL—Data Definition Language, used to define database objects under the DBMS.

Delta Management—System of transferring only data that has changed when using Remote Function Call (RFC).

Dialog Module—A group of dialog steps in a program.

Direct Cost—Costs that are directly and fully identifiable with a reference object according to the costs-by-cause principle.

Distribution (Controlling)—A business transaction used to allocate primary costs. The original primary cost elements are retained on the receiver cost center. Information on the sender and the receiver is documented in the cost accounting document.

Distribution Key—Contains rules on how the costs are to be distributed. It is used in planning to spread costs over the planning period.

DLL—Dynamic Link Library, which is integral to the functioning of the Windows architecture at runtime.

DMS—Document Management System.

Domain—A description of the technical attributes of a table field, such as the type, format, length, and value range. Several fields with the same technical attributes can refer to the same domain.

Dynpro—A dynamic program that controls the screen and its associated validation and processing logic to control exactly one dialog step.

EBCDIC—Extended Binary-Coded Decimal Interchange Code.

EDI—Electronic data interchange. A standardized scheme for exchanging business data between different systems via defined business documents such as invoices and orders.

Enqueue Service—An SAP R/3 system mechanism for the management of locks on business objects throughout client/server environments.

Entity—The smallest possible collection of data that makes sense from a business point of view and that is represented in the SAP R/3 system.

Entity Relationship Model—Entities may be linked by logical relationships that have business significance. Entities and their interrelations can be used to build static models of the enterprise, which are portrayed in the respective computer application with its tables.

Environment Analyzer—A help program that generates a list of both the development objects that belong together and the boundaries between development classes.

EPC—Event Driven Process Chain. A process chain describes the chronological and logical relationship of functions of the R/3 system and business system statuses, which initialize the functions or are generated as a result of function execution.

Equivalence Number—A specification of how any given value is to be distributed to the different receiving objects.

Event (Reference Model)—A status that has business relevance. It can trigger an SAP system function, or it can be the result of such a function.

Event (Workflow Management)—A collection of attributes of objects that describes the change in the state of an object.

External Activities—Non-stock components and/or activities in a production order that are produced or performed outside the company.

Float—A period of time that permits you to start a network or activity at a later date without incurring a delay in scheduling.

Follow-up Costs—Incurred after the actual manufacturing process has been completed; for example, costs of rework and warranties.

Foreign Key—Defines a relationship between two tables by assigning fields of one table (the foreign key table) to the primary key fields of another table (the check table).

Forward Scheduling—A way of scheduling a network, starting from the basic start date and adding durations to determine the earliest start and finish dates for successive activities.

App
A

Free Float—The time that an activity can be shifted into the future without affecting the earliest start date of the following activity or the end date of the project. Must not be less than zero or greater than the total float.

Function Module—A program module that has a clearly defined interface and can be used in several programs. The function module library manages all function modules and provides search facilities in the development environment.

Function-Oriented Cost Accounting—Assigning costs to a business function for the purpose of analysis.

General Costs Activity—A type of activity in a network that plans general costs incurred during the lifetime of a project. Examples of such planned costs are insurance, travel, consulting fees, and royalties.

GUI—Graphical User Interface. The SAPGUI is designed to give the user an ergonomic and attractive means of controlling and using business software.

Hypertext—Online documentation that is set up like a network, with active references pointing to additional text and graphics.

IDOC—Intermediate document. The SAP R/3 system EDI interface and the ALE program link enabling standardized intermediate documents to communicate.

IMG—Implementation Guide. A component of the SAP R/3 system that provides detailed steps for configuring and setting the applications.

Imputed Costs—The value changes that do not represent operational expenditure or correspond to external expenditures in either content or timing (for example, depreciation and interest).

Indirect Costs—Costs for which one single receiving object cannot be directly and fully identified according to the cost-by-cause-principle. The following are examples:

- Indirect expenses, such as building insurance
- Indirect labor cost, such as supervisor wages
- Indirect materials cost, such as coolant cleaning materials

Initial Cost Split—Cost component split for raw materials procurement, showing such details as the following:

- Purchase price
- Freight charges
- Insurance contributions
- Administration costs

Inventory from Which Revenue Can Be Generated—The revenue expected in view of the costs already incurred can be divided into capitalized costs and capitalized profits. This is calculated as Calculated Revenue minus Actual Revenue. Results analysis calculates the inventory for sales orders.

Job Order Cost Accounting—An instrument for the detailed planning and controlling of costs. Serves for the following:

- Collecting
- Analyzing
- Allocating the costs incurred for the internal production of non-capitalized goods

Kerberos—A technique for checking user authorizations across open distributed systems.

Library Network—A generic network structure that can be used by many projects. Used in a project system for repetitive processes or for process planning.

Line Item—A display of posting according to activity and document number.

Logical Database—A set of predefined paths for accessing the tables in a specific database system. Once defined and coded, they can be used by any report program.

Logical System—A system on which applications integrated on a common data basis run. In SAP terms, this is a client in a database.

Loop—A circular path through activities and their relationships.

Lot-Size Variance—Variances between the fixed planned costs and the fixed allocated actual costs that occur because part of the total cost for an order or a cost object does not change with output quantity changes; for example, setup costs that do not change no matter how long the operation takes.

LU6.2—The IBM networking protocol used by the SAP R/3 system to communicate with mainframe computers.

LUW—Logical Unit of Work. An elementary processing step that is part of an SAP transaction. A logical unit of work is either executed entirely or not at all. In particular, database access is always accomplished by separate LUWs, each of which is terminated when the database is updated or when the COMMIT WORK command is entered.

Make-to-Order Production—Type of production in which a product is generally manufactured only once and to a specific customer order.

MAPI—Messaging Application Programming Interface. Part of the Microsoft Windows Open Service Architecture (WOSA).

Master Data—Data relating to individual objects; remains unchanged for a long time.

Matchcode—An index key code attached to the original data that can be used to perform quick interactive searches for this data.

Material Requirements Planning—Generic term for activities involved in creating a production schedule or a procurement plan for the materials in a plant, company, or company group.

Material Type—An indicator that subdivides materials into groups (such as raw materials, semi-finished materials, and operating supplies) and that also determines the user screen sequence, the numbering in the material master records, the type of inventory management, and the account determination.

Measuring Point—The physical and/or logical place at which a status is described. Examples follow:

- Temperature inside a reactor
- Speed of revolution of a wind wheel

Menu Painter—An SAP R/3 system tool for developing standardized menus, function keys, and pushbuttons in accord with the SAP Style Guide.

Metadata—Information about data structures used in a program. Examples of metadata are table and field definitions, domains, and descriptions of relationships between tables.

Mode—A user interface window in which an activity can be conducted in parallel with other open modes.

Modified Standard Cost Estimate—A costing type that uses the quantity structure that has changed during the planning period to recalculate the cost of goods manufactured for a product.

Moving Average Price—Value of the material divided by the quantity in stock. Changes automatically after each goods movement or invoice entry.

Network—In SAP R/3, a structure containing instructions on how to carry out activities in a specific way, in a specific order, and in a specific time period. Made from activities and relationships.

Network Type—Distinguishes networks by their usage. The network type controls the following:

- Costing variants for plan, target, and actual costs
- Order type
- Number ranges
- Open items
- Status profile
- Authorizations

Object Currency—The currency of cost accounting objects. The currency of the controlling area is the default currency of a cost accounting object, such as a cost center, an order, and so on.

Object Overview—Customized list of data and line-display layout (for example, routings, inspection plans, maintenance tasks, and networks).

ODBC—Open Data Base Connectivity. A Microsoft standard based on SQL Access Group definitions for table-oriented data access.

OLE—Object Linking and Embedding. A Microsoft technology to enable the connection and incorporation of objects across many programs or files.

Open Item—Contractual or scheduled commitment that is not yet reflected in financial accounting but will lead to actual expenditures in the future. Open-item management provides for early records and analysis for cost and financial effects. Also referred to in SAP as a commitment item.

Operating Concern—An organizational unit to which one or more controlling areas and company codes can be assigned. Certain criteria and value fields are valid for a specific operating concern. The criteria define business segments, and the value fields are then updated for these objects.

Operating Level—The planned and/or actual performance of a cost center for a period; for example, output quantity, production time, and machine hours.

Operating Rate—The ratio of actual operating level to planned operating level. Measures the effective utilization of a cost center or activity.

Operating Resources—The personnel and material necessary to carry out a project. Can be used once or many times. Defined in value or quantity units. Planned for a period or a point in time. Includes, for example, materials, machines, labor, tools, jigs, fixtures, external services, and work centers.

Operational Area—A technical term used to signify a logical subdivision of a company for accounting or operational reasons and therefore indicated in the EDM-Enterprise Data Model. An operation area is an organizational unit within logistics that subdivides a maintenance site plant according to the responsibility for maintenance.

Operations Layout—List, sorted by operations, of costing results from product costing and final costing.

Order—An instrument for planning and controlling costs. Describes the work to be done in a company in terms of which task is to be carried out and when, what is needed to carry out this task, and how the costs are to be settled.

Order Category—The SAP application to which the order belongs; for example, SD.

Order Group—A technical term for grouping orders into hierarchies. Used to create reports on several orders, to combine orders, and to create the order hierarchy.

Order Hierarchy—Hierarchical grouping of orders for processing at the same time as in order planning and order reporting.

Order Phase—A system control instrument for the order master data. Allows and prohibits operations on orders, depending on the following phase or stage: opened, released, completed, or closed.

Order/Project Results Analysis—A periodic evaluation of long-term orders and projects. The o/p results analysis evaluates the ratio between costs and a measure of an order's progress toward completion, such as revenue or the quantity produced. The results analysis data includes the following:

- Cost of sales
- Capitalized costs or works in progress
- Capitalized profits
- Reserves for unrealized costs
- Reserves for the cost of complaints and commissions
- Reserves for imminent loss

Order Settlement—The complete or partial crediting of an order. The costs that have accrued to an order are debited to one or more receivers belonging to financial or cost accounting.

Order Status—The instrument to control whether an order may be planned or posted to. Reflects the operational progress of an order along the sequence of Released, Revenue Posted, Fully Invoiced, and Completed. Determines the following:

- Whether planning documents are created during cost element planning
- The transactions allowed at the moment (phase), such as planning, posting actual costs, and so on
- When an order may be flagged for deletion

Order Summarization—Allows you to summarize data by putting orders into hierarchies. Also allows you to analyze the order costs at a higher level, such as by product or plant.

Order Type—Differentiates orders according to their purpose; for example, repair, maintenance, marketing, or capital expenditure.

Overall Network—Network resulting from the relationships between all the existing networks.

Overhead—The total cost of indirect expenses, indirect labor, and indirect materials (indirect costs). Allocated to cost objects by means of overhead rates.

Overhead Cost Management—The entirety of cost accounting activities for planning and controlling the indirect costs, as follows:

- Responsibility-oriented overhead cost management by cost centers
- Decision-oriented overhead cost management by action-oriented objects, which are orders and projects

Overhead Costing—Most common method in product cost accounting. Method as follows:

- Assign the direct costs to the cost object.
- Apply the indirect (overhead) costs to the cost object in proportion to the direct costs, expressed as a percentage rate.

Overhead Group—Key that groups materials to which the same overheads are applied.

PA Settlement Structure—To settle costs incurred on a sender to various business segments, depending on the cost element. The Profitability Analysis settlement structure is a combination of assignments of cost element groups to business segments.

Period Accounting—One basis for Profitability Analysis. Costs are identified in the period in which they occur, irrespective of the period in which the corresponding revenue occurs.

Plan Version—Control parameters for comparative analyses in planning in cost accounting. The plan version determines whether the following actions occur:

- Planning changes are documented.
- A beginning balance is to be generated.
- The planning data of another version can be copied or referenced.

Planned Activity—The planned cost center activity required to meet the demand, measured in the corresponding physical or technical units.

Planned Delivery Time—The number of days required to procure the material via external procurement.

Planning—Assigning estimates of the costs of all activities required to carry out the business of an organizational unit over the planning period.

Planning Document—The line item for documenting planning changes.

Planning Element—The work breakdown structure (WBS) element in which cost planning can be carried out.

Pooled Table—A database table used to store control data, such as program parameters, or temporary data. Several pooled tables can be combined to form a table pool, which corresponds to a physical table on the database.

Price Difference Account—Records price differences for materials managed under standard prices, or differences between purchase order and billing prices.

Price Variance—Occurs if planned costs are evaluated in one way and the actual costs in another. The planned standard rates for activities might change in the meantime, for example. Can also be the result of exchange-rate fluctuations.

Primary Cost Planning—Planning of primary costs by values and quantities of activities.

Primary Costs—Incurred due to the consumption of goods and services supplied to the company from outside. Costs for input factors and resources procured externally; for example, as follows:

- Brought-in parts
- Raw materials
- Supplies
- Services

Process Manufacturing—A production type; continuous manufacturing process from raw materials to finished product.

Product Costing—Tool for planning costs and setting prices. Calculates the cost of goods manufactured and the cost of goods sold for each product unit using the data in the PP-Production Planning module.

Product costing based on bills of material and routings is used for calculating production costs of an assembly with alternatives for the following:

- Showing the costs of semi-finished products
- Detailed estimate of the cost components, down to their lowest production level

Production Costs, Total—The costs of finished products bought for resale, or the costs of goods manufactured plus sales overhead, special direct costs of sales, and administration overhead.

Production Cycle—A manufacturing process in which the output of the final manufacturing level (or part of it) becomes input for lower manufacturing levels of the same process (recycle).

Production Order—Instruction for the Production department to produce a material. It contains operations, material components, production resources and tools, and costing data.

Production Resources and Tools (PRT)—Needed for carrying out operations at work centers. Assigned to activities for whose execution they are necessary. Stored as various master data in the form of material master, equipment master, or document master.

Includes the following:

- Job instructions
- Tools
- Test equipment
- Numerically controlled programs
- Drawings
- Machinery

Profit Center—An area of responsibility for which an independent operating profit is calculated. Responsible for its own profitability. Separate divisional result is calculated.

Profit Order—An order whose planned revenue is greater than the planned costs. Results analysis uses the profit percentage rate of a profit order to calculate the inventory from which revenue can be generated, and to calculate the cost of sales.

Profit Percentage Rate—Planned revenue divided by planned costs of an order.

Profitability Analysis—In SAP R/3, accomplished by cost-of-sales approach or period accounting.

Project Definition—Framework laid down for all the objects created within a project. The data, such as dates and organizational data, is binding for the entire project.

Project Management—An organizational structure created just for the life of the project, to be responsible for planning, controlling, and monitoring of the project.

Project Structure—All significant relationships between the elements in a project.

Project Type—Capital spending or customer project, for example.

Q-API—Queue Application Program Interface, which supports asynchronous communication between applications of different systems by using managed queues or waiting lines.

Quantity Structure—The quantity-related basis for calculating costs. The bill of material and the routing form the quantity structure for product costing and the preliminary costing of a production order.

Quantity Variance—Difference between the target costs and the actual costs, which results from the difference between the planned and actual quantities of goods or activity used; for example:

- More raw materials from stock for a production order
- Fewer activities from a cost center than were planned

Rate of Capacity Utilization—Ratio of output to capacity. Fixed costs can be divided into used capacity costs and idle time costs.

Realized Loss—Usage of reserves for imminent loss by results analysis. Loss can be realized when actual costs are incurred and/or when revenue is received. Results analysis realizes loss as the difference either between the actual costs and the calculated revenue, or between the calculated costs and the actual revenue, as follows:

- Actual costs minus calculated revenue
- Calculated costs minus actual revenue

Reference Date—Using the reference dates and the offsets, the start and finish dates of the sub-operation or the production resource/tool usage are determined.

This is a time within an activity (for example, the start date). Reference dates also are used to determine usage dates for production resources/tools.

N O T E You can enter time intervals for reference dates.

Relationship (Project System)—Link between start and finish points of two activities in a network or library network. In SAP R/3, the relationship types are the following:

- SS—start-start
- FF—finish-finish
- SF—start-finish
- FS—finish-start

Repetitive Manufacturing—A production type. Many similar products are manufactured together on the same production line, using more simplified functionality than that for production orders. In SAP R/3, bills of materials and routings are created for each product.

Reserves for Costs of Complaints and Sales Deductions—Inventory cannot be created for certain costs, such as costs arising under warranties or because of sales deductions. For such costs, results analysis creates reserves equal to the planned costs. These reserves are then used when (and if) actual costs are incurred.

Reserves for Imminent Loss—Results analysis creates reserves equal to the planned loss. These reserves are reduced as (and if) this loss is realized.

Reserves for Unrealized Costs—Calculated in results analysis by subtracting the actual costs from the cost of sales.

Resource-Usage Variance—Occurs if the used resource is different from the planned one; for example, the actual raw material used is different from the planned raw material.

Results Analysis—Periodic evaluation of long-term orders. Results analysis compares the calculated costs and the actual cost of an order as it progresses toward completion. It calculates either inventory (if actual costs are greater than calculated costs) or reserves (if actual costs are less than calculated costs).

The data calculated during results analysis is stored in the form of the following:

- Cost of sales
- Capitalized costs
- Capitalized profit
- Reserves for unrealized costs
- Reserves for costs of complaints and commissions
- Reserves for imminent loss

Results Analysis Account—A General Ledger account that records the figures calculated during results analysis.

Results Analysis Data—The outcome of an evaluation of the costs and revenue in relation to the quantity of goods or services in an order. The results are reported in the following format:

- Work in progress and capitalized costs
- Reserves
- Cost of sales

Results Analysis Key—Determines the following for results analysis:

- Whether revenue-based, quantity-based, or manual
- Basis on which it is carried out (planned or actual results)

- How profits are to be realized
- Whether to split inventory, reserves, and cost of sales

Results Analysis Version—Describes the business purpose for which results analysis was carried out. Determines the following, for example:

- Whether the business is in accordance with German and American law
- Financial accounting purposes
- Profitability analysis
- Results analysis accounts to be posted
- How the life cycle of an object is to be broken down into open and closed periods

Revenue—The operational output valued at market price in the corresponding currency and sales quantity unit.

Quantity * Revenue–Sales

RFC—Remote Function Call. A protocol written in ABAP/4 for accessing function modules in other computers. RFC-SDK is a kit for integrating PC applications so that they can access SAP R/3 functions.

RPC—Remote Procedure Call. A protocol for accessing procedures residing in other computers from C programming environments. Corresponds to RFC.

Scheduling, Network—Determines earliest and latest start dates for activities and calculates the required capacity, as well as floats.

Screen Painter—An ABAP/4 Development Workbench tool that can be used to create, modify, display, and delete dynpros.

Secondary Cost Element—Cost centers require services from other cost centers to produce activity of their own. These are secondary costs. Planned assessment is used to plan the secondary costs. Activity input is used to plan the secondary cost quantities.

Settlement Parameters—The control data required for order settlement, as follows:

- Allocation group
- Settlement cost element
- Settlement receiver

Simultaneous Costing Process—Displays the actual costs incurred to date for such things as an order. The process describes all costings of an order in the SAP system, including order settlement. These costings come in the form of preliminary costings and actual costings. The values can then be analyzed in final analysis.

Spooling—Buffered relaying of information to output media, across multiple computers if necessary.

SQL—Structured Query Language. Defined by American National Standards Institute (ANSI) as a fourth-generation language for defining and manipulating data.

Standard Cost Estimate—Calculates the standard price for semi-finished and finished products. Relevant to the evaluation of materials with standard price control. Usually created once for all products at the beginning of the fiscal year or a new season. The most important type of costing in product costing. The basis for profit planning or variance-oriented product cost controlling.

Standard Hierarchy—The tree structure for classifying all data objects of one type. For example, the cost centers belonging to a company from a cost accounting point of view are represented by a standard hierarchy copied from the R/3 Reference Model and then customized.

Standard Price—The constant price with which a material is evaluated, without taking into account goods movements and invoices. For semi-finished and finished products calculated in product costing.

Style Guide—A collection of the SAP design standards for uniform design and consistent operation routines for SAP applications.

Summarization Object—An object containing data calculated during order summarization, project summarization, or the summarization of a cost object hierarchy. A summarization object, for example, can contain the costs incurred for all the orders of a specific order type and a specific responsible cost center.

Surcharge—A supplement, usually as percentage, used to apply overhead in absorption costing.

Target Costs—Calculated using the planned costs, along with the following:

- ☐ The actual activities divided by the planned activities (for cost centers)
- ☐ The actual quantities divided by the planned quantities of goods manufactured (for orders)

Task List Type—Distinguishes task lists according to their functionality. In production planning task lists, for example, a distinction is drawn between routings and master recipes.

TCP/IP—Transmission Control Protocol/Internet Protocol. The standard network protocol for open systems.

Time Interval—A period of time between at least two activities linked in a relationship. The relationship type determines how start and finish times are used in the calculation.

Total Float—Time that an activity can be shifted out into the future, starting from its earliest dates without affecting the latest dates of its successors or the latest finish date of the network.

Transaction—The series of related work steps required to perform a specific task on a business data-processing system. One or more screens may be required. From the user's point of view, it represents a self-contained unit. In terms of dialog programming, it is a complex object that consists of a module pool, screens, and so on, and is called with a transaction code.

Transaction Currency—Currency in which the actual business transaction was carried out.

Unit Costing—A method of costing in which bills of material and routings are not used. Used to determine planned costs for assemblies or to support detailed planning of cost accounting objects such as cost centers or orders.

Usage Variance—Difference between planned and actual costs caused by higher usage of material, time, and so on.

User-Defined Field Types—A classification code used to interpret the meaning of a user-defined field. For example, a user may designate a specific field as one of the following types:

- General field of 20 characters to be used for codes or text
- Quantity fields with a unit
- Value fields with a unit
- Date fields
- Check boxes

User-Defined Fields—Entry fields that can be freely defined for an activity or a work breakdown structure element (Project System) or an operation (Production Planning).

User Exit—An interface provided by an SAP R/3 application that enables the user company to insert into a standard R/3 component a call to an additional ABAP/4 program that will be integrated with the rest of the application.

Valuation Date—The date on which materials and internal and external activities are evaluated in a costing.

Valuation Variant—Determines how the resources used, the external activities, and the overheads are to be valued in a costing (in other words, at what prices).

Variance Category—Distinguishes variances according to their causes, such as the following:

- Input: price and usage variances
- Yield: scrap, mix variances, labor efficiency variances, schedule variances
- Output or allocation: fixed-cost variances, over-absorption variances, under-absorption variances

Variance Key—Technical term. Controls how variances are calculated. Assigning a variance key to an object determines, for example, whether variances are calculated for the object by period or for the life of the object. The object may be a cost center, an order, or a cost object identifier (ID).

Variance Version—Technical term. Specifies the basis for the calculation of variances, as follows:

- How the target costs are calculated
- Which actual data is compared with the target costs
- Which variance categories are calculated

App
A

View—A relational method used to generate a cross-section of data stored in a database. A virtual table defined in the ABAP/4 Dictionary can define a view by specifying how information is selected from whichever tables are targeted.

Volume Variance—Cost difference between the fixed costs estimated for the products (based on standard capacity) and the allocated fixed costs that are either too low or too high due to operating either below or above capacity.

WBS—Work Breakdown Structure. A model of a project. Represents in a hierarchy the actions and activities to be carried out on a project. Can be displayed according to phase, function, and object.

WBS Element—A concrete task or a partial task that can be subdivided.

Work in Progress—Unfinished products, the costs of which are calculated by subtracting the costs of the order that have already been settled from the actual costs incurred for the order or by evaluating the yield confirmed to date.

Work Order—Generic term for the following order types:

- Production order
- Process order
- Maintenance order
- Inspection order
- Network

Work Process—An SAP R/3 system task that can be assigned independently to, for instance, a dedicated application server; for example, dialog processing, updating a database from change documents, background processing, spooling, and lock management.

Workflow Management—Tool for automatic transaction processing used in a specific business environment. ◉

A Consultant's Perspective

In this chapter

This book has tried to offer a comprehensive and accurate guide to the FICO modules. For the experienced consultant, this book should be a good reference manual; for the new consultant, this book should be more of a companion, referred to on a regular basis. For many readers going through their first implementation, or working with FICO modules for the first time, you don't have the benefit of experience. This appendix contains the experience of skilled and seasoned consultants.

The views expressed in the following sections are entirely individual and are not necessarily those of the other contributors to this book. Consultants with very different backgrounds have anonymously donated them. They are meant to be honest opinions, perhaps more subjective than objective. In the space given, there isn't room to cover all aspects of FICO, but it is generally believed that one's first comments are useful indicators. By making the contributions anonymous, it is hoped that the consultants were able to say what they really think, and not necessarily what they think people want to hear.

Analyzing SAP from Consultant One's Perspective

His SAP experience spans over 7 years. Initially coming into contact with SAP with the R/2 mainframe product, he was a user as an accounting supervisor in the general ledger and intercompany accounting areas. He then moved on to a business support group role for SAP R/2, acting as a trainer and help desk support for R/2 users, and helped develop and extend the functionality in the Accounts Receivable area. After that, he became a consultant. The rest of this section is his view of SAP.

The Finance function in SAP is delivered within four main modules. These are:

- Financial Accounting (FI) dealing with external (statutory or legal) accounting
- Controlling (CO) dealing with internal (management) accounting
- Enterprise Controlling (EC) with enterprise-wide accounting
- Treasury (TR) dealing with cash management and cash budgeting

It is unlikely, therefore, to find a single consultant who is versed in the implementation of the entire financial application in SAP. The core of the system, however, is FI and CO. It is common for financial implementations to include FI and CO at the same time, providing the entire scope of financial controls and reporting.

Let us consider, then, each of these modules in turn, and then discuss the points and issues of integration between the two. We will then conclude with some observations on the remaining financial modules.

Using FI

Financial Accounting is broken down into the following components:

- General Ledger
- Accounts Payable

- Accounts Receivable
- Fixed Assets
- Consolidation
- Special Purpose Ledger

Using Organizational Structures within FI

In the implementation of FI, the organizational structures are the Company Code and the Business Area. The Company Code presents little configuration difficulty, being readily identified by the legal reporting entities. The use of the Business Area is somewhat more complex. Where there is a requirement to report internal balance sheets and profit and loss accounts within a Company Code or across Company Codes, the Business Area is the correct organizational tool. Consideration of the strategic product lines within an organization can usually identify Business Areas. It is essential that the number of separate Business Areas remains limited due to the volume of automatic adjustments needed to prepare true Business Area balance sheets. The allocation of cash items between the relevant Business Areas remains a thorny issue in this regard. For most organizations though, this is normally accepted as an organizational issue rather than a system one.

Using the General Ledger

In the implementation of the General Ledger, the vital component is the definition of the Chart of Accounts which identifies all the account numbers that are to be used to record financial transactions. Indeed, the importance of this stage extends to every single SAP module because all other modules rely on account assignment to reflect the value flows in accounting, based on the quantity flows of logistics.

This of course presents problems in an implementation, because often agreement of the definitive Chart of Accounts, especially in international implementations, is not necessarily straightforward. Complications also exist where there is a requirement to consider the provisions for local statutory accounting and consolidated accounting. Completion of the Chart of Accounts also includes configuration of all the numerous automatic account assignments.

Once this step is completed, the remaining implementation stages are relatively easier. Adapting standard SAP-delivered document types and posting keys provides you with all the necessary steps to record financial transactions in the General Ledger.

Using Subledgers (Accounts Payable and Accounts Receivable)

The treatment of the subledger applications of Accounts Payable and Accounts Receivable are almost identical. This is not surprising as they represent two sides of the same coin—trading. For this reason, SAP also refers to customer and vendor master records collectively as Business Partners.

In Accounts Payable and Accounts Receivable, the important stages are the definition of the master records and the financial programs for payment and dunning (receivables payment reminders).

The master records present design considerations because they are integrated master records that are used by logistics. A Phase 1 FI/CO implementation may give rise to a Phase 2 logistics implementation. Therefore, consultants need to consider the possible requirements for sales and purchases in the future when configuring customer and vendor master records.

Of all the FI configuration steps, the payment program is probably the most complex. There are many stages to complete, and in certain countries there is no definitive standard recognized for the format of the electronic bank transfer.

An effective FI implementation also relies on configuration of the display formats for accounts analysis of General Ledger, Accounts Payable, and Accounts Receivable balances to meet the informational needs of the organization.

Outside of the main components of an FI implementation, there may also be requirements for Fixed Assets and Cash Management functions.

Using Fixed Assets

Fixed Assets requires the correct definition of General Ledger accounts to record the Acquisition and Production Cost (APC) and cumulative depreciation accounts on the Balance Sheet, the depreciation charge, and gain or loss on disposal accounts in the profit and loss.

A further organizational structure must be defined, the Chart of Depreciation, which identifies the depreciation values to be calculated. This is linked to the Company Code. Care must be exercised if parallel currencies are being implemented in Financial Accounting to ensure the Chart of Depreciation is compatible with these currencies.

The requirement to identify asset types, together with the depreciation methods and the automatic account assignments, completes the scope of Assets Accounting. Normally it is the data transfer side and reporting side, which can cause the main implementation headaches for this area of FI.

Cash Management and Cash Budgeting

Cash management and cash budgeting is often a Phase 2 or even Phase 3 part of an SAP implementation. It is relatively easy to configure on top of the standard at a later date. It is also necessary to have the SD and MM modules already implemented to use the full functionality of cash management.

Cash management draws in information from Accounts Payable and Accounts Receivable for short term forecasting, but can also access, in an integrated SAP system, sales and purchase orders for medium-term forecasting. Implementation of cash management requires establishing the correct settings on the relevant General Ledger and customer and vendor master records.

Cash budget management provides the ability to analyze the cash flow statement and requires the definition of commitment items, which must be assigned to the relevant General Ledger accounts. A further organization structure, the Funds Management Area, must also be created and assigned to each relevant company code in turn.

Using CO

The previous management areas considered the use of FI Financial Accounting which provides the required functions for External Reporting which, due to statutory regulation, is reasonably uniform for most organizations. In contrast, the functions of Internal Reporting and control need a more flexible approach. This is ably provided by the CO module.

If we now consider the CO module, we see again a series of sub-modules within CO that are all designed for a specific task in mind. Thus the configuration issues vary, depending on which part of CO is being implemented. CO provides different information requirements for different analyses of profit and cost control and performance. It also causes more design issues than FI. Within FI, the business requirements for standard functions (General Ledger, Accounts Payable, and Accounts Receivable) are broadly similar in most organizations. With CO, however, the requirements will vary widely between organizations, especially in different industry sectors. Even organizations operating within the same industry can have particular requirements for management accounts unique to their organizations. Thus, obtaining information about cost management and profit responsibility requires good input from Financial Controllers within the organization. They need to identify the costing methods adopted and the requirements for analyzing the results.

Controlling Overhead Cost

Controlling overhead cost is the core part of CO. All organizations have a requirement for cost control. Cost center accounting typically allows divisions of costs across departments and product lines. Internal order allows the identification of costs for discrete events.

Within CO, cost centers and internal orders are the main cost collectors used to control and report overhead costs.

Using CO-CCA Cost Center Accounting

Cost centers identify where costs are spent and who has the responsibility for those costs. Cost centers need to be organized in a logical structure, which is enforced in SAP via the standard hierarchy. A company can typically identify a standard hierarchy based around its organizational structure. Alternative hierarchies may also be required to identify a grouping of cost centers from a different viewpoint (for example, geographically). A decision must also be made concerning the use of activities in a non-production implementation. Activity types provide useful mechanisms for cost allocation and allow divisions of cost into fixed and variable, which is essential to certain costing methods. They are also a necessary inclusion where SAP production planning is implemented because they provide the cost drivers for product costing.

We also need to identify the relevant cost accounts from FI that should be created. This is important because creation of a cost element necessitates the need for a cost object which can have a dramatic impact on automatic account assignments in CO. Revenue elements should only be created if Profitability Analysis is also being implemented. Revenue elements require a real cost object assignment of which a business segment in PA is the expected default.

The analysis of how detailed planning is conducted and how this relates to the budget allocation must be defined. The quality of the planning information and, hence, control is directly related to the planning effort expended. SAP allows the creation of planning layouts, or user-defined screens, which can facilitate planning. It is also necessary that the correct authorizations be assigned to these layouts in order to maintain confidentiality and consistency of plan data.

Finally the methods of allocation for shared overheads must be established. The appropriate statistics required for allocation are identified for direct recording on the cost centers, or are possibly transferred from the Logistics Information System. The cycles for these allocations must be maintained and tested. Good naming conventions for segments within a cycle should be adopted to ease maintenance and understanding. It is also a good idea, with complex allocations, to plan these methodically on paper first, before executing them.

Using CO-IO Internal Orders

The nature and use for internal orders can be undertaken in parallel with the cost center activity. Internal orders are very flexible cost collectors, and it is possible that certain types of orders are constantly being created, while others are infrequent. This will all be dictated by the nature of the organization's business. Broadly speaking, they are used to collect costs temporarily for events, jobs, or small projects in an organization. The nature of the final allocation of the order also needs to be addressed. This can identify judicious use of statistical orders that will prevent the added complication of settlement for these orders.

Order statuses for each order type need to be determined, and this can give a good deal of control over the life cycle of an order but involves detailed configuration. This must be tied to the internal procedures and associated business transactions that are to be undertaken at each stage in an order's life.

As for cost centers, we need to define how the organization plans and budgets internal orders. This can include configuration of budget availability, budget supplements, and budget returns, as well as integration into the overall capital-spending budget.

Settlement structures and layouts need to be defined, and it is important that this is coordinated with the cost element creation. Configuration inconsistencies arise quickly where development of the interrelated parts of CO is not coordinated.

Internal order and cost center relationships need to be established and built. The plan integration between these areas in CO also needs to be tested.

Controlling Profitability

Having established the main components of overhead management, the organization needs to consider the area of profitability. There is a need to measure profitability on a cost-of-sales basis, period-basis, or both. There is also the need to focus on the external and internal view of profitability.

Given these requirements, SAP offers within CO the Profitability Analysis (CO-PA) module and Profit Center Accounting (CO-PCA) module.

Using CO-PCA Profit Center Accounting

CO-PCA provides the internally focused analysis of profit, and there are similar considerations to cost center accounting. Profit Centers need to be organized into a standard hierarchy. Alternative hierarchies may also need to be constructed. Considerations for planning and plan transfer from other modules need to be addressed.

A further decision regarding Profit Centers is whether it is required to record certain balance sheet items. It is possible to assign fixed and working capital items. This allows for return on investment reporting, and a Profit Center used in this way could be thought of as an Investment Center. Profit Center accounting provides powerful associations between SAP cost objects and the related Profit Center, which must also be assigned. This assignment allows the inclusion of overhead costs in a Profit Center.

App
a
D

Using CO-PA Profitability Analysis

CO-PA is a powerful and flexible tool for Sales and Marketing, focusing on the external view of profit. The challenge posed by CO-PA is that the database has to be designed to suit each individual organization. It is imperative that this is designed in the most efficient manner possible if the database performance is to remain manageable. There is also complex configuration between the areas of Sales and Distribution (SD) and Product Costing (CO-PC). For this reason the use of CO-PA without SD is usually not recommended. This requires building details of a sales order into the financial accounting (FI) document.

The key impact of all the CO modules is only realized with the provision of effective reports. Without effective reporting, we end up with a system that could be described as "Data rich, information drip." The SAP modules provide efficiently designed databases, or the tools to define your own, in CO-PA. This data storage is limited, however, unless proper attention is spent on the analysis of information requirements and the creation of effective reports. SAP delivers standard interrogation and drill-down reports in all of its CO modules, but these can be greatly enhanced and added to with the Report writing tools available in CO.

Integrating FI and CO

A discussion of the main integration points of FI and CO is now relevant. In the organizational setup, the Controlling Area in CO is linked to the Company Code in FI. Multiple Company Codes may be assigned, which allows cross-Company Code controlling. This is only possible, however, when all Company Codes are assigned to the same Chart of Accounts. This is because a Controlling Area is designed to analyze by cost object the cost and revenue elements, which must be uniform.

Therefore, the creation of cost elements is dependent on the creation of certain General Ledger accounts. Tools exist in CO that allow the automatic creation of cost elements.

Where there is a requirement to analyze FI accounts by business area, the cost objects in CO can be assigned to the relevant business area. As well as the product strategic business areas, there should also be a general business area for assignment of non-product specific costs.

Using Other Functions in FI

Two remaining functions in FI to mention are Special Purpose Ledger and Consolidation.

Special Purpose Ledger, FI-SPL, is used in the definition of specific ledgers which are necessary to meet a unique reporting requirement that is not fulfilled by any other standard SAP financial module. The term ledger is used to signify that we create a ledger to analyze account balances by a non-standard reporting field. In the creation of these ledgers, the correct definition of the reporting dimensions and the corresponding set up of the ledger and data transfer are critical to ensure the efficiency of the reporting.

Consolidation, FI-LC, provides functionality to support legal consolidation of organizations. FI-LC in turn relies on purpose-built ledgers defined within FI-SPL to capture the data from individual Company Codes and perform the necessary inter-company elimination. In order to achieve this, we require proper coordination of the Chart of Accounts. This must consist of group account numbers which, in turn, must be linked and related to financial statement items. Collectively, these items form a financial statement version, the tool used to report the balance sheet and profit and loss account. A decision must also be made as to whether data transfers to the consolidation ledger should be in real-time or performed at period-end. Where data exists in different clients, the latter method would be the only choice for cross-client data transfer.

Using Other Functions in CO

CO consists of one final module, EIS or Executive Information System. This can be regarded as a stand-alone module as it provides the capability to define a series of databases that are capable of storing and reporting all information that is vital and relevant to an organization. Note this includes more than just the SAP data sources. Indeed, it is important within an organization to collect information from other internal systems, and also external sources, regarding the competition and markets. SAP facilitates data transfer from existing SAP systems into the EIS databases. It provides a standard tool for building data transfers from other sources. While providing a version of the Report Painter tool for reporting, EIS is also well supported by a Complimentary Software Product, Insight. This provides a visually intuitive and integrated front-end for information processing.

It can be seen, from the insight into FI and CO, that these modules contain a vast variety of applications to assist an organization and challenge a consultant. It is seldom likely that the entirety of FI and CO is implemented at one time. Certain parts of an FICO implementation may also take place during different phases.

Finally, a good FICO consultant has a mind for the information requirements of an organization and the best financial SAP tool to suit a particular requirement.

Good luck with your FICO implementation.

Analyzing SAP from Consultant Two's Perspective

I was attracted to specializing in SAP for two main reasons. First, I had spent at least 10 years on contracts at different companies around the world. I spent this time struggling to master the custom systems that clients had written (often at phenomenal expense). After one or two years learning a system—thinking I had mastered something useful—I would then go to another project and almost have to start all over again. This eventually became tiresome. Secondly, I saw something new in SAP that I did not see in other packages. It was the determination of SAP to try and produce a suite of modules which reflected "best in class" practices as well as a mass-market attitude. I realized that it was only a question of time before all the major companies would at least evaluate SAP, as they looked to retire their ever-aging legacy systems, and take the opportunity to downsize their IS staff to reduce costs.

As a Certified Accountant by training, I was always closer to working in finance areas, rather than manufacturing, sales, logistics, and so on. I therefore naturally gravitated towards the FI/ CO modules, or to be precise, they gravitated towards me. Getting a break in SAP is a bit like the "chicken and egg situation;" you cannot get in because you don't have the experience, and you can't get the experience because you can't get in. I got my break while on a project for a global customer who was switching to SAP R/3 and retiring about 100 systems in the process. They were prepared to "bite the bullet" with me, but the learning curve was steep and there was no formal training. That opportunity, which lasted about 6 months, opened more doors. Thereafter it got easier, but took time. Most of the consultants I see these days either joined a consultancy and received SAP or internal training or learned their SAP skills at their employers, and then, for whatever reason, left to join the ever-growing consulting market.

App

I find that there are generally two types of SAP projects. The first type is a brand-new implementation. This type often replaces made-to-order legacy systems with R/3. It is normally done just in a division of a company—rarely the whole company at one go. These require a lot of knowledge, either about the client's industry and/or the client's systems. And by the time you arrive, most of the analysis work is done already. They expect you to "hit the deck running," even though they've been working on it for months or even years. Typically, there are also many interfaces to other systems passing and receiving data, which complicates things.

The second type of project (and these seem to be more R/2-related) is where the client has been using SAP for a few years and wants to change the configuration because their business has changed. These bring new problems to the consultant because staff are trained to use the system only in a specific way, and any process changes are difficult to introduce. At some point, these clients will have to migrate to R/3 or R/4, so there will always be a lot of work in this area—perhaps increasingly so over the next decade.

One of my biggest problems, and something with which I still struggle, is knowing all the possibilities of the system. The modules are so vast and cover so much, that a detailed knowledge can often only be learned by "on the job training" over many years. Unfortunately, the system documentation is of limited help at times, but it pays to ask around because on a large project, somebody else will often know something about it. Unfortunately, from my experience some of the delivered SAP processes/functionality (for example, European VAT handling, Activity Based Costing, Management Reporting) don't work well as yet. But, as an integrated Transaction Processing system, R/2 or R/3 takes a lot of beating, so SAP must also be a compromise.

FI/CO are the more passive modules, by that I mean they're used more for record keeping and historic analysis, and often where the processes are more standard in all organizations.

However being at the back-end of the chain, this also presents a new problem because if anything goes wrong with the financial numbers, it is often largely due to somebody in SD or MM changing a flag or using the wrong order type. Because of the tight integration, there is an immediate impact all over the system, and often there is no "undo" button. Sometimes you don't even see the error until the end of the month. This can be both a strength and a weakness of SAP. It comes as no surprise, therefore, that the most critical time for these types of errors is just after going live—when users experiment in the Production environment. Therefore, good training and documentation are prerequisites that should not be overlooked.

Management generally sees the FI module as a cornerstone to their business, but it is often not the most important. Good sales, logistics, and materials handling will be of far more value to any company. However, all these modules need, at some point in a process, to access FI for information, the cost of writing many interfaces becomes prohibitive. The FI module, in my experience, is always implemented. The U.S., in particular, extensively uses the Special Purpose Ledger (SPL) to combine SAP and Non-SAP ledgers, often to feed a management reporting database or consolidation system. Use of the SPL is not as widespread in Europe, but growing.

The CO module has differing uses, and is not always implemented. In a manufacturing organization, you can take specific advantage of the links with cost objects like Production Orders (CO-OPA), which are closely linked to MM and PPS (Production Planning & Scheduling) so that you can, for example, determine the Profit or Loss per Production Order against a standard cost. In a more service-related organization, perhaps CO-CCA Cost Center accounting is more relevant in enabling all costs to be settled onto Cost Centers so managers can monitor their spending. Often, both are used.

CO can be added later, if required, and FI has the ability to validate Cost Centers even if CO is not present. Tools also exist to retrospectively populate CO with Cost Center data. Both FI and CO have budgeting capabilities, but it is more common to set detailed plans at a cost-center level in CO than on an account number level in FI. The FI function exists purely to support the financial statement version.

I have not yet seen or heard of an organization that uses SAP without some additional modifications. These modifications involve either writing new tables and new ABAPs, so as to get the system to do what they want, or at least writing new reports to get the system to show what they want. The larger the company, the more complex the solution often becomes. On top of this, SAP rarely replaces everything in an organization, so there is inevitably the payroll interface or the feed to a consolidation system or something similar to consider. Again, the larger the organization, the more legacy environments that are being gradually replaced, the more interfaces there are to consider. These processes never fail to impact the FI/CO configuration and operation. Fortunately, there are some processes, more so within FI, which are fairly static. For example, the functions in Accounts Payable, Accounts Receivable, and Monthly Closing don't radically change from company to company, and, once mastered, are not forgotten.

Because SAP is changing all the time, it is always exciting to see what new things they find to bring out with which to test us. ●

Index

G

GAAP
  Accounts Payable, 91
  certificates of compliance, 381
general costs activity, 416
General Ledger, 18
  Accounts Receivable, 64
  areas, 23
    chart of accounts, 23
    company codes, 23
  balance sheet, 28, 51
  chart of accounts, 24
    common chart of accounts, 29
  closing
    operational structure, 51
    subledgers, 46
  closings (year-end), 36
  controlling, 206
  currencies (parallel), 129
  currency, 34
  daily closings, 35
  extended (chart of accounts), 20
  Financial Accounting, 431
  Financial Accounting Application, 26
  financial document interfaces, 52
  Financial Information System (FIS), 53
  financial statements, 50
  functions, 28
  languages, 33
  master data, 24
    checking, 25
  monetary values, 37
  monthly closings, 35
  numerical values, 37
  posting, 44
    data entry, 46
    subledgers, 45
  profit and loss, 28, 51
  profitability, 27
  reporting, 47
    output, 49
    Report Painter, 48
    Report Writer, 48
    standard reports, 47
  rules, 35
  special, 28
  special purpose ledger, 37-38
    actions, 40
    allocation, 57
    centralized planning, 43
    comparing ledgers, 56

    decentralized planning, 43
    distribution, 41, 57
    distribution keys, 59
    functions, 55-57
    inflow, 40
    interface, 57
    planning, 39, 58
    planning parameters, 59
    reporting, 60
    scope, 59
    set concept, 42, 58
  subledgers, 27
  transaction data, 26
  transaction log, 19
  transactions, 18
  year-end (closing), 28
  year-end results (anticipating), 26
Generally Accepted Accounting Principles (GAAP), 376
goodwill (investment Consolidation), 178
graphical user interface (GUI), 416
graphics (project analysis), 302
gross operating profits (Profitability Analysis module), 323
group assets (classes), 112
group valuation, depreciation (special valuation), 125
group-wide planning (Consolidation), 154
groups (transferring data), 171
guarantees, Accounts Receivable (special transactions), 80
GUI (graphical user interface), 416

H

head office (company codes), 32
head office accounts
  Accounts Receivable, 68
  vendors (Accounts Payable), 95
hierarchies
  assets, 109
  cost objects, 244, 413
    product-related, 246
    responsibility-related, 246
  standard, 426

history sheets (assets), 113
  reporting, 145-146
hypertext, 416

I

IAC (Internet Application Component), 379
identifying (assets), 110
IDES (International Demonstration and Education System), 377
IDOC (intermediate document), 416
IM-Investment Management, 13
IM-FA Tangible Fixed Assets, *see* **Tangible Fixed Assets**
IM-FI Financial Investments, *see* **Financial Investments**
IMG (implementation guide), 416
imminent losses (reserves), 424
implementation
  Business Engineer, 387
  training completed, 400
implementation guide (IMG), 416
implementing software (avoiding mistakes), 3
imputed costs, 416
  accruals (cost elements), 200
  calculation objects, 201
  surcharges, 200
  target = actual procedure, 201
imputed interest, depreciation (special valuation), 124
in-house courses (FICO education and training), 394
indexing (matchcode), 417
indirect allocation of costs, 250
indirect costs, 416
  product costs, 235
individual, depreciation (special valuation), 126
industries (cost objects), 233
Industry Solution for Insurance and Real Estate Management, 349

L

languages (General Ledger), 33

launching (training program), 398
- application skills, 390
- information skills, 391
- learning zones (FICO), 390
- management skills, 391
- technical skills, 390

leased assets (special transactions), 144

ledger-based period accounting (Profitability Analysis module), 326
- structure, 327

ledgers
- comparing, 56
- reconciliation (cost elements), 201
- reconciliation, 8
- special purpose, 9
- subsidiary, 4

letters
- Accounts Receivable, 85
- dunning (Accounts Receivable), 83

levels (dunning), 82

library networks, 417

limiting (credit), 88

line items
- Accounts Receivable, 80
- assets, 113
- reports (projects), 299

line-item, 417

liquidity, 336
- analyzing, 337

liquidity forecast function (Cash Management), 333

locks (enqueue service), 415

logical databases, 417

logical system, 417

logical unit of work (LUW), 417

logs (Activity Logs), 409

loops, 417

losses (realized), 423

lot-size variance, 417

LU6.2, 417

LUW (logical unit of work), 417

M

mainframes (LU6.2), 417

maintenance (depreciation area assets), 122

maintenance levels (assets master records), 115

make-to-order costing, 225

make-to-order production, 417

make-to-stock costing, 225

management (project), 423

management accounting, see controlling

management consolidation, 162

management skills (FICO education and training), 391

managerial leadership (FICO education and training), 392

managing assets internationally, 148

manual input (unit costing), 237

manufacturing
- co-products, 411
- process, 422
- production cycles, 422
- repetitive, 424

manufacturing view (projects), 267

MAPI (messaging application programming interface), 417

margin analysis (Profitability Analysis module), 324

Marginal Costing, 10

marginal costs (controlling), 191

Market Risk Management module, 341
- cash plan, 342

mass change procedure (assets master records), 116

mass retirements (fixed assets), 138

master data, 417
- Accounts Receivable, 65
- General Ledger, 24-25

master records
- assets, 113
  - accounting, 361
  - archiving portfolios, 116
  - classes, 111-112
  - elements, 114
  - maintenance levels, 115
  - mass change procedure, 116
  - numbering, 115
  - parameters, 115
  - portfolios, 116
  - screens, 114
  - substitution conditions, 115
  - time-dependent data, 115
  - validation conditions, 115
  - viewing, 115
  - workflow, 116
- Consolidation, 164
  - business areas, 164
  - FS Items Catalog, 165
  - statistical lines, 166
- orders (data formats), 256
- vendors (Accounts Payable), 92-93

master sheets (credit), 89

matchcode, 417

material requirements planning, 417

material types, 418

Materials Management
- availability checking, 287
- view (projects), 268

measures (Capital Investment), 357, 364
- allocating activity costs, 367
- cost centers, 367
- cost elements, 366
- external accounting, 371
- final settlement, 370
- internal accounting, 370
- internal activities, 368
- investment support, 369
- overhead, 367
- posting down payments, 368
- settlement functions, 369

measuring point, 418

menu painter, 418

messaging application programming interface (MAPI), 417

metadata, 418

milestones (project structures networks), 279

Why Join the ASAP team?

We are a fast growing dynamic group of companies operating globally in an exciting new virtual environment. We have the simple aim to be the best at what we do. We therefore look to recruit the best people on either contract or permanent basis

If you are any of the following, we would like to hear from you.

1. Highly Skilled and Experienced SAP Consultant.

You will have been working with SAP systems for many years and will be a project manager or consultant of standing in the industry. If you are willing to assist in the training and development and perhaps recruitment of your team, then we will be able to offer you exceptional financial rewards and the opportunity of developing the career of your choice.

2. Skilled in Another Area and Looking to Cross Train

You may be a computer expert or a business person with expertise in a particular area, perhaps, logistics, finance, distribution or H.R. etc., and/or with a particular industry knowledge. If you are committed to working with SAP systems in the long term, we will be able to offer you SAP cross training and vital experience. You must have a proven track record in your field and must be prepared to defer financial advancement whilst training and gaining experience. If you have the commitment and the skill you will in time be able to receive from us the high financial rewards and career development choice above.

3. A Person who has worked in a functional job
for an End User Company and who has been involved in all aspects of an SAP project from initial scoping to implementation and post implementation support.

You will have an excellent understanding of the industry or business function you are in. You are likely to have a good degree, ambition, drive, flexibility and the potential to become a top SAP consultant. You will thrive on the prospect of travel and living and working in other countries, jetting off around the world at short notice and working as part of a highly motivated and productive team. You must be committed to a long term career working with SAP. We will be able to offer you an interesting and rewarding career, giving you training and experience in a number of different roles. If you can prove yourself, you can expect rapid career development, with excellent financial rewards. Your only limit is your ability and your aspirations.

How To Contact Us

ASAP World Consultancy, ASAP House, PO Box 4463,
Henley on Thames, Oxfordshire RG9 6YN, UK
Tel:+44 (0)1491 414411   Fax: +44 (0)1491 414411

ASAP - 24 Hour - Virtual Office - New York, USA
Voice Mail: (212) 253 4180 Fax: (212) 253 4180

E-Mail: info@asap-consultancy.co.uk

Web site: http://www.asap-consultancy.co.uk/index.htm

A S A P
WORLD CONSULTANCY™

ASAP Worldwide
Enterprise Applications Resourcing & Recruitment

The company established in July 1997 has ambitious plans to become the world's largest global recruitment company specialising entirely in "the placement of permanent, temporary and contract staff who will be engaged in the implementation, support, training and documentation of systems known as enterprise applications". These include: SAP, BAAN, Peoplesoft, Oracle Applications, System Software Associations, Computer Associates, JD Edwards, Markam, JBA etc.

The company benefits from:

- Detailed knowledge of the market, its requirements and dynamics.

- Use of one of the world's most advanced recruitment systems.

- Access to large databases of candidates.

- A global approach to the staffing problems of a global market.

- Unique and innovative solutions for solving the staffing problems of a high growth market.

- A commitment to offer clients and candidates a professional, efficient and high quality service that is second to none.

- A commitment to the continual development of the services that we offer.

- Reciprocal partnership arrangements with other recruitment companies worldwide.

WORLDWIDE

Services to companies looking for staff

Permanent, Contract & Temporary Recruitment

ASAP Worldwide has a deep understanding of the enterprise application resourcing market, its requirements and dynamics. Whether your requirement is for a single individual or a team of hundreds, we offer the best practices and standards of service you would expect from one of the world's most professional recruitment companies to solve your staffing requirements.

In such a high growth market where the right people are at a premium, it takes a very different approach to find and place candidates. We offer a unique range of services to companies of all sizes and in all sectors worldwide. We leave no stone unturned in our search for candidates and we have unique techniques for selecting the very best candidates to offer you. We offer originality and innovation that make us stand out from the crowd.

Service to people looking for work

We believe that there is far more to our work than simply trying to fill job vacancies. We believe that we are providing a service of equal value to both employers and candidates looking for work. We are genuinely interested in your personal and career development and we undertake to try our very best to find you the work that best meets your requirements. Because of the size of our network, we are able to offer a truly global service, so whatever part of the world you would like to work in, whatever the type of employer and whatever the type of work you would like, we believe that we are better placed to give you what you want.

Send us a copy of your C.V./resumé and receive a free copy of our "Career Development Programme" booklet, designed to help you advance your SAP career.

How to contact us:

ASAP Worldwide
PO Box 4463 Henley on Thames
Oxfordshire RG9 6YN UK
Tel: +44 (0)1491 414411
Fax: +44 (0)1491 414412

ASAP Worldwide - 24 Hour - Virtual Office - New York, USA
Voice Mail: (212) 253 4180 Fax: (212) 253 4180

E-Mail: enquiry@asap-consultancy.co.uk

Web site: http://www.asap-consultancy.co.uk

A.S.A.P
WORLDWIDE